Curzon in India

2. Frustration

DAVID DILKS

Curzon in India

2. Frustration

TAPLINGER PUBLISHING COMPANY
New York

First published in the United States in 1970 by
TAPLINGER PUBLISHING CO., INC.
29 East Tenth Street
New York, New York 10003

© David Dilks 1969

Library of Congress Catalog Card Number 70-88619
SBN 8008 2107 6

Printed in Great Britain

For Jill

Contents

List of Illustrations

The frontispiece is reproduced by kind permission of the National Portrait Gallery, and all other illustrations by courtesy of the Secretary of State for Foreign and Commonwealth Affairs.

Foreword

THIS SECOND VOLUME of *Curzon in India* attempts to tell the story of his last three years as Viceroy, a time of sorrow in private life and of frustration in public affairs. Some aspects will, in all probability, remain obscure for ever. Occasionally, a few forgotten letters may shed a gleam of fresh light upon the extraordinary episodes which I have tried to chronicle. It has been necessary to compress into a comparatively short compass a vast quantity of papers; but the main features of the story are, I hope, justly presented.

My kind friends and colleagues, Roy Bridge, Ian Nish, John Hutchinson and Zafar Imam, have unearthed German and Russian sources; and my pupils Rhys Hall and Horst Jaeckel have shared the fruits of their researches. Mrs J. Farquharson, Miss W. Edwards, Mrs P. Johnston, Mrs G. Knott and Miss J. Hayers have coped cheerfully with my calligraphy. I wish to renew my thanks to those who have allowed me to use copyright material, and to acknowledge the helpfulness and patience of my publishers, especially of Mr Francis Pagan. To my wife I am more indebted than I can say.

For the selection of documents and for the views expressed in these volumes the responsibility is mine alone. I have not concealed my admiration for Curzon's gifts, or my conviction that he was ill-used in 1905; but so far as possible the story has been left to tell itself.

DAVID DILKS

Principal Characters

AMPTHILL, Baron:
Governor of Madras, 1899–1906; Viceroy, 1904.

ARNOLD-FORSTER, Rt Hon. H. O.:
Parliamentary Secretary, Admiralty, 1900–3; Secretary of State for War, 1903–5.

BALFOUR, Rt Hon. A. J.
(later Earl of Balfour):
Chief Secretary for Ireland, 1887–9; Leader of the House, 1891–2, 1895–1905; Prime Minister, 1902–5.

BRODRICK, Hon. St John
(later Earl of Midleton):
Financial Secretary, War Office, 1886–1892; Under-Secretary of State for War, 1895–8, and for Foreign Affairs, 1898–1900; Secretary of State for War, 1900–3, and for India, 1903–5.

CLARKE, Sir George S.
(later Baron Sydenham):
Member of the War Office Reconstruction Committee, 1903–4; Secretary of the Defence Committee, 1904–1907; Governor of Bombay, 1907–1913.

COLLEN, Lt-Gen. Sir E. H. H.:
Military Member of the Viceroy's Council, 1896–1901.

CRANBORNE, Viscount
(later 4th Marquess of Salisbury):
Under-Secretary for Foreign Affairs, 1900–3; Lord Privy Seal, 1903–5.

CURZON, Rt Hon. G. N.
(later Marquess Curzon):
Under-Secretary for India, 1891–2; for Foreign Affairs, 1895–8; Viceroy, 1898–1905; Foreign Secretary, 1919–1924.

DANE, Sir Louis W.:
Secretary to Government of India in the Foreign Dept., 1902–8; in charge of British mission to Kabul, 1904–5.

DAWKINS, Sir Clinton E.: Finance Member of the Viceroy's Council, 1899.

ELGIN, Earl of: Viceroy, 1894–9.

ELLES, Lt-Gen. Sir Edmond R.: Adjutant-General, India, 1900–1; Military Member of the Viceroy's Council, 1901–5.

ESHER, Viscount: Permanent member, Defence Committee; chairman of the War Office Reconstruction Committee, 1903–4.

GODLEY, Sir A. (later Baron Kilbracken): Under-Secretary of State for India, 1883–1909.

HAMILTON, Rt Hon. Lord George: First Lord of the Admiralty, 1885–6, 1886–92; Secretary of State for India, 1895–1903.

HARDINGE, Rt Hon. Sir Arthur H.: Minister at Teheran, 1900–5.

HARDINGE, Hon. Charles (later Baron Hardinge): Secretary of Embassy at St Petersburg, 1898–1903; Assistant Under-Secretary for Foreign Affairs, 1903–4; Ambassador at St Petersburg, 1904–5; Viceroy, 1910–16.

HAVELOCK, Sir Arthur E.: Governor of Madras, 1895–1900.

KITCHENER, Field-Marshal Lord (later Earl Kitchener): Sirdar, Egyptian Army, 1890–9; C-in-C, South Africa, 1900–2, and India, 1902–9; Secretary of State for War, 1914–16.

KNOLLYS, Viscount: Private Secretary to the Prince of Wales, later King Edward VII, 1870–1910.

LAMINGTON, Baron: Governor of Bombay, 1903–7.

LANSDOWNE, Marquess of: Governor-General of Canada, 1883–8; Viceroy, 1888–93; Secretary of State for War, 1895–1900; Foreign Secretary, 1900–5.

LAWRENCE, Sir Walter R.: Private Secretary to Curzon, 1889–1903.

LOCKHART, Gen. Sir William: C-in-C, India, 1898–1900.

MCDONNELL, Hon. Sir Schomberg: Principal Private Secretary to Salisbury, 1888–92, 1895–9, 1900–2.

MINTO, Earl of: Governor-General of Canada, 1898–1904; Viceroy, 1905–10.

NORTHCOTE, Baron: Governor of Bombay, 1899–1903.
PALMER, Gen. Sir Power: C-in-C, India, 1900–2.
ROBERTS, Field Marshal Earl: C-in-C, India, 1885–93, South Africa,
                                 1899–1900; C-in-C, British Army,
                                 1901–4.
SALISBURY, Marquess of: Secretary of State for India, 1866–7,
                                 1874–8, and for Foreign Affairs, 1878–
                                 1880, 1885–6, 1887–92, 1895–1900;
                                 Prime Minister, 1885–6, 1886–92,
                                 1895–1902.
SANDHURST, Viscount: Governor of Bombay, 1895–9.
SELBORNE, Earl of: First Lord of the Admiralty, 1900–5;
                                 High Commissioner in South Africa,
                                 1905–10.
SPRING-RICE, Rt Hon. Sir Cecil A.: Chargé d'Affaires at Teheran, 1900;
                                 First Secretary at St Petersburg, 1903–
                                 1904; Minister at Teheran, 1906–8.
YOUNGHUSBAND, Sir Francis E.:   Resident at Indore, 1902–3; British
                                 Commissioner to Tibet, 1902–4.

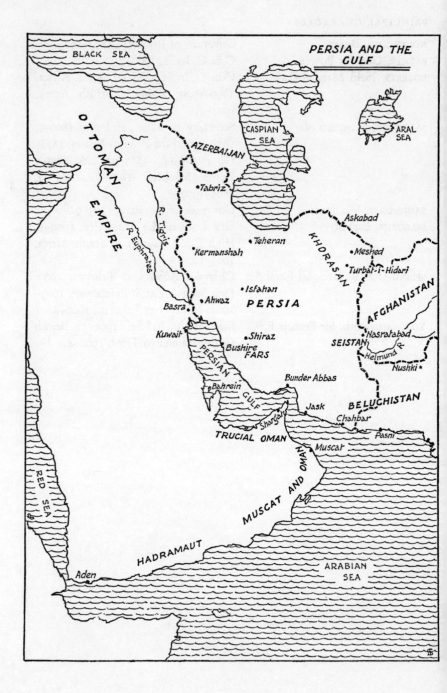

PERSIA AND THE
GULF

BLACK SEA

OTTOMAN
EMPIRE

CASPIAN
SEA

ARAL
SEA

AZERBAIJAN

Tabriz

KHORASAN

Askabad

Teheran

Meshed

Kermanshah

Turbat-i-Hidari

AFGHANISTAN

Isfahan

PERSIA

R. Tigris

R. Euphrates

Ahwaz

Basra

Kuwait

Shiraz

SEISTAN

Nasratabad

Bushire

FARS

Helmund R.

Bahrein

Nushki

Bunder Abbas

BELUCHISTAN

PERSIAN GULF

Jask

Chahbar

Sharjah

Pasni

TRUCIAL OMAN

Muscat

RED SEA

MUSCAT AND OMAN

HADRAMAUT

ARABIAN
SEA

Aden

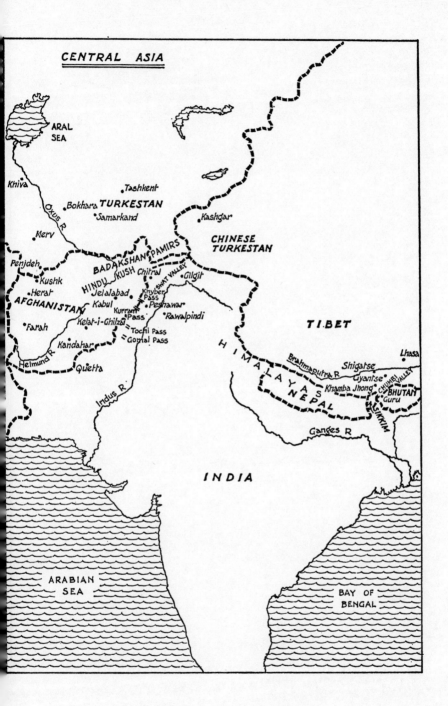

ONE

Kitchener's Debut

... Kitchener, whom he thought to possess ...

IT IS CLEAR that Kitchener felt hostile to the Military Department well before he arrived in India. On his way out, he indicated to Cromer that he intended to act; and at Bombay the outgoing C-in-C, Sir P. Palmer, complained of the Military Department. Palmer was smarting under a personal grievance against Elles and, as Kitchener later confessed to Curzon, poisoned his mind against him.[1] To Walter Lawrence, who had realised that Simla would do its utmost to make bad blood between the C-in-C and Viceroy, Kitchener spoke of the muddled division between administrative and executive work in the army. Lawrence liked his candour and receptivity, observing that 'if he adheres to his resolution to regard the V[iceroy] as king all will go well'.[2] Curzon was impressed by his first contacts with Kitchener, whom he thought to possess honesty, directness, commonsense and a combination of energy and power:

> I feel that at last I shall have a Commander-in-Chief worthy of the name and position. Hitherto I have dealt with phantoms. He knows perfectly well how disloyal to me the Army has been, and how everything distasteful or unpopular has been thrust on to my shoulders. He says that he will stop this pretty sharp.

Kitchener seemed rather apprehensive about his position and powers. It appeared, he said, that he should have come out as Military Member; yet he believed the C-in-C should be the chief military adviser. Curzon asked him to wait a little to see the system in practice, for paper rules would yield to the force of character and circumstance. The position of the C-in-C depended not upon definitions of prerogatives but on his own personality and it was not likely that India would fail to profit from the counsels of the first soldier of the day.[3] This was exactly in line with the advice Hamilton had already given. Lady Curzon felt somewhat less confident. She asked Kitchener to take the military load off Curzon's shoulders: 'I suppose you know that the prayer of the soldier has been that the two giants would fall out – and it will be a grief for them to see you work in harmony, and to know the intense satisfaction it is to George that you are here at last.'[4]

Kitchener said immediately that he wished to effect a complete change in the military arrangements, including the virtual abolition of the Military Department. When Curzon expressed astonishment that such a proposal should emanate from a C-in-C who had barely set foot in India, Kitchener undertook not to raise the matter again until he had some experience of the system. Very soon afterwards, however, Kitchener indicated to Elles that he wished to take the Ordnance, Supply and Transport and Remount Departments into the C-in-C's care.[5] The manœuvres, which Kitchener had just attended, struck him as 'a mere farce'. He described them scathingly in the first of a long series of letters to Lady Cranborne, daughter-in-law of Lord Salisbury, wife of the Under-Secretary at the Foreign Office, friend and relation by marriage of the new Prime Minister, Balfour. These letters were regularly copied by her and sent to him. The character and significance of the link will emerge. 'I dare say you will gather' Kitchener now wrote to her, 'that there is some waking up to be done and that I shall have considerable difficulties with the present organisation of the War Department in India…there is a sort of feeling among the best officers in the Army that I must face it if the army is to be made in any way efficient.'[6]

Within a few days the new C-in-C had committed himself to the view that the Indian Army would come to grief in a big war; that no material improvement could be expected under the existing system; and that the deployment of the army must be altered to cope with the Russian menace rather than with internal upheaval.[7] Kitchener's proceedings in these first weeks caused Curzon to remark that he seemed to imagine the military government of India was to be conducted by a concordat between the two of them:

> He comes and pours out to me all sorts of schemes to which he asks my consent. It is all so frank and honest and good-tempered that one cannot meet these advances with a rebuff. Here and there I head him off, or steer him into more orthodox channels. But of course as yet he does not know the ropes.[8]

A fortnight afterwards, Kitchener told Lady Cranborne that although Curzon was 'all that one could wish and as kind as possible' the system was useless. According to him, Curzon had justified it on the ground that if the C-in-C had anything to do with the machinery he would become too powerful; between the two the civilian elements got control. He, Curzon, was satisfied with the results. 'When one sees however the deplorable state of the organisation of the Army I am astonished at the satisfaction expressed…As to power, I do not want more power outside the Army, but I do want power to do good in the Army. If I am incapable why appoint me, if I fail get rid of me, but why keep on a dead level of inefficiency or drift backwards because you won't trust the person you appoint to do good?'[9] This was written in January, 1903. A few days later, Curzon reported Kitchener to be 'settling down and...delighted with the country and work'. There followed a brief skirmish about an order which the Military Department wished to issue and to which Kitchener objected. He hinted at resignation[10] and then challenged officially the division between executive and administrative work in the army. The executive function of the command, he asserted, was the administration of its fighting power. Supply and transport were of supreme importance in time of war. Kitchener described at length what seemed to him a system of checks on all military proposals, scouted any possibility of rash innovation if a single military adviser were supreme, stated that much money could be saved and said the present organisation meant endless discussion. Under it no consistent military policy was feasible. It must collapse in time of war. He proposed that the Military Department and Army headquarters should be brought together in one building. The Military Department would 'remain' the military bureau of the Viceroy. The C-in-C, however, would be the dominant military adviser. This, Curzon said, meant the suppression of the Military Department. He suggested that since Kitchener's experience of the system had lasted but a few weeks, it would be better to wait until he had been a year in India, when he might have discovered merits which he did not for the moment discern.[11]

Roberts, with whom Kitchener was in regular correspondence, told him that when C-in-C in India he had always managed well enough with the Supply and Transport Department under the Military Member. Kitchener, however, would not be put off. The difficulties of getting anything done, he replied, were heartbreaking:

> I never thought Englishmen could be so influenced by their...surroundings as to lose their character and become very much like the baboos of the country as I find at every turn here.
> The only thing that excites officials out here is to get some of their relations or friends pushed into some billet or other or to arrange that some particular lady is stationed where they are.
> They all seem to come to this state of things in time...[12]

Curzon, believing that Kitchener would not raise the matter of the Military Department again until 1904, was in cordial, if slightly apprehensive, relations with him. The new C-in-C, he told Cromer, was beginning to make himself felt: 'A very self-centred man. He has acquired a good deal of urbanity of manner since the old days, but his language and his indifference to public opinion still retain their pristine frankness and charm.'[13]

Early in May, however, Curzon advised Hamilton privately that he was 'a little nervous about Kitchener', who had hitherto been in a position of undisputed command where his voice was supreme and where military considerations dominated political. The C-in-C had now let it be known that he did not expect his proposals to be criticised in the departments by officers of inferior rank; and had advanced a scheme which would place Indians in charge of mobile guns. This had never been allowed since the days of the Mutiny and the Secretary of State had often stated emphatically that field artillery must remain in British hands. Curzon had to oppose the idea[14] and did not doubt that it would be rejected, at which Kitchener would be proportionately vexed. He cited this example to show that Kitchener had failed to assimilate Indian conditions and to adapt himself to Indian methods of procedure:

> Though I have the greatest respect for his character and talents, and am firmly resolved to make the most of both of them in the proper channel, I shudder to think of what he might do were not a very strong hand kept upon him, and were he at liberty to translate all his new and impulsive theories in a country like India into practice.[15]

Meanwhile, some of the ramifications of Kitchener's private correspondence were becoming known in London. A representative of the War Office remarked to Lord George at the Defence Committee: 'Great changes are impending in the Indian Army.' 'I know of none' replied the surprised Hamilton, 'except the renumbering of regiments.' He was told that letters passing between the War Office and India showed that various other reforms were on the *tapis*. Long before Kitchener arrived, this habit of direct communication had caused trouble. Curzon had more than once asked that documents should not pass independently of the India Office and Viceroy. Hamilton and Lansdowne, then Secretary for War, agreed. In 1901, Hamilton had protested stiffly to Brodrick against the same practice, which was ordered to cease.[16] He now asked Curzon to tell Kitchener that 'although communications between the two C-in-Cs are always recognized, any changes of an important nature must be referred through the Indian Government and the India Office here. Otherwise we shall have a double set of communications which will be a source of great embarrassment and personal friction...'

Curzon explained in his covering letter to Kitchener that the India Office controlled the Indian Army as much as the ICS and was most tenacious of its prerogative. Nothing disturbed the Office more than to know that a high official was writing about important proposals to other departments. Confidential letters between Kitchener and Roberts were not only customary but 'most desirable'. If, however, Kitchener adumbrated to him large schemes upon which the Government of India had not given an opinion, the India Office were 'sure to think that you are going behind their backs and they are apt to become antagonistic'. Kitchener answered that he had sent a copy of his paper on the Military Department to Roberts. Lacking Indian experience, he had thought it right to consult him on a matter 'which I recognise may possibly necessitate my having to resign my present command'.[17]

Curzon repeated that he thought it most natural and desirable that the C-in-C in India should be in frequent private consultation with his opposite number at home, not least because Roberts was the greatest living master of that Indian military experience which Kitchener did not yet possess. He asked that when Kitchener was writing of ideas not yet submitted to or agreed by the Government, Roberts should be told clearly that the views were purely personal, at least for the moment. Kitchener replied he was sure he had always made this clear but would be very careful in future. He thanked Curzon for the kind way in which he had written,[18] and promptly begged Lady Cranborne and Roberts to keep what he wrote quite private. 'It seems rather petty when Imperial interests are in the balance,' he grumbled, 'but of course there is nothing for it but to be very circumspect... I do not think the Imperial Defence Committee will be able to do very much unless they are able to communicate with the man on the spot.' This statement, of course, misrepresented the facts. Nothing prevented the IDC from communicating with Kitchener. Roberts misunderstood the situation and told Kitchener that he should not pay too much attention to the 'wigging'. 'It would be very unfortunate if we could not write freely to each other.'[19] It is not clear whether Lady Cranborne realised the truth any more correctly. Anyhow, the warning made no difference to Kitchener's procedure, excerpt to cause him to adopt more secret methods.

These events moved Curzon to write again to Lord George about the C-in-C, who, as he rightly judged, regarded the Military Department 'as an insufferable and odious obstruction, which must be temporarily tolerated, but which is to be swept away as soon as he is firm upon his legs'. Curzon thought that he and Kitchener were unlikely to quarrel, partly because they were good friends, partly because without the Viceroy Kitchener knew he could do nothing. But he had no doubt that Kitchener was looking forward to his early departure, when he could assume in India the place he had filled in Egypt and South Africa: 'He thinks that when I go, he will get rid of the Military Member, and with a new Viceroy, ignorant of India, and probably less strong-willed than himself, that he will be the ruler of the country in everything but name.'

Kitchener had hinted at resignation if he did not prevail and Curzon admitted to Hamilton that the situation was already 'fraught with great difficulty'. If it could be handled for the remainder of 1903 by a frank interchange of opinion and continuance of cordial relations, well and good. This was the line Curzon intended to pursue:

> Kitchener is an extraordinarily lonely man: being unmarried, he has nobody in his house except young officers greatly his inferiors in age and standing; he takes no advice from anybody; he spends his whole day in thinking over his own subjects and formulating great and daring schemes; he will not go and talk them over with the Military Department because he looks upon the latter as his sworn foe; he will not make friends with other Members of the Government, some of whom he cordially despises and openly criticises; he stands aloof and alone, a molten mass of devouring energy and burning ambitions, without anybody to control or guide it in the right direction.

Curzon had now spoken to Kitchener about his recent tours on the frontier, saying that an officer of his prodigious prestige could not rampage along the borders without exciting the wildest apprehensions on the other side. The chance of a visit from the Amir must not be jeopardised by any further explosions and he asked Kitchener not to undertake his contemplated journey in September on the Northern frontier, where the peace of the area round Chitral must not be disturbed. Curzon praised warmly Kitchener's desire to acquaint himself with the whole frontier. All this the C-in-C took extremely well. He said that it had never entered his head that he should tell the Viceroy where he was going or that any ferment could be produced by his appearance.[20]

This letter had hardly been sent off when Kitchener told Lady Curzon that he intended to resurrect the question of the Military Department. Curzon wrote to him at once, remarking that a most disagreeable situation would arise if that Department opposed the C-in-C and were supported by the Council. Would Kitchener say privately what was proposed? Then, if he foresaw storms, Curzon might advise postponement till the autumn, 'when your familiarity with the work, and consequently the authority of your advice, would be proportionately increased. I am sure you will see that this advice is offered with the best intention.'[21]

It transpired that the occasion of this particular onslaught upon the Military Department was the correction by them, without reference to Kitchener, of an ambiguity in an order seen and approved by him. The C-in-C's indictment, Curzon told him, was factually inaccurate. He must oppose it if it were officially put forward, and he thought the Council unlikely to agree with the C-in-C. To Curzon's amazement, Kitchener replied that he had very good hopes that Elles would support what amounted to a proposal for his own extinction. This was simply put to the test. Elles, who had only two days before confided to Curzon his grave apprehensions about Kitchener's designs on the Military Department, said at once that these proposals would reduce the Military Member to the level of a staff officer to the C-in-C. He must fight them at every point. Curzon passed this information to Kitchener, reflecting privately on his apparent inability to see any side but one of a question in which he was interested.[22]

The Viceroy also told him that the India Office would, he thought, decline to revolutionise the government of India on the recommendation of a C-in-C who had been only six months in the country. Should he not, therefore, wait and see how the machine worked? The particular incident of which Kitchener complained had been investigated. It was of the most trivial nature, easily explained and unworthy of mention in a State paper. All this does not mean that Curzon failed to understand the difficulties. He realised Kitchener's reluctance to see his schemes criticised and possibly upset by the Military Department. Yet this danger could be avoided, at least to some degree. Before submitting the finished schemes to the Military Department, Kitchener might send for Elles and discuss it with him, or send Duff to talk the matter over with Barrow, Elles's deputy. If the C-in-C himself decided not to proceed with a particular scheme, it need not be printed in the departmental files or circulated. This would prevent the publicised rejections of which Kitchener had complained. Curzon asked him to believe that Elles was intensely anxious to help.[23]

At dinner on 20 May, Kitchener told the Viceroy that there were only three possible positions for a C-in-C. He could do nothing, in which case he would be universally popular; or he could put forward his proposals and carry them, in which case he would be respected though perhaps disliked; or he could put them forward and have them rejected, in which case he would be despised. Kitchener said that he intended to be found in the second class. Curzon approved entirely; but the difficulty, as he observed to Lord George, was to know how to steer him into that class. According to

Curzon's account, written the next day, he asked Kitchener point-blank: 'What is at the bottom of it all? What do you object to? You admit that you have no case against the Military Department, from your own experience, and yet you want to destroy it; where does the grievance come in?'

Kitchener said he could not endure that his proposals should be criticised or rejected by subordinate authorities. 'You may be unable to understand it, for it is all a question of military feeling and military discipline. Civilians do not have the same sensitiveness, but as Commander-in-Chief I cannot afford to have my opinions criticised, and possibly overturned, by military officers of lower rank than myself.'

As Curzon remarked to Hamilton, here was a claim

> to absolute dictatorship in all military matters for the Commander-in-Chief, and it is drawing a razor across the throat of the Military Department and cutting it from ear to ear. That is undoubtedly what Kitchener came out here to do; what he has had in his mind ever since; what he may desist from attempting for the present under pressure from me; but what he will bring up again, either during my time or the moment that I have gone.

That judgment proved to be correct in every particular. Curzon was not prepared to take part in the decapitation of the Military Department, which, he now believed, did useful and necessary work. The presence of a Major-General at its head did not detract from the prestige of the C-in-C. Curzon knew from earlier experience that good relations could be maintained. The position of the C-in-C depended upon his own personality and no constitutional check could prevent a man of character and capacity from becoming the most prominent military personage in the land. If he were discreet in dealing with the Military Department, the C-in-C would find them eager to work for him; for, to put it at the lowest, the promotion of all of them was in his hands.

Whether counsels of commonsense could be pressed upon Kitchener Curzon felt unsure. Apart from the vexation and worry entailed in keeping matters straight in future, Curzon had been shocked at the light cast by these incidents 'upon the personality of a man whom I have constantly seen described in the papers as a diplomatist and a statesman, but who seems to me, in so far as I have yet been brought into contact with him, to be strangely deficient in some, at any rate, of the essential attributes of both'.[24]

Kitchener reported to Lady Cranborne by the same mail his version of the story. He had decided, he wrote, to let the matter wait for a year, 'as I can I think do a little good here. I shall then resign on a very similar proposition, so if Curzon gets a year's extension, as everyone here seems to think probable, you may see me again in London about this time next year...I am sure you will be careful that *nothing* comes from me and that my name is never used'.[25]

Within a day or two, however, Kitchener had threatened immediate resignation in an extraordinary letter which showed either that after six months' experience he had completely failed to understand the system or that he was determined to misrepresent it. Curzon had explained, in response to Kitchener's request for 'a ruling', that all orders went forth in the name of the government or of the Governor-General in Council. Many must be issued without reference to the Council or to individual members of it. Most of the military orders were in fact drafted by Kitchener's staff and sent to the Military Department for despatch. No order of any importance, to Curzon's belief, had gone out without reference to the C-in-C. Until evidence to the contrary were forthcoming, he did not propose to alter the system. Kitchener replied that if the Military Department could issue orders to the army without the cognisance of the C-in-C or HQ staff, the executive command of the Army had passed out of the hands of the C-in-C. If Curzon's present 'opinion' were 'a final ruling', he felt he must resign his command. Curzon replied patiently that it was not a ruling but a description of the system. Kitchener had still produced no case in which executive orders to the army were issued without the knowledge of the Commander-in-Chief or the Headquarters Staff. Any question of a 'new ruling' must be a matter not for the Viceroy but for the Government of India. Kitchener should state his views fully to the Viceroy's Council, and might rely upon him for full support against any attempt to deny the C-in-C full executive control of the army.[26]

Some of Curzon's entourage told him that Kitchener was bent on leaving India anyway and was merely seeking a plea. Until now Curzon had not credited this theory, for the C-in-C had seemed to be so tumultuously keen about his work and he, Curzon, had felt a warm interest in the man's dynamic power and a desire to save him from pitfalls. No unfriendly words had passed. In the space of six months he had spent more hours listening to Kitchener's 'torrential expositions' than in the company of Lockhart and Palmer in four years. But he did now concede that Kitchener was manifestly disappointed with his position in India. He had come after being the autocrat of South Africa and the darling of England and had started by believing that he could trample on all opposition. For the first time in years, he found himself the servant of a highly organised government. He could not understand why the Viceroy was so much more splendidly housed and equipped than himself. Having obtained permission to add a billiard-room

at Snowdon, Kitchener also built, at a cost to the Indian taxpayer of nearly
£2,000, a large panelled hall; and was annoyed that the government would
not pay at once another £2,000 to put in electric light. He disliked Anglo-
Indian society which, Curzon admitted, was in many respects appalling:
'He abominates our files and departmental method of working. In fact, he
is just like a caged lion, stalking to and fro, and dashing its bruised and
lacerated head against the bars.'

Curzon well understood Kitchener's mortification at finding himself a
poor second to the Viceroy, a novel and painful experience for a man in his
fifties and of imperious temper. All this was explained in detail to the
Secretary of State, for the crisis might come at any time:

> I want you also clearly to recognise that no effort on my part shall be wanting
> to prevent such a stupid disaster as the loss of Kitchener's services. I am not
> looking at it from the point of view of public opinion alone, though I know
> well that however trumpery the issue on which he might elect to go, public
> opinion in England (though certainly not in India) would side with him, and
> say he had been driven out by me, or by the bureaucracy, or by anything but
> the real cause. I am regarding it from the point of view of the advantage of the
> Empire. If only we can tide over his first year, by the end of which he must to
> some extent have learned the ropes, all may yet be well.

Curzon's instincts lay with the strong man who found obstacles in his
path; yet Kitchener had forced him into the position of championing the
Military Department, which Curzon had never thought possible, and of
putting the brake everywhere on his plungings. He begged Hamilton to
keep this quiet for the moment. The only safeguard was that the Viceroy
and C-in-C should remain friends. Once they were estranged, or public
opinion began to think they were quarrelling, the crash was certain to
come.[27]

Early in June, a new incident of friction arose. Sir E. Elles desired to
appoint to the vacant post of Director of Military Works, which was in the
Viceroy's gift, a certain colonel. Kitchener ran another candidate. Nothing
would induce him to accept the colonel; he telegraphed without authority
to Roberts, extracted a recommendation of his own candidate and then
quoted it on the file. Curzon decided in favour of Kitchener's man, expect-
ing Elles's resignation at every moment. The description of the latest
military fracas had now become a regular feature of Curzon's letters to the
Secretary of State. He told Lord George that he felt the position most
deeply. For over four years he had managed with two Cs-in-C and two
Military Members, with little difficulty:

Now I provide a Tom Tidler's ground on which these two turkey-cocks fight out their weekly contests—each clamouring to get me on his side and threatening me with resignation if I take the other. Moreover, it is all so unnecessary and so stupid. If only Kitchener would show a little grace and tact, and think a little of the difficult position in which he is constantly placing me, things would go better. As it is, I am the focus of a perpetual turmoil which I have done nothing to provoke, and of which I am a mortified but helpless spectator. I am told too that all sorts of fresh combats are ahead, to which I look forward with an almost sickening apprehension.[28]

Accepting Curzon's early diagnosis of Kitchener's character as absolutely true, Hamilton hoped that his zeal for reform might be associated with established methods of procedure. Lord George was shocked by the casual manner in which Kitchener had tried to reverse the policy of keeping field artillery in the hands of Europeans. He doubted if Kitchener's Egyptian experience was of any real use in India; on the contrary, it seemed to excite him into sudden and single-handed action of a kind which no Commander-in-Chief, however experienced, would be justified in taking.[29] It was in organisation, reconstruction and administration that Kitchener excelled. As a strategist and tactician he was reputed to be much inferior to less able men. Hamilton, to whom his proceedings evidently caused grave worry, agreed that the powers of the Military Department could not be truncated to the degree suggested by Kitchener. Undue concentration of work in the hands of the C-in-C at home had been one of the prime causes of inefficiency. Like Curzon, Hamilton understood the annoyance of an autocrat, so long cock of the walk in Egypt, at finding his plans subject to criticism by junior officers. But since Kitchener was surrounded by British officers with no special experience of India, and since he knew nothing of Indian traditions and practice, he could not be given the free hand which he seemed to demand:

I sympathise with you very much [Hamilton wrote gloomily] in this trouble, and I do not see its solution. He evidently has an animus against the Military Member and his department, and, when he gets a dislike or suspicion of this kind into his mind, it is almost impossible to subsequently eradicate it.[30]

Lord George rightly detected that although the Viceroy's personal influence with Kitchener would count for much, it would be difficult if not impossible for him to placate the C-in-C without truncating the Military Department. Curzon noted that Kitchener seemed to have no grasp of, or interest in, administration. Though alleged to pride himself on financial capacity, he seemed to confuse finance with arithmetic. The one idea seemed to be to frame an estimate and keep within it.[31] Nonetheless, the atmosphere changed completely for a while in the summer. Kitchener was in the Viceroy's camp at Naldera as the weekly letter was penned on 9 July. 'Not a cloud flecks the sky' wrote Curzon, who had heard that Kitchener had earlier been convinced the Viceroy would oppose him. Kitchener now realised his misapprehension, and the change of mind might prevent trouble in future.[32] Kitchener's own letters of this period reflect his altered view: 'The Curzons, both of them, have been *very* kind and nice to me' he told Lady Cranborne, '…he is really a first-rate Viceroy and we work together much better now, quite cordially in fact.' And again, in the following week: 'I am getting on very well with Curzon. I think my having shown him there was an extreme point of endurance that might be reached has done good.'[33]

The mood did not last. Soon the complaints of obstruction, delay and friction were resumed. If war came, Kitchener told Roberts, there would be chaos and breakdown. In three years' time, he wrote to Lady Cranborne, Russia would be rapping at the door with a double line of railway. If nothing had been done in the meanwhile

we shall deservedly go to the wall. Under the present Military Department system it is almost impossible to get anything done and as the Viceroy supports the system I feel perfectly hopeless about the future. Is it not therefore a waste of time to stop here?…

The Curzons have been *very* kind and the weather is delightful in the rains —everything beautifully green—but I feel no pleasure in life while the Service suffers.[34]

Here Kitchener was striking a sure note. The conviction of Russian advance formed the basis of Balfour's strategic thinking. This letter, like most of the others, was passed to him. A week later, Kitchener told the same correspondent that by the spring of 1904 it would probably be time for him to pack up. He complained at length of the Military Department, suggesting that Cromer might be put into the government at home and himself into Cromer's place at Cairo.[35]

It would be wrong to leave an impression of unbroken wrangling between Curzon and Kitchener. The C-in-C received Viceregal support in the renumbering of regiments; the creation of a staff college for India; the increase of kit allowances; a juster system of disablement pensions; the improved efficiency of the police. Kitchener found the frontier militias which Curzon had created efficient. The Viceroy, desiring to spare Kitchener embarrassment, ordered that any military proposals emanating from him should not be noted upon by junior officers in the Military Department but should go directly to the Secretary. This was a treatment not accorded to the Viceroy himself or any other member of the Council. A new category of Army Orders, to be issued by the C-in-C, was instituted. The Viceroy's Council even recommended Kitchener's scheme to form homogeneous infantry brigades in place of those composed half of British and half of Indian troops. The opinion of the military authorities at home was hostile, and Kitchener withdrew the proposal.[36]

Above all, Curzon was relieved beyond measure to have found a fearless man who would support him in suppressing brutal attacks by British soldiers upon Indians. When in the course of one week four instances of unprovoked assault, three of them resulting in death, came before the C-in-C, he realised what it was that Curzon had been trying to fight:

> Now thank God he has taken the task off my shoulders, and the generals and colonels who used to snap their fingers at me are dancing timorously to the new tune. Nobody ever dares tell the inner side of things in India…I have scoured out a good many of these cesspools. But hitherto I have had to do it entirely alone. You can scarcely credit the sympathy with wrongdoing that there is here —even among the highest—provided that the malefactor is an Englishman.[37]

* * * *

With St John Brodrick, Curzon had corresponded almost every week until the temporary rupture which followed the Cabinet's willingness to accept his resignation in November, 1902. Brodrick, though slightly Curzon's senior in age, was his junior in public status, political achievement and mental capacity, and knew it. A tinge of wistfulness, perhaps even envy sometimes creeps in. 'Five years yesterday since we upset the government!' he wrote on 22 June, 1900. 'What a lifetime of work you have crowded into it. As good a five years as any man could ever hope to do. Hardly a day lost—great achievements—fame. I wish I had such a record.'[38] Curzon would reply sympathetically, understanding only too well Brodrick's difficulties under Lord Salisbury at the Foreign Office: 'I know what an uphill job it is: with the Parliamentary Under-Secretary, so to speak, outside the show and with that strange, powerful, inscrutable, brilliant, obstructive deadweight at the top.'[39]

Often mutual friends would tell Curzon of Brodrick's doings. Lord George said that he was trying to cultivate humour, 'which is rather an effort and not always quite successful'; and Alfred Lyttelton wrote in the summer of 1900 that Brodrick's sense of 'the infirmities of his friends, their want of judgment, wisdom, morals, deepens—though his real loyalty and kindness of heart repairs some (not all) of the breaches which he makes in our reputations'.[40]

In 1901, Lady Hilda Brodrick died suddenly. Curzon's memory turned to the days when he lived near the Brodricks and seemed 'to be part of your happy life and you of mine. Do you remember it? So sequestered, so peaceful, so confidential, so serene...think...how her spirit (if you believe in such things, which I do) will always be about you, watching your path, perhaps even inspiring your action...'

To him, Curzon wrote, the news of her death had brought a day of horror and gloom:

> I think only of you with your broken heart and crippled life, of your poor children, Muriel just on the threshold of her young existence, the rest standing so much in need of a mother's care. It makes my heart bleed to think of your solitude and anguish in the future.
>
> You know...that all my thoughts and prayers are with you: and that there is no one in the world nearer to your heart in its sorrow than
>
> Your affec.
> George[41]

'Your letters' Brodrick answered 'have gone to my heart—they are so understanding and comprehensive—I feel you take in more than any but one or two how intensely one has to suffer.'[42]

Brodrick had throughout this time to cope with all the multifarious and often unpleasant business of the War Office, interspersed with an abundance of Parliamentary duties. Early in 1902, he confessed to feeling the strain a good deal. He had given up his home and kept at work all day, returning to a solitary room only for a few hours' sleep: 'As you truly say, one settles down to a great loss. It is nearly eight months now and I have got accustomed to going about alone and doing mother as well as father...' And again a few weeks later: 'Every place I go to has memories of her, and I often show a cheerful face and retire at night to the hopeless collapse of fatigue and loneliness.'[43]

The Prime Minister's Private Secretary, Sandars, acknowledging Brodrick's industry, administrative ability and lucidity in speech, observed that nature had endowed him with 'a strange and unhappy genius for producing strained situations in his conduct of public business'. He seemed to rejoice in a duel, especially with a distinguished member of his own party or with a newspaper proprietor, whose journal he would treat as a criminal organisation. With an artless manner went a *mauvaise plaisanterie* so finely developed as to bring joy to the connoisseur, amusement to colleagues and, eventually, disapproval in the Lobby. 'He had indeed something of the temperament which made Lord Houghton ask Cardinal Wiseman to meet Mazzini at breakfast.'[44]

Since succeeding Curzon at the Foreign Office in 1898, Brodrick had worked Sundays and weekdays alike. There seems to be no doubt that he interfered much in matters of detail and took upon himself more than he could sustain. Schomberg McDonnell reported his habit of overwork, and his impetuosity, to be growing. 'It is of no use to keep a pig and do all the squealing yourself.' Clinton Dawkins, with the freedom of Balliol friendship, described Brodrick as 'very industrious and very high-minded... more obstinate than any other animal in the world...not without vanity, and has not really the mind, or imagination, necessary for the War Office, let alone India.'[45]

In view of the central and tragic rôle played by Brodrick in this story, these indications of his character and methods are worthy of attention. The consciousness of inferiority which he often betrayed – 'I admit your power to beat me over any country'—appears to have made little difference for the moment, to the quality of his friendship with Curzon. They remained until 1903 upon the closest terms. When, a little more than a year after Lady Hilda's death, Brodrick became engaged to marry Madeleine Stanley, he told Curzon before anyone else.[46]

Perhaps Brodrick's later attitude to Curzon was influenced by his desire to become the next Viceroy. Curzon heard of this from Selborne and from the King's Private Secretary; very probably Brodrick knew that he had been told. When the extension was being discussed, Brodrick expressed himself as 'very contented to wait a bit longer', as though he had some kind of reversionary interest.[47] He may have abandoned this ambition willingly. It is equally possible that he felt wounded by the Viceroy's expressed wish that Selborne should succeed.

All this, however, lay in the future; the immediate question was whether Brodrick could remain at the War Office without bringing down the government. In 1900, he had refused Lord Esher's offer to become Permanent Under-Secretary. Esher, an intimate friend and confidant of the King, had nevertheless played a large and unwelcome rôle in military questions. In his converse with men highly placed, wrote Brodrick long afterwards, he was 'always shrewd and sometimes helpful'; but by the time a decision had reached the point when it could be laid before the sovereign, 'the issue had been largely prejudged, on the incomplete premises of an observer who had no official status'.[48] The position of the Secretary of State during the

Boer War was inevitably an uncomfortable one, and especially in the case of Brodrick, who had so long a connexion with the War Office as Parliamentary Under-Secretary. Revelations of confusion, disloyalty and even corruption caused much anger. In a private letter to Esher of 16 October, 1902, King Edward described the Office as a mutual admiration society and the inadequacy of the Intelligence Department as 'one of those scandals which ought to hang Lords Lansdowne and Wolseley and Sir Evelyn Wood'.[49]

Moreover, the large rise in the Army estimates, the plan for six Army Corps, and the failure of recruitment to come anywhere near the expected total, raised much Parliamentary discontent. 'Now, Mr Brodrick,' said *John Bull* in the cartoon, 'am I an Island or a Continent? If I am an Island, I require a strong Fleet and a small Army; if a Continent, I require a large Army and a small Fleet; but I can't afford both.'

Curzon, who had warmly defended Brodrick during the past two years, heard a good deal from his visitors and correspondents of the hot water in which his friend was currently wallowing at the War Office. He supposed that St John's 'tactlessness and clumsiness, which even his dearest friends know to be phenomenal, have more than compensated for the great conscientiousness, rectitude, and industry, with which he addresses himself to his most difficult task'.[50]

Lord George reported that the Secretary for War, disliked by civilian and military officials, had contrived, quite unconsciously, to annoy and humiliate many of those with whom he had to do business. For this Hamilton felt sorry, thinking Brodrick a good fellow and hard worker, with the interests of the Army genuinely at heart:

> but his deafness has greatly grown upon him, and that, combined with a certain tactlessness, prevents him from understanding the gist of personal conversations, and to this physical failing rather than anything else may be attributed the very unjust opinion, which, I fear, almost universally prevails concerning him.[51]

Brodrick's unpopularity had indeed reached such a pitch that the Prime Minister described it as the most serious menace to the government.[52] A week or two later, at the end of February, Hamilton told Curzon that in a long parliamentary experience he never remembered seeing so much animus shown against a Minister as against Brodrick during the debate on his Army scheme. Lord George still could not fathom the cause. Brodrick was able, extremely industrious and, though tactless, not discourteous; but Hamilton thought the real failing must be that his facility in exposition greatly exceeded his powers of organisation. He was extremely self-opinionated, and so deaf that he did not hear other people's opinions. By contrast,

Selborne, liked by everyone, was not only carrying out reforms but had managed to associate public opinion with him. He seemed by instinct to get to the bottom of the questions he investigated; whereas Brodrick 'obtains a very rapid, surface grasp of the immediate difficulty, and has a rare power of bringing all kinds of somewhat strained and extraneous arguments in support of his scheme'.

These qualities, coupled with an indomitable push, had enabled him to run up army expenditure to 'terrific proportions', for, in the next budget, defence would cost £70m. Almost certainly conveying a hint about the Viceroyalty, Hamilton wrote that some posts for which he had once thought Brodrick suitable now seemed beyond his capacity.[53]

On the same day, Brodrick told Curzon that he was in serious difficulty at the War Office. Lord Roberts had aroused hostility by his handling of the scandal in the Grenadier Guards. A group of young officers were simultaneously trying to oust Brodrick, who, though believing himself to have accomplished more than any Secretary of State since Cardwell, offered his resignation to the Prime Minister. Curzon, whose correspondence with him had only just been resumed after the row over tax remissions at the Durbar, replied kindly that he was very sorry to hear of these troubles and felt intensely for Brodrick. Parties, he observed, search for scapegoats.[54] Meanwhile, critical debates had been taking place in London. Hamilton wrote that he could not recollect such general complaint of the chaos prevailing at the War Office. Brodrick's ample powers of speech had induced him to overstate his proposals and, as Lord George nicely put it, 'undoubtedly in one or two cases the figures which he has produced in the House of Commons and which had a great effect in determining a debate, have proved to be not altogether accurate'.

Balfour had so strong a hold within the House that he could pull the Government out of any mess and Hamilton remarked that if it were not for his confidence in the Prime Minister's capacity he would have predicted a ministerial collapse upon the question of the army estimates.[55] However, the government got through with a good majority, largely because many Irish members abstained. Hamilton admitted to an uneasy conviction that in substance the assailants were in the right. In Hamilton's view, Brodrick had been badly at fault in trying to initiate reforms during the war, before he had time to take stock of the needs and of the best methods. To justify the vastly increased estimates, both Brodrick and the Prime Minister made free use in debate of Indian requirements and of the large reinforcements which India would need in the event of an assault on the North West frontier. Lord George was not much pleased.

He conceded that for dialectical purposes the argument answered, but neither he nor anyone at the India Office had been consulted when additions to the establishments were made. At no time since 1895 had he or the government of India asked for a substantial addition to the Indian Army. The only request in that time had been one made by Curzon for an extra 5,000 men, and that on the condition that the British treasury would pay. The India Office analysed the increases of Indian and British establishments since 1890. The number of white troops in India during that period had gone up by 3,000 and at home by 63,000. It was therefore clear that the additions had not been caused by India, but partly by increased requirements in the colonies (notably South Africa) and still more, Hamilton commented unkindly, by 'the ambition aroused in the military mind of being able to take part in a big continental war'.[56]

The immediate crisis of confidence had now passed, though a much more violent storm was soon to gather. Curzon heard from Schomberg McDonnell, who saw much of political life from within, that the government had fallen into considerable disrepute:

> The phenomenal feature...is the hatred of St John: granted that he is tactless and rude, and that the indecent rejoicing over his second marriage has shocked many of his friends—that does not account for the malignity with which he is regarded by his own party in the House of Commons: men cannot be got to admit now that he is even able: and in his office he is even more detested than in the House.

The Ministerial team, wrote McDonnell, was a poor one: Lansdowne weak, Hamilton stale, Gerald Balfour useless, Londonderry ludicrous, Stanley a standing joke. Selborne, however, had done very well:

> I don't think my dear George that you will have much difficulty in running into your own place when you return—already people talk of you as the next P.M. You have a reputation for *strength* which is everything now; at this moment the public chooses to think that Arthur Balfour is weak and not hardworking.[57]

★   ★   ★   ★

A few weeks after the decision to increase British soldiers' pay, Curzon learned that a Cabinet committee (Balfour, Devonshire, Chamberlain and Brodrick) had been appointed to investigate Army expenditure. This really meant, as Hamilton commented, putting the War Office into commission and he feared that three of the four would make proposals placing additional expense upon India.[58] Chamberlain had returned from South Africa very keen to keep there a considerable reserve, upon which India would have first call. This scheme might well be sanctioned by the committee. Six weeks later, Brodrick wrote of Chamberlain's determination to have in South Africa a permanent garrison of 30,000 men. That would raise the total of British troops serving abroad to 150,000, a number at which the War Office blenched somewhat. The reconstituted Defence Committee had been investigating Central Asian strategy. It estimated that if Indian forces had to meet a Russian advance by moving to Kabul and Kandahar, India would need 15–30,000 men as rapidly as possible, with another 70,000 to follow. If France supported Russia, it would not be easy to send large numbers of troopships through the Mediterranean and Suez. Until the French fleet could be annihilated, India could be certain of receiving troops only from South Africa. Would it not be worthwhile, Brodrick asked the Viceroy, for India to pay something for a reserve of 15,000 men held absolutely at her disposal in South Africa, whence they could arrive within three weeks of the outbreak of war? Chamberlain insisted that South Africa should not contribute a farthing towards this permanent garrison. He had apparently threatened resignation more than once.[59]

Curzon replied that this was not a good moment to put the scheme forward, when India had just, by the decision of the Lord Chancellor, been saddled with extra military expenses of £786,000 a year. Moreover, large reinforcements for India could not be wanted yet, for Russia was unable to strike until she had built the Orenburg–Tashkent railway. In the interim, India could spend her money more advantageously than upon keeping 15,000 men for whom she would have no need.[60] On 16 July, a telegram from London announced that Britain wished to maintain in South Africa a garrison of 25,000 men, of whom one half would be ready to proceed to India in emergency. For this privilege India would pay £400,000 a year, half of the extra cost of quartering these men in South Africa. If the British garrison in India were augmented, the cost would fall entirely on India; on which ground Hamilton recommended the new proposal.

Before this message had been deciphered, the plan had been announced with approval by Brodrick in Parliament. Such a procedure, Curzon protested, hardly treated him as a colleague, put him in the invidious position of having to oppose a measure already made public, and undermined British rule by treating India unfairly. Kitchener, fresh from two and a half years in South Africa, minuted that he did not believe it would be possible, in emergency, to withdraw half the garrison.[61]

This proved decisive. The government of India refused to take part in

what they called a one-sided bargain which would almost certainly break
down at the crucial moment. Curzon remarked privately to Hamilton that
the British Empire had drawn most freely upon Indian troops for wars all
over the place without paying a penny in advance; now the Cabinet wanted
India to pay large sums for a hypothetical claim. India had provided what
was really a reserve for Imperial wars. It seemed to Curzon an almost
priceless advantage to England. Moreover, the latest incident was one of a
series. He had never denied that India was a subordinate government, a fact
being borne in upon him every week:

> But we are a very important Government and we have a very important
> constituency behind us and putting the matter on the lowest basis, treating it
> from the point of view of expediency alone, I often feel tempted to ask His
> Majesty's Government why they should not, in their own interests, adopt an
> attitude of somewhat greater consideration, and facilitate the progress of the
> machine by pouring in a little oil...

The proposal, Curzon urged, should be abandoned, for the announcement
had been freely condemned in India and persistence would do serious harm
to the position of the British Government. The view he had first put to
Brodrick was endorsed by his colleagues; that India had better military
uses for the money. And would it not be more reasonable for the home
government to pay part of the cost of the Army in India upon which it did
not 'hesitate or cease to indent for campaigns with which India has no
connection'? In any case, the 12,500 troops would be wanted not to defend
India but to fight Russia on the Helmund or Hindu Kush. That would be an
Imperial war, comparable with fighting the USA if she invaded Canada.
Yet no one would dream of making Canada pay, either at the time or in
advance.[62]

Before the debate, Curzon learned, Brodrick had said he must indicate
the possibility of an Indian contribution; to which Hamilton replied that
the government of India must not be committed. All it was necessary to
say was that the two governments were in touch. By blurting out the
opinion that India ought to pay, Brodrick put the least palatable part of the
scheme in its most objectionable form. The Cabinet, however, were 'very
much annoyed' at India's refusal and at a press leakage of the fact in Simla.
Hamilton admitted that Brodrick had spoken ineptly; but 'this clumsy
method of dealing with a difficult question is one peculiar to Brodrick'
who had now been subjected to severe attack.[63] To him Curzon had already
observed that the War Office, and the government at large, did not understand how to treat India:

You seem to think that we are merely a sort of Department who can be ordered to do this or that, as though we were the Board of Trade or Agriculture or some similar institution. Neither do you seem to me to set any count upon public opinion in India. Even the India Office does not realise that India is changing every day, that opinion here is educated and articulate and that the old tyrannies and jobs that used to be perpetuated at the expense of India are no longer capable of repetition.

Curzon detailed a considerable number of instances in which India, as he believed, had been poorly treated. As for this latest issue, he had never known the Indian press so united in denunciation:

I cannot conceive anything more unfortunate than the impression which British Governments are steadily building up in India, viz. that India is always to be treated from the selfish and Shylock point of view by the people at home and that it is to the Viceroy alone that she can look for defence of her interests. This puts the [Viceroy] into a position of quasi-antagonism to the Government at home, of which you are always telling me that he is a colleague...[64]

The rest of this correspondence contains some points of importance. Brodrick wrote, 'Your policy in Persia and Afghanistan and Thibet appears to us to make "big battalions" a necessity.' Curzon replied that his policy did nothing of the kind. Admittedly, he wanted to anticipate the Russians at Lhasa; but as India was very close to Lhasa and Russia was not, there was no need for big battalions. It was from India, said Brodrick in another letter, that the demands for more troops came. Curzon pointed out that India had not asked for any troops at all, though plenty had been requested from her.

The leakage at Simla had brought sharp comment from London. Curzon answered that it was far worse in the Cabinet; and the departments in India were manned by those to whom five shillings was an important consideration. The Cabinet, he added lightly, almost seemed to imagine that leakages were deliberate. Though Curzon did not realise it for some considerable time, that was exactly what Brodrick and various others did believe. Yet not a word had transpired in the press about the Indian government's opposition to the soldiers' pay increase; no one knew that the decision to make India pay the charges at the coronation had been contested; Curzon himself had been bitterly criticised for failure to announce the tax remissions at the Durbar. At the wink of an eyelid all this could be altered.[65]

The letters leave no doubt that Brodrick, who had endured a year of severe Parliamentary battering, felt aggrieved. 'If you knew' he wrote to Curzon 'the time, trouble and loyalty which I have expended on supporting your policy by what all your military supporters here consider to be necessary preparations, you would I think realise that I deserve something better than to be represented simply as a raider of your revenues.' He had already promised to do all he could to stop the bitterness growing up on the British side. As for the £786,000, he treated the issue as a constitutional one. Was the Cabinet master or not? He could not see how business was to be carried on if the Viceroy, being represented in the Cabinet by the Secretary for India, was to review all Cabinet decisions. Would Brodrick apply this to Chamberlain and the Colonies, Curzon retorted? 'It is because the government of India see themselves so constantly treated in a way that they know no Home Government would dream of applying to the meanest constitutional Colony that they feel hurt and angry.'[66]

*   *   *   *

Salisbury had realised before the end of the Boer War that the Conservative-Liberal Unionist alliance was unlikely to last much longer. 'Things will be in a very fluid state' he said 'soon after my departure.'[67] Lord George, who had already noted the effects in connexion with Afghanistan, explained to the Viceroy in May how the departure of Salisbury, Goschen and Beach had upset the old balance of opinion. Chamberlain was now much stronger, and much as Hamilton admired his qualities he feared lest the Colonial Secretary press some proposition so startling that the government might break up. Certainly Chamberlain's position was a curious one. The strongest individual in the Cabinet, he had little sympathy with its military, educational and financial policy. Hamilton judged, rightly, that there must soon be a serious collision. A few days afterwards, he was telling Curzon that 'the want of internal cohesion and of general motive power amongst the Cabinet.. does not augur well for the duration of the government. The machine has got out of gear, though its creaking at present is only heard by those engaged in its management.'[68]

At the Prime Ministers' Conference of 1902, a resolution urging preferential treatment in the United Kingdom for colonial goods had been passed. For revenue purposes, Sir M. Hicks Beach had imposed a shilling duty on corn during the Boer War. In the autumn, before Chamberlain left upon his visit of reconciliation to South Africa, the Cabinet had apparently resolved that the shilling duty should be remitted on corn imported from the British Empire. Balfour reported this decision in explicit terms to the King; other Ministers, however, do not seem to have understood anything so definite. It is another instance of the confusion arising from lack of proper records and from unbusinesslike conduct of the Cabinet's work. The Chancellor, C. T. Ritchie, an avowed supporter of free trade, determined to repeal the corn duty in his forthcoming Budget. The matter had to be settled at a single Cabinet immediately on Chamberlain's return. Ritchie had his way. Presumably the alternative would have been his resignation, and Balfour felt that he could not afford to lose two Chancellors of the Exchequer in swift succession.[69] Anyhow, Ritchie announced the repeal in terms which made nonsense of the arguments which Balfour, Beach and others had used when the tax was imposed. Three weeks later and a few days after Lord George had confided to Curzon his fears about the Colonial Secretary's love of a big splash, Chamberlain spoke at Birmingham of the need for a fiscal system which would allow favours to friends and retaliation against rivals. This speech came as a clarion-call to some of the younger Conservatives. The Tariff Reform League was formed at once; and Balfour realised that the government were trapped. 'As public opinion is at present in England' he wrote, 'deliberate protection of foodstuffs would be an impossibility. It is a great misfortune that it is impossible either to retain the tax or to withdraw it without offending many good supporters of the Government.'[70]

These developments, indeed, threatened to transform the whole political situation. Less than three months before, the most serious danger Mr Balfour had foreseen had been Brodrick's unpopularity. Now there had arisen an issue explosive among the electorate, divisive amongst the government's following but providing a heaven-sent opportunity for the opposing forces to rally upon an issue of the utmost respectability. Lord George, who conceived himself to possess a sure grip of fiscal and financial questions, thought the whole idea unpractical and predicted the annihilation at the next election of the party advocating Chamberlain's policy. 'The middle class will not look at it, and the great bulk of the working class will repudiate it. Landlords, farmers and exporting manufacturers will be its supporters, and what are they among so many?'[71]

At this stage, Curzon's extension of office had just been agreed in principle. The controversy now beginning in England might even put a Liberal government into office before it took effect; and that aspect apart, the position of India in relation to the new proposals had to be weighed, though Chamberlain seemed to have given it little enough consideration. Curzon, who had thought the abandonment of the corn duty an act 'of great levity', was kept well informed of the developments within the Cabinet. Early in June Brodrick sent dismaying news:

I fear Chamberlain is leading to the biggest smash the Tory party has had for 50 years...His first proposal in the Cabinet was to free Canadian corn *and not India*—so little had he considered it. Even now he has only an idea—not a scheme, and goodness knows how the flesh and blood are to be put on to the bones... My own impression is J.C. wishes to go. He is very loyal but overstrained—He dislikes the Budget—Education Bill—G. Wyndham's Bill and my Army scheme. It is only a question if we can get through this Session...[72]

Meanwhile, Chamberlain, stung by interruptions, had committed himself in Parliament more definitely than at Birmingham, contradicting the speech Balfour had delivered earlier in the evening. Many assumed that preference was part of the government's policy. Hamilton, like others, was not prepared to go so far.[73] Though the dissolution of the party was staved off for a few months, the cleavages had become manifest. The pure free traders were numerous on all sides of the House; pure protectionists few; retaliationists well represented, devotees of Imperial preference influential but not numerous. Balfour realised that the fact of known division within the Cabinet 'greatly weakens our position, and gives the Opposition a new and unexpected advantage in the Parliamentary game'. He still hoped to avert, or at least defer, any crisis which might bring down the government.[74] His uncle, Lord Salisbury, spoke privately to Hamilton in that month, June, of his deep concern at the political position, saying that any party proposing to put a permanent tax on food would in the end be knocked to pieces. It was probably on this occasion that Salisbury condemned the dual leadership of Balfour and Chamberlain as contrary to the spirit of Parliamentary government. It would bring any party thus conducted to real disaster. Another visitor, Hicks Beach, also found Salisbury 'angry with Balfour for allowing Joe to master him so much'.[75]

By the end of the session, the Parliamentary supporters of the government had divided into 'tariff reform' and 'free food' sections, with a variety of permutations. 'We issue leaflets' wrote Ian Malcolm to Curzon, 'of infinite inaccuracy and revile each other as only happy families can. The position is damnable: and you may well be glad that you are out of it.' Balfour no longer had any hopes of holding the Cabinet together but seems to have believed that Chamberlain would fall in with the scheme of fiscal retaliation which he intended to announce. He felt confident of being able to carry on as Prime Minister.[76] Hamilton, who was spending these last weeks of his political life at Harrogate, undergoing a water-cure associated with perpetual rain, cold and gloom, told Curzon on 20 August that the government's disintegration could not be long delayed. The worst feature in the political situation was Chamberlain's omnipotence in the inner councils:

If he was Prime Minister, our people would know whom they were following; now Arthur's diaphanous drapery is around him and the public are not keen sighted enough to see what is the figure inside. The machine is out of gear. Everything connected with the self-governing Colonies is put up on a pedestal to which the rest of the Empire is to bow down.[77]

This chimed with the view Curzon had often expressed. He thought Chamberlain would certainly be beaten on the first round; and did not agree with an approach which professed to pull the Empire together while apparently ignoring India, far and away its largest constituent part:

I do not believe that the continued existence of the Empire depends upon Preferential Tariffs (though I am personally ready to throw away any number of 'fly-blown phylacteries'), but it looks to me as if the future existence of the Unionist Party, for some years at any rate, were likely to be compromised by the manner in which the question has been raised.[78]

That letter was written on 10 September. Four days later, the crucial Cabinet was held. Balfour, having decided that preference was not practical politics for the moment, now realised that he must lose Chamberlain, who had already offered his resignation in writing. At the outset of the meeting, Balfour stated that he regarded the dissolution of the Cabinet as inevitable. He must have the loyal and cordial support of all his colleagues. Ritchie and Lord Balfour of Burleigh, who had put in memoranda disputing the Prime Minister's fiscal policy, were curtly dismissed. Lord George Hamilton, with Lansdowne's support, proposed that the speech Balfour was shortly to deliver at Sheffield should be awaited. He refused at once.[79] This Cabinet has been the subject of many conflicting accounts, which it is unnecessary to collate here. The main question at issue has been whether the free traders, Hamilton, Ritchie and Balfour of Burleigh, were kept in ignorance of the fact that Chamberlain too was about to resign. According to a memorandum written a few days later by the Prime Minister, Chamberlain told the Cabinet that if preferential duties were dropped there were reasons personal to himself which made it impossible for him to stay. Austen Chamberlain's recollection agreed with this version.[80]

Whether Chamberlain announced his resignation or not, there can now be no doubt that the fact was not understood by Hamilton and others. No mention seems to have been made to the Cabinet of Chamberlain's letter of resignation, in which he had explicitly admitted that preference for the colonies could not be pressed immediately. If Chamberlain's resignation was supposed to be known to everyone, it is very hard to understand why Balfour asked the Duke of Devonshire to keep the possibility strictly to himself. In a letter to Curzon of 16 September, Lord George, who had sent in his own resignation, described the proceedings in terms which show clearly that he had no idea that Chamberlain's departure was already settled, if indeed it was. The Balfour-Chamberlain alliance, he wrote, was an impossible combination for those used to Chamberlain's ideas about protection and preference. The Prime Minister differentiated, posed as a free trader and put forward protectionist principles, with limitations which must disappear if the principles were carried. Chamberlain, while ready to resign, had stated that he must adhere to the preferential scheme, whether he were in office or not, adding that he was not Prime Minister and that his colleagues should not necessarily be bound by what he said. However, if the Prime Minister would not repudiate Chamberlain's theories, then the lesser men had no choice but to go. Balfour, Hamilton thought, could not afford to part with Chamberlain just now. If the protectionist movement failed, the Prime Minister would be most severely censured; if it succeeded, Chamberlain would get all the credit. A little more firmness and a juster appreciation of the issues involved, if shown in the earlier phases, would have saved him from his present dilemma:

> His closest advisers think too much of the Party machine, and too little of the principles with which he has to deal. The machine should never dictate the policy, but the policy ought to be so handled as not to break the machine. We have contrived to break up the machine, and yet to go to the country with a policy which is foredoomed to failure.[81]

A few days later, Hamilton was telling Curzon angrily that the free-trade ministers had apparently been befooled, since Balfour had in his pocket at the Cabinet the resignation of Chamberlain and the withdrawal of his proposals for taxes on food. It appeared that the only object of the meeting was to lure into resignation certain Ministers, so that Chamberlain might take his opponents with him. As it happened, the resignation letters of Hamilton and Ritchie stated clearly that the preferential tariff was one of their reasons for departing. Hamilton's letter had been sent in with the approval of Devonshire, who intended to follow suit immediately. The Prime Minister, according to Hamilton's information, played the Duke along until the resignations of Ritchie and himself were received and then told the Duke of the scheme he had pre-arranged with Chamberlain. Devonshire had not gathered at private meetings with Balfour on 14 and 15 September that Chamberlain was definitely to go. When to his astonishment he learned this fact on 16 September, he said, 'then George Hamilton, who resigned on my advice and under a misapprehension of the actual state

of things, ought to be told, as he might wish to reopen his case.' Balfour
refused. The first information Hamilton received of the changes was when
he read a newspaper containing the acceptance of his resignation. Since
Balfour knew that he was ready to go at any moment, this behaviour
seemed the more unpardonable.

> Poor fellow, he is a child in Joe's hands, for the trick played on us emanated
> from that worthy. The agitation, which Balfour is to head, is assuming a purely
> Protectionist character, and his finicking definitions and limitations will soon
> disappear...I am only too pleased to be out of office, though I can never forget
> the mean trick practised upon me by an old and valued friend.[82]

This, then, was the disagreeable end of nearly five years' co-operation
between Hamilton and Curzon, a period which, with every passing week
under the new régime, stood out the more pleasantly in Curzon's memory.
Hamilton had more than once felt angry with the Viceroy, who in his turn
had lamented the other's inability to keep the India Council in better order.
All the same, they had, with conspicuous success and across a gap of seven
thousand miles, put through a programme of reshaping and reform unequalled in any quinquennium since the time of Dalhousie. Saying handsomely that it had been a real pleasure to work with Curzon, whose steady
expansion in the post of Viceroy he had watched with delight, Hamilton
praised his high motives, fearlessness in facing unpopularity, phenomenal
powers of work, command of the written and spoken word. These were
rare gifts, which should enable the Viceroy to do at home things as big as
those he had achieved in India. The Secretary of State added a friendly
word of advice:

> Try and suffer fools more gladly: they constitute the majority of mankind.
> In dealing with your colleagues and subordinates try and use your rare powers
> of expression in making things pleasant and smooth to those whom you over-
> rule or dominate. Cases have more than once come to my notice where persons
> have been deeply wounded, and gone from you full of resentment, in conse-
> quence of some incautious joke or verbal rebuke, which they thought was
> harshly administered.

Curzon felt genuinely grateful for Hamilton's kindness and forbearance
and told him so. His words of criticism and advice were perfectly sound.
'I am quite certain' he went on solemnly, 'that no Viceroy ought ever to
indulge in chaff or in a joke; and I have no doubt that my propensity to
both forms of recreation (in a life of excessive tedium and burden) is a
snare.' The press in India, European or native, uttered no word of appreciation of Hamilton's eight years' service. What Ampthill described, with

despair and disgust, as 'a sort of howl of savage exultation' went up.[83]

*   *   *   *

The crisis in the War Office, merely postponed in the spring, broke out afresh before the upheaval of September. In August, it appears, Esher took it upon himself to indicate that Brodrick should go. Lord Roberts had come to believe, as Wolseley had done three years before, that the C-in-C could get nothing done. Accordingly he hinted at, or threatened, resignation. Brodrick gave assurances of support for desirable changes, and advocated that a post be created for Kitchener, whose driving power would speed up the administration of the Office. Roberts's view was not shaken. It is clear that Roberts thought Brodrick unsuitable; difficult to work with, prone to interfere with discipline and to waste time over details, viewing everything from the House of Commons aspect. 'I could not get him to understand that it is a Cabinet Minister's rôle to teach the House and not to let the House dominate him.' Moreover, Brodrick had increased the difficulties of the C-in-C's position 'by an unfortunate failing of never being able to trust, or believe in, any one, with the inevitable result that no one cared to work for him...to my mind a man with such a failing is totally unfit for any position of authority or responsibility'.[84]

As it appeared to Brodrick, the diminished position of the senior military member, if an Army Board were established, must be unsatisfactory to Roberts, who wanted an increase of power which he could not obtain under any system. 'I saw the knot was getting too tangled' Brodrick explained to Curzon, 'and told Arthur I thought my mission had been carried as far as I could carry it.'[85] This was probably anticipating the inevitable. The King, to whom Brodrick was *persona ingratissima*, indicated that he must leave the War Office and would be very suitably placed at the India Office. On 28 September Balfour called on Brodrick at Gosford, after leaving Balmoral. He gave the impression that a Board would be established at the War Office on the lines of the Board of Admiralty, a procedure warmly approved by the King. The Prime Minister refused to allow Brodrick's retirement, offering the Secretaryship of State for India. This was accepted at once. As for the War Office, Balfour had apparently determined upon an appointment acceptable to the sovereign. According to Brodrick, the Prime Minister tried Selborne, Wyndham, Cromer and Esher, failed with them all, and had to settle upon the one man, H. O. Arnold-Forster, against whose appointment he had inveighed most strongly.[86] Balfour told the King that although Arnold-Forster lacked charm he had knowledge, industry, zeal for reform and intimate acquaintance 'with the administrative methods of the Admiralty which Your Majesty is so rightly desirous of introducing into the War Office'.

The King at first refused, preferring Akers-Douglas or Selborne, but gave way when Balfour insisted.[87] Brodrick wrote despondently to Curzon. Cromer and Milner were both supposed to have refused any office at all; Selborne and George Wyndham had refused the India Office; Arnold-Forster was much disliked. Everyone was a *pis aller*. Balfour wanted his cousin Salisbury (just succeeded to the title) to join the Cabinet, which, observed Brodrick 'is Hotel Cecil with a vengeance...It can surely not last long'.

It need hardly be said that Curzon took a very poor view of most of the proceedings, though he thought highly of Arnold-Forster and looked forward to working with Brodrick,[88] who received his strictures without the least surprise. The situation, as the latter remarked, was a very curious one. Between 1895 and 1900, not a single vacancy occurred in the Cabinet. Since then a regular shift had taken place; in 1900, 1902 and now in the autumn of 1903. Of the latest appointments, only one—the substitution of Earl Percy for Salisbury at the Foreign Office—had strengthened the government. As Salisbury had 'failed completely' as Under-Secretary, his promotion had astonished everyone 'and it is in keeping with the determination to put magnates into every position, which I have detected in the Chief's conversation. For instance, it was all I could do to prevent his offering the Secretaryship for Scotland to the Duke of Montrose who has never even spoken in the H. of Lords.'

Brodrick did not doubt that the 'Hotel Cecil' feeling had been substantially strengthened: 'the idea that blue blood is the only passport has received some real encouragement (the two new Whips are both eldest sons) and our bench is unmistakably weaker than it has been at any time since 1895.'[89]

The Cabinet had lost, in little more than a year, Salisbury, Hicks Beach, Lord James of Hereford, Chamberlain, Ritchie, Balfour of Burleigh, Hamilton and Devonshire. At the end of September, before the Duke's resignation, Balfour had thought that the new Cabinet compared favourably in reputation and capacity with the old, though admittedly nothing could entirely compensate for the loss of Chamberlain.[90] How Balfour could believe that Arnold-Forster, Alfred Lyttelton, and Graham Murray would be an improvement on the departed ministers must remain a mystery. What is certain is that Balfour's personal position became, after the recriminations which followed the ministerial crisis, an unpleasant one. Ian Malcolm told Curzon that respect for the Prime Minister seemed to have disappeared; he was openly accused of sharp practice and of moral cowardice in appearing as a free trader while pushing the free traders out of the Cabinet. Then came, on top of the feeling that all had not been above-board, the resignation of the Duke of Devonshire and the publication of the somewhat painful letters exchanged between him and the Prime Minister. Nevertheless, it was thought that Arnold-Forster could do well at the War Office, to judge by the oaths uttered by the soldiers who heard that he might be going there. Austen Chamberlain and Alfred Lyttelton would be good Parliamentary performers; but Brodrick's appointment was described by an M.P. as 'dumping *in excelsis*'.[91] Hamilton had warned the Prime Minister that he would be an indifferent choice for the India Office; and, knowing Brodrick's habit of rubbing up those with whom he dealt, wrote to Curzon, 'I doubt whether you will find him easy to get on with or if he will handle the Council well.'[92]

The Viceroy thought they would find no difficulty in working together but realised that loyalty to India would require Brodrick to abandon many points of view he had championed at the War Office. 'On the other hand, he is a man with a wide grasp of public affairs, with Imperial views and with a strong sense of duty...' Brodrick telegraphed immediately on his appointment:

> Judging from the past that I am likely to be in sympathy with you, I trust this arrangement will commend itself to you. Apart from personal affection, no Member of the Cabinet more fully realises the greatness of your work in India and his own inexperience. Be sure of all possible support from me.
>
>   St John[93]

*   *   *   *

Curzon reacted cautiously to the fiscal controversy, observing that while everyone but the Liberals had abandoned the old cast-iron orthodoxy, no one talked in anything but generalities. He wanted to see what would happen in the first concrete case. When the Russians increased their duty on Indian tea, he telegraphed to London, offering to raise the Indian tax on Russian petroleum. Russia then threatened to raise some other tax. The government did not adopt his offer.

Again, what would the colonies actually accept? Would the British working man accept the same thing? And was each British government to present to Parliament each new commercial treaty, based on different fiscal principles according to the views of the party in power? Or would there be a general system of higher tariff, with relaxations?

The British Empire is capable of being held together by a number of bonds, political, administrative, military and naval, commercial, sentimental. If these are to be worked up into a genuine Union, there must in time be some organisation for the purpose. But I have always heard that the Colonies do not want a Council at present, because they think it will mean some loss of independence and considerable increase of burden. I have therefore always felt disposed to wait. I am far from averse from a fiscal union: but no one has convinced me that it ought to come first, still less am I persuaded that without it the entire fabric will fall asunder.[94]

As for the special interests of India, her import duties upon British and other Imperial goods would presumably have to be abolished, at heavy cost. Moreover, a large proportion of Indian exports went to countries outside the Empire and would certainly suffer discrimination.[95] In an official letter of 22 October, 1903, Curzon and his colleagues stated that without any system of preferential tariffs India already enjoyed a large, probably an exceptionally large, measure of advantage in the free exchange of imports and exports. From the position of economics only, India had something, perhaps not much, to offer the Empire, very little to gain and a great deal to risk or lose. From the financial point of view, the danger of reprisals against India, even if they proved unsuccessful, was so serious and their results would be so disastrous that she would not be justified in launching out in a new policy unless assured of greater advantages than any thus far apparent.

To this judgment the Finance Member, Sir Edward Law, entered a dissenting minute. Though he too thought it to India's interest to leave matters as they were, he judged that it might be hard to show that preference would injure the country. The risk of reprisal was generally small. These views came before a Committee of the Cabinet, to which the Chancellor, Austen Chamberlain, argued that India was in a strong position to negotiate and that her exports might benefit largely under a preferential system. Most members of the Committee disagreed. Two draft despatches were prepared. One, on Brodrick's orders, controverted the view of the government of India. The other, on the orders of the Committee, generally accepted it. In the event, no reply was sent.[96]

*   *   *   *

The autumn of 1903 was for Curzon a time of partings. Lord Salisbury's

death and Hamilton's resignation were followed by Walter Lawrence's
return to England. Curzon's pressure upon him in 1898 to resume his Indian
career had been amply justified. The two had been known as 'the iron
hand and the velvet glove'. Before the private dinner of farewell at Simla,
Lawrence, knowing his master's habits on such occasions, said, 'I hope you
will not jest.' 'Jest!' he exclaimed, 'I am far nearer to tears.' Curzon's
tribute praised Lawrence's knowledge and love of India, discretion and tact:

> He has brought me confidence and sympathy where I might not have been
> able to acquire them for myself; he has smoothed down the rough places and
> converted frowns into smiles; he has been known and trusted from one end of
> India to the other, and in all things he has been to me the soul of fidelity and
> devotion.

Lawrence replied that hardly a day had passed without some act on
Curzon's part of generosity, sympathy with those in trouble, some proof of
courage, energy, prevision:

> But what has most endeared him to me and has won my affection, and my
> absolute devotion, has been his invariable consideration. My work has been a
> daily pleasure, a daily lesson and a daily tonic.

All in all, Sir Walter had much to reflect upon that night. He sat up
talking with his dear friend Sir Pertab Singh, who confided that he wanted
to annihilate the Moslems of India, some sixty millions in number. Lawrence spoke of mutual friends among the Moslems. 'Yes' said Pertab,
'I liking them too, but very much liking them dead.' In the early hours,
Lawrence went up to Curzon's room to say a last goodbye. He was at the
desk, working out a minute on education.[97]

TWO

The Buffer States

AFTER NEARLY five months' silence, the Amir wrote on 27 November, 1902, that he still intended to visit India as soon as urgent internal affairs allowed, though he did not think there was anything to discuss. He argued as usual that the agreements were not personal to his father, and that the British should supply more arms and money. There was no hint of rupture, or of inclination to make terms with Russia. Accounts of the position at Kabul seemed to reveal three actual or potential factions. First, the Amir and his following: Habibullah's rule alternated between sensual idleness and a cruelty notable even by Afghan standards, while his letters spoke of the turbulence of his people. Next, his brother Nasrullah, who would probably support him until it were convenient to defect; and third, Abdur Rahman's widow and her son.

The Amir was reputed to have communicated with the Russians about frontier questions. Realising that the sterner policy might have made him suspicious, Curzon neither believed that he had made any agreement with Russia nor wished to precipitate the issue. The previous history of missions to Kabul had been a most unhappy one and no emissary could possess the Viceroy's authority. While the Amir's position remained weak, he dare not concede anything; the despatch of a party to his capital would be taken as proof of anxiety to settle and could hardly produce anything better than a confirmation of the terms agreed with Abdur Rahman.[1] Two years later, this prophecy proved exact.

Meantime, Russia's interest in the buffer states became more marked. As for Afghanistan, Lamsdorff appeared to regard old promises as invalid. 'I did not detect' wrote the British Ambassador, 'any symptom of a sincere desire to try and avert misunderstandings by a free and frank exchange of confidential views.' The official Russian reply, distinctly brusque in tone, hinted at the despatch of agents to Afghanistan. Curzon thought this was probably a bluff, but agreed that local correspondence might be allowed if the Amir wished it. So far, he had expressed no desire for such changes.[2]

The Cabinet, weary of friction with Russia in Central Asia, asked Lansdowne to seek a *modus vivendi*. King Edward observed that Russia could not be trusted, for she had only one desire: to increase her power in Asia. Curzon's view was broadly similar. He judged that the Russians would no more leave Afghan foreign relations in British hands out of respect for treaties than they had continued to honour the Black Sea clauses after 1870.[3] The Foreign Secretary himself told the Russian Ambassador that manifestations of a desire to intervene one day in Tibet and the next in Seistan

> were of a nature to afford us serious food for reflection...were we to assume that Russia claimed throughout the Asiatic continent a kind of 'overlordship', in virtue of which she thought herself called upon to raise these points in regions remote from her own possessions and in which she had apparently no concern? Count Benckendorff ridiculed the idea...[4]

An agreement, the Viceroy remarked, would curtail Russian ambitions. But with a policy as fitful and vacillating as Britain's, Russia had only to wait to get her way in Southern Persia. Where, then, was the incentive?[5] Lord George's recent letters had confirmed his poor view of the Cabinet's resolution in Asiatic questions. Fear of any international complication, wrote Hamilton, had made his colleagues unduly timid,

> except when a question arises of India advancing money to Persia, or taking some obligation entirely upon her own shoulders, and then they are courageous enough. And I am afraid they look upon me both as obstructive and a curmudgeon because I object to propositions which are put forward which, whilst they might occasionally get the Imperial Government out of a Parliamentary difficulty, would be clearly indefensible from an Indian point of view.[6]

In April, 1903, Lansdowne had high hopes of an understanding with the Russians, who seemed to have behaved straightforwardly about Tibet. Benckendorff had now admitted that the matter of frontier relations could be decided only with the Amir's consent; and so long as such relations were clearly defined, Lansdowne did not wish to be too stiff. If Habibullah would steadfastly refuse all facilities for Russian agents, the British position would be a very strong one.[7] At that very moment, however, various Russian officials were making approaches to the Governor of Herat about boundary pillars and other questions; a rash of tiresome incidents broke out along the north-west frontier; the Military Attaché at Teheran believed that Kushk and other places on the Russo-Afghan border were being made ready as bases; and the Amir, who had intimated again that he would soon visit Curzon, assured him that there would be no correspondence with the Russians. Indeed, Habibullah protested at the irregularity of their actions, and wondered whether they were hoping that some accident would befall their emissaries? Curzon professed himself entirely satisfied by this attitude, and, having rejected a suggestion of the Foreign Department to threaten a British agent at Herat, felt justified.[8]

The horizons of the Czar, as described by Kuroptakin, were not narrow. He wished, it appears, to take Manchuria, Korea, Persia and the Straits, dreamed of bringing Tibet under Russian control, and complained that Ministers did not carry out their master's wishes with sufficient fidelity. Though a liberal discount must be made for Kuroptakin's irritation at court intrigue, his sharp reference to 'each Bezobrazov who sings his song in unison with the Czar', when related to the developments later in 1903, indicates that this account may represent the substance of the Emperor's mood.[9] For whatever reason, the better understanding desired by the British Cabinet did not mature.

★   ★   ★   ★

The military discussions after the Shah's visit to London had produced, in the first instance at least, a general recognition at the War Office that Seistan was the focus of British interest in Southern Persia. An inter-departmental conference advised that if Russia invaded the north, British reaction must be limited to the occupation of Seistan and Bunder Abbas. Arthur Hardinge, who had hoped that south-western Persia and even Isfahan might be held, found this a daunting conclusion; but as Roberts observed, such issues knew no local boundary:

> Any resistance on land in Persia to a movement by Russia would almost certainly result in the violation of some portion of Aghanistan, with the object of threatening India, which would necessitate the concentration of all our available forces for the defence of that country.

The Foreign Office, India Office and Admiralty had agreed on the naval action to be taken should Russia try to seize a coaling-station in the Gulf. It was not clear, Brodrick minuted, that France would wish to establish Russia in the Gulf, nor to Germany's interest that those two powers should monopolise the trade of that region. If war resulted, Britain was 'exceedingly unlikely to stand alone'; if an understanding with Germany were sought, however, she would claim Kuwait as a terminus for the Baghdad railway.[10] Yet amidst all the shoals and reefs a policy had to be found if the British position were to be salvaged. The Russian loans of 1900 and 1902 seemed to portend the demise of Persia as a power with any pretension to inde-pendence. Hardinge believed that his political superiors in London scarcely realised the darkness of the outlook, which could no longer be met by temporising:

> Fortunately these ancient Eastern Governments, in the dry desiccating air of Upper Asia, rot slowly, like Egyptian mummies, and retain a certain semblance of their old outward form when the vitals within are already dust...The northern tide is running so strong against me that it is well nigh impossible to make way against it, and the most I can do is to keep the boat from being carried further down...[11]

To do justice to Lansdowne, he did understand that a more definite note must be struck; but his brother-in-law at the India Office gave Curzon little reason to expect a change of policy, suggesting that Indian authorities were apt to overlook the ubiquity of the Foreign Office's interests. Was it wise to threaten a weak power already in the clutches of a stronger, the game that had failed in Turkey and China? In Persia, cajolery and rewards had been tried, yet the Shah, breaking his promise, had just accepted without consultation a new tariff favourable to Russian trade and injurious to British. The corollary was plain enough, an understanding with Russia, earmarking all the country between Seistan and Bunder Abbas for Britain, but allowing Russia to reach the Gulf: 'Time is on Russia's side' ran the familiar refrain, 'the longer we delay coming to an arrangement, the worse the settlement for us will be...De Witte and the Emperor both want to come to terms and Germany is becoming fast in Russian eyes an object of mistrust and even of menace.'[12]

Lord George pointed out to Godley that if Britain and Russia were on friendly terms, Holland would be safe from Germany.[13] His desire for an agreement with Germany, or his belief in its feasibility, had evaporated, while the First Lord explained to Curzon that the Navy Estimates were

> a simple question of national existence. We must have a force which is reasonably calculated to beat France and Russia and we must have something in hand against Germany. We cannot afford a three power standard but we must have a real margin over the two power standard...

This policy the Cabinet had now adopted. The German Navy was becoming very formidable. It represented a derogation from what might otherwise be even greater power on land, where alone a struggle against Russia and France would be decided. Therefore, Selborne remarked, 'without losing one's judgment and balance altogether...certain conclusions force themselves on one.[14] Shortly after this, the decision to build a new naval base on the Firth of Forth was announced.

According to rumour in the early part of 1903, Russia had offered Persia

£½m in return for political concessions. When Hardinge learned that the Persians would be glad of three or four hundred thousands within a couple of months, the discussion of October, 1901, repeated itself: Hamilton wanted to see some tangible security; Curzon stood out for a recognition of British primacy in Southern Persia; Lansdowne wished neither to increase British commitment there nor to lose the opportunity. Although the mission to confer the Garter had been received with ceremonious courtesy at Teheran, the attitude of the Persians towards the British did not reveal much gratitude. The Shah, Curzon noted without surprise,

> appears to be applying the very leg upon which the Garter has just been bound...to that part of our person for which no respect is entertained by the subalterns of the Grenadier Guards.[15]

The King directed Knollys to tell the Prime Minister that it would be 'inconceivable if Hamilton and the Indian Council were allowed to influence the only wise decision at which we could arrive'. If the loan fell through, 'the conferring of the Garter will be even more useless than he [the King] has always believed it to be.'[16] The Cabinet thereupon decided that money must be lent, entirely from India's resources and through the Imperial Bank, with the home government sharing the risk on capital and interest. £200,000, the first instalment, was paid on 8 April, secured on the Caspian fisheries and the customs of Fars and the Gulf ports. M. Vlassof, the Russian Minister, said it had been 'un grand coup'. He offered a sum which would extinguish the British advance. The Grand Vizier refused.[17] This loan saved his political skin for the moment. It had been known for some time that the Shah wished to take the waters in Europe, and equally well known that he had not the wherewithal. Moreover, the wages of the army, months in arrears, could now be paid.

In the autumn of 1902, Valentine Chirol of *The Times* had travelled extensively in Persia. He found that Russian ascendancy had replaced British influence at Teheran, where the Legation lacked trained staff. One employee happened to be the brother of a confidential servant of the Grand Vizier, who betrayed in jocular vein a singularly intimate knowledge of the diplomatic strings which Hardinge presumably believed himself to be pulling in secret. Other Persian notables complained of the British Minister's passivity. Concurrence in the establishment of the Belgian customs administration had been universally interpreted as a sign that Britain accepted Russian preponderance throughout Persia, and a senior Belgian official told Chirol that his instructions were framed in consultation with the Russsian Ministry of Finance.

Forwarding these observations to Lansdowne, Curzon commented that he knew Chirol to be right on one point. Britain's policy towards the Belgians had been misconceived from the start. As for Hardinge, whose acuteness and finesse were acknowledged, 'he always thinks that he has everybody in his pocket and is never so happy as when he is being successfully hoodwinked by Naus or someone in that gallery'. Since the policy of wheedling the Persians was futile, 'a good show of the boot now and again is very essential'. The scandalised Sanderson said he did not see that this particular boot had any nails. Lansdowne admitted a part of the impeachment, adding that Hardinge was perhaps unduly fond of trying to meet the Persians with their own weapons. Nevertheless he had achieved something at Teheran, with few cards.[18]

India's money had been offered, Curzon wrote, not out of regard for Persia, or interest in the Shah ('a selfish driveller') or the Atabeg ('a convinced and inveterate Russian partisan') but only to delay the final doom, and because the British government lacked the courage to do it on their own account. Hardinge's reply expressed astonishment that the Viceroy should suspect any Persian statesman of harbouring convictions. The sole conviction of the Grand Vizier was that he must stay in office. Now he was ready, provided his own skin were not at risk and it were worth his while, to betray Russia. It was a waste of time, the Minister found, to talk to Persian Ministers about Persia's interests. One consideration interested them in foreign questions: 'What can I do to remain a Minister, or Governor, or favourite of the Shah, and make *mutakhil* in that capacity for myself and my family?'[19]

Curzon remained unpersuaded. To him, it seemed that Hardinge lived in an aura of imaginary defeats of the enemy and victories for himself, while India paid. 'He is always flattering himself over cajoling Naus or stroking down the Atabeg. But I know on good authority that he is only laughed at for his pains.'[20]

It was not only the activity of Russia that raised doubts about British paramountcy in the Gulf. The project of a railway through Anatolia to Baghdad and thence to the Gulf seemed likely to be realised. Germany, having secured the first concession, could not raise the whole capital singlehanded. In the autumn of 1902, after the second Russian loan and the Shah's unhappy visit, the departments believed that the railway would provide the most effective check on Russian progress and should therefore be encouraged, on condition that Britain could secure a proper share in the control of the line and of its southern terminus.[21] Though the whole question was of high importance to India, it was handled entirely in

London; but as Clinton Dawkins was one of the three British financiers involved, Curzon was well-informed.

Initially, Lansdowne empowered them to say that if their German counterparts furnished suitable assurances, the Cabinet would pledge good offices. The assurances were given, whereupon *The Spectator* and *The National Review*, both violently anti-German, opened fire. The Foreign Secretary then retreated: he had earlier spoken for the Cabinet without consulting them, had never dreamed that they would doubt his policy, feared there was a divergence of view. Luckily, Dawkins and the others had not committed him as fully as he had authorised.[22] Lansdowne, who called the outcry 'insensate', had no objection to an unfortified free port at Kuwait, whereby Russia would gain innocuous access to the Gulf. The Russians, however, seem to have thought that the purpose of the proposal was to give Germany an unhealthy degree of preponderance in Asia Minor. Dawkins, with his own sources of intelligence, had reason to believe that the material appearing in the British press originated with the Russian Embassy in Paris.[23]

At all events, the Cabinet felt they must bow before the storm. Early in April, Balfour had at last announced that Great Britain had special treaty relations with Kuwait. This was what Curzon had requested in 1899, and meant that no terminus could be found in the Sheikh's territory without British goodwill. On 5 May, after the negotiations had collapsed, Lansdowne told the Lords that the British government would 'regard the establishment of a naval base or of a fortified port in the Persian Gulf as a very grave menace to British interests, and...we should certainly resist it with all the means at our disposal.'[24]

The declaration, made with the agreement of Balfour but not of Lord George, delighted Curzon, who had wanted such a statement for ten years and more. Russia, Benckendorff affirmed, did not intend to establish a base in the Gulf, followed a policy of free commercial competition in Persia and was most unlikely to build any railway threatening India from the Beluchistan flank. This hardly seemed to accord with the new tariff or the Russian surveyors in Southern Persia, and Curzon credited none of it. Lansdowne, whose talks about Afghanistan had so far proved nugatory, asked whether an understanding might not be reached, Britain recognising Russia's preponderance in Northern Persia, Russia acknowledging Britain's special interest in the Gulf, Southern ports and Seistan.[25] But this approach too met no response.

The Baghdad railway project did not recover from its sharp setback. Since it would apparently bring no great advantage to British or Indian interests, Curzon was not sorry. The railway, he thought, would diminish British influence in Mesopotamia and Arabia, which must sooner or later break away from the Ottoman Empire. Turkey in Asia might well become a seedier version of that public nuisance, Turkey in Europe. Nor did he want to see Germany in the Gulf:

> Many people say, 'Oh, make friends with the Germans as a set-off to the Russians.' Yes, but what sort of friends? The German Emperor would sell us tomorrow for a wink from Russia's eye; and I predict that before many years had passed you would see a Russo-German combination devised to push us out of the Gulf...I would not let the Turks and the Germans make any clandestine agreement to sell us behind our backs by arranging for a port at Basra or in Khor Abdulla or anywhere else.[26]

$$\star \quad \star \quad \star \quad \star$$

The search at Cabinet level in 1903 for an Afghan, Tibetan and Persian policy caused ministers to realise more fully what would be Britain's liability in a war with Russia. The results, as reported to the Viceroy, could hardly be called inspiring. Hamilton's letters indicated an extreme reluctance to face any risk and the assumption of an increasingly significant role by the Defence Committee. While the soldiers seemed to follow outdated ideas, the politicians, with the exception of Lord George, were ignorant of the elementary facts about British relations with Afghanistan or Russian movements in Central Asia.

In Hamilton's mind, two conflicting forces, both political, ruled the situation on the North West frontier. If the British sat still and allowed Russia to advance, they would invite disturbance in India and perhaps even shake the loyalty of some native regiments. Yet the Afghans were only likely to be on the British side because they dreaded the Russians rather more. If India's army acted prematurely, its erstwhile allies might join the opposite camp. An advance to Kandahar and Jelalabad seemed to balance these considerations.

The War Office, Hamilton noted with amusement, drew alarming pictures of the hundreds of thousands of troops whom Russia could deploy, especially after completion of the Osenburg–Tashkent railway, yet declared that the British could not under existing conditions feed 30,000 at Kabul. Russia had to contend with a desert and the Pamirs, while India possessed a rail network and the resources of a continent. He believed that without an effort which would bankrupt her Russia could not expect to win. Not until many years were past could she recoup by conquering India. Surely there were more alluring propositions on offer? Moreover, if invasion of India were part of a fixed Russian policy, she would have moved when the British army had been entangled in South Africa.[27]

Balfour too had been contemplating the Afghan question. His views suffered a sea-change between December, 1902, and April, 1903, when he privately enunciated the thesis that if the Amir were loyal to the British connexion, his territory, including Herat, should be practically guaranteed. He distinguished between fighting for Herat and at Herat by saying that the Russians would be turned out not necessarily by an attack at that point, but by bombarding Cronstadt, if it were feasible. 'Then' asked Godley, 'you are prepared to lay down a Monroe doctrine in respect of Afghanistan?' Balfour replied that he was, though he could not speak for the Cabinet.[28] Though Balfour soon changed his mind about the possibility of putting pressure on Russia in Europe, his resolve that she must be kept out of Afghanistan did not falter.

As the discussions proceeded, the difficulties Russia must surmount to wage war in Central Asia assumed, in Hamilton's eyes at least, most satisfying dimensions. The worst situation, one to which Curzon was alive, would be the installation of Russia at Kabul as the protector of the Amir, well placed to excite the tribes. By this token, Habibullah's goodwill became more than ever important.[29] West of his territories, Balfour argued, development of agriculture or transport would assist Russian advance. He wanted sterilisation. Hamilton objected that British policy in Asia was justified by the promotion of civilisation and prosperity 'and we cannot now go back and insist on having a desert all round us, because the improvement of the country between us and Persia or the Russian frontier might some day or other be of use to them for military purposes'.

Lord George feared lest the conclusions of the Defence Committee become mandatory and thus determine the spending of India's money. He watched with interest the mental processes of the Prime Minister, who swiftly picked up the main facts about Indian defence but, having the material for decision, discussed hypothetical contingencies, many improbable and some impossible.[30] Balfour composed a memorandum, of which Hamilton surmised that it would probably resolve itself into an attempt to increase India's establishments. No member of the Cabinet, he observed, understood the political perils which might spring from excessive taxation or realised that the size of the obligatory garrisons was largely governed by the feeling of the people when an advance was made beyond the frontier.[31]

Russia, ran the Prime Minister's argument, had practically unlimited numbers of troops, while India had not; hence the importance of the territory dividing them. Afghanistan was valuable not merely as a buffer, to take the brunt of aggression, but as a 'non-conducting' territory, lacking railways or good roads, and thereby debarring Russia from bringing to bear her numerical superiority at a vital point. In war, British forces must nevertheless occupy the line Kabul–Kandahar; to that extent military and political expediency coincided. Unfortunately, Afghanistan did not provide an ideal buffer, for it was riven by internal feuds and discontents, deriving such unity as it possessed from the rule of a despot 'whose methods of discouraging opposition are too thoroughly Oriental to harmonise with Western sentiment'.

Balfour described in terms similar to those employed by Curzon the unsatisfactory state of British relations with the Amir, who refused a European representative at Kabul, kept the agent a virtual prisoner, would give no information and build no roads or railways. 'And though we may be called upon to strain the whole resources of the Empire to repel any invader of Afghanistan, no man can be sure that the armies despatched for this purpose might not have to fight their way through Afghan troops to the positions it would be desirable for them to occupy.' As for a Russian advance by way of Seistan, Balfour argued on the lines which Hamilton had already described: that since a railway from Nushki to Seistan would be militarily disadvantageous if it provoked a Russian line to Nasratabad via Meshed the best plan would be to seek an agreement with Russia to defer for as long as possible all railway building in Eastern Persia.

The Defence Committee judged that unless the obligatory garrisons could be reduced, the field army of India would need to be supplemented by 30,000 men in the first four months of war, by 70,000 more within another six months and probably by a further instalment by the end of a year. These figures assumed that Russia and Britain would have completed the lines to Tashkent and the Afghan border respectively.[32]

On his visit to the frontier in the spring of 1903, Kitchener had realised that Seistan was a vital position. He did not wish to occupy it, but to be able to turn the Russians out if they tried to take the region. India heard rumours of Russian engineers surveying railway routes to the Indian Ocean, and it is known that there were plans for a railway to run due south to the sea from Meshed. The Belgian customs officials behaved, in Curzon's view, as Russian tools; and further north the Russians had established a cordon, professedly as a precaution against plague, which effectively hampered Indian trade. After a futile protest, the Cabinet appointed a British consul, with armed escort, at Turbat-i-Hidari.[33]

The trend of the reply to Balfour, written entirely by Curzon but also

signed by Kitchener, was to prune down India's requests for reinforcements, even though they thought that Russia could bring to each railhead
on the Afghan frontier, and maintain there, more than the 100,000 men
estimated by the Prime Minister. Russian supremacy in Seistan would provide enhanced opportunities for an attack on Kandahar, and for unsettling
and embroiling the Beluch border. She would then be driven southwards.
Engineers and irrigation experts whom Curzon had sent to the valley of the
Helmund discovered that its waters, properly used, were liquid gold. They
estimated that more than three million acres in Persia and Afghanistan
could be made to blossom as a rose, as Curzon had long hoped; and by
drawing off the water, the party controlling a certain stretch of the Helmund
could command the water supply of Seistan. Curzon and Kitchener hoped
that the Amir might grant a lease of this area. Balfour's suggestion that
Russia might begin a line to Meshed if the railway were pushed forward
from Nushki was accepted; and that extension should not be undertaken
for the moment, unless the Amir would agree.[34]

*　　*　　*　　*

Despite the British loan of April, supplemented by a further £100,000 in
July, discontent had not been allayed at Teheran. An agitation by the
mullahs, amongst whom Arthur Hardinge had probably spent some money,
was laid at his door by the Russian Minister in conversation with the
Atabeg. This formed part of a strenuous but abortive Russian campaign
against Hardinge. It may be that M. Vlassof's influence had been reduced by
a *gaffe* of a few months before, when he had accused the Grand Vizier of
telling a lie. Normally it would have been safe enough, but it happened that
on this occasion the Grand Vizier had strayed into a demonstrable truth.
He put on no mean display of righteous indignation. When, in the summer,
the Persian government announced that 12,000 men would be assembled
for manœuvres, the Russians were said to have produced £55,000; but in
the event only 2,000 men turned up, and before then the Shah had spent the
cash on a trip to the hills.

Lawlessness and the government's patent inability to suppress it might
provide Russia with a good opportunity to intervene; but by now Hardinge
was better placed. He said that if Russian troops entered Azerbaijan or
Khorasan, on whatever pretext, a corresponding step would be taken in
Seistan or the Gulf. This information, almost certainly conveyed to the
Russian Legation, cannot have failed to strengthen the hands of the Persian
government. Hardinge repeated the statement a few months later. By then,

the Grand Vizier's long reign was over, probably because he could not
provide his master with yet more money. His policy had been one of
borrowing until every security was exhausted. Asked what would happen
then, he shrugged and replied 'God is merciful'.[35] His successor, the Ain-ed-
Dowleh, was on rather distant terms with the British Legation but also
with the Russians.

After Lansdowne's announcement of 5 May about the Persian Gulf,
Curzon said that he would like to pay an official visit to British posts there.
India's money had provided the two loans of 1903, secured in part on the
Gulf ports; and, on the Arab shore, Muscat, Bahrein and Kuwait were more
or less under British protection. The Cabinet, nervous lest Curzon should
make new agreements, agreed 'with some little hesitation'[36] to the tour,
arranged for November.

Just before the Viceroy's party sailed, the new Secretary for India,
St John Brodrick, warned him against leaving any impression of British
desire to alter the *status quo* in the Gulf or at Muscat. The Sheikh of
Kuwait would doubtless be keen to receive additional assurances of sup-
port, but Britain had repeatedly agreed that Kuwait lay within the Turkish
Empire. Curzon merely minuted 'They must say something'.[37]

The first port of call was to be Muscat, where Russian and French cruisers
had arrived earlier in the year. During the spring a fresh fracas with the
French had broken out there. Three prisoners, claiming French protection,
had been taken. A week or two after Lansdowne's declaration of 5 May,
Cambon presented terms amounting almost to an ultimatum. Lansdowne
offered arbitration at The Hague, agreeing that the Sultan should be
advised to release the prisoners if the French would furnish a definitive list
of flag-holders and agree to issue no more emblems of protection. The
slavers were let out while a French gunboat stood off Muscat. Eventually,
the award at The Hague conceded the substance of the case for which
Cox and Curzon had fought. By then, the French and British governments had found other reasons for co-operation; but desire to allay the
Sultan's discomfiture was one of the Viceroy's main reasons for visiting
him.[38]

The entry into Muscat Harbour Curzon thought magnificent. From a
distance the land was shrouded in the haze of heat. The towering crags
seemed to drop sheer into the sea; suddenly a cleft opened in the rock,
concealing a sheltered anchorage, ringed round with cliffs. On the narrow
shore at the far end of the inlet clustered the gleaming Arab houses, 'like a
seagull's wing against an angry sky'. Two buildings, the British Consulate
and the Sultan's Palace, stood out, linked by a line of flags six hundred

yards long. Curzon's big white ship dropped anchor before six British men of war.

The Sultan made a most favourable impression. He did not plead for any further pledge, though he did say that he would gladly invite Britain to assume the protectorate. His demeanour was rather that of 'a loyal feudatory than that of an independent sovereign'. He took Curzon's hand, swearing eternal fidelity and devotion. The trade of Muscat was practically all British; Major Cox, to whose skilful management of the Sultan Curzon paid high tribute, was almost the ruler of the place; and 1,300 Indian subjects lived there. The French equality at Muscat looked more farcical than ever, for the only evidences of French interest were an attenuated consul, 'very like a polite haircutter', a coal-shed, 'which they only secured because we were weak enough to give it to them' and a gun-runner.[39]

At Shargah, where a ground swell of six feet was running, the Trucial Chiefs of the Pirate Coast attended a Durbar on s.s. *Hardinge*. So completely had they forsworn the habits of their immediate ancestors that several were prostrated by sea-sickness. The Viceroy, who had caught cold while exploring the strategic possibilities of Cape Musandim, conversed with the sheikhs in sepulchral tones through an interpreter and then gave presents; gold-mounted swords, rifles and gold watches with chains which seemed large enough to tie up an elephant. No new engagements were asked or needed. In his address, Curzon recalled that the British had on this coast found strife and created order:

> We opened these seas to the ships of all nations, and enabled their flags to fly in peace. We have not destroyed your independence but have preserved it. We are not now going to throw away this century of worthy and triumphant enterprise; we shall not wipe out the most unselfish page in history. The peace of these waters must still be maintained; your independence will continue to be upheld; and the influence of the British Government must remain supreme.[40]

At Kuwait, Sheikh Mubarak made elaborate arrangements. A victoria, the only wheeled vehicle in the place, had been brought specially from Bombay. The visitors were to land some three miles from the town, so that a suitably impressive entry might be staged. On shore could be seen all the armed forces, cavalry, camel-cavalry and foot, together with the Sheikh and his courtiers. Curzon exchanged greetings with Mubarak, who had dyed his moustache and whiskers black in honour of the occasion. The two climbed into the victoria and set off smartly with an escort of the camel-corps, some of whom sported suits of chain-mail. In the van fluttered the Sheikh's flag. Its motto read *TRUST IN GOD*

Here was a timely message, particularly for the rest of Curzon's party, mounted on mettlesome Arab horses with tall saddles. The procession bowled along in streaming clouds of dust, to the accompaniment of fierce war-cries, exploding crackers and the shouts of the running crowd. Groups of women uttered shrill noises reputed to signify joy. The horsemen, firing ball-cartridge wherever they pleased, tossing their spears about merrily, were having the time of their lives. Glancing back, Curzon saw Sir A. Hardinge flicked deftly to earth over the head of his horse. 'Nothing daunted, he courageously resumed his seat and, amid a hail of bullets, continued the uneven tenor of his way.'

The Sheikh made no bid for the extra assurances against which Brodrick had warned. He spoke of his attachment to Great Britain and his coldness towards Russian and French overtures, asking whether he could not have an allowance and an honour, now that he had come under British protection. Admittedly he had the Turkish rank of Pasha, with an annual grant of 120 tons of dates, for which he found not much use. Mubarak said he had severed all connexion with the Turks, except to pay a yearly tribute. Curzon considered carefully whether he was merely playing off one party against the other, but concluded that the Sheikh's professions were a genuine reflection of his indebtedness to the British, without whose help he would long since have lost his throne. Committing himself neither to the title nor to the subsidy, he warned Mubarak against adventures in the interior of Arabia, where Britain could give no help. The Sheikh said he understood this perfectly.

At the official reception, Curzon presented a sword to the Sheikh, who asked to gird it on at once as 'a military officer of the British Empire'. He seemed, the Viceroy wrote to Brodrick, 'by far the most masculine and vigorous personality whom I encountered in the Gulf, with acute intelligence and a character justifying his reputation for cunning and explaining the method by which he had attained his position (wholesale murder of competitors).'[41]

The departure from Sheikh Mubarak's residence proved to be a good deal less imposing than the arrival. During the private interview, rending sounds of plunging, whinnying and crashing came from without. With exquisite forbearance neither side inquired what was going on. After the interview, Sheikh and Viceroy descended to the street. The two Arab horses had disappeared. So had the victoria. All that remained was a heap of matchwood. The dignitaries picked their way through heaps of filth to the shore.[42]

Only one incident marred the success of this tour in the Gulf. Before the party arrived at Bushire, it had become known that the arrangements previously agreed with the Persians were in doubt. Arthur Hardinge tele-graphed to Teheran without reference to his host, to whom he expressed confidence that everything would be easily settled. But it was not. The Persian passion for etiquette obtruded itself. Curzon believed that the Persians were now trying to make him play second fiddle to their man at Bushire, which he declined to do. The boat lay offshore while messages passed. After a day Curzon gave it up.[43] His only official contact with the Persian authorities, therefore, was made at Bunder Abbas and Lingah, where he competed with the Governor of the Gulf Ports to see which could produce the more flowery compliments while keeping a straight face.

The true object of these calls was to assess the strategic position at the entrance to the Gulf. The British and Indian governments were more or less agreed that if Britain acted in Southern Persia, the four islands com-manding the approach to Bunder Abbas would be seized. This area, it transpired, provided a fine natural anchorage which, properly used, would prevent Russia from taking that port. Russia in the Gulf would presage Russia in Arabia and a warm-water port, though not vital to Russian trade, would mean the economic closure of Persia to Indian and British trade, besides providing another point of pressure upon India and the British Empire. 'I cannot see' Curzon had commented, 'why we would connive at either issue. Not even Admirals can close our eyes to the teachings of common sense.'[44]

The mishap at Bushire, of which the Persians gave Lansdowne a garbled account, caused Curzon to mistrust more than ever Hardinge's assurances of Britain's recovered influence at Teheran.[45] Valentine Chirol, having accompanied Curzon in the Gulf, was able to tell the Foreign Secretary the facts. Lansdowne spoke generously of the admirable services the Viceroy had rendered in shaping British policy there and in other Imperial questions like Aghanistan and Tibet, adding pointedly that he feared his estimate of Hardinge was right.[46]

The tour, Curzon believed, had produced a conviction of British supremacy in the Gulf and of determination to sustain it; and he hoped that the many talks with Hardinge might embolden him in his dealings with the Persians, and with the Belgians, by whom he had been hum-bugged. 'He treats Persia in every respect as the finished reproduction of a European Power; whereas it is the tottering survival of a doomed Oriental type.' Curzon pressed the need for robust defence of British interests in Seistan and generally for a less subtle line. 'You know these countries...'

3

he wrote to Hardinge's cousin Charles, 'and you therefore know that the only diplomacy for them is to have a mind and state it, instead of doubling backwards and forwards through the tortuous mazes of a statecraft at which they are much better than ourselves.'[47]

*　　*　　*　　*

During August and September, 1903, some unsatisfactory discussions took place with Russia about Afghan affairs. Cecil Spring-Rice, then chargé at St Petersburg, guessed that Russia would avoid Central Asian complications only if they brought a danger of war. Diplomacy was as useful as an attempt to make a wooden horse pass water. The question was simply a military one:

> Nothing...but a *fact* has any effect...Don't trust in any form of diplomacy or representation, but make your calculation of what you can *do*, counting all the risks of such a deed...The only security is the power to defend ourselves.
>
> No one who lives here can doubt that Russia is a purely aggressive power — a growing organism convinced of its conquering mission — and that whatever we do in the way of friendliness in South-East Europe we shall never be forgiven the crime of possessing what Russia wants to have.[48]

A few weeks afterwards, the Russian government restated their 'firm decision' to establish direct relations with Afghanistan. After the 'frank explanations' already given, they considered the question closed. In practice, Spring-Rice commented, Russian and Afghan agents were already dealing with each other, and Russia had now notified her intention to send agents into Afghanistan at a time to suit herself.[49] Curzon had again offered to meet Habibullah at Peshawar in October. Russian wishes, the Amir responded, were no longer veiled: 'they want to possess the whole world for themselves, and to have everyone with them; but who is the person who desires to be with them?' Nevertheless, he did not understand the purpose of a meeting. His people would not submit to the political influence of any foreign power. If the Russians advanced, the real object would be India. Any damage would be suffered by the Afghans and by India:

> Although Your Excellency's friendship for me is evident, yet in reality the fruit and benefit of this friendship go to the exalted Government of India. It is clear to Your Excellency that to render aid to the Government of Afghanistan is really to render aid to the illustrious British Government...

Habibullah also claimed that the consolidated subsidy, the disposal of which he alone must determine, formed part of the existing agreement.[50] All this had an intimate bearing on the memoranda written by Balfour a

few months earlier. Curzon felt sure that the Amir had deliberately misrepresented the conditions upon which the subsidy was granted. At his
instance, the government of India represented to London that the annual
subsidy of 18½ lakhs was beyond Afghanistan's needs. If it were handed
over without question, the Indian authorities would still know nothing of
the military resources and equipment of a country they were supposed to
defend. The money apart, Habibullah drew such advantages from the
agreements that he was most unlikely to imperil them; but his tactics were
'intentionally dilatory'.[51]

This important despatch, to the line of which Curzon consistently
adhered, was sent after much disquieting news had reached Simla. The
agent at Kabul was being supplied with a good deal of intelligence by one
Abdul Ghani, English translator on the Amir's staff. No one seemed to
know whether this Abdul Ghani was a traitor or a spy. According to his
information, a representative of the Amir had been communing for some
time through an agent with Russian officers at Tashkent and Samarkand.
It was said that the Amir dare not leave Kabul for fear of losing his life, a
hypothesis to which one of Habibullah's own letters lent colour. Curzon did
not know what all this might mean. If Abdul Ghani were acting on his own
behalf, or on Habibullah's, it was hard to discern the object. Nor was it
easy to see what profit the Amir could derive from intriguing with the
Russians. 'The whole situation' the Viceroy commented, 'is one more
illustration of the extreme and mortifying absurdity of a system under
which we know nothing whatsoever of what is going on at the capital of a
subsidised ruler and so-called ally within 150 miles of the Indian border.'[52]

Somewhat later, the agent reported that Habibullah had made an alliance
with Russia. Curzon disbelieved it. He advised that the Amir should be
asked yet again to negotiate a new arrangement with the Viceroy. The
worst of all policies would be to give way on any vital point, whereas the
Cabinet had been willing to sacrifice almost anything in Afghanistan for the
sake of a quiet life; yet no real sacrifice should be needed. If the Amir were
disaffected, nothing could be done to stop him. If he were loyal, he would
not be lost because the mailed fist was occasionally shown.[53]

The Foreign Secretary spoke seriously to Benckendorff about Anglo-
Russian relations. Russia's attitude in the Afghan question had created
'a most unpleasant impression'. The Ambassador protested that Russia had
now abandoned any intention of sending agents into Afghanistan; but when
he spoke, later in November, of Russia's anxiety about Tibet, Lansdowne
retorted that Tibet was nowhere near any Russian territory. By this time
Russia would have been at Lhasa, and it was

beyond measure strange that these protests should be made by the Government of Power which had all over the world never hesitated to encroach upon its neighbours—for instance, Manchuria, Turkestan and Persia—when circumstances seemed to demand it.[54]

Lansdowne's earlier proposal for spheres of influence in Persia was effectively rejected, as Curzon had always said it would be. However, Benckendorff did mention that Russia might well require a commercial outlet on the Gulf, though she would admit Seistan, Afghanistan and Tibet to be entirely within the British sphere. On 25 November, Lansdowne took this up, observing that Russia's predominant interest in Manchuria might be recognised. This conversation foreshadows in rough outline the Anglo-Russian agreement of 1907. Curzon called Lansdowne's proposals 'most admirable', but doubted whether Russia wanted an arrangement. For the moment the Foreign Secretary thought that the Russians, though irritated about Tibet and 'George Curzon's splashings in the Persian puddle', might come to terms. Lamsdorff professed himself satisfied with the British attitude, but intimated darkly that in case of need Russia had 'certains moyens de modérer la jeunesse ambitieuse de Lord Curzon'.[55]

Simultaneously, India's despatch about Afghanistan was being considered. The Cabinet felt that if Habibullah were forced into nominal concessions he would merely be frightened into intrigue with Russia, which a meeting with the Viceroy would not prevent. 'I think' wrote Brodrick, 'the Cabinet wishes to sit still, unless some very essential question makes interference necessary.' Balfour said, and Curzon readily agreed, that there should be no effort to extort roads or railways, for the Amir must be induced to believe that the British respected his independence.[56] It would be legally justifiable, but impolitic, to withhold the subsidy from Habibullah, who appeared on the whole loyal both to the letter and the spirit of the old agreement...We admit that that agreement is in some respects defective and unsatisfactory; but it seems dubious whether international relations would be improved by attempting for the same amount of money to get more out of the son than we got out of the father.'

With the Cabinet's consent, but with little confidence in the outcome, Curzon once more invited the Amir to a conference on the frontier. If there were no result, he proposed to consult with the authorities in London during his forthcoming leave about the despatch of a mission to Kabul.[57]

★   ★   ★   ★

Russian railway penetration of Manchuria began with a concession of 1896, which Stalin was forty years later to sell to the Japanese. The opportunity provided by the Boxer rebellion to place troops in crumbling China proved irresistible, as did the temptation to leave them there. Of more immediate concern to Japan, Russia seemed to be making a puppet of Korea. In August, 1903, the creation of a new Far Eastern Viceroyalty under a notorious enthusiast for expansion, and the retirement of Witte, showed that the crisis might now be very near. Lamsdorff was assured that this new organisation did not mean the curtailing of his responsibility. 'The supreme authority' said the Czar, 'rests with me, and in regard to foreign policy you and I are inseparable.' Soon, however, Benckendorff let Lansdowne see that over a good deal that was happening Lamsdorff had no control. This was true enough. Bezobrazov and his circle formed a group – 'the black cabinet' Kuropatkin dubbed it – independent of the Foreign Ministry. Before his fall, Witte too seems to have maintained a separate intelligence and diplomatic organisation.[58]

By the end of 1903, the prospect of a Far Eastern war bade fair to upset the distribution of power not only in Korea or China or Eastern waters, but in Central Asia and far beyond. If France should support Russia, Britain must under the treaty of 1902 fight with Japan. Balfour thought that risk remote. Russia was unlikely to crush the Japanese who, even if defeated at sea, could carry on, and Russia herself could hardly emerge unscathed from a sea battle. There was no call, therefore, to force upon Japan unpalatable advice which, by arousing resentment, would diminish the value of the alliance. Even if Russia captured Korea, she would not be the more formidable. If she chose to squander her limited resources in ships and money at the other side of the globe, she would be making herself impotent elsewhere.

Lansdowne, attaching more importance to the preservation of peace, would have liked Britain to act as honest broker;[59] but he and the Cabinet seem to have been convinced by Balfour's view that for all the rôles in which Britain feared her—as ally of France, invader of India, master of Persia, possible disturber of European peace—Russia would be the less fitted after taking Korea. She would be financially enfeebled, with her fleet tied to the East to watch over 'at least one unsleeping and implacable enemy'. Though Russia's value to France against Germany might not be much impaired, 'her value to France in a war with us would be greatly reduced, and her whole diplomacy, from the Black Sea to the Oxus, might be weakened into something distantly resembling sweet reasonableness...'[60]

Five weeks later, without declaration of war, Japan attacked. Already Lansdowne's talks with the French, to which the Far Eastern developments will have lent a spur, were substantially complete. In that month Selborne reminded the Cabinet that the two-power standard related to the two naval powers which happened to be the strongest. Even if the Russian navy were much reduced in the tussle with Japan, that fact would make little difference to British building, for the German navy had been steadily overtaking the Russian. The First Lord, citing the preamble of the Navy Law of 1900, repeated his 'conviction that the great new German navy is being carefully built up from the point of view of a war with us. This is also the opinion of Sir Frank Lascelles [British Ambassador in Berlin], and he has authorised me to say so.'

The value of British seaborne trade was £1,200,000,000 per annum. It included the food and raw materials without which the economy would quickly die. Lansdowne had already told the Cabinet that Britain could not afford to relax, presently or prospectively, her efforts to strengthen the Empire by land and sea.[61]

That the possessor of the most efficient army in Europe should also be building a first-class navy was necessarily alarming, and it certainly predisposed Lansdowne in favour of a composition with France and then, as he hoped, with Russia. Had the Russians' answers earlier in 1903 been more accommodating, it is quite likely that an agreement would have been reached. It would have been done with Curzon's goodwill and it might have prevented his resignation. As it was, the Russo-Japanese war killed the talks for the time being. Though Lamsdorff and the Emperor were said to be well-disposed, there seemed to be no directing will at St Petersburg;[62] and the decision to press on vigorously at such a time with the Orenburg–Tashkent railway played straight into the hands of those who regarded Russia as Britain's most inveterate enemy. Balfour had by now realised that Russia would not be easily got at. 'I do not...believe' he wrote in April, 'that Russia is vulnerable in any mortal spot except her Exchequer, and this I hope will be seriously weakened by the present hostilities.'[63]

Curzon was always less frightened than his Cabinet colleagues of Russian strength in Central Asia or Southern Persia. He did not believe that France would feel impelled to fight with Russia if Britain took a port in the Gulf, or that Britain would in war have to occupy most of Southern Persia while Russia took the north. Persia was unlikely to be the only or the chief theatre of war, and Russia's record did not indicate any desire to swallow Persia or supplant the dynasty. On the contrary, wrote the government of India,

her policy everywhere, at Constantinople, at Teheran, at Khiva and Bokhara, at Lhasa, at Peking, and at Soül is to maintain the existing authority and to support the reigning sovereign, but to reduce him to a state of vassalage to herself. The control of Central Asia from the Caspian to the China Seas already places a tremendous strain both upon her military and financial resources: and she has, as we read her intentions, no ambition for the present to annex more territory or to subjugate more peoples by force of arms.

Rather, she would use the established régimes as a means to political and commercial control:

> What she has successfully done in the Central Asian Khanates she would like to do in Persia (and doubtless also in Afghanistan). For these purposes it is necessary that the unit with which she is dealing for the time being should be so weak as to be dependent, but not so weak as to fall absolutely to pieces...

This analysis may profitably be compared with the directions laid down by Lamsdorff in the same year:

> Not permitting the predominance of a third power, to bring Persia step by step under the influence of the Czarist government but without destroying her autonomy in internal or external matters, to turn Persia into an obedient and useful adjunct, sufficiently strong yet a tool in our hands; economically, to preserve the Persian market for the free flow of Russian labour and capital...[64]

Curzon recommended that a minor Russian encroachment on the north, a much more likely occurrence than full-dress invasion, be met by a limited response in the south, coupled with an invitation to think again.[65] Balfour agreed with that policy and even wrote that if Persia were effectively taken over by Russia, the British position in India would become hardly tenable. This was putting the danger rather higher than Curzon did; and beyond that point the two parted company somewhat, for the Prime Minister consistently ruled that Seistan should not be fertilised or built up. Spring-Rice reported large Russian plans for railways in Persia, and an agent in the pay of the British Embassy at Petersburg got hold of the surveyors' reports. Other documents, which may well have been planted, indicated that the Russians would use a British railway to Seistan, notwithstanding the break of gauge, for a flank attack on Kandahar.[66] Kitchener, who had doubtless learned of Balfour's opinion, privately dissociated himself from Curzon's desire to turn Seistan into a granary. In signing the joint note, he had 'merely meant to say that if you change the face of nature it will be time enough to discuss the subject when you begin to do so'.[67]

Though Hardinge and Curzon had agreed on most issues during their talks in the Gulf, their difference of view about the right handling of the Persians remained; and friction between McMahon's mission, the Belgian customs officials and the Legation drove Hardinge to complain early in 1904 that 'with this succession of combative Captains, whose only notion is

to fight everybody all round, and to telegraph copious reports of their
battles to Calcutta and Teheran, we shall always be in the hot water which
the Russians delight to prepare for us—and in which they watch us, puffing
and wriggling, with a perfectly intelligible enjoyment'.[68]

All the officers, on the other hand, thought the Minister lukewarm in
their defence. Curzon asked them to be more tactful and him to take more
interest. The fact that the Belgians did not favour Britain's efforts to build
up her interest in Seistan Hardinge attributed to the extra trouble they had
been given by the Nushki route, while McMahon said that they had done
their best to kill it and to place every obstacle in the way of British influence. The officers, Sir Arthur guessed, wrote to suit Curzon's known views,
which were thereby confirmed; but the French chargé described the
customs administration as 'complètement inféodée aux intérêts russes'.[69]

In general, Hardinge proved more than a match for Vlassof, who cannot
have been best pleased to find himself in a position resembling that of the
British during the Boer War. At the news of Japanese victories, the
Persians displayed indecent joy. When the Russian Legation complained,
Ministers politely regretted their inability to control the ignorant public's
exhibition of its sentiments.

In May, the Shah had a fit, brought on by an attempt to eat in a recum-
bent position. However, he soon recovered sufficiently to ride and shoot
quail at his country palace, and had ordered, through his Minister in Paris,
a *cocotte*, for whom he sent £2,000. The Minister intercepted £1,500.
The lady thereupon cancelled the contract. The Pivot of the Universe
recalled the Minister. When M. Vlassof died suddenly, the Shah merely
observed 'C'était un mauvais homme'. That evening, as the diplomats
returned from the private funeral, they had to pass the Palace. The King of
Kings had chosen to stage a huge firework display. Rockets and squibs shot
up everywhere. The Russian Legation were much offended; but Sir A.
Hardinge felt sure that the Shah had not meant to be inconsiderate.[70]

Naturally enough, the Russians did their utmost to create friction between Britain and Persia. A secret memorandum, of which a British agent
purloined a copy, stated that Habibullah, incited by the British, was about
to advance in the east. Persia must send troops; if money were needed,
Russia would give half a million roubles. More interesting still, this document confirmed the suspicion, long held by Hardinge and Curzon, that
Russia and Persia had some five years before reached an agreement for
mutual assistance.[71] Hardinge managed to dissipate these and other rumours;
and in September a further British loan of £100,000 was made. Even in the
last days of the Atabeg, Persian policy had not, he believed, been dictated by

Russia; and the Ain-ed-Dowleh, though most ignorant, suspicious, reactionary and obstinate in British affairs, was still more obstructive in Russian. Delight at Russia's impotence and humiliation outweighed distaste at the successes of an Asiatic but idolatrous state.[72]

There is no question that Curzon's persistence in pressing for a policy, allied with a willingness to find money, had done much to revive the British interest in Persia. The trade route to Seistan flourished, and the telegraph penetrated there. Consuls or vice-consuls were appointed to Kermanshah, Bunder Abbas, Pasni, Mohammerah, Ahnaz and Shiraz, and political agents at Bahrein and Kuwait. A cable connected Muscat with Jask and later with Bunder Abbas. The mail service in the Gulf was improved, and a new trade route to Isfahan developed.

For the moment the Russians would not make an acceptable agreement. Vlassof's successor was instructed to steer away from any division of Persia into spheres of influence, work for the reform of the Persian army with Russian instructors and press Russian interests in the Gulf. Russia's political and economic aims, Lamsdorff commented, interlocked. Not until 1907 did Isvolsky ask his colleagues to abandon the conviction that 'Persia must come entirely under Russian influence, and that Russia must press onward to the Persian Gulf...'[73] It was only then, after Tsuschima, the Peace of Portsmouth and her troubles at home, that Russia would recognise British predominance in the South.

THREE

Younghusband's Mission

THE REALITY of Russian relations with Tibet in 1902 is still unknown and will probably remain so; at the time, it was necessarily a subject for guesswork based upon snippets of intelligence. Dorjieff had certainly been in close relations with the Dalai Lama for some years and seems to have told him that the Czar might embrace Buddhism. Another Buriat Mongol, Zerempil (alias Bogdanovitch) had been trained by the Russian General Staff for clandestine duties in Asia. Together Dorjieff and Zerempil were to give substance to the revived Russian interest in Tibet by transporting arms and ammunition to Lhasa. Each took charge of a caravan, one traversing the Gobi Desert with two hundred camel-loads of rifles, the other proceeding with horses and yaks through Koko Nor. Both reached the capital by the late autumn of 1902.[1]

Though these details were hidden from Curzon and his colleagues, menacing rumours reached them from many quarters. Charles Hardinge, who had sent such circumstantial evidence to the Foreign Office, felt certain that Russian expeditions to Tibet and coquetting with a Tibetan mission at Petersburg were not directed to the pursuit of science or religion. Even the cautious Sanderson conceded 'indications of some hanky-panky'.[2] When the Prime Minister of Nepal, who had been preoccupied with the task of deposing his brother, discovered that one of Dorjieff's missions had passed through his country, he felt anxious to keep in touch with Curzon about Tibet, to which Nepal stood in a special relationship. The reports of the Nepalese agent at Lhasa provided, in default of an alternative, the bulk of India's information.

On 31 December, the Prime Minister told Curzon at Delhi that he thought there were several Russian agents at Lhasa. Russia in Tibet meant goodbye to the independence of Nepal, and he offered co-operation in any mission that the British might send. This friendliness, representing a substantial change of attitude, pleased Curzon,[3] whose view of the issue coincided with that of the military authorities in London. As Lord Roberts minuted, Russian predominance in Tibet would be not a direct military danger but a serious disadvantage.[4] Like him, the Viceroy could not credit that the home government would allow the creation of a rival political influence in Tibet. As India became the strategic frontier of the British Empire, pressure of European powers upon the glacis beyond the mountainous ramparts became more perilous. It did not seem likely that Russia would undertake large military operations in Tibet, though even a small force could probably take the country without a battle and could unquestionably show up the weakness of the North-East frontier.

China had recently proposed a conference. Curzon wanted to accept, to hold it not on the frontier but at Lhasa and to insist upon promptitude. He would have preferred that China, the nominal suzerain, be left out, for there was now in the shape of the adult Lama a responsible Tibetan authority. The talks should culminate in the appointment of a British agent at Lhasa, and the mission be accompanied by an armed escort 'sufficient to overawe any opposition that might be encountered on the way, and to ensure its safety while at Lhasa. The military strength of the Tibetans is beneath contempt, and serious resistance is not to be contemplated.'

These views were accepted by the government of India and incorporated in a despatch of 8 January, 1903.[5] Simultaneously Viceroy and Secretary of State were conducting a spirited argument about the foundations of British policy in Central Asia. At first, the prospects for an agreed line on Tibet looked fair. Though doubting that a mission could reach Lhasa without a fight, Lord George realised that Russia could not make any significant intervention on the Tibetans' behalf for the time being. The distances between Russian territory and Lhasa were vast, the country inhospitable in the last degree. The matter wanted attending to; but there was no taste in London for advance and South Africa must absorb a large part of the Army for some years.[6]

The charge that decisive policies in these regions carried risks, because they brought other great powers on the scene, Curzon did not deny; but supineness in the early stages often produced the same result, as witness the events at Kuwait and Aden. A rival allowed to presume indefinitely upon British feebleness could hardly be brought to realise that patience might have a limit. Nor did he dispute Lord George's lament that the British did not seem to handle Asiatic powers very successfully. But how could they expect to carry a policy when they did not know what it was, or when it changed daily, or when the stand, if made at all, came too late? Though the policy of drift must be abandoned, surrender was not the sole alternative. Curzon asked Hamilton to excuse the feeling with which he wrote of this

subject, which he knew well and had most at heart. No doubt Downing
Street regarded him as a monomaniac about Asia, though Asiatic experts
spoke in unison on these subjects:

> I have a sort of consciousness that my arguments do not produce the smallest
> effect. If a Government means to sit down...no amount of kicking, even on the
> most sensitive spot, will induce it to rise; and I contemplate now, as I have
> always contemplated and wrote in my book about Russia thirteen years ago,
> that we shall steadily throw away all our trump cards...[7]

Curzon could scarcely believe that after nearly a hundred years of
diplomacy devoted to keeping Russia out of Afghanistan, she would be
allowed without a struggle to plant her influence in Tibet. It did not meet
the point to say that India was ringed round on the side of the Himalayas
by towering peaks and icy passes. So were Gilgit, Hunza and Chitral; but
just as the Russian advance on the Pamirs had compelled fortification of the
frontier there, the establishment of Russia in Tibet would compel similar
precautions in Sikkim, Bhutan and Assam. There would be one more
point at which Russia could apply pressure, and a source of possible intrigue
between Russia and Nepal, which provided some of the finest soldiers of
the Indian Army.[8]

Meanwhile, Russia had made a move. A note left at the Foreign Office on
2 February stated that according to a reliable source a British expedition
was marching north into Tibetan territory. It might cause 'a situation of
considerable gravity' and force Russia to protect her interests in those
regions. Lansdowne protested at the minatory tone of the memorandum
and asked for explicit assurances about the rumoured secret treaty between
Russia and China and the intended presence of a Russian agent in Tibet.

Although Lord George persistently refused to accept that Britain possessed
the strength to curb Russia's progress even in Southern Persia, he did not
doubt that the opposite applied in Tibet. If, with a good case and material
power, the Government would not act there, it seemed hopeless to try to
restrain Russia in any part of Asia. There were obvious difficulties; and
unless they could be met, the Cabinet might well dither until it became too
late to send an expedition in 1903.[9] A few days later, the proposal for an
escorted mission to Lhasa was duly refused. It is enlightening to trace the
stages by which the Cabinet reached this decision.

In the India Office, Curzon's policy would have been accepted. But when
Hamilton and some members of the India Council discussed Tibet with
Balfour, Lansdowne, Devonshire and Ritchie, a very different attitude pre-
vailed. Lord George urged the need for despatch. He argued that British

power in India rested upon prestige, that if the Russians placed an agent at Lhasa while British efforts to communicate with the Dalai were spurned, a 'most unfortunate impression' would spread over northern India. In Tibet the usual conditions were reversed, for Britain could bring irresistible force to bear. The effect of all this was the exact opposite of that intended. The Ministers shied immediately from the conclusion, evidently apprehensive of the vulnerability to Russian pressure of British interests elsewhere. Two other considerations carried weight. Balfour feared that since Tibet was theoretically a part of China, other powers might interpret a mission to Lhasa as an attack on Chinese integrity and then claim compensation; the Foreign Secretary felt that to send a force while he was awaiting Russia's reply to his inquiry might smack of sharp practice.

Hamilton protested in vain, and again at the Cabinet on 19 February,[10] after which Balfour wrote to the King that Curzon desired to send a mission 'with a large military escort'. But the Cabinet felt that there would be no danger in delaying 'heroic measures' until the need were proved. A British agent at Lhasa would need 'a large permanent guard'. Such a policy must lead to a protectorate, which might engender European complications:

> Moreover there are many difficult questions pending between us and Russia in connection with her Central Asian ambitions. An arrangement with her is most desirable—but no such arrangement is possible if we irritate her unnecessarily about Tibet, and at the same time play our best trump prematurely.

Lord Lansdowne was to seek some means of diminishing Anglo-Russian friction in Central Asia.[11] With the authority of the Cabinet, he told Benckendorff that any Russian activity in Tibet would be followed by a more than equivalent display of British activity. If Russia sent a mission, Great Britain would send a stronger one. Benckendorff denied any designs on Tibet. Lansdowne, by intimating that notes like those recently received about Tibet and Seistan must cease if friendly relations were to continue, caused Hamilton to reflect upon the contrast with Salisbury. When in 1895, Russia asked what the British were doing in Chitral, Salisbury had been induced only with extreme difficulty to reply that movements within British territory did not concern other governments; whereas Lansdowne, exasperated by the duplicity of the Wilhelmstrasse, had just sent a curt letter accusing Germany of deliberate lying.[12]

If the decision had been swiftly made, Curzon believed, a mission could probably have penetrated to Lhasa unopposed. Even if resistance were met, nothing like an expedition or campaign need ensue. He predicted accurately enough that the Cabinet would be obliged, at much greater cost and in face of international difficulty, to do what they had just refused to do.[13] Hamilton commented that in no Asiatic question would the advantages lie more clearly on Britain's side. If the Cabinet would not move over Tibet, they were never likely to risk complications unless some gross insult were offered to the British honour or flag. The decision, he thought, must be taken 'to a large extent as governing our future policy in Asia'.[14] Curzon replied simply that the British Empire could not be sustained under those conditions:

> If we are not to defend our own frontiers, to ward off gratuitous menace, to maintain our influence in regions where no hostile influence has ever yet appeared, until the national honour has been grossly affronted, the practical result will be that you will be unable to take a step upon your frontiers until they have actually been crossed by the forces of the enemy.[15]

The argument about Chinese integrity seemed academic. How had Russia been able to move into Manchuria, Japan into Korea and France into Tongking? Britain had fought Nepal and occupied Hunza, which acknowledged Chinese suzerainty each year. The Cabinet, however, had authorised only an announcement that talks with the Chinese and a Tibetan representative would begin. It was also promised that British influence should be recognised at Lhasa 'in such a manner as to render it impossible for any other Power to exercise a pressure on the Tibetan government inconsistent with the interests of British India'; but the means of securing such recognition remained unspecified.[16]

Russia's reply, which eventually arrived on 8 April, stated that she had made no agreement relating to Tibet and did not intend to send agents thither. If 'a serious disturbance of the status quo' occurred, Russia might have to act, not in Tibet but elsewhere. Curzon agreed that the denial must be accepted, though he doubted that such a volume of smoke had arisen simultaneously at so many points without fire. Probably the agreement had been tentative.[17] Lord George took the Russian assurances to allow a free hand short of protectorate. He suggested that Curzon should push forward the negotiation with the Chinese and Tibetans, and warn them that the convention must be ratified by the supreme authority in Tibet, whose sanction India would secure by force if necessary.[18] The delegates were to meet at Khamba Jhong, the nearest inhabited place on the Tibetan side of the frontier.

*   *   *   *

Thus it came about that in May, 1903, Francis Younghusband listened beneath the deodars at Simla as Curzon rehearsed the long tale of Tibetan encroachments, refusal to receive letters and rumoured flirtations with Russia. He asked whether his visitor would lead the mission at Khamba Jhong? Younghusband accepted at once, recording his pride at being selected and his consciousness of the risks they were both running. The two had long been friends. Younghusband, who felt more affection for Curzon than for anyone outside his own family circle, had been chosen for knowledge of Central Asia, of orientals and especially of the Chinese, for reliability, equanimity and good temper. The line favoured by Curzon, indeed the only one available, was to play upon Tibetan and Chinese aversion to British advance upon Lhasa.[19] The Cabinet, preoccupied by recent events in Somaliland, Aden and Manchuria, refused to press for an agent at Gyantse or Lhasa, despite Hamilton's pleadings. He feared that their attitudes would make it harder to secure even trading concessions; but if the negotiation broke down, disapproval could only take the shape

with little inconvenience and certainly no risk of future complications, of either a blockade or of the occupation of the Chumbi Valley. Both Lansdowne and I pointed out to the Cabinet that it was an 'enclave' in British territory which, without the slightest difficulty, could be occupied...[20]

Early in July, a detachment of the mission crossed into Tibet and, after brushing aside hints by the Jongpen (magistrate) from Khamba Jhong at the dire consequences of advance, camped at more than 15,000 feet beneath the fort. There Younghusband joined them. He refused urgent appeals to leave; the Tibetans refused any kind of negotiation. Fruitless appeals went to Lhasa. The mission lay becalmed. Younghusband, mystic, student of religions and lover of the solitary places, was in his element. At sunrise, when all below was still clad in a steely grey, he would be up to see the first rays touch the sparkling summit of Everest. Then by stages the range of peaks would catch the light and glisten pure white. Tints of blue and purple, with constant mutations, played over the mountains till the glow of dying sun lingered on the pinnacles. Younghusband delighted in the limpid quality of the light and the incomparable intensity of the colours; reds like the blood-orange or the ruby, blues of deep sapphire, greens like emerald and amethyst.

Political prospects looked less exciting. Mr Ho, the Chinese representative, apologised for the Tibetans' ignorance and obtuseness. A gay individual, addicted to cards and opium, with one wife at Lhasa and another at Yatung, Mr Ho was understandably bored to death at Khamba Jhong. Younghusband remarked with a straight face that since he found the fresh mountain air delicious a lengthy stay would be quite acceptable. He hunted busily around for fossils and flora. The Chinese Resident (Amban) at Lhasa put no pressure on the Tibetans and was reputed to spend each day in contemplation, twiddling a prayer wheel. Captain Parr of the Chinese customs service telegraphed pithily to Pekin:

> Tibetans truculent refuse negotiate here. Ho useless. Amban indifferent. Recommend Yamen exert pressure, otherwise trouble inevitable.[21]

Mr Ho had announced himself to possess high qualifications in the shape of the Double Dragon and the Peacock Feather, but it transpired that the cook of a member of the mission also sported the Peacock Feather. Parr told Younghusband that all efforts would be wasted until the British insisted on an agent at Lhasa. All this confirmed Curzon's belief that the Tibetans had not yet begun to take the business seriously. Each letter from Khamba Jhong showed them to be relying on Russian support. Younghusband, he told Lansdowne, 'has the patience and the immobility of a pyramid. But you will find that nothing whatever is done until we move or threaten. I will postpone it as long as you like. But sooner or later it is inevitable.'[22]

Though the Dalai Lama was supposed to have sanctioned talks at Khamba Jhong, nothing was happening. Mr Ho made off for more congenial pastures. The Nepalese Prime Minister provided animals and supplies and advised the Tibetans to make terms, while Curzon warned the Amban that Younghusband might otherwise seek more convenient quarters for the winter. Any move must be made by the end of November. 'The Tibetans' Curzon telegraphed, 'have no conception of our power and rely implicitly upon Russian help, which, Lhasa informant tells us, they have sent officials to invoke.'

This phase coincided with the Cabinet crisis. On 20 September, 1903, Hamilton wired that the proposal to advance into the interior was 'regarded with grave misgiving'. The government thought that in the first instance the occupation of the Chumbi Valley would convince the Tibetans of British seriousness.[23] China's reply to Satow's representations at Pekin was predictably unsatisfactory; and on 1 October Curzon was told that if a complete rupture occurred, the home government were, after all, prepared 'to authorise the advance of the Mission to Gyantse, provided you are satisfied that this measure can be safely taken, as well as the occupation of the Chumbi Valley'. [24]

Summoned to Simla, the commissioner was catechised for two hours by Curzon, who, after raising every conceivable objection to an advance and finding the answers sound, adopted his arguments in Council. Young-husband, who attended, wrote, 'I fancy from what I saw and have heard that nobody says much against the Viceroy. He does not so much invite discussion as lay down the law and almost defiantly ask if anyone has any objection. If anyone *has* he is promptly squashed...'[25]

After the meeting, the government of India asked for the advance to Gyantse, since the Chinese were being dilatory and the Tibetans preparing for war:

> The policy which has been pursued towards Tibet...for the past quarter of a century has utterly broken down, and has only resulted in our patience being mistaken for weakness, our overtures being rejected with scorn, and our strength being despised.[26]

This message led to a gloomy exchange of letters between the new Secretary of State and the Prime Minister. 'From his letters' wrote Brodrick, 'I know that George intends ultimately to go to Lhasa.' Balfour replied that he strongly deprecated 'permanent entanglements' in Tibet; partly because there were already commitments enough, partly because 'if we "Man-churianize" what is technically a part of the Chinese Empire, we may greatly weaken our diplomacy in the Far East'. If war broke out between Russia and Japan, who would lay long odds that Great Britain would not be at loggerheads with Russia in six months? In that event, even small complications in Tibet might prove 'exceedingly embarrassing. If I were sure that these considerations were present to the mind of the Indian government I would have more confidence in their estimate of the Tibetan situation.'

The Prime Minister remarked also on the perennial difficulty of govern-ing the Empire:

> The rulers in its outlying portions have great local knowledge, but no responsibility and little thought for the general situation; and we at home are naturally reluctant to over-rule people on the spot who say, and often with truth, that their policy is the only one which will save bloodshed and money in the long run!
>
> I suppose we must assent to George Curzon's suggestion; but surely we might wait for a week for Cabinet sanction? If military considerations render this inexpedient I authorise you to approve—but I do so reluctantly.[27]

Thereupon Brodrick telegraphed a message which revealed a situation of which Curzon had previously been unaware. Discussion in the Cabinet, it said, had shown a 'strong and unanimous feeling against any permanent entanglement in Tibet'. Brodrick doubted if the telegram of 1 October, giving conditional authority for an advance to Gyantse, would have been acceptable to the Cabinet. That vital telegram, which virtually committed the Government to the Tibetan expedition, had been sent in curious circumstances. Hamilton, having resigned the India Office, continued to fulfil routine duties there but refused to approve the draft. Lansdowne consulted Balfour, who realised that if a rupture occurred some form of coercion must be applied, and authorised its despatch. Perhaps Balfour, having been preoccupied with the Cabinet resignations, failed to realise at the time the true situation at Khamba Jhong.[28]

Brodrick now represented that no rupture of negotiations had taken place, and that an advance would probably be opposed by the Cabinet and India Council.[29] His own memorandum to his colleagues described the risks of the expedition, the obstacles to the maintenance of a mission at Lhasa, which he asserted to be Curzon's object, the international effects of violating China's territory, and the critical state of Far Eastern affairs.[30] Curzon, who had understandably read parts of his telegram with astonishment, pointed out that the rupture had occurred. Since the first meeting the Tibetan delegates had refused to exchange a word with Younghusband. The Dalai Lama, asked in June to send a counsellor of state, had not replied. Armed Tibetans surrounded the mission. A new Amban, specially appointed eleven months previously to conduct the negotiations, was still proceeding leisurely towards Lhasa. Acquiescence in this humiliating position would have a bad effect on Nepal, Bhutan and Tibet, but the presence of a force at Gyantse, a considerable trade mart on the road to Shigatese and Lhasa, should ultimately bring the Tibetans to reason.[31]

After the Cabinet's meeting Brodrick telegraphed on 6 November that they had agreed to advance

> but they are clearly of opinion that this step should be taken purely for the purpose of obtaining satisfaction; that it should not be allowed to lead to occupation or to any form of permanent intervention in Tibetan affairs; and that it should withdraw as soon as reparation is obtained. They consider the action proposed necessary, but the question of enforcing trade facilities must be considered in reference to the above decision, and His Majesty's Government are not prepared to establish a Mission in Tibet permanently.

Brodrick also wired privately that the Far Eastern situation, together with the logistic difficulties and small potential gains in Tibet, provided sufficient reason for not interfering. Much opposition had been expressed.[32] The Cabinet, wrote Balfour to the King, felt 'apprehensive that the Viceroy entertains schemes of territorial expansion or at least of extending responsibilities which would be equally detrimental to Indian interests and to the international relations of the Empire'.[33]

In his private letters, the Secretary of State urged that even if Russia placed a consul at Lhasa, Britain could still challenge her or send an expedition. At the Cabinet it had been argued that unless it were intended to establish a protectorate Russian intrigue could not be prevented by anticipation at Lhasa:

> It becomes, therefore, a question whether advanced posts beyond the line of the Himalayas are a weakness or strength to us, quite apart from the political difficulty, as the Cabinet conceive it, of occupying Chinese territory, and giving Russia a handle for encroaching on other portions of Chinese territory... I think we should require a very long and patient experience of Gyantse before any kind of further movement would be entertained.[34]

Curzon promised officially and privately that he had no desire to invade or permanently occupy Tibet. There was no quarrel with the Tibetan people, who had shown themselves friendly, but only with the obstinate monks at Lhasa. Two British subjects, arrested at Shigatse, were reported to have been killed.[35] However, the terms of the Cabinet's authority to move to Gyantse indicated the divergence of view. Its purpose, in Curzon's eyes, was not to obtain reparation but to sign a new convention and to ensure observance. It was not clear for what the Tibetans were supposed to make reparation; nor did the Cabinet seem to understand that since 1890 they had enjoyed the right to station a British officer at Yatung. The idea of marching to Gyantse as a punishment for the Tibetans' recent attitude, Curzon foretold, and then of marching back again, would be found unpractical. He could not gauge how far the Cabinet's attitude had been coloured by the trouble brewing between Russia and Japan, but that factor should weigh in favour of boldness:

> Pray believe that I am not in the least anxious to effect any *coup de théâtre* in Tibet: I neither want frontier fighting, nor am I concerned about the extension of the frontiers of Empire. But what I want to secure is that our present intolerable and humiliating relations with the Tibetans shall not continue, and that they shall be sufficiently impressed with our power as to realise that they cannot look to any other quarter for protection.[36]

Brodrick, who did not deny the disagreement, remarked upon the intractable problems confronting the Cabinet; the uneasy situation in South Africa, the seemingly endless campaign in Somaliland, disquiet in Macedonia and Morocco, the raging tariff controversy, the loss of four of the ablest Ministers, the whole defence organisation in the melting-pot.[37]

These were the circumstances in which a Tibetan policy had to be framed at the end of 1903. Elsewhere the omens promised no more propitiously. The information of the Nepalese agent at Lhasa indicated that Dorjieff was there and had promised Russian support.[38] Unlike most of his predecessors, the Dalai had survived to manhood, largely because he had the wit to murder the Regent before the Regent could murder him. When his Ministers advised a composition, he dismissed them. 'Why' he asked the ruler of Sikkim, 'do the British insist on establishing trade marts?...The British, under the guise of establishing communications, are merely seeking to over-reach us. They are well practised in all these political wiles.'[39]

The degree to which the Dalai placed his trust in Russia will remain a matter of dispute. It may be that Dorjieff interpreted liberally assurances of goodwill from St Petersburg. Czar Nicholas sent a Captain to find out what the British were doing and to incite the Tibetans against them, concealing these orders from the Foreign Minister. If Kuropatkin, the War Minister, is an accurate guide, his master's ambitions on the eve of the Russo-Japanese war were not of a modest scope:

> He wants to seize Manchuria and proceed towards the annexation of Korea; he also plans to take Tibet under his rule. He wants to take Persia and to seize not only the Bosphorus but also the Dardanelles.[40]

*   *   *   *

The mission crept towards Gyantse by way of the Chumbi Valley. On the first night, the thermometer registered 50° of frost. Younghusband and the escort, under General Macdonald, took up quarters at a dismal hamlet called Tuna, consisting of a half-dozen stone cottages and swept by perpetual blizzards. The Tibetans showed themselves friendly enough, although emissaries from Lhasa said that should they fail to prevent the mission from advancing, they would rely upon another power. They repudiated the connexion with China. Accompanied only by an interpreter and a young officer, Younghusband rode unarmed to parley with the Tibetans at Guru. The 'Generals' were amenable, the lamas hostile; greetings were exchanged and buttered tea consumed; but the negotiations made no progress. Younghusband, having come through many crises unscathed, had felt confident that he could so bear himself that the Tibetans would not use force. Afterwards the three rode back to the mission's camp, lucky to have escaped arrest or death.[41]

Curzon refused to be flustered by these vexing circumstances. The

Tibetans were behaving as he expected. There was no need to rush onwards. 'When we are at Gyantse and have made no further progress in
negotiations it will be time enough to talk about open rupture, and
slaughter, and advance to Lhasa.'[42] Doubtless basing himself on Brodrick's
remark that the Cabinet would require a very long experience of Gyantse
he reminded Younghusband that neither of them had authority to bluff
about Lhasa: 'We may ultimately have to go there, and you may be right
in thinking that no other solution will be practicable. But, for the present,
the limit of our orders is Gyantse, and this also should be the present limit
of our threats.'

Moreover, the mission was advancing, in the Cabinet's view, not because
of Dorjieff or Russian intrigue, but because of Tibetan transgressions. A
hostile reader of two recent letters from Younghusband, Curzon told him,
would pounce upon the obsession with Russia and say that the real object
was to reach Lhasa before the Russians. This was neither the whole truth,
nor that part of the truth which it was desirable to emphasize; and the
mission must not fire the first shot, however much the monks might frown
or scowl:

> Remember we do not want to kill the Tibetan peasants, even when they are
> armed with rusty matchlocks. Our enemies are the monks and so far they have
> not attacked you.

Younghusband replied:

> There is nothing I would not do for you; and if you asked me to eat dirt
> before the Tibetans for the next six years and expunge the words Russia and
> Lhasa from my vocabulary altogether, I would do it, knowing quite well that
> it could only be for the best...[43]

The Viceroy stood, then, in an intermediate position, on the one hand
enjoining obedience to the letter of instructions, on the other earnestly
representing that no hampering pledges be given. An informant, who
stayed with Curzon in January, 1904, said the highest Russian authorities
had openly told him that Younghusband's advance had frustrated their
plans; and since it was not clear how far the mission would have to go,
nothing should be promised about early retirement or keeping no agent in
Tibet or abstaining from intervention there.[44] However, the plea went
unheeded. A Blue Book published during February contained the crucial
telegram of 6 November, against the ambiguity of which Curzon had
protested at the time.

The Tibetans showed no sign of negotiating, though some Lamas of
special distinction turned up and cursed the camp for five days. Curzon

grew impatient for the move to Gyantse, but it was not till the last day of March, five months after the Cabinet gave authority, that the main column set forth from Tuna. After a few hours, a Tibetan force was met, blocking the road. Younghusband refused to shell the position, but warned the opposing General that his force would be disarmed. As this process began, the General shot an Indian. Firing immediately began. Very soon the Tibetans had been routed. Of some 2,000, 840 were killed, wounded or taken prisoner. The remnant simply turned and walked away with bowed heads. One of their Russian rifles was captured by a newspaper correspondent, who sent it to the Viceroy.[45]

While Brodrick said he was not sorry the Tibetans had suffered a smashing defeat, Curzon confessed himself sickened at the carnage. Probably there had been little choice once the first shot came from the other side, but the military had seized the occasion swiftly and the appetite for slaughter, once roused, was not easily slaked. In another skirmish the Tibetans again suffered heavily and were pursued for ten miles. On 11 April the mission, without further fighting, took Gyantse where Younghusband established good relations with the magistrate and abbot and stayed for some weeks. No Tibetan negotiators appeared.[46]

Seven thousand miles away, the House of Commons debated Central Asian affairs. A number of the Government's back bench supporters threatened, according to Brodrick's account, that if the policy of 6 November were not reaffirmed they would go into the other lobby. The Chief Whip advised that such defections would leave the Government most uncomfortably placed, whereupon Balfour delivered a speech which, as Brodrick realised, went further than Curzon would have wished.[47] This determination in London to treat the whole Tibetan issue as one of local frontier politics necessarily made the execution of policy a delicate business. Younghusband still wished to go to Lhasa, believing that Tibet could not raise another serious force and that the monks would promptly curl up, for militancy and buddhism did not chime.[48]

The longer the mission remained in Tibet, Curzon judged, the more possible would it be to convince the Cabinet that India's terms might be obtained. An agreement must contain guarantees against a revival of trouble, and should be signed by the Dalai Lama, even if negotiated at Gyantse. This the Cabinet might perhaps allow, though they would certainly be hostile to any forward military policy. Nor did Curzon wish to fight a way through to Lhasa. If London would agree, he wanted a British agent there; if not, a high-ranking Nepalese might represent India. The Chumbi Valley should be retained, probably for good. It dominated

Bhutan and offered the best road to Central Tibet; its inhabitants were not
Tibetans, were friendly and dreaded the Tibetans' return. These views, put
by Curzon to the Council before he left for England, met with general
acceptance. The Chinese, Satow reported from Pekin, regarded the military
incidents of the advance with indifference, if not satisfaction, as conducing
to the recovery of their authority.[49]

'I can scarcely believe' Curzon wrote to Brodrick, 'that many people
really think that, after five years characterised by the caution which I have
displayed on the North-West frontier, I should want to snatch a doubtful
laurel by a policy of precipitate and emotional aggression on the North-
East.'[50]

★   ★   ★   ★

Early in May, the mission's camp at Gyantse, defended at that moment by
less than two hundred troops, was attacked by a much larger number, who,
after reaching the wall unnoticed, were beaten off. Even the Bengali head
clerk did great execution with a shotgun. In two hours' fighting the
Tibetans lost about 240 dead and wounded. Younghusband telegraphed
that the assault showed the Lhasa government to be irreconcilable. Every
overture had been rebuffed and the mission should advance to Lhasa, where
the real power lay.[51] Military preparations would take a month. The
Council, now under Ampthill, agreed. 'I fear' he telegraphed, 'a change of
policy will be forced on His Majesty's Government.' On this the King
minuted 'I hope Col. Younghusband will be supported and our position
will suffer grievously if we submit to such treatment...'[52] But there was
now a fresh consideration. If the European governments' assent could be
obtained, the Anglo-French agreement, just signed, would provide relief
from that dependence on others' goodwill in Egypt imposed by Gladstone's policy twenty years before. In exchange for Russian adhesion,
M. Cambon suggested, the Cabinet should renew their assurances about
Tibet. Curzon again asked that the British position, one of unique advantage, should not be compromised. Russia, not a neighbour of Tibet, could
advance no claims parallel to those of Britain, whose political influence there
must be supreme, and secured, if absolutely necessary, by a protectorate.
The key lay in Russia's hands. If she did not interfere in Tibet, there would
be no protectorate.[53]

The Cabinet, however, confident that Germany would take full advantage of the opportunity for blackmail, hoped to isolate her.[54] Lansdowne
accordingly offered Russia the bargain. Rejecting annexation or a permanent

mission, the Cabinet nevertheless decided that 'to sit still at Gyantse, and to wait indefinitely until it pleased the Grand Lama to permit the Amban to come to our camp, was an impossible policy; and that if the Tibetan Government refused to negotiate there, we should be driven to advance and negotiate at Lhasa itself.'[55]

This was what the Government of India had requested sixteen months earlier, but amounted to a denial of the terms they wished to obtain. Brodrick alleged that his colleagues were 'quite prepared to take a firm stand with Russia' but observed that it was an unlucky moment. The Russians showed a sensitivity about Tibet, he allowed, which went some way to justify Curzon's belief that he had anticipated them there.[56] Russia was emphatically assured that so long as no other power interfered in Tibet, there would be no annexation, protectorate or attempt to control its internal administration. Though there was a saving clause, it could carry little weight when coupled with so categorical a statement. The Czar, grumbling privately that British undertakings would satisfy him only if Curzon did not return to India, accepted them. On landing in England, Curzon learned that the advance to Lhasa had been sanctioned. 'I hardly think you can realise' said Brodrick, 'how little appetite there is in England at this moment for another little war of any description.'[57]

Meanwhile, tensions between the home government and the commissioner at Gyantse began to grow. At the end of April Brodrick had warned Younghusband against undue eagerness to reach Lhasa. As he had already been messing about in Tibet for ten months without result, Younghusband thought this as ludicrous as the provision of a further opportunity for negotiation at Gyantse, where the mission was under attack night and day. But for personal devotion to Curzon, he wrote, he would resign at once rather than serve a government so supine. Though the Tibetans' valour and tactics improved at Gyantse, where Zerempil is supposed to have fought, they made no attempt, unaccountably, to sever the tenuous line of communication, or the telegraph, to Chumbi. Younghusband reported that many more Lhasa-made rifles and Russian arms had been used. The Tibetans, were they not receiving Russian support, 'could not possibly defy us like this'.[58]

While these messages passed to and fro, a curious situation had developed at Simla. Neither Kitchener nor Elles cared for civilian command of the mission. The C-in-C minuted that Younghusband's attitude might 'lead us unnecessarily into very serious complications in Tibet'. Ampthill refused Elles's request that when military operations began, General Macdonald should take political control. Macdonald had been selected by Curzon, on

the military authorities' advice, for his qualities as an engineer. At that time
the problems had been chiefly those of road-building and communication.
Now he was at loggerheads with Younghusband, who thought he could
winter at Lhasa. Macdonald said it was impossible. If that were so, Younghusband telegraphed, it would be better not to go there at all. It happened
that Ampthill too believed, for the moment at least, that the expedition
should clear out of Lhasa as early as might be, and not interfere thereafter,
unless it became inevitable, in the affairs of Tibet.[59]

Younghusband received what he called 'a very God-Almighty-to-a-
blackbeetle style of telegram', reminding him that proposals should 'as far
as possible' conform to the policy of the Cabinet. In a kind private letter,
the acting Viceroy explained that international considerations must predominate and Russian resentment be diminished. Even the failure of the
mission would be 'better than the certain prospect of war with Russia from
the point of view of the whole British Empire'. This was written at the
time when India was receiving alarming reports of Russia's military activity
in Turkestan and Transcaspia. Before the letter arrived, Younghusband had
represented that if reparation were the sole purpose, only a punitive expedition need be sent; but if an agreement were desired, he might have to stay
the winter at Lhasa. He was put out to discover, after a month's continuous
bombardment and four night attacks, that the British government thought
these events unimportant. He resigned on 16 June.[60] Ampthill persuaded
him to withdraw.

Kitchener favoured a punitive expedition and swift withdrawal. This
line, as he knew, accorded in substance with that of the Cabinet and he was
careful to inform Lady Salisbury of his belief that an agent left at Lhasa
would be murdered.[61] On this issue, therefore, Curzon and Kitchener
disagreed, though not with acerbity. Curzon's first weeks at home were
fully occupied and he did not receive all the Tibet papers. At some point
in the latter half of May, however, he had a private talk with Lansdowne.
Having implored the Government not to go on repeating promises about
Tibet, Curzon understood from him that the undertaking not to annex
Tibet or interfere in its internal administration need not rule out a permanent occupation of the Chumbi Valley or a 'somewhat prolonged' occupation of Lhasa. Curzon at once told Ampthill and Younghusband of this
conversation,[62] and we know that it affected the conduct of affairs at Lhasa
soon afterwards. Whether Curzon overbore the Foreign Secretary in
conversation, or misinterpreted him, or correctly reported him, we are
unlikely to discover for sure. Perhaps Lansdowne was trying to assuage
Curzon's anger at the Egyptian bargain and his reactions were anyway apt

to be more robust than Brodrick's. Certainly Lansdowne told Roberts at this moment that though he doubted the wisdom of placing an agent at Lhasa 'we ought not to come away, until we have effected a really satisfactory settlement with these obstinate barbarians'.[63]

That the Cabinet had been able to think of no alternative to a negotiation at Lhasa fulfilled Curzon's predictions with some exactitude. Each Minister, he wrote to Ampthill, 'admits to me in private that the Cabinet have been wrong, but shelters himself behind the collective ignorance and timidity of the whole...'[64] The arguments he placed before the Cabinet did not vary in any important particular from those he had expressed from the beginning. Each halt of the spasmodic advance had encouraged Tibetan obstinacy. It was now apparent 'that no objective has from the start been possible but Lhasa, and that it is useless to pursue the ordinary diplomatic forms in dealing with so intractable and archaic a people'. Curzon surmised correctly that Younghusband would reach Lhasa at the end of July or early in August, and that the Dalai would have fled. If the National Council had also vanished, the talks would be protracted, probably through the winter. As the mission could not simply walk away with a piece of paper, the best guarantee would be an agent at Lhasa, most of the objections to which rested upon an incorrect analogy between fierce Afghans and the Tibetans, whose religion did not inculcate fanaticism or xenophobia. In short, the intention to withdraw from Lhasa before October seemed ill-related to the facts:

> That it will be possible within the space of two months, after fighting has ceased at Lhasa (1) for Colonel Younghusband to frame...an agreement; (2) to secure the assent to it of any responsible Tibetan authority; (3) to send it to Simla; (4) for the Government of India to discuss and approve it, and (5) for the draft to be forwarded to England and approved here, when opinion about the most vital provisions is still uncrystallised, seems to me out of the question. Do not these probabilities also greatly enhance the likelihood of a temporary occupation of Lhasa?
> ...the best method of converting the sullen opposition of the Tibetans into a more friendly feeling will be, in my opinion, to give them any guarantees that may be suggested for the uninterrupted exercise and prestige of their religion.[65]

The opinion of the Cabinet, with whom Curzon conferred at length on 1 July, differed at almost every point. They would not make 'a large annual sacrifice' to keep an agent with proper support in Tibet, but would make considerable sacrifices to prevent the establishment of Russian influence there. They would go to Lhasa, but solely to obtain reparation and satisfaction:

In our judgement [wrote Brodrick], the mere fact of a British force marching to Lhasa and slaughtering a great number of Tibetans on the way ought even without a treaty to establish our claims and show our power...

...If on arriving at Lhasa we find no Dalai Lama and no one with whom we can negotiate, it would still be open to us to raze the arsenal and the wells and destroy any fortification, to take such indemnity as we can get in specie, to destroy all arms which we may capture and to remain in occupation of the Chumbi Valley...[66]

Curzon was evidently not impressed by this discussion. The idea that the expedition should proceed to the holy place of Buddhism, wreak the maximum of damage and then retreat completely, he regarded as a sterile substitute for a policy. As for the Cabinet, they were 'naturally ignorant of anything but large and frequently incorrect generalisations; and the discussion wanders about under imperfect control. It is a very difficult business and hesitation and difference of opinion are both justifiable.'[67]

The view of the government of India accorded largely with Curzon's, except that the military authorities had persuaded their civilian colleagues that the mission could not winter at Lhasa. A despatch of 30 June described at length the evidences of Russian intrigue and activity in Tibet, which the Chinese Minister at Petersburg likened to the policy Russia had previously pursued in his country. Ampthill and his colleagues asked for a resident agent, a prolonged occupation of Chumbi, and exclusive political influence.[68] Instructions in a contrary sense from London put some parts of this document out of court before its arrival. The telegram of 6 November, 1903, had attained in the eyes of the Cabinet what Curzon called an almost canonical sanctity. 'I read your despatch' he wrote to Ampthill, 'which I thought a very good one. But it produced no more impression in Downing Street than it would have done had it been read in the streets of Lhasa.'[69]

Consideration of this despatch by the British Government coincided with the acute apprehensions arising from Russian attacks on British merchant shipping. Ampthill's line had not been an entirely consistent one, particularly in respect of an agent at Lhasa; a fact which Younghusband quickly realised to his chagrin. Some members of the Cabinet, including Lansdowne, feared that an agent there would merely be shut up, as at Kabul, and even Curzon said that if a guard of more than five hundred were needed, the officer had better reside at Gyantse.[70] The Cabinet were also divided, and, in Brodrick's phrase, 'a little hampered by pledges given to the Russians', on the question of the Chumbi Valley. But if it were not occupied for a time, asked Curzon, how would Tibetan observance of the terms be ensured? How would the Cabinet secure the condition, described in 1903 as indispensable, that British influence should be recognised at Lhasa in a manner which would prevent the exercise of pressure inconsistent with India's interests?[71]

*   *   *   *

The Tibetans had been warned that the advance would begin on 25 June, but it was not until early July that the Gurkhas and Royal Fusiliers stormed the fort at Gyantse, previously taken without a struggle and then handed back. Younghusband remained on distant terms with Macdonald, whom he characterised as one of those sound people so appallingly safe that they never do anything, sucking in every rumour and laying out his plans 'as if the Tibetans were commanded by a Napoleon and were the most blood-thirsty people in the world'. Though the Tibetans resisted long in the skirmish at Gyantse, the commissioner was confirmed in the opinion that they were not to be taken seriously as a fighting force. Some 2,500 had now been killed, for the loss of fewer than 40.[72]

In mid-July the column at last moved off for Lhasa, past the turquoise depths of the Yam-dok lake and across the Brahmaputra. A last stand was broken by the Gurkhas. Futile parleys took place at intervals. It became clear that Tibet was not merely an arid waste. The plain lay three or four miles broad, well-cultivated and flourishing. 'I don't know', wrote Young-husband, 'where in the whole length of the Himalayas you would find a more prosperous looking country.' He did not relish the thought of the Russians in command of such resources.[73]

The mission met no stern resistance. Early in August they reached a smiling valley, covered with trees and cornfields. On the crest of a little hill gleamed in the sunlight the golden vanes and pinnacles of the Potala, palace and monastery of the Dalai Lama. Younghusband and his escort camped outside the walls of Lhasa. Accompanied by the Amban's body-guard and two companies of the Royal Fusiliers, he processed through the heart of the forbidden city, seen by only one Englishman since the days of Warren Hastings. Crowds of apathetic Tibetans looked on. There was no sign of fanatical feeling amongst the people, who did not seem 'to care a twopenny damn whether we went there or not'.[74] The Dalai Lama had fled to Mongolia, confiding his seal to an elder of the Buddhist hierarchy, the Ti Rimpoche.

Just as Younghusband's party reached Lhasa, the home government's despatch on the Tibetan terms left London. It rehearsed the Cabinet's long-standing reluctance to intervene, and the European reactions of India's

policy in the buffer states. It stated again the central doctrine of the Defence
Committee and Cabinet in Balfour's time: that the British Army existed
largely in order to defend India. There should be an agent, with purely
commercial duties, at Gyantse. The indemnity should be within the
Tibetans' capacity to pay in three years. British influence, the Cabinet still
believed, 'must be duly recognised at Lhasa, so as to exclude foreign
pressure'.[75]

Uncertainty surrounded the commissioner's position at every point.
Macdonald was longing to quit Lhasa, although Younghusband had no
doubt that a resident could settle there peaceably and that the military risks
had been wickedly exaggerated. He did not have precise instructions on
many of the important points. No one could tell whether he would find at
Lhasa any authority with whom to bargain. The resources of the country
were unknown. Messages took five or six days to Gyantse, and then some
hours to Simla. If a telegram needed decision in London, the interval at
Lhasa between despatch and receipt could hardly be less than a fortnight.
According to military opinion, the party should leave early in September.
It must be conceded that these were not promising circumstances.

Younghusband began his negotiations by being rather stiff. The Council
of Ministers, four of them, seemed quite at a loss, planets deprived of their
sun. Talks moved very slowly. Captain O'Connor, who bore the whole
brunt of translation, would find little bags of gold dust mysteriously
deposited upon his table. With a twinkle, the commissioner gravely
advised him to stand out for something worth having. Though the lamas
understandably detested the mission, the people became friendly and
established a huge bazaar outside the camp. The arsenal proved to be a
very small affair, but Younghusband saw a copy of a purported treaty
between Russia and China, and the Amban, the Nepalese agent and
the Tibetans themselves talked of a written compact between the Dalai
Lama and the Russians. China 'temporarily' deposed him at the request of
the Amban, who declared to Younghusband that the only way to deal with
such impossible people as the Tibetans was 'to take their heads and knock
them on the floor'.[76] The Prime Minister of Bhutan, the agent of Nepal,
the Chinese Resident and even the Ti Rimpoche put pressure on the
National Assembly towards the end of August. Younghusband spent a
good deal of time trying to convince the Tibetans that Russia was not
nearer than India.

In view of the sharp disagreement which soon developed it is important
to realise how far the Cabinet had diverged from the policy recommended
by Curzon and Ampthill. On 15 August Balfour informed the King that

the mission could not retire without striking some blow at an enemy which refused to keep its old engagements or to discuss new ones:

> The Cabinet decided that, if the Lama refuses even to consider our very reasonable and moderate offers, we have no choice but to turn the expedition from a peaceful into a punitive one: and with every regard to the religious feelings of the Tibetans, to destroy such buildings as the walls and gates of the city, and to carry off some of the leading citizens as hostages. This course is painful; but apparently inevitable.[77]

Brodrick hoped that Younghusband would be able to bring away a substantial indemnity, while the Viceroy was wondering whether Younghusband would contrive to secure anything. Macdonald seemed to be thoroughly ill and unfit to command the force, devising pretexts for an early retreat. His portentous telegrams about want of supplies caused Ampthill much difficulty with Kitchener, who favoured draconian measures, beginning with an assault on the monasteries. Younghusband showed that the difficulties about supply and the absence of warm clothing had been greatly magnified. The medical staff were then cited by Macdonald as agreeing that early retirement was desirable. This Ampthill dismissed as 'rank nonsense', together with further reports about snowfalls, growing cold, the rising of the Brahmaputra and the Tibetans' possible renewal of war.[78]

Younghusband had good reason to believe that the military arguments would prevail. After the Cabinet's meeting on 15 August, Brodrick had laid it down that Macdonald, in communication with the commissioner, should decide the date of departure. On 31 August, the General said that unless Simla ruled otherwise he intended to go in a fortnight. The next day, Younghusband held a large meeting in the presence of the Amban, presented a draft and said that he expected signature within a week. £500,000, the indemnity he demanded, was based on a proposal of the government of India. After inquiry, Younghusband thought the Tibetans could manage this; but cash was not abundant, and they repeatedly asked to pay in ponies, or barley, or silk. The Ti Rimpoche and the Prime Minister of Bhutan begged that the sum might be disbursed over a period of seventy-five years, instead of the three years proposed in the draft and laid down by the Government in London.

This would mean, at first sight, the occupation of the Chumbi Valley for the same period, but Younghusband knew that the Government need not be so bound. Their troops could leave Chumbi at any time, with the right of reoccupation if the payments were not forthcoming, and a reduction of the indemnity could be made more suitably by the Viceroy than by him. Moreover the Commissioner had not forgotten Lansdowne's view that pledges to Russia would not prevent an occupation of the valley. Indeed, he had not expected to obtain a treaty at all, in which case that would have been the only possible reparation.[79]

The Lhasa convention was signed on 7 September in a fine room at the Potala Palace. Younghusband, the lamas, the Amban, the envoy of Nepal and the Prime Minister of Bhutan, all in formal dress and accompanied by their staffs, settled to the protracted business. Behind stood two hundred British and Indian troops. The agreement had been set down in three languages, written in parallel columns on an enormous sheet of paper. Nine copies, three for each party, had been prepared. The seals of the Dalai Lama, the Council of Ministers, the National Assembly and the three great monasteries were solemnly affixed.

This agreement marks the beginning of direct Anglo-Tibetan relations. It kept foreign agents, commercial and diplomatic, out of Tibet. It did not provide for interference with the internal administration, or mean a protectorate as that term is usually understood. If the Tibetans chose to live apart, nothing prevented it. As for trade they were in substance to do what they were already obliged to do by the previous agreements. Having received orders not to propose access to Lhasa for the trade agent to be stationed at Gyantse, Younghusband struck that provision out of his draft. Finding that the Tibetans raised no objection, he made a separate agreement on that point, allowing access for commercial matters which could not be settled at Gyantse. This he failed to report by telegraph to Simla.

When the news of the main convention reached him, the Viceroy advised that it should be accepted as it stood, despite the provision about seventy-five years. If the Tibetans paid more than a lakh of rupees a year, so much the better; otherwise the amount could be reduced in return for good behaviour or further trade facilities. The King, without consulting Brodrick, immediately expressed high approval of the 'admirable manner' in which the mission had been brought to a 'happy conclusion'. Brodrick himself telegraphed on 12 September, 'I heartily congratulate Colonel Young-husband on conclusion of agreement with Tibet. His action will be supported.'[80] Presumably he had failed to grasp the purport of some of the terms.

As these events were soon to be fiercely debated between Simla and London, were to blight Younghusband's career and to have a most damaging effect on Curzon's relations with Brodrick and the Cabinet, it is important to trace the last stages. The telegrams from London had repeatedly emphasised aversion to the mission's remaining at Lhasa a moment longer than was essential. 'Please consider' Brodrick wired to Ampthill on 13 September, 'whether it would not be possible without prejudice to the signed Agreement to intimate, as suggested in your telegram...that a reduction will be made if the terms are duly fulfilled, and if further trade facilities are given.'[81]

Younghusband had promised the Tibetans that he would leave promptly and the military were keen to leave. On the eve of departure he received Ampthill's authority to remain until mid-October, and learned that a much smaller indemnity, and another trade-mart, were desired. This created a most awkward position, for he did not wish to upset good relations by staying on. It did not appear that he could reopen the talks and still get away before winter cast its barrier across the passes. Younghusband decided to go.[82] The Ti Rimpoche presented a special gift, saying, 'It is not the custom of our country to give the image of the Buddha to strangers, but you have shown such courtesy and peace-making that we ask your acceptance.'

Neither Brodrick nor Ampthill knew the exact date of departure. On 16 September the former approved the proposal to reduce the indemnity in return for concessions, but expressly ordered that 'in no case should the force remain longer at Lhasa for the purpose of improving the bargain which has already been arrived at'.

He did agree later that Younghusband might, after all, remain at Lhasa if the government of India were satisfied of his safety; but the issue was academic. The messenger met the mission on 24 September, as it marched towards the Himalayas. Younghusband felt that he could not now turn back:

> Had I attempted to alter at this stage a settlement made with such solemnity, we might. .have failed to attain our object, while it is certain that the present good feeling, which is the best basis for our future relations, would have been lost.[83]

*   *   *   *

These events had demonstrated what Curzon had told the Cabinet in June; insistence upon Younghusband's return before the winter meant that a settlement could not be thrashed out at Lhasa, properly considered in Simla and London, and modified on the spot. Given the distances and the primitive communications, it was impossible. However, Brodrick immediately asserted that Younghusband, imbued with 'the whole of Curzon's ideas as regards our permanent occupation of the country' had deliberately flouted his instructions and had been writing to Curzon letters uncomplimentary to the home government's Tibetan policy. This correspondence, and others which Curzon had carried on since he came to England, had caused him 'the utmost embarrassment'. The reference is presumably to letters to and from Ampthill and Dane, communications which seemed to the Secretary of State 'wholly improper'.

Brodrick, exactly like Younghusband, judged that the government had power to remit the indemnity and that it would be 'very unwise to start a fresh negotiation at Lhasa at the moment'. Less than three weeks later he was to censure Younghusband for failing to do this; two months after that, he reverted to his first opinion.[84] A further difficulty was caused by the telegrams which had passed between Ampthill and the King, who had been urging an honour for Younghusband. The latter, Brodrick stated baldly, had got hold of someone in the Royal entourage:

> It would have been unseemly, seeing the warmth of the royal congratula-
> tions on Younghusband's achievements, to take any step which would enable
> Younghusband, with the King and the government of India apparently on his
> side, to take the opportunity of kicking up his heels at the expense of the
> government here.

The India Office had calculated that Tibet might pay a lakh, or two lakhs, of rupees (i.e. about £6,650 or £13,300) for three years. 'Although this would have been a comparatively small amount, it would have been sufficient to mark our sense of their conduct. Personally' Brodrick added with no apparent awareness of contradiction, 'I should have thought that £100,000 was as much as we should be in any way wise to demand...' He did not explain why Younghusband had not been instructed to work to any of these figures.

'What makes me fear that a great deal more has been written to Young-husband than could possibly be right' Brodrick concluded, 'is that, despite the fact that I have letters on various subjects from Walmer every day, no allusion has been made to the Tibetan terms in any communications.'[85] It is not clear what this sentence was intended to convey. If Brodrick was saying that at no time had Curzon written about possible terms of settle-ment with Tibet, it was untrue. If he merely meant that Curzon had not commented on the terms of the Lhasa convention, that was hardly sur-prising, since they had not yet reached him. When they did, Curzon expressed admiration of Younghusband's achievement. 'I hope at any rate' he wrote drily, 'that we shall hear no more of the Somaliland analogy

4

which I think need no longer darken the vision of the Cabinet.'[86] At this
stage Curzon had no means of knowing that Brodrick in effect attributed
to him the deliberate overthrow of the Cabinet's Tibetan policy. Between
these severe strictures on Younghusband's action and Brodrick's desire to
carry away a large indemnity there had elapsed only a fortnight. It was
exactly a month since Balfour had written, after the Cabinet, of the seeming
inevitability of widespread destruction at Lhasa and the taking of hostages.

The terms of the Lhasa convention soon began to leak into the press.
Charles Hardinge, Ambassador at St Petersburg, had been emphasising
for some weeks the value of adherence to British promises about Tibet.
Failure to honour them would invite Russia to repudiate hers about
Afghanistan; and British relations with the Amir remained unsettled. A
breach of good faith would be interpreted as taking advantage of Russian
embroilment with Japan. Lansdowne too felt anxious to strengthen
Lamsdorff's hands.[87] Once the Lhasa terms became known, the Russians
began to complain, especially of the provision for the occupation of
Chumbi. 'They are in an extremely sensitive condition' wrote Brodrick,
'with a great tendency to stable their horses with Germany.' Lansdowne
showed no undue alarm. He invited the Russian chargé d'affaires to refer
to his own country's agreement about Manchuria. Once again Hardinge
pressed for the strictest interpretation of British pledges. Otherwise Russia
would do as she pleased about Persia and Afghanistan. Perhaps she would
do so anyway; but scrupulous observance of pledges would make the
British position much stronger.[88]

The importance of behaving well towards Russia, at a time when the
Far Eastern war raged, when the Osenburg–Tashkent railway had just been
opened and the British military problem was far from solution, doubtless
weighed heavily with Balfour. On 4 October, having just seen Brodrick,
he told Lady Salisbury as a fact that Curzon had been 'constantly corresponding, behind our backs, with Younghusband, and, in my belief,
endeavouring to upset the Tibetan policy of the Government'. After a
further interview with Brodrick, the Prime Minister noted

> Younghusband has got us into a most abominable mess: I wish I could be
> sure that he has not done so deliberately, and under the full impression that he
> was pleasing...G. C. [urzon]! I think Younghusband will have to be publicly
> repudiated.[89]

Why Balfour had taken three weeks to reach this conclusion is not plain.
Certainly his contact with Brodrick seems to have produced an invigorating
effect. On that day, 4 October, he wrote another furious note about

Younghusband's disobedience, which had 'touched the honour of his country'. Hostile critics, he feared, would say that the British government had taken a leaf out of Russia's book by giving promises and then encouraging a breach of them.[90] It may be that Brodrick had impregnated the Prime Minister with his own conviction that Younghusband was exercising a baleful influence on the King, to whose Private Secretary they wrote on successive days. Brodrick had no doubt that Younghusband had gone to Tibet 'fully determined on the policy of our staying there and controlling the policy of Tibet'; Lord Lansdowne had said that the indemnity and the term of payment must be reduced at once. A letter written by Lansdowne on the previous day to Charles Hardinge shows his attitude towards the other terms, however, to have been robust. If there were to be any intervention in Tibet it must be by the British alone; Great Britain must have first call on concessions; there was nothing new in the trade regulations. We went to Lhasa to exact reparation and we cannot be content with a mere promissary note.'[91]

Balfour, in his note to Knollys, dilated on the importance of containing Indian military responsibilities at a time when they were being increased by Russian railway building to the borders of Afghanistan. Moreover, Britain stood pledged to the integrity of China, 'perhaps the most sensitive spot in international diplomacy', and to the Russians, whose assent to the Khedival decree had been of great value. The Prime Minister wrote as though Younghusband had been given absolutely plain terms in good time for his talks. He felt that alteration of a part of the convention would be most unjustly attributed to Russian pressure and not to consideration for international principle:

> The only chance of any permanent arrangement with that power in Central Asia depends on the mutual confidence that engagements will be adhered to, and if, as I fear, Colonel Younghusband in acting as he has done, wished to force the hands of the Government (whose policy, doubtless, he disagrees with), he has inflicted upon us an injury compared with which any material loss to the interests affected by our Tibetan policy is absolutely insignificant.[92]

As usual, Chirol of *The Times* enjoyed excellent sources of information. 'I believe' he wrote, 'Brodrick has done a lot of mischief, partly out of crass stupidity, and partly out of jealousy of Curzon. His attitude towards Younghusband, and his tendency to back up Macdonald against Younghusband, are otherwise inexplicable, and there are other circumstances equally suspicious.' Having known General Macdonald in China, Chirol could imagine no one less suitable. 'He has deliberately put every spoke he could in Younghusband's wheel and the meanness of the subterfuges he has had recourse to—we have had tangible proofs of it in connexion with his exercise of the Press censorship—is almost past belief.'[93]

A telegram of censure greeted the return to India of Younghusband who now regretted undertaking such a negotiation and asked permission to represent the position personally to Balfour and the King. Ampthill found him, at their first meeting, unpleasantly resentful and sullen. But after long talks and a good dinner Younghusband thawed out, and Ampthill's appreciation of the achievement at Lhasa deepened. The government of India renewed their support of the convention, [94] while the Viceroy wrote warmly of Younghusband's great courage, tact and patience, which had turned the Tibetans' hostility into an apparently genuine friendliness.[95]

It was not until the latter part of October that Brodrick mentioned to Curzon his conviction that Younghusband had been encouraged in disobedience by the belief that he was thereby serving another set of opinions. Curzon gave an assurance that he had not written to Younghusband about the amount of the indemnity or the term of occupation of the Chumbi Valley. He also told Brodrick that the Government had been unfair to Younghusband. The order that Chumbi must be evacuated at the end of three years seemed to contain the maximum of disadvantage. 'Of course the general policy that you defend is everywhere reducing your great agents abroad to relative impotence. I have no doubt that the Empire will suffer for this in the long run.'[96]

By now the text of the second convention, allowing occasional access to Lhasa for the trade agent, had reached London. Brodrick hoped, or so he informed Ampthill, to endorse it, but found almost all his colleagues hostile. Since the Cabinet considered it on 3 November, immediately after the acute phase of the Dogger Bank crisis, desire not to give any possible offence to Russia probably played a part. The convention was accordingly rejected, the Foreign Office feeling that it would otherwise be impossible to prevent Russia from sending a commercial agent.[97]

Sir Arthur Godley adopted a less serious view of Younghusband's conduct. He even took it upon himself to remind Brodrick that until a few months before the Government had believed they would come back from Lhasa with tails between their legs and with the prospect of sending another expedition in 1905. The actual situation was a very different one. He thought the Cabinet should show some gratitude to the man largely responsible for their escape from so awkward a position. The Cabinet, needless to say, showed nothing of the kind. Godley feared they would insist on 'a public wigging'.[98]

Brodrick still judged Younghusband to be a wire-puller, not least in the King's entourage, and remarked on the strong feeling in London that Indian officers should be taught a lesson in 'correct behaviour'. He circulated a memorandum to the effect that Younghusband believed he would be supported by Simla and could ignore the home government. Nevertheless, the Secretary of State avowed to Curzon that while his own draft virtually exonerated Younghusband, the colleagues demanded something stiffer. Several of the more influential members, whom Brodrick did not name, spoke against any reward for Younghusband.[99] In the end, it was agreed that a KCIE, the lowest possible award, should be given. The despatch stated that India's frontier policy must be laid down by the Cabinet alone and criticised the 'serious nature' of Younghusband's 'disregard of the instructions he had received'. Ampthill and his colleagues had referred to the attempt of May to 'secure an amicable settlement with Russia by deferring to her views about Tibet'. On the special instructions of Balfour, a formal despatch was sent to Calcutta, declaring that the Cabinet's Tibetan policy had been 'guided throughout by the interests of India'.[100]

FOUR

Kitchener's Threat

THE SHORTCOMINGS revealed during the Boer War provoked irresistibl[e] demands for inquiry and reform, for, as Milner observed, an avalanche o[f] military incompetence had nearly swept the Empire away.[1] Great Britain'[s] 'usual luck', Balfour recognised, had held. Though her army was seve[n] thousand miles distant, she had not suffered serious diplomatic squeezing let alone foreign intervention.[2] A commission under Elgin criticised th[e] confusion, incompetence and even corruption which had prevailed. Thre[e] members, including Lord Esher, suggested that the War Office be reor[-] ganised under a Board, on the lines of the Admiralty's system.

Having refused the War Office, Esher became chairman of a committe[e] of three, apparently at the King's instance.[3] Brodrick rightly predicted tha[t] the wholesale changes in the Army would bring trouble. All, he tol[d] Curzon, were dictated by Esher, 'a potentate without portfolio'.[4] The wor[k] of the triumvirate was soon done, Esher evidently presuming a good de[al] upon his intimacy with the King and with Balfour, who failed to asse[rt] himself. On the morning of 1 February, 1904, three of the highest dig[-] nitaries at the War Office learned from personal letters written by Arnold Forster, and simultaneously from *The Times*, that their posts were to b[e] abolished. They were, as Lord Roberts expressed it, 'naturally taken aback[.]' A week later Roberts himself, C-in-C of the British Army, found in h[is] paper the names of the new Army Council and was told that the Warra[nt] instituting the Council, and the Patent, had been issued. Arnold-Forste[r], assuming that Roberts knew, did not mention that this Patent abolished th[e] post of C-in-C. Roberts only found out five days later.[5]

Esher took it upon himself to send officers to the displaced officia[ls,] requiring them to leave forthwith. Roberts protested angrily. Having mad[e] grovelling apologies for the pain caused to him, Esher, feeling 'rath[er] enfeebled' by recent events, retired to Scotland for a few days.[6] Very soo[n] afterwards, the Cabinet received on a Saturday the triumvirate's latest pr[o-] posals. On Monday morning they appeared in the press. According t[o]

Roberts's accounts, the King admitted that a C-in-C was needed only when the sovereign happened to be a woman. King Edward, Roberts felt confident, had made up his mind to become, with Esher's ready help, the effective head of the Army.[7]

Kitchener judged the object of these reforms to be a divorce between the administrative and executive functions in the Army, to which, quite consistently, he was entirely opposed:

> In peace time the feeling in the Army of W.O. administration will be accentuated, and in War time the Army in the field will have absolutely no confidence in a civil administration assisted by some officers who may be entirely out of touch with the Army and know practically nothing of the necessities of a campaign.[8]

Esher's committee had also been examining the co-ordination of defence and foreign policy at the highest levels. The Defence Committee had been, wrote the Duke of Devonshire in 1900, 'nothing more than an informal Committee of the Cabinet' and had not played the role intended. It had met rarely, with no definite agenda, calling in the professionals for advice only, keeping no minutes. Selborne described it to Curzon as 'a farce'.[9] Salisbury's mind, as his nephew Balfour realised, did not bite upon such questions; but in 1902 the change of leadership and the end of the Boer War offered a chance.

Arnold-Forster, then a junior minister at the Admiralty, submitted to his superior, Selborne, a memorandum arguing the need for a more coherent and expert machinery and for 'the creation and growth of a body of opinion with regard to Military questions which will command respect because it is the outcome of scientific method and research'. He proposed a preliminary committee under the Prime Minister, to be followed by a permanent body investigating the central questions of Imperial defence. Shortly afterwards, Brodrick and Selborne circulated a paper on somewhat similar lines, proposing a committee under the Prime Minister or the Duke, with the two service ministers and four senior officers as the other permanent members. If Brodrick's account is correct, the alternative was the resignation of himself and Selborne. In December, the committee was reconstituted, the Duke remaining Chairman. Its meetings in the following year were attended at various times by eight Cabinet Ministers, the Canadian Minister for War, and seven soldiers and sailors. Much of their time passed in informal discussion, without decision.[10]

After Devonshire's resignation in October, 1903, Balfour took charge at every meeting until his government fell more than two years later. Esher and his two colleagues, Sir J. Fisher and Sir G. Clarke, urged that the Prime Minister should always preside, with complete freedom to determine the membership of the committee. A small department would be set up under his control, to give continuous study to ever-changing questions of strategy. The new body was intended to provide consistent planning in peace and a well-founded action in war. Previously there had been no machinery, outside the Cabinet itself, for harmonising the policy of the departments. It was, as the first Secretary, Sir G. Clarke, once wrote, no one's duty to look ahead on such issues. Questions of Imperial defence were never properly focused. The result had been a policy spasmodic, ill-regulated and wasteful.[11]

Unlike any other element in the British constitutional machine, the Defence Committee might be made to include representatives of the oversea colonies. 'It thus contains' wrote Balfour in 1903, 'the potentiality of being an "Imperial Council" dealing with Imperial questions.'[12] Though the Committee provided the Prime Minister, for the first time, with an embryonic department of his own, it did not become an executive body. On that condition alone could there be any chance that the principal countries of the Empire would take part. 'It has no power' said Balfour, 'to give an order to the humblest soldier in His Majesty's Army, or the most powerless sloop under the control of the Admiralty.'[13]

In practice, the position was less clear-cut. Apart from the Prime Minister, the Committee was regularly attended by the Secretary for War, the First Lord, the Secretary for India and the Chancellor of the Exchequer, and intermittently by the Foreign Secretary; among officers, Roberts, the First Sea Lord, the Chief of the General Staff, the Director of Naval Intelligence and the Director of Military Operations were normally present. It was unlikely that the Cabinet would upset a broad decision of Imperial defence policy reached by its senior members and their most distinguished professional advisers. This soon became apparent in relation to India. Not only did the Committee's conclusions about, say, Persia or Afghanistan become the basis of British policy, but it also trespassed inevitably into the fields of diplomacy and politics and tended, in Curzon's view, to usurp functions properly belonging to the executive as a whole.[14]

*   *   *   *

Official relations between Curzon and Kitchener, after the stormy start, remained for some months on a more or less even keel. Both went on tour in the autumn of 1903, and Kitchener then suffered a serious accident which confined him to bed for some months. The crisis, however, was merely postponed. Curzon's extension of office, announced in early August, meant that Kitchener would in all probability force the issue of military administration. The ground had been carefully prepared, week after week, through Lady Cranborne and Roberts. Kitchener's personal staff were utterly devoted to him and pressed forward his cause. Hubert Hamilton and Frank Maxwell, his ADCs, wrote intermittently to Lady Cranborne letters which exuded unquestioning loyalty to K. of K., fanatical belief in his powers, denigration of Curzon and the Military Department. Any opposition to the chief's proposals was attributed to jealousy, incompetence, red tape or folly. Hamilton had not been in the country nine months before he discovered Curzon to be, though an admirable Viceroy, 'dangerously ambitious for himself because of self *rather* than as God's agent for the good of his country. So different from Lord K. who never thinks of himself or how things may affect him personally...'[15]

For her part, Lady Salisbury (as she became in August, 1903) had convinced herself that Kitchener was the only man who could reform the War Office and the Army,[16] a belief shared in varying degrees by Rosebery, Brodrick and Esher, but not by Kitchener himself. Through her Kitchener had the ear of the Prime Minister for over two years before the Military Department could make any reply. Curzon probably knew that this correspondence was going on,[17] though he did not realise its intensity or character. Nor did he have any idea that in December, 1903, Balfour himself had written secretly to Kitchener:

> My own personal conviction is (at least as at present advised) that the existing division of attributes between the Commander-in-Chief and the Military Member of the Council is quite indefensible...
>
> I cannot say how thankful I am that we have got you, in this critical and in some respects transitional period, as our military adviser and guide to the problems of Indian Defence.[18]

Kitchener's opinion of the system and his attitude towards Elles did not change. Each complained of the other to the Viceroy, who warned Brodrick on 14 January, 1904, that it was proving most difficult to keep the peace between Kitchener and the Military Member:

> The former most unreasonably and unjustly dislikes and despises the latter and writes most unfairly about him and his schemes in the departmental notes. He wants to break and destroy the Military Department and thinks, I fancy, that the best way to do it is to force Elles to resign. This would be a great misfortune...[19]

Curzon told Brodrick in the following month that he would be very glad to discuss at home the Indian system of military administration. 'It seems to me to be on the whole well adapted to ordinary men in ordinary times, which is perhaps as good a criterion as any that could be named. If an exceptional C-in-C or an exceptional Military Member comes along, no doubt he resents the intrusion or influence of the other party...' Kitchener acknowledged to Lady Salisbury that the Viceroy was 'very friendly to me', but thought him largely in the hands of the Military Department.[20]

Kitchener's unauthorised procedures, of which another instance occurred in late March,[21] caused annoyance to the Viceroy, who remonstrated frequently:

> He cannot resist, however, having his little scores off the Military Department or some other traditional foe, and I am afraid he will go on committing these irregularities to the end of the chapter. Fortunately it is always quite possible to discuss these matters with him in a friendly way, and I am now spared the constant anxieties with which I used to be threatened during the first six months...[22]

This confidence was quickly shown to be premature. Immediately before Curzon left for his holiday in England, Kitchener completed a revised version of his proposals for the military administration of India. A Military Member would be retained as deputy to the C-in-C, would attend Council but would not vote if his chief were present. The bulk of the memorandum was occupied with the now familiar complaints of delay, antagonism and friction, coupled with the wholly incorrect assertion that projects were laid before the Viceroy and Council if the Military Member thought fit. This paper was sent 'quite privately' to Roberts and to Mullaly, whom Kitchener sent home in response to Curzon's request that a competent officer should be present in London for discussions about Indian defence. Mullaly handed it to Balfour.

In conversations with his successor, Ampthill, Curzon spoke of the difficulties between Kitchener and Elles. Ampthill, who hardly knew Kitchener, felt confident that he was 'far too loyal to think of taking advantage of Lord Curzon's absence'.[23] What is noteworthy is that in these circumstances Ampthill should have formed and upheld an opinion essentially identical with Curzon's. Very soon the C-in-C was pressing for administrative control of the Supply and Transport Department. After careful study, the new Viceroy judged that Kitchener was using this demand simply as a means to the abolition of the Military Department.

Were it granted, there would be no logical reason for refusal to transfer remounts, ordnance and medical stores.

'Lord Kitchener's proposal' Ampthill wrote to Brodrick, 'is in effect to revert to the system of combining executive and administrative functions under one head, a system which no longer exists in any other army in the world, which India abolished fifty years ago and which has at last been finally and emphatically condemned in England. I can see no reason for making even one step in this retrograde direction...' He had therefore urged Kitchener to accept a compromise intended to strengthen those executive powers of control over the Supply and Transport Department which he already possessed.

Ampthill recognised gloomily that his appeal was unlikely to succeed, for Kitchener was 'desperately keen' on the subject, to which he referred on every possible and impossible occasion. He had even managed to drag it into his minute on a file relating to the incidence of disease among camels. Ampthill hoped that this issue would not spoil his otherwise harmonious relations with the C-in-C,[24] who, however, flatly refused the compromise. He continued to insist that the Military Member had executive control over supply and transport. It was explained that he had not, but without effect. As Elles observed, no system could function when the man responsible for enforcing the orders—in this instance the C-in-C—declined to do it.[25]

The issue had now to go to Council, most members of which had already expressed sympathy with Kitchener's position. 'I am sorry to say' wrote the unfortunate Viceroy, 'that the Commander-in-Chief has imported a personal note into the discussion which I had been at pains to keep out of it, and I rather dread what may happen when it comes to verbal debate in the Council Chamber.' Kitchener had already intimated that the price of an adverse decision would probably be his resignation.[26]

Elles warned his colleagues that this was not a simple matter. It threatened the established system of military administration. Kitchener, vowing that Elles had drawn a red herring across the trail, deprecated the attribution of views which he did not hold.[27] Ampthill disbelieved this from the start. Brodrick himself observed that if Kitchener took a part of the Military Member's work, he would end by taking the whole.[28]

It had been arranged that Curzon should attend the Defence Committee in London on 15 June. Among the memoranda he found, to his astonishment, the revised proposal for the demotion of the Military Member which Kitchener had put forward at Simla seven weeks earlier. It was not the Committee's business, Curzon protested to the Prime Minister, to discuss the constitution of India. Brodrick supported him and the paper was withdrawn. Balfour said he had not intended it to be circulated and would not think of allowing the Committee to pronounce an opinion upon it, though some questions of Indian defence must be considered.[29]

Brodrick sent Kitchener's memorandum in strict secrecy to Ampthill, who commented sternly:

> I think that it is indisputably wrong that he should propose to them [the Defence Committee] a great constitutional change without the knowledge of the Secretary of State and behind the back of the Viceroy who is the head of the Army in India. If a similar privilege were accorded to other Members of the Viceroy's Council, there would be an end to all possibilities of good government...

Ampthill reported that Kitchener did not understand argument but resorted to mere declamation; that he did not look at a tithe of the papers he was supposed to deal with personally, while complaining constantly that he had not been shown this or that document; and that his staff, with the exception of General Duff, were ignorant of administration, inexperienced, prone to hero-worship and unthinking acclamation. By the same mail, Kitchener informed Lady Salisbury that he was getting along capitally with the Viceroy![30] Within a fortnight, Ampthill's poor opinion was reinforced by two proposals made from the C-in-C's office. The first — that Indian soldiers be trained as artisans to build barracks for themselves and British troops — made no reference to the sound reasons for which a milder suggestion had been turned down in 1903. The second was that the area of cantonment be extended to a radius of fifteen miles from each barracks. Nobody in Kitchener's office had worked out that this would mean a tract of about one thousand square miles, in which the Commanding Officer would have authority over the civil population. Both proposals were rejected.[31]

The immediate problem, about supply and transport, was overcome with some difficulty. Elles commented shrewdly that while he felt bound to oppose Kitchener on some questions, 'with his prestige it is rather a hopeless task, as whether right or wrong he will probably get his own [way] through his influence at home. I have no personal feeling in the matter, and if it was ever desired to make him supreme, I should be glad to make way by resigning my appointment with the reflection *Quem Deus vult perdere prius dementat.*'[32]

Kitchener's draft order showed that he wanted both executive and administrative control over transport and supply. He then told the Viceroy that he desired only the same powers as over cavalry and artillery. This he practically possessed already and Ampthill soon made proposals acceptable to the whole Council. Kitchener noted that before accepting executive control he would be glad to see it defined. As Ampthill commented to the Secretary of State, Kitchener did not really know what he wished or even what he had, and his staff were quite unable to help him form an opinion. Eventually the C-in-C accepted the suggestion, previously made by Elles and rejected with contumely, that a small committee should thrash out the details. So it was arranged. Financial control, and supply of animals and stores, remained with the government of India, acting through the Military Department. 'I have done all in my power to hasten matters' Kitchener assured Lady Salisbury.[33]

★   ★   ★   ★

During 1903, both the War Office and Indian Army HQ had been estimating movements of men and supply in the first months of a war against Russia. Their calculations varied alarmingly. Balfour, writing to the C-in-C, tactfully ascribed the discrepancy to the lack of reliable information about the North-West frontier, and professed himself disturbed at the nature of military relations between England and India, which seemed to make effective common action difficult. Yet the investigations of the Defence Committee were tending to prove the successful invasion of Britain impossible. If this conclusion were accepted and made public, it would be inferred that the British Army existed for small expeditions, just conceivably for use in Canada, for the retention of South Africa, but principally for the defence of India.

'I know' wrote Balfour, 'George Curzon thinks that we are always trying to rob him, and the Press and Public here are ever ready to take up the cry that this powerful and wealthy country is bleeding a poor and subordinate Dependency with cynical selfishness. My impression is that the wrongs are all the other way...'

India paid nothing for the Navy, without which reinforcements could not be sent, and little for an Army 'which exists chiefly on her behalf'. Admittedly the Colonies paid even less; but though India was the brightest jewel in the Imperial Crown, not to say an excellent customer, it was from a strictly military point of view nothing but a weakness: 'Were India successfully invaded, the moral loss would be incalculable, the material loss would be important—but the burden of British taxation would undergo a most notable diminution!'[34]

Curzon was not told of this letter, but knew Balfour's view in general terms. He rejected the belief that the British Army existed only to strike in Afghanistan; and even if it did, that was no reason for India to pay. 'The Army would be fighting there for the Empire and not for India alone. The frontier of Afghanistan happens for the moment to be the Achilles' heel of the Empire. But that does not make it an exclusively Indian interest.'[35]

Behind these discussions loomed the shadow of the Orenburg–Tashkent railway. Though the motives for its construction were partly economic, British attention naturally concentrated upon the fact that it would permit Russia to deploy her vast reserves of men in Turkestan and Transcaspia, and thus to create on the borders of Afghanistan a menace so serious as to call forth the whole armed strength of India. Kitchener called it 'a factor of the most supreme importance', enabling Russia, as if in chess, to check Britain on the Afghan frontier while making the next move on Persia. Despite her acute financial and political embarrassment, Russia set aside at the end of 1903 further sums for the speedy completion of the line and for an extension to the Persian frontier. Like Curzon, Kitchener thought this told its own tale. Russia might, he noted in February, 1904, be 'absolutely ready for action within two years'; and he did not lose the opportunity to link this prospect with the alleged inefficiency of the Indian Army.[36]

The government of India heard in May of troops and guns being moved towards Tashkent. An agent in Central Asia, a European in whose reports implicit trust was placed, reported Russian garrisons to have been increased. The Russian army in Turkestan he believed to be fully mobilised. Everywhere great activity was manifest. Railway building went forward rapidly. Early in June, the spy reported accurately that the new railway would be open not in 1905 or 1906, but by September, 1904, and in full running order by Christmas. The Russians at Tashkent claimed to have an understanding with Habibullah and with Indian princes.[37]

The Military Attaché at St Petersburg was told by the Russian General Staff that there was no question of mobilisation in Central Asia, where the situation was normal. 'A barefaced lie' said Ampthill. Kitchener too preferred his own sources of intelligence. Brodrick observed that though the military preparations in Turkestan probably had a double object, there was a genuine fear in Russia of risings in her Asiatic Empire after the Far Eastern setbacks.[38] Within a few weeks, Russian cruisers began to seize British merchant shipping. On 21 July the Viceroy and Kitchener were asked to consider in secret what steps should be taken if Britain and Russia went to war.

Understanding the problems at Petersburg, Lansdowne determined not to fuss unduly. 'Benckendorff is contrite, and so, I suspect, is Lamsdorff, and we must blacken their faces as little as possible.' Russia's explanations, however, were so haughty, and the internal unrest there so marked, that the Defence Committee decided to spend some £660,000 at once in preparing the Indian Army for mobilisation. Balfour wondered what might happen on the Russo-Afghan border if the neutral powers had to settle matters between Russia and Japan; and seizures of merchant shipping might recur. The concessions eventually made, it was believed in London, had owed a good deal to the timely move of the Mediterranean Fleet.[39]

Brodrick commented in mid-August that the extreme haste with which the railway was being pushed on appeared 'to indicate an intention of threatening us on the North-West frontier of Afghanistan'. However, Count Lamsdorff denied knowledge of any concentration of troops. Noting the Russians' stiff attitude about cruisers and contraband, Curzon had thought it 'quite conceivable that they wish deliberately to provoke us on the Afghan frontier'. A little later, when Russia seemed to court a rupture, he added: 'No Russian Minister can ever believe that a British Ministry is in earnest: and they seldom are.'[40] Though Kitchener learned privately from St Petersburg that the danger of war was real and imminent, Ampthill had not found in the Foreign Office papers cause for such grave anxiety.[41] In all probability he was right; but what matters is the belief in London that war with Russia was at least possible, a belief which strengthened Kitchener's position at a crucial moment.

Even before the completion of the Orenburg–Tashkent railway, it had been realised that should India's demands be fully met in time of war, there would be no organised force of Regulars left at home. The Defence Committee decided in the spring that if naval conditions altered, and if South Africa remained quiet, 30,000 men could go promptly to India, followed in six months by a further 69,000. 'India,' observed Balfour, 'represents the weak spot in our Imperial armour, and, therefore, gives the measure of our needs.' Arnold-Forster said the problem was insoluble, and the idea of relying upon the militia for Indian garrisons in time of stress ridiculous. Some battalions would 'simply lie down and be cut to pieces'.[42]

The Secretary for War was still struggling to create a viable system. While Brodrick and Balfour tried to achieve a closer harmony between Indian Army HQ and the War Office, the Chancellor asked the Cabinet to recognise that Britain's financial resources were 'inadequate to do all that we should desire in the matter of Imperial Defence'. Well and good, replied Arnold-Forster, but 'I cannot reduce money, unless you will let me reduce men...'[43] In that midsummer of 1904, the military question created turmoil in the Cabinet, which on one occasion sat until 12.30 a.m. The Prime Minister would have liked to delay reform of the army, but felt that the urgency of the Indian needs, and financial pressure, made early decision essential. He did not think Arnold-Forsters', or any other, scheme would produce the economies anticipated by the public:

> But if his plan prevents the growth of Army Estimates which would otherwise occur; if it provides a Striking Force; if it supplies ordinary drafts for India; if it supplies Indian reinforcements in time of war; if it supplies an adequate reserve; and if it prevents the otherwise inevitable augmentation of our annual expenditure, it will have done much.[44]

This may be described as an understatement of heroic proportions. The Defence Committee, having accepted that Britain should maintain in peacetime forces which would allow 100,000 men to go to India in the first year of war, learned in July that the C-in-C now desired 135,614 officers and men within nine months, assuming the doubling of the Field Army of India and the opening of the railway to Tashkent.[45]

*   *   *   *

Kitchener is said to have remarked, at this time of overwhelming popularity, that he could apparently do no wrong, an excellent situation of which he intended to take the fullest advantage. 'But' he would add, 'I know they will round on me some day as they did on Lord Roberts.'[46]

Though Lady Salisbury's letters to Kitchener have not survived, it is clear that Balfour was asking questions by this method. On one occasion Kitchener explained, for his benefit, that if the C-in-C were in the field with the Army, his deputy would stay at the seat of government. An independent Military Member could never work smoothly with the C-in-C or his staff, and might dominate the civilian Council in virtue of being on the spot. 'This is why under the present system I would not take command in the field against Russia.' While Kitchener was also using Lady Salisbury as a link with other members of the Cabinet, Brodrick, taking advantage of Curzon's leave, had begun a direct and secret correspondence with him.[47]

During the spring and summer, the C-in-C kept up the stream of complaints to which his confidants must by now have grown accustomed. His most telling argument, which gained added force during the Far Eastern struggle, was that in serious war the Indian system must disintegrate. Money voted for the Army, he wrote,

> is wasted out here just as much as, if not more than, at home; but they all seem to like it, and efficiency is the last thing that appeals to anyone except the Viceroy. What has been done in the past is right, and nothing must on any

account be altered by horrid innovators from benighted England—be they Viceroys or Commander-in-Chief! Curzon has done a great deal, but there is still so much to do.[48]

Kitchener's friends certainly put their information to good use in London. Major Marker, now private secretary to Arnold-Forster, explained to Leo Amery of *The Times*, who passed the information to the newly-appointed Secretary of the Defence Committee, that Kitchener had nothing to do with the preparations for the Tibetan expedition. He also spoke, in a sense that does not need description, of the relations between Army HQ and the Military Department. Clarke had already concluded that the Indian system was wrong in principle, though he did not believe that the C-in-C would allow an Army Council of the kind just established in England: 'K. is an ultra centralizer and if he got his way, he would get everything into his own direct power. He rather likes personally to manage Army administrative services, instead of concentrating upon training and organisation...'[49]

Clarke approved most of Kitchener's proposals, but condemned his new staff arrangements as wholly unsound: 'as his influence is out of all proportion to his judgment, I look upon a trained staff as denied to us. If the Press had not taught the country that K. is a God-sent administrator, it might have been possible to make progress in obtaining a staff qualified to direct operations of war.'[50]

Colonel Mullaly, sent home by Kitchener to assist the Defence Committee, seems to have worked chiefly through Balfour, Lady Salisbury and Clarke who, after a long talk with him, advised the Prime Minister in July of friction and of a monstrous and useless departmental correspondence in India.[51] Curzon, although willing to go a long way to meet the C-in-C, remarked that Kitchener's idea of rule was Kitchener, and that it was not possible to rely on a series of Kitcheners. With this view Esher agreed. He had little choice, for it had been the basis of his own recent proposals for army reform.[52] This was the state of the parties when, on 4 August, 1904, Balfour, Brodrick, Roberts, Godley and Curzon met in the Prime Minister's room at the House of Commons to discuss the military administration of India.

On the question of placing supply and transport under the C-in-C, all except Curzon concurred. He agreed, however, that if the change had been made by the time he reached India, he would loyally work the new system. According to Curzon's account, written immediately afterwards, Balfour and Brodrick pressed for abolition of the Military Department and the concentration of all military power in a single department under the C-in-C. They asked him to institute a commission, which would propose a new scheme. He refused, saying that any such step must be taken by his successor. He could not understand why the administration of the Indian Army, like that of the British, should be thrown into the melting-pot every second or third year, knew of no general dissatisfaction with it, or breakdown, in India, and saw no reason to destroy the system in order to please Kitchener or anyone else. On the whole, Roberts took his side; and the result, so Curzon imagined at this stage, was that nothing would be done.[53]

To outward appearances, the subject rested at that point for some time. But various documents passing in the next few days show how the forces in London were grouping themselves. Sir A. Godley told Brodrick that he hoped for an early inquiry into the relations of the military authorities and 'the desirability of concentration and unification'. If this awaited Curzon's return, he would have no difficulty in eliciting views favourable to his own, or in so managing matters as to make all reform difficult or impossible for many years. It was obvious, to Godley, that Curzon was strongly influenced by the personal considerations, not wishing to put more power into Kitchener's hands; whereas Godley believed that for every mistake Kitchener might make, he would carry out a dozen useful reforms.

Brodrick agreed, and told Balfour so.[54] He expounded to Ampthill a scheme for an Indian Army Board, the officers of which would administer the departments with more freedom than those currently serving under Kitchener. How they would secure and preserve this freedom he did not explain. Now that the post of C-in-C had been abolished in England, the tendency would be for the best men in the British Army to look to India; and he did not believe that the best soldier of the day could work effectively with 'a major-general of very moderate field services, but who has at present the power to check him at every turn'. Balfour had been very much impressed with the Indian Army's inability to hold the Field Force of four divisions in readiness, and was 'quite unwilling to face a Russian war with two War Offices in India'.[55]

Meanwhile, Clarke had received a paper, written by General Sclater and generally approved by Kitchener, which suggested a system analogous to that just established at home. Clarke being one of the authors of the reorganisation, this was shrewdly aimed, and it may account for Brodrick's temporary adoption of a similar plan. Clarke informed Balfour baldly that the Indian system was abundantly proved to work ill.[56] Marker had established close liaison with Colonel C. à Court Repington, Military Correspondent of *The Times*, whose army career had been abruptly cut short by a love affair with Lady Garstin and who later became notorious as an able but unscrupulous intriguer. Repington was supplied with information by

Marker and, no doubt, by others. He deeply admired Kitchener, whom he wanted as Chief of the Staff in England, and detested the Indian system. Kitchener corresponded regularly with Marker. 'I am perfectly sick' he wrote in mid-July, 'of the present state of affairs. The Military Member is the real C-in-C...and as to getting things done it is almost hopeless. If any redistribution scheme is accepted at home I feel quite sure it will be wrecked out here by the interference of the Military Department in every detail. Peg away at this whenever you get a chance. I see a possible chance of resigning before long but I fear it will be blocked as Ampthill would not like my going in his time. Keep this to yourself...'[57]

It appears that Colonel Mullaly made it clear during the summer that his chief would soon break loose on some issue or other; and Kitchener learned from Roberts, after the meeting of 4 August at the House of Commons, that he doubted whether Curzon and the civilian colleagues would allow abolition of the Military Membership. Ampthill wrote, with relief, that he and Kitchener had become very good friends,[58] but the C-in-C's lack of method was causing delays. 'He will not record his opinion in writing and wants an absolutely free hand. He does not comprehend our constitutional responsibilities and if he is expected to do more than announce his opinions verbally and casually he considers it mere "red tape".'

'I wish' Kitchener had just written to Lady Salisbury, 'I had been created so that I could look on senseless obstruction, useless delays and multiplication of work with perfect equanimity; but then I am afraid I was not built that way, worse luck.'[59]

His main work thus far had been to bring into a more coherent relationship the variety of India's armed forces: the Imperial Service troops, the police, the reserves and the regular army. The policy of scattering large garrisons about the country, as a safeguard against mutiny or riot, he abandoned in favour of concentration on the frontier. By this method, and with the expansion of some units, the field force would rise from four to eight or nine divisions. In short, the redistribution scheme reflected confidence in the tranquillity of India and a conviction of imminent Russian menace.

It has already been recorded that preliminary moves in this direction had been made in 1902. Curzon praised Kitchener's more thoroughgoing plan as 'a statesmanlike attempt to deal with the question on broad lines' and recognised that the existing distribution and organisation were faulty, obsolete and wasteful. He said at once that Kitchener's estimate of the cost, £1⅓m., was absurd, and forecast £6½m., warning that even the improved state of India's finances would not stand this in the near future. Before the

Viceroy went on leave, the whole scheme had been exhaustively discussed.
Kitchener was gratified to find that almost all the local civilian authorities
approved.[60]

Those parts of the scheme relating to the increase of the field force were
promptly considered by the Finance and Military committees at the India
Office, who, Brodrick observed, were 'evidently very much disinclined to
overrule Lord Kitchener'. Godley and the Parliamentary Under-Secretary,
Hardwicke, agreed. So Brodrick, who preferred eight divisions and
blenched at the expense of raising another, found himself in a minority of
one at a table of ten.

The full scheme meant an extra three battalions of British troops, for
which India must pay, and on the new terms. Apparently the Councillors
did not mind about the expense. Mullaly said that if Kitchener did not have
the nine divisions he would probably abandon the whole plan. Whether he
was authorised to make this threat is not clear.[61] The proposals simultaneously leaked into the London press. Given Kitchener's methods of
handling such matters, this is unlikely to have been an accident. Brodrick's
account of the universal unwillingness at the India Office to contradict
Kitchener must have given Curzon food for reflection. Nonetheless, he
refused to commit himself to so large an expenditure without consulting
his colleagues in India. As Clarke pointed out to the Prime Minister, Russia,
her power crippled by the Japanese war, could not for some years develop
her strategy on the North-West frontier.[62]

At Simla, the government of India had been considering the whole plan.
In mid-September, Ampthill asked at the Council whether their recommendations could now go forward to London? Kitchener then accused the
Military Department of sloth. The exchanges, recorded by the Viceroy, ran
on these lines:

> KITCHENER: 'I say that it is perfectly monstrous that the Government of India
> should take so long about a matter of such vital importance; I can't think
> what we are waiting for.'
> ELLES: 'We are waiting for Your Excellency's opinion on the replies from
> Local Governments, which were sent to you six weeks ago.'
> KITCHENER: 'Oh, that's all right. I have agreed to everything that the Local
> Governments say.'

When Elles again remarked that nothing to this effect had been learned
from Army HQ, the C-in-C retorted that it was mere 'red-tape' to require
formal letters. If the government of India were to be conducted on such
lines, it might as well shut up shop. Ampthill said that in the transaction of

all business written assent was needed. Thereupon Kitchener asserted that
the documents had not been received:

ELLES: 'They were sent to you six weeks ago, Sir, and we have not heard
anything of them since.'
KITCHENER: 'I have never had them, but I have told you all that I agreed with
the Local Governments.'

Immediate inquiry showed that the papers had indeed been in Kitchener's
office since the beginning of August.

I think [wrote Ampthill to Brodrick], that this little narrative will give you
some idea of the difficulties of working with the great Kitchener of Khartoum
and explain what I mean when I say that he cannot brook constitutional
methods. My personal relations with him, however, are all that I could wish
and I have no fear of a misunderstanding with him; my only fear is of a hopeless
breach between him and the Military Member in spite of the conciliatory and
deferential manner adopted by the latter.[63]

It will be obvious that among Kitchener's many qualities scrupulous
regard for truth and accuracy was not the most prominent feature. He does
not seem to have realised that the Viceroy would be sending home letters
and documents which, to put it at the kindest, showed in a different light
the events he purported to describe. Often the hiatus passed unnoticed, for
the correspondence with Lady Salisbury was not seen by Brodrick, and
Balfour possessed neither the memory nor the knowledge of India to supply
his own corrective. But at this time, when Kitchener was in direct touch
with the Secretary of State, the discrepancies became ludicrous. On the
same day, Brodrick received from Ampthill the letter just quoted and from
Kitchener a letter accusing Elles of deliberate obstruction and denouncing
the Military Department, which should devote itself entirely to finance:
'Since last January the scheme has been in the hands of the Military Department…the baboo department will not and cannot be made to move.'[64]

When that letter was written, the whole matter had in fact been settled
except for one issue, that of homogeneous (i.e. wholly British or Indian)
brigades or mixed brigades. Elles asked that Kitchener should not press his
preference for homogeneous brigades, a departure from tried tradition and
likely to weaken the good feeling and loyalty that arose from fighting side
by side. Ampthill agreed, wishing to run no avoidable risk of discontent.
Kitchener pronounced the homogeneous brigades 'vital to the scheme' but
could produce no argument in Council. Sir E. Law took Kitchener's side as
usual. The Council was evenly divided. It must have seemed hardly
credible that Kitchener could not recall the reason for his opinion on a

matter described by himself as vital. 'You will be surprised to hear it,' Ampthill informed Brodrick, 'but Lord Kitchener really does not know the ins and outs of his own scheme which I cannot believe to be his personal work so far as the detail is concerned.'[65]

Immediately the C-in-C created a crisis. It chanced that he had dismissed a Volunteer Adjutant, before ascertaining that he did not possess the power to do it. The Military Department asked him to rescind the order, since the appointment of this particular officer rested with the local government. Kitchener then telegraphed to the Secretary for War, Mr Arnold-Forster, that his position had for some time been one of great difficulty, 'owing to the existing system of dual control'. The Military Department's action, based on 'a mere question of procedure' made him feel that he could no longer be responsible for the discipline of the Indian Army. He therefore resigned, and wished also to retire from the Army.[66] It may not be a coincidence that this telegram was sent on the day when the indefinite postponement of Curzon's return became known.

Only after the message had gone to London did Kitchener write to Ampthill, who, for the first time in five months, was taking a weekend off, and who reacted with a decision and firmness that may have surprised him. The Viceroy pointed out immediately that it was not a question of failure to uphold Kitchener's action. If he objected so strongly, why did he give no warning? The first impulse of the Council would have been to defer:

> Can you honestly say that your authority as Commander-in-Chief is impaired because the Government have asked you to withdraw an order concerning Captain Swan of the Nilgiri Volunteers?...
>
> I cannot accept your resignation on such grounds. I could not accept your resignation in any circumstances without a much fuller explanation and far more cogent reasons than those which you have given me.[67]

This language implied that Ampthill did not believe the reason given by Kitchener, and he telegraphed to Brodrick that it was a mere pretext, the resignation having been submitted 'in a fit of childish temper because we did not accept his opinion in Council on a point in the reorganisation scheme, for he claims to be infallible on all matters which concern the Army'.

Ampthill commented curtly on the discourtesy, folly and lack of patriotism displayed by Kitchener,[68] whose next letter made it clear that the real ground of resignation was 'dual control', whereby the Military Department was

> practically the principal military adviser to the Viceroy as well as the authority

that transmits the Viceroy's personal orders or issues orders in his name to the Commander-in-Chief.

...the Commander-in-Chief...is treated in all such matters as if he...did not form part of the Government of India.

Thus it is quite evident that the Military department can themselves at any time render the position of any Commander-in-Chief an impossible one.

Ampthill rejoined that to the best of his knowledge Army HQ and the Military Department had worked well together. In the matter of supply and transport that Department had yielded to Kitchener's view at Ampthill's own instance, while the reorganisation scheme had been accepted 'with an unquestioning confidence in your judgment and deference to your views which I am sure have never been accorded to any previous Commander-in-Chief'.[69]

In London, the news of Kitchener's resignation fluttered the dovecots. Arnold-Forster, judging Kitchener to be probably right, sent on the telegram to Balfour, who wired immediately to the C-in-C:

Must beg you in public interest to take no hasty action.

Brodrick promised that the fullest consideration would be given to any cause of complaint, and appealed earnestly for time. These messages crossed a telegram from Ampthill:

Lord Kitchener shows signs of relenting. Please leave him to me and do not do anything from home unless I ask you.[70]

Kitchener said when they met that he was not in the habit of resigning. His action had been taken only after very deep consideration, and it would seem 'puerile' if he now withdrew it. The Viceroy thought it prudent not to say that he knew of Kitchener's earlier resignations and that it had been puerile to resign anyhow. He noted that Kitchener 'argued very well on this question with which he is very thoroughly acquainted', undertook to tell Brodrick that the system should be examined, and was convinced that something must be done to meet Kitchener's views if he were to be retained. It became apparent that the discussion in Council about mixed brigades had deeply hurt the C-in-C, who asserted several times that Elles had accused him of proposing to make the Native Army disloyal. On each occasion Ampthill pointed out that this was a most unfair misrepresentation. Eventually Kitchener admitted that he was not entirely just to Elles. 'You can see' Ampthill wrote to Brodrick, 'the difficulty of dealing with a man who is seized with such curious ideas concerning the proprieties of debate and the privileges of the Commander-in-Chief.'[71]

Knowing nothing of Kitchener's private correspondence, Ampthill ascribed the incident merely to an outburst of temper. This may have been the immediate occasion; but it was a test case. News of the resignation was immediately telegraphed to Mullaly, who explained to Balfour that the position of the Military Department, and fresh objections raised by them 'after a delay of nearly eleven months' to Kitchener's large schemes, made it impossible to go on. 'He tells me that he thinks that either Sir E. Elles or himself will have to go; and if his resignation is accepted he intends to retire from the army.' Mullaly was simultaneously describing to Lady Salisbury the 'astonishing obstruction' of Kitchener's work. The C-in-C had telegraphed that Ampthill was completely in the hands of the Military Department. Mullaly, writing on War Office paper appropriately headed 'Mobilisation and Intelligence Department', inveighed against the whole Indian system. He believed, quite rightly, that Kitchener would not be allowed to go. Lady Salisbury, transmitting the letter at once to Balfour, assumed pardonably but wrongly that 'the papers which were to be sent home by the Indian Council [*sic*] containing the schemes without which... the India Office cannot act, are what Elles is procrastinating about and on which he wants another Committee, and that at last K. in despair has thrown up the sponge'.[72]

Kitchener himself told her that after taking the plunge he had felt 'quite a young man again instead of a worried preoccupied old cripple'. He expressed sorrow that his hand should have been 'forced by the Military Department' at a time so inconvenient to himself. For the moment he withdrew the threat, on promise of an early inquiry. This, and the patent unwillingness even to contemplate his departure, must have indicated plainly to Kitchener how strong a position he occupied. Ampthill, who realised that Kitchener would be satisfied only if vested with Papal infallibility in all military matters,[73] was soon to regret his part in preventing the resignation.

*   *   *   *

Reports of activity in Central Asia reaching London during September convinced the Director of Military Intelligence that a reinforcement of Russian troops had indeed taken place. Denying any aggressive intent, Benckendorff admitted the fact, hinted broadly that another division might be sent and suggested that the more the British Government avoided unexpected decisions, such as the refusal to allow the Baltic Fleet to coal in British territory, the more favourable would be the prospects. If a further

division were sent, Gen. Grierson calculated, Russia would have in
Central Asia some 114,000 combatant troops, of whom nearly three-quarters
would be available as a field force.[74]

The Orenburg–Tashkent railway, completed just at the time of
Kitchener's resignation, meant a vastly increased power of concentration. Kitchener's staff calculated that within two months of the outbreak
of war, Russia could put 60,000 men on a northern line of advance and a
similar number on a southern. In six months' time, wrote Brodrick,

> Russia will have exactly double the railway power for decanting troops into
> Aghanistan which she now has into Manchuria. The stations on the new lines at
> fixed intervals are provided with kitchens for cooking food for 1,000 men at
> the same time.[75]

It is certainly true that Russian forces in Central Asia were being
strengthened, for which the Defence Minister had asked in August. The
motive may have been, as a document by Lamsdorff suggests, to deter
Britain from pushful measures in Seistan; perhaps to give a counterweight
to the fact that the Russian Fleet staggering out to the Far East was entirely
within British power; or generally to dissuade the British, by pressure at the
most vulnerable point, from joining Japan.[76]

As for the military reorganisation at home, Arnold-Forster had sur-
mounted the first Parliamentary hurdles but was perpetually at loggerheads
either with the King, or with his professional advisers, or with Cabinet
colleagues. The Army, he told Curzon in a doleful letter, was 'conservative
to the core, and, be it said with bated breath – not actively intelligent…Our
military condition is deplorable, a standing peril for the nation…At present
half – more than half – of the troops we maintain are unfit to take the field.
We are trying to meet others' "best" with our "worst" and that will spell
disaster one day…'[77]

These were the circumstances in which members of the Cabinet had to
face the likelihood of Kitchener's resignation. Curzon, learning after the
event what had happened at Simla, favoured a stern attitude. Brodrick
naturally considered the likely reaction. 'I am inclined to think that if
Kitchener resigns and tells his tale, the ipse dixit of even such a Viceroy
as George will not satisfy the public.'[78] He was convinced that Kitchener
must be met in some way, and had inexplicably persuaded himself that the
Indian system was identical or similar to that recently abolished at home:

> If you have a position in which our greatest Military Organiser feels he cannot

remain, which the Prime Minister thinks is in principle indefensible, and which has been abandoned in England, it makes it very difficult to resist a change.[79]

To Lady Salisbury, the Prime Minister sent early in October a letter which merits some comment and attention. Curzon's refusal to alter the Indian military system seemed to him 'an excellent illustration of what George Hamilton always used to say...that he would never work any plan but one that he himself had originated'. As for Kitchener, he had been fighting 'by every means in his power, legitimate and illegitimate' against the system. On the main question, Balfour agreed with him

and could I have foreseen the development of events and the attitude which George Curzon has taken up, I should have made it a condition of any renewal of the tenure of his office that he should make a genuine attempt to reform the system. My hope now is that he will give up his appointment in April...

Balfour did not feel unqualified admiration for the methods of Kitchener, whose first plan, it appears, had been to tide quietly over the remainder of Curzon's tenure by agreeing to 'some of his most preposterous strategic suggestions; and I do not think Mullaly denies that K. by no means holds *some* of the opinions to which he has solemnly put his hand'. At this stage of Balfour's argument, it should be observed that Curzon's refusal to alter completely the military system may or may not have been an illustration of Lord George's dictum; but that is hardly the point. Curzon had repeatedly said, from the time of Kitchener's arrival, that he would not suppress the Military Department, as Balfour knew quite well. Even at this stage he could easily have prevented Curzon from returning to India. The phrase 'preposterous strategic suggestions' presumably refers to the Helmund lease and is not without its humour; for the Defence Committee, in deciding under Balfour's inspiration that the principal purpose of the Army was to meet Russia in Afghanistan, were preparing for the wrong war in the wrong place, while nothing could have been more preposterous than the size of the forces Kitchener soon proposed to deploy across the North-West frontier.

Clearly, Balfour had seen through the circumstances of the latest crisis. Kitchener was trying to 'force everybody's hand by an absurd resignation'. Mullaly, it seems, confessed that the real motive had been 'to compel us to adopt his policy at the point of the bayonet. There is an element of slimness in our only General which slightly diminishes my respect, though in no sense my liking, for that great man.'

The words 'our only General' are noteworthy. Balfour thought that a Viceroy taking up Indian military reform would find the weight of official opinion against him, because Ampthill agreed with Curzon, and for some unexplained reason he took Ampthill to be representative.[80] A day or two later, Balfour pressed Brodrick for the prompt transfer to Kitchener of supply and transport: 'if Elles and Ampthill have been anxious, and able, to block this most necessary reform, it is a further proof (if further proof were required) that Kitchener's complaints of the existing system are well-founded'.

Let it be recorded to Brodrick's credit that he immediately corrected the Prime Minister on the facts, pointed out that Ampthill was ' "playing up" admirably' and passed on some of his letters, so that Balfour could savour the more fully Kitchener's methods.[81] 'If it were not' Brodrick wrote to Ampthill, 'that most of us consider the present relative positions of the Commander-in-Chief and Military Member to be the cause of divided responsibility, we should I think be more disposed to resist his demands.'[82] It is not known whether the Viceroy was able to extract any meaning from this utterance.

Very soon afterwards, Great Britain and Russia were on the brink of war over the Dogger Bank incident. The Czar told Charles Hardinge that he had countermanded a proposal to move a full division of troops on the Tashkent line. War with England, the Ambassador believed, would be welcomed throughout Russia, which would patch up a peace with Japan and 'so free the Russian Army to concentrate its entire energy and forces in a determined attack on India'. The Military Attaché found no evidence in Central Asia of immediate preparations, but the officer commanding the Odessa military district spoke openly in the opposite sense. The Chief of Staff at Tashkent remarked that India was the only place where the British could be got at and if, when Japan was beaten, they wanted another Berlin Conference, there would be war in Central Asia. Significantly, Lamsdorff reproved the War Minister for his subordinates' loose chatter. Under existing conditions, he wrote, it was the basic task to preserve friendly relations with neutral powers.[83]

Kitchener's resignation, Brodrick remarked to Curzon during the crisis, 'would be regarded more anxiously at this moment than any other'. Curzon was composing a note which stated explicitly that he opposed Kitchener's desire to centralize the military administration of India in his own hands. He considered the C-in-C's presence on the Council 'simply invaluable, both because of his unique authority and experience and because, in India, I think that the government ought never to decide upon military questions without hearing the executive head of the Army'. But that officer already had extremely onerous duties and must spend much time on tour. Military proposals must also be judged by other than military criteria. Hence the value of the Military Membership. These opinions were at once circulated to the Prime Minister and Cabinet.[84]

On 3 November, Balfour sent Curzon a crucial letter, arguing that though India had not hitherto been threatened, in the era of British rule, with invasion, the extension of Russian railways had transformed that situation. The government had despatched to India 'the soldier who certainly commands a greater amount of confidence than any other English General, Lord Roberts excepted', who insisted that the system would not stand the test of war. If it were not altered he would leave. 'I feel...certain that, if he resigns, he will make public the ground of his resignation and that the ground will be the one I have stated.' Whatever the merits, it would then be found that the vast weight of British opinion would side with Kitchener. Closer examination might show that Curzon and Roberts were right; but if no commission were appointed, if Kitchener thereupon left and if war broke out with Russia, 'both at home and in India an impossible situation would be created'.[85]

On the same day, Curzon offered his resignation to the Prime Minister:

> If you find it easier to carry out the views of the government about India with a new Viceroy you have only to say it to me and I will make way. This is not an ultimatum à la Kitchener. It springs from a sincere desire not to be a source of trouble.[86]

Balfour did not take this up. After a long talk with Curzon on 9 November, he thought that in practice 'the whole argument in favour of an independent Military Member really reduces itself to the necessity of having some military check on the otherwise too absolute power'.

He was, however, not sure that Curzon would admit this; in which supposition he was justified, for Curzon's argument was not so simple. According to his own record, Balfour said that he cared little for the system of checks and distrusted dual control. The Viceroy and his Council should be strong enough to curb extravagance, and a properly constituted War Office would supply the Commander-in-Chief with sufficient criticism to prevent blunders. But, Curzon interjected, Kitchener frankly avowed that he could not for an instant tolerate commentary and discussion on his policy among his subordinates. Balfour answered that if this were so 'it was only an exaggeration of a common failing among soldiers—a failing which made them greatly inferior for administrative purposes to civilians of equal ability'.

Curzon proposed that the home government should send a despatch, stating that Kitchener was understood to be dissatisfied and asking the government of India to investigate. He told Balfour that to the best of his belief the only member who took Kitchener's view was Kitchener. The government at home would then consider the question and, if they wished, appoint a commission. Balfour thought this a good plan:

> It would be impossible for us from here to make a revolutionary change in the Indian Government against its wishes and without consulting it, and even after consulting it, we could not force our views upon it without making independent inquiry.[87]

Brodrick tried to placate Kitchener, asking that any difference on small questions be laid aside: 'There is no one so anxious as I am to smoothe your path.' He also pointed out that many authorities favoured the Indian system. Kitchener's reply expressed disappointment. If nothing was likely to be done, he should be released before overstrain broke down his health completely and would hope to leave India, and the Army, as soon as possible.[88]

In the meantime, Repington and Marker had been discussing the next steps. The former, hearing that Curzon would return to India for six months only, suggested that Kitchener might wait till he had gone. On this Marker noted that no delay could be admitted if the Indian Army was to be efficient in time. Two years of Kitchener's tenure had now passed; if he acted as soon as a new Viceroy arrived he would be accused of trying to 'rush' him. 'Curzon is the *real* obstacle to the removal of the present dual control and I am for going for the key to the position, as soon as may be.' Repington realised that the system Kitchener wished to institute was basically the one just unravelled in England. However, he produced a list of those who should be influenced and induced to write to the press. 'You can manufacture a public opinion if you go the right way to work.'[89]

*   *   *   *

The cost of Kitchener's redistribution scheme had risen in eight months from £1⅓m to £8½m, excluding strategic railways and cantonments. The whole basis of the plan was to fight Russia in Afghanistan, 'a contingency which,' Curzon noted, 'though it has been contemplated for nearly 70 years, has not yet arisen (I admit that it is more likely to arise in the future), while the security of the country is an obligation that is present with us every day.'

Evidently he took a cooler view than the colleagues he was about to rejoin. Military spending in India had been rising rapidly since 1901. It was not plain that a balance had been struck between the claims of military redistribution and others, for instance, irrigation, education and the police. If these were to be stinted in order to provide funds for Kitchener's scheme 'great popular irritation and agitation must be faced'. Curzon feared that unless care were exercised, Indian military spending would be carried forward on a wave of prodigality which might provoke a reaction and a sharp reversal by an incoming Liberal government. He doubted whether the expense of £20m or £30m on frontier railways, which Kitchener wanted to build on a massive scale, would be of much value, since Russia would still be able to take Herat and Afghan Turkestan. Physical conditions must confine British strategy to the early seizure of the line Kabul–Ghuzni–Kandahar. Should Russia break out from the zone of her unavoidable success, as much of the Indian army as possible must be massed to meet her.[90]

He agreed that the urgently necessary schemes, and the costs for 1905–6, should be sanctioned at once. As Brodrick observed, 'if war should take place with Russia, and we had postponed action, we should incur heavy responsibility.'[91] The desire for an extension of railways was rooted in a belief that the logistic problems would otherwise be insuperable. In 1879–80, Roberts's 13,000 men had in ten months consumed all the available food near Kabul. Yet Kitchener was proposing to place there a force of 80,000 or 100,000 needing more than three million pounds of food a day. At least 234,794 camels would be required for this carnage alone; but all available animals must be used to bear stores and ammunition.

India's demands for reinforcements in time of war rose sharply during 1904. Before Curzon left England in November, the figure had reached nearly 150,000. But even if 100,000 were sent, there would be no British troops left for any other Imperial purpose. The Defence Committee refused to guarantee any such total. Compliance, Clarke told Balfour, might well make India the predominant partner in Imperial defence, and the only explanation of the vast increase was Kitchener's Kriegspiel of 1903. Like Gen. Grierson, Clarke believed that vital factors of supply and communication had been 'either ignored or absolutely miscalculated. Great masses of men are moved across the most difficult country in the world as if they were pawns upon a chess board.' Railways were assumed to traverse this terrain at prairie speed, up to a mile a day. All that part of the scheme should be discarded, and no more than 60,000 men promised.[92]

The place which India now occupied in the ruling conception of British strategy is exemplified in a note by Balfour of December, 1904. The British Empire, according to him, needed 209,000 soldiers. Of these, a mere 27,000 were allotted to home defence; 30,000 for colonial garrisons; and 152,000 for drafts and reinforcements to India.[93]

FIVE

Interlude in England

WHEN St John Brodrick succeeded Hamilton at the India Office in the autumn of 1903, Curzon explained the lines on which he hoped they would work together. He complained of dilatory procedures at the Office:

> The pace strikes me as leisurely in the extreme, and your Councillors compound for the little work that many of them have to do by doing it with a sobriety of movement that reminds one of a London bus in Cheapside.

The Council, though necessary as a check upon an otherwise irresponsible government of India, should not be allowed to defeat the Secretary of State and Viceroy, constitutional allies, once they were agreed. After nearly five years as Viceroy, Curzon, feeling that he had a knowledge of the whole country which no one else had had the luck or opportunity to acquire, placed a corresponding confidence in the judgment of himself and his Council. India looked to the Secretary of State as her champion, paid his salary and that of every man in the Office: 'and nothing causes warmer resentment here than the idea that this huge and costly machinery is not always or exclusively devoted to her own interests.'

In Curzon's judgment the serious dangers to British rule arose from the 'racial pride and the undisciplined passions of the inferior class of Englishmen in this country' and from the impression, should it gain a substantial foothold, that indifference was shown to India's cause in London:

> It is better to make a stand for India and to be beaten by your colleagues, than to make no stand at all...the number of things that can be done at the expense of India...is diminishing year by year...India will become more and not less clamant in the future: and in every case of divergent interest that I have been called upon to examine, it is my conviction (though I doubt if at present it is yours) that justice is on her side...[1]

When Brodrick described the War Office as a shop to which India might go, with the liberty, if dissatisfied, to go elsewhere, Curzon pointed out the fallacy:

But that is precisely what we cannot do. We go to the shop because it is the only establishment with which we are permitted to trade, and we go there, not on equal terms with the man behind the counter, but with the knowledge that he has the authority to overrule us in any conflict that may arise.[2]

A few days afterwards, Curzon received at Bahawalpur two telegrams from Brodrick. The first requested information within four days on the crucial question, alleged to have been before the Indian authorities for nearly four years, of reinforcement in time of war. It had not been before them at all; Kitchener, awaiting figures from Roberts, was far distant; and Curzon had to explain that Brodrick wanted the impossible. 'It is much as if Balfour at Bordighera were asked to frame a fiscal policy by telegraph with the Chancellor of the Exchequer at Lisbon, neither of them having any papers with them, or ever having gone into the matter in advance.'

The second message related to coolies for the Transvaal, 20,000 of whom were needed for railway work. Again an answer was demanded within four days. Brodrick observed that it would be 'undesirable' that the Cabinet should be forced to override the government of India on this subject. The responsible member of Council, Ibbetson, was in Assam. Curzon telegraphed at once to him, meanwhile warning Brodrick sharply:

The name of South Africa stinks in the nostrils of India. The most bitter feeling exists over the treatment meted out to Indians in the Transvaal and Natal. Any attempt to ignore or override this feeling would produce a commotion greater even than that over the South African garrison, while the recollection of the latter would tend to inflame it...We are not in the least anxious to send Indian coolies to work upon railways in the Transvaal or anywhere else...

Already tens of thousands of Indians lived in South Africa, subject to invidious, and sometimes odious, disabilities. Only a fair bargain, as Ibbetson independently advised, would be tolerable; and as for overruling by the Cabinet

Surely you do not mean to order the government of India to send coolies to the Transvaal whether they like it or not?...I cannot without a good deal of thought and study swallow the proposition that, having saved South Africa at the outbreak of the war, it is now the duty of India to develop it.

Dilating upon the importance of Indian opinion, Curzon pointedly repeated that there were some things that home governments could no longer do at India's expense. For five years he had been preaching the doctrine of Empire; but Indians were disposed to think it a farce

for in practice it means to India a full share of the battles and burdens of Empire
5

but uncommon little of the privileges or rights. For instance, intense resentment is caused at the complete omission of India in all the home speeches about Fiscal Reform. This sort of indifference sinks down and it gnaws at the roots of the loyalty and contentment which we are doing our best to inculcate.

By telegram, Curzon dismissed the proposed terms of indenture as quite inadequate and refused to throw away India's bargaining counter.[3] The response at home was illuminating. Members of the India Council advised Brodrick that no outcry would arise in India against the recruitment of coolies 'on good terms' unless it were known that Curzon was hostile. 'You may conceive' wrote Brodrick, who evidently credited this, 'how it handicaps me in the presentation of your views to the Cabinet that they have every reason to believe that you individually are placing yourself athwart them at a moment of extreme difficulty, when it is no doubt in your power to invoke public feeling in India in your support...'

The Secretary of State also urged Curzon at least to appear to study the India Council a little more. 'You regard them as hostile to you, and they, so far as I can judge, think you undervalue them.[4] Again Brodrick asked that the question of coolies should not become a conflict between the two governments. The Cabinet might well 'take the bit between its teeth'; and there would in any event be repercussions in the future if a friendly solution were not found. He argued that since Britain was now held to be safe from invasion, India remained as the main justification of the British Army. The task of feeding 'a great Indian force' in peace, and of providing a greater one in war, embarrassed British finance, formed an abiding focus of Parliamentary trouble and wrecked War Ministers and Commanders-in-Chief:

> I do not want to put it too high, but you will no doubt see that, as India is for ever on our lips, it is possible for people here to take the view that you, who above all others promote a strong frontier policy which requires large armaments and reserves, should assist us where you can.[5]

Nevertheless, the government of India decided that Indian labourers would not be sent unless definite assurances of a change of heart in the Transvaal were received. When the home government said that the conditions could not be met immediately, Curzon replied that the Indians could not go.[6] China therefore continued to furnish South Africa with the coolies and British history with one of its more effective election-cries.

This correspondence did not form a happy augury. Curzon must have been taken aback to learn that Brodrick and the leading lights of the India Office imagined that he could shape Indian opinion on a subject so sensitive merely by expressing himself in public. Walter Lawrence found that

Godley, though very cordial, apprehended a change in relations between India and the Office. It seemed that Brodrick regarded himself as a success at the War Office and wished to be equally successful at the India Office. He and the new Cabinet thought Curzon too powerful and too strenuous. McDonnell and Dawkins confirmed this impression. 'I suppose' said Lawrence, 'they see another possible Chamberlain as Viceroy?' Godley assented. 'These jealous chattering pygmies depress me' Lawrence wrote to Curzon; but the rest of his letter was, perhaps, more unexpected. He had been summoned by Brodrick, who quickly showed that he believed Curzon to lead or inspire the Indian press, presumably in its attitude to the various issues on which Viceroy and Cabinet had differed. Lawrence replied that Curzon stood aloof from the press. Though a hint or a nod would raise a storm in cases where England overruled India, it was never given; at which Brodrick appeared to be convinced.[7]

Curzon could scarcely believe his eyes. The best course, he remarked to Godley, was to laugh at fables so absurd:

If anyone started the story that you were secretly a Mormon and had six ladies strewn about at different watering places in Wales, you would probably burst out laughing, not swearing...Suffice it to say that, in five years, I have not had a single conversation with a single Indian press man: that during that time I have not written, inspired, or suggested a single communication in the Press (other than official communiqués officially issued): that my attitude towards the Indian press...has brought me many enemies: and that I will take off my hat to any public man at home who can show a similar record.[8]

With that, Curzon probably dismissed the matter from his mind, for the moment at least. Any effect produced in London by his denial was temporary. With Lawrence's letter came an appeal from Godley, probably provoked by the refusal to supply coolies, for an effort to remove the impression 'that you are inclined when there is a difference of opinion to carry your protest beyond the recognised official limits, to bring pressure to bear to force the hand of the Government at home. You will say at once that the impression is most incorrect and unfair. Still, I venture to urge you to remember that it exists.'

As for Brodrick, 'I am quite sure that you would be wrong if you were to count on his being either ductile or malleable.'[9] This indicated, in rather more oblique terms, what Walter Lawrence had already said. Curzon remarked that if he were to be suspected of unworthy motives every time he disagreed with the Cabinet, then it would be pointless to continue as Viceroy.[10] Soon afterwards arrived another letter, conveying Godley's belief that there were 'strong reasons for thinking it would have been better if you had not exceeded the normal term'. Curzon did not know how to take this. He tried to explain how these dark hints caused him anxiety and distress, seeming to indicate storm-clouds ahead. Did Godley think his work in India done? Would it be better to have no definite policy in Tibet, Persia and Afghanistan? Was it, as many friends at home had said, that the Viceroy had become too powerful and did not fall in readily enough with the views of the Cabinet; or that he was a source of disquiet to a Secretary of State anxious to make his authority felt? Curzon admitted that there might be some truth in all these suppositions, but believed that his work was not yet finished. He was proud of his record in India and of being reappointed, and had no intention of running away or being hustled out because Brodrick was more assertive or the new Cabinet more suspicious or the India Council more hostile:

> All three can of course combine—having the superior authority—to render my position untenable...and in that case I shall not hesitate to write to the Prime Minister and place my resignation in his hands...I leave you to judge whether such a situation would redound to the credit of the Ministry or of the Secretary of State. When he was appointed, many of our mutual friends did not give the combination six months. I replied that, in view of our old relations, I saw no reason why it should not last for six years. Nor in anything that has yet passed between us do I see the signs of that disruption which you appear to portend.

Nonetheless, Curzon understood that things were being said and done in London of which he knew nothing beyond hints from Godley, who should realise that there was 'a proud and sensitive nature' at the other end.[11] Sir Arthur replied that his apprehensions were of a general kind. The new Cabinet's views on some important subjects seemed to be strongly held and at variance with the Viceroy's. The India Council differed from Curzon on many subjects. Brodrick, though loyal and friendly to him, formed his own opinions and liked to act upon them. All of them believed that the Viceroy was the mandatory of the home government; that India was ultimately governed from England by the King; that the Cabinet alone was responsible to Parliament for every detail of administration, which responsibility meant control. At the other end was a man of brilliant achievements but with a different view, held as strongly as the Cabinet's. Did uneasiness need more explanation?[12] Absolute control, Godley held, must lie with the Cabinet, the Prime Minister and the Secretary of State. He could see no reason why

what is called public opinion in India should have any more overwhelming weight either with Your Excellency's Government or with the Secretary of State than it had 10 or 15 years ago.[13]

Curzon expressed delight at 'so wholehearted a statement of the finest old crusted doctrines'. But when Godley said that responsibility was also absolute and unshared, they parted company. Did he mean that if there were a war with Afghanistan the Viceroy would be held free of all responsibility? Surely not; rather, the doctrine was conveniently pulled out of the cupboard 'when it is thought necessary to reduce the Viceroy to proper subjection. But at other moments it is discreetly left on the shelf'.

As for Indian public opinion, while it seemed clear to those in England that there was no change since the time of Dufferin, it was to Curzon plain

> that there is all the difference in the world. What is the great difference at this end? It is that public opinion has been growing all the while, is articulate, is daily becoming more powerful, cannot be ignored. What is the origin of mistakes sometimes made at the other end? It is that men are standing still, with their eyes shut, and do not see the movement here...to contend that [public opinion] does not exist, that it has not advanced in the last 15 years, or that it may be treated with general indifference, is in my view to ignore the great change that is passing over this country, and which I believe that history will recognise myself as having done much (whether wisely or unwisely) to accelerate...the lifting of India from the level of a dependency to the position which is bound one day to be hers, if it is not so already, namely that of the greatest partner in the Empire.

From another proposition of Godley, that the real government of India lay in the House of Commons, Curzon also dissented. For everyday purposes, India was governed by the Cabinet and Secretary of State at one end, and the Viceroy and his Council at the other. The former admittedly had superior authority, but the aim should be co-ordination:

> Of course in matters of Foreign Affairs involving other Powers the Home Government must be supreme. They may be mistaken: but the power is theirs... In internal affairs I should myself let the pendulum swing the other way: and I would as a rule let the man on the spot decide...[14]

Godley remained unmoved. He conceded that in case of war with Afghanistan, Curzon would be held responsible in the sense that he would be praised or blamed by public and press. But this was not 'properly speaking, responsibility at all'. If the Viceroy acted with the Cabinet's consent, the responsibility would be theirs; 'they must defend you, and unless Parliament censures and rejects them, you are safe'. Godley still saw no material change in Indian public opinion since Dufferin's time. India was already the greatest member of the Empire, and had been before Curzon went there. She was, and must remain, a dependency. If Curzon intended that India, with her 'despotic and bureaucratic' government, should become as independent as Canada, with her constitution and Parliament,

> if you mean that we are to send out a series of carefully-selected autocrats and then let them do what they please—in that case all I can say is that I believe you have not, and I am sure you ought not to have, the slightest chance of seeing your ideal realised. For one thing, where are we to get our autocrats?... Curzons, I assure you, don't grow on every gooseberry bush.[15]

There the debate stood adjourned. Godley urged upon Lady Curzon that her husband should now leave India for good.[16] Though he had no intention of so doing, Curzon reflected that Brodrick seemed to launch upon ill-founded schemes, and then to complain bitterly when India would not help the Cabinet over various stiles:

> His Council are delighted to have got a new man, who does not know anything of India, and they knock spots off us with the keenest satisfaction. The Secretary of State, though personally very loyal and friendly to myself, does not at all like being merely my echo, and I think rather enjoys spreading the impression that I am a very difficult person to handle, and that it is a good thing for the Cabinet to sit upon me from time to time. All this will disappear when I get home, and meet these suspicious gentry at a table. I think I can soon blow away the atmospheric conditions that have transformed me into a sort of Spectre of Brocken of exaggerated and inhuman proportions.[17]

*   *   *   *

At some time early in 1904, Curzon received from Brodrick an 'ultra secret' manuscript note. The Parliamentary situation, it said, was very bad. 'Chinese slavery' provided a good cry; Austen Chamberlain had 'jumped up too quick and shows it' and had anyway an impossible task, for Selborne had put £2½m on the Navy estimates and Arnold-Forster's reforms brought no economies; Balfour's 'extraordinary penchant for the ultra-great' had been shown by his support of the candidature of the Duke of Connaught for the post of Inspector-General, with control of all army appointments, 'which will of course transfer the influence from the working soldiers to the highest quarter.'

Brodrick therefore anticipated a collapse during the summer, in which event Curzon's reappointment could not be guaranteed.[18] However, there was nothing to be done about that aspect. Despite the outbreak of the Russo-Japanese war early in February Curzon judged that the Russians were unlikely to do anything in Central Asia sufficiently serious to upset his leave. He was impatient to reach England in order to make the acquaintance of the newly-arrived baby daughter; and the nature of the Viceroy's duties, coupled with the excruciating boredom of Simla, lent enchantment to the prospect of more lively society:

> All sorts of clouds seem to roll up between the present and the dim delightful past. [He wrote to one of the Souls] Where are those days gone? Gone, burned, only a faded memory—but an eternal spell...I am going home to see if I am remembered and to save myself from dying here. Will anyone know me or care for me? Or shall I find a grey-haired company trudging with myself to a common end?[19]

The Governor of Madras was to replace Curzon. Their relations had improved markedly in the latter part of 1903, after the trouble about the Durbar. After expressing himself on controversial subjects with the utmost vigour, Ampthill had been relieved, and perhaps a little surprised, to receive a reply 'as kind and indulgent and indeed flattering as possible'. Admiration for the Viceroy, he told Godley, had never wavered during their disagreements and had now ripened into warm attachment.[20] For his part, Curzon took endless pains to rehearse the business with his successor, whom he forewarned against the vagaries of the Foreign Department and the designs of the C-in-C. Ampthill, having been in the last stages of fatigue, felt refreshed by his contact with Curzon, whose 'personality, ideas and marvellous powers are certainly most inspiring, and I have never had such interesting conversations in my life as those which I had with him before his departure. I am approaching my work with a kind of fearful joy, for it is beyond imagination interesting, absorbing, and exciting.'[21]

Sir Denzil Ibbetson thanked Curzon for unvarying courtesy, hospitality and kindness, and for the education of working under a master courageous and confident, stimulating and unfaltering, devoted to India. In the early hours of his last morning in Simla, Curzon wrote a reply of equally warm praise and gratitude, especially for willingness to discern

> behind the often deceptive screen of external manner and conduct, and through the blurring shadows cast by personal foibles and transparent mistakes, an earnest longing to do my duty in a calling that I always think has been laid on Englishmen from on high.[22]

* * * *

Curzon's homeward passage was cheered by two developments in foreign affairs, the steady success of Japan in her war with Russia and the signature

of the Anglo-French agreement. Some nine months before, Delcassé had
hinted that should an arrangement be reached, he would restrain Russia
and intimate that if she picked a quarrel with the British, French support
might not be forthcoming.[23] Lansdowne advised the Cabinet that an
Anglo-French understanding would 'not improbably be the precursor of a
better understanding with Russia, and I need not insist upon the improvement which would result in our international position, which, in view of
our present relations with Germany as well as Russia, I cannot regard with
satisfaction'.[24]

Resolution of the persisting antagonisms in Egypt, Morocco, West
Africa and Newfoundland held obvious advantages. Although the talks
with Russia petered out in the autumn of 1903, the crisis in Manchuria and
Korea, followed by the outbreak of war in February, 1904, made a treaty
more desirable than ever, since the French were allies of Russia and the
British of Japan. Moreover, it was realised that Germany's swiftly growing
fleet was designed for combat in the North Sea and Channel. The sole
object of German naval policy, the First Lord advised Balfour, was to
possess battleships which might intervene with decisive effect on one side
or the other during a war in which England was engaged with France or
Russia.[25]

The detailed terms of the agreement, signed in April, seemed to Curzon
a poor bargain. Muscat was omitted; and he judged, rightly, that in the
long run France would be supreme at Bangkok and Tangier. Yet he
remembered the bitter relations with France during his time as Under-
Secretary, and the violent feeling displayed during the Boer War: 'I cannot,'
he wrote to Lansdowne, 'conceal my admiration for the extent and value
of what you have achieved and I should like to add my own to the many
congratulations which have been showered upon you.'

In the prevailing circumstances, Curzon surmised, it would not be
feasible to reach a similar agreement with the Russians, who wanted all and
thought they could get it by waiting. Britain must keep what she had in
Asia. 'The utmost that we can do is to promise not to advance.'[26]

On reaching home in mid-May, Curzon received a generous welcome.
Almost every newspaper carried an appreciative article; some said that his
record stood comparison with that of any predecessor, even Dalhousie,
Wellesley, or Hastings. Having greeted a throng of friends at the station,
he was driven immediately to Buckingham Palace for a conversation with
the King.

At Oxford when taking an honorary doctorate, at Eton on the fourth of
June, at Dover on his installation as Lord Warden of the Cinque Ports,

Curzon spoke of India, the excellence of the ICS, the need to preserve the buffer states and the causes for pride in British achievement. These orations, reported far and wide, aroused much interest. The most notable was delivered when he received the Freedom of the City of London in July:

> To me the message is carved in granite, hewn of the rock of doom: that our work is righteous and that it shall endure.

Reminding the audience forcefully of the debt they owed to India for help in recent campaigns, he did not attempt to claim a complete identity of view in India itself:

> No one is more ready to admit than I that if you put side by side the rulers of a European race and the ruled of an Asiatic, and particularly such races as the Indian and the English, where you have a small minority face to face with a vast alien conglomeration, you cannot expect to have complete coalescence. On the one side you have pride of race, the duty of self-protection, the consciousness of power; on the other you have struggling sentiments and stifled aspirations. But...a bridge must be built between the two, and on that bridge justice must stand with unerring scales.[27]

'George' exclaimed his old friend Selborne, 'it was the best speech you ever made.' Characteristically, Sir A. Godley wrote at once to say that the awakening of British interest in India would be undesirable, since it must infallibly lead to Parliamentary interference in detail with its government.[28]

★   ★   ★   ★

The standing of Balfour's administration, which Brodrick had described in such gloomy terms, did not improve during Curzon's leave. In the early part of the year, Brodrick evidently spent a good deal of time criticising Arnold-Forster's proposals, which inevitably reflected upon his own work at the War Office. Lengthy documents were exchanged. In late February Arnold-Forster replied in a detailed paper, the nub of which was that his predecessor had misunderstood some of the plans and had misinterpreted others. Two months later, his difficulties had still not abated. Having received memoranda and endured a long interview with Brodrick, he wrote wearily that the latter seemed to object not to the new policy but to the fact that his own was being altered or abandoned, on which account the press made fun of him. To dislike this state of affairs was natural:

> but the odd part is that he does not see that I cannot possibly arrange all my scheme so as to preserve everything that he has done, in view of the fact that my sole raison d'être is to alter what has been done.'[29]

Curzon heard a good deal of all this during his first weeks at home. It helped to explain slackness at the India Office: 'Brodrick is engaged in an internecine struggle with Arnold-Forster in the Cabinet; and ... as this occupies 3/4ths of his time and the whole of his attention, our interests suffer.'[30]

The disagreements became public property in a fashion with which Curzon was soon to be familiar. Early in July, Arnold-Forster read in *The Standard* an article based on one of his Cabinet memoranda. 'It is sad to think' says his diary, 'that wherever there is a thief there is a receiver... Brodrick, said to be responsible, denied it. On a later occasion, *The Times* carried details of a Cabinet decision on short-service battalions. The Secretary for War asked Esher point-blank whether he had given the facts to Col. Repington. This was a justified question, Esher admitted, but he had not done so, never gave confidential information to journalists, and hardly ever saw Repington. Arnold-Forster reflected sourly that in fact Esher constantly communicated with newspapers and with Repington, who, however, confessed that on this occasion he had received the Cabinet memorandum from another source. 'This is cheerful' noted Arnold-Forster, 'and is one more example of how persistently I am betrayed, and my work rendered difficult by all this backstairs intrigue, of which there seems to be no end.'[31] Given the intimate relations now known to have flourished between Kitchener's confidants and *The Times* and *The Standard*, it is possible that Major Marker, Arnold-Forster's private secretary, may have had a hand in all this.

The conduct of business in London left a poor impression upon Curzon, who attended the reconstituted Defence Committee for the first time in May. 'It is a very simple matter' he reported to Ampthill. 'I do not think they know anything, certainly not much, about India, and I do the talking while they ask questions.'[32]

Lansdowne was promptly addressed about the dozen or so Indian cases awaiting attention at the Foreign Office. The reactions of officials seemed flabby:

No one here remembers anything. In the India Office they do not know to what despatch one refers. The Secretary of State has only the dimmest knowledge of any of these subjects, and the Foreign Office cannot remember whether they have been consulted or not. After seeing the working of the departments here, I am really surprised that we ever get an answer at all. No one is concerned in getting anything done. They are all anxious about the Parliamentary existence of the Government.[33]

Though full of admiration for Balfour, Curzon thought he had ceased to control a hopelessly unwieldy Cabinet. The ill-defined powers of the

Defence Committee might also become a source of anxiety, for Indian affairs were freely discussed there by 'a body of men barely one of whom has ever been in India, among whom the sailors are very strong and where the only representative of our interests is the Secretary of State who knows nothing about India at all'.

Nor was he reassured after a later meeting of the Committee to discover that he was recorded as making three statements about Afghanistan, none of which he had uttered and each of which was inaccurate.[34]

*   *   *   *

Writing in March, Godley attributed Curzon's difficulties with the Cabinet and the India Council to his inability to put himself in others' shoes or to imagine how others saw him. In this judgment there was indubitably truth, but not the whole truth, for his troubles in London sprang more from disagreement about the merits of various questions than from lack of sensibility. The India Council, Godley told Ampthill later, though not admirers of Curzon, were 'a very good set, straight and patriotic, strongly conservative', often believing that Curzon's proposals did not really represent the views of the government of India.[35]

As a curtain-raiser to his holiday, Curzon learned that Brodrick had been defeated by the India Council on three issues to which both attached importance, the retention of Cooper's Hill College, the Famine Fund and the Savings Bank Fund. The Viceroy had also pressed hard for permission to publish the Police Commission's report, which was necessary to the implementation of its proposals. However, Brodrick refused publication of some parts and Curzon had to explain publicly that there would be a delay. Five days later, *The Times* carried the gist of those parts. Godley observed to Ampthill that so far as he could discover, the Councillors at the India Office seldom disagreed with previous Viceroys, who had, on the other hand, deferred somewhat to the views held there. Curzon began his Vice-royalty on a different theory; he had a great work to do, with previously expressed opinions. 'He has consequently sledge-hammered men on points on which they were quite sure not to yield, till they became in their turn unyielding in regard to questions to which he had given great attention. I believe the process has been quite unconscious on both sides, but it has led to the Councillors here discussing many things *de novo* with a freedom which the House of Lords would rarely exercise with regard to a Bill sent up from the House of Commons.' He hoped that personal communication between Curzon and the Council might achieve much.

To Godley's mind, nothing that others urged affected Curzon's judgment in the least; then, the next time a clash of opinion occurred, others unconsciously assumed that Curzon had 'again got into an untenable position'. This proposition he illustrated from a discussion on Seistan, in which Curzon had maintained his long-held view and the home authorities theirs. Sir Arthur does not seem to have realised that his example applied with equal force in reverse. To Brodrick's mind, Curzon's fault was to press far too much. Having obtained 80 per cent, he contended vehemently for the rest; whereas in the Cabinet the Foreign Secretary's policy was often modified in most important particulars.[36]

Balfour had agreed with Curzon that the Act of 1858 needed revision and asked whether he could draft a bill, which might pass in 1905. Godley, with whom Curzon discussed this, had long believed that the Secretary of State should be master in his own house, but advised Brodrick that such a reform should not be introduced at a time when it would be attributed to the inspiration of a strong-minded Viceroy. Moreover, the Cabinet must have the power and the will to push it through. At the end of the year, Curzon made detailed proposals, which could not affect him materially. Balfour replied that he too did not believe 'in these systems of elaborate checks and counterchecks...I can well imagine how irritating it must be if, and when, schemes long thought out and elaborately prepared by the central and provincial governments in India are squashed without appeal in Whitehall'. Whether the government could do anything in the coming session was, however, doubtful.[37] It proved, for whatever reason, impossible.

A goodly part of Curzon's relations with the home government during this summer naturally turned upon the Afghan and Tibetan developments. On the first issue he believed, and had every reason to believe, that he and the Cabinet were at last agreed; on the second, their views diverged, partly because, as it appeared to him, gratuitous and inconvenient pledges had been given to Russia. Godley, acknowledging Curzon's extraordinary qualities, even conceded a touch of genius. Yet he conceived him to 'revel in the popular side of a strong foreign policy' without facing the unpopular expenditure, and to have given a colour to Asiatic policy which demanded a material increase in fighting power.[38] This observation, which seems to ignore the rapid increase of military spending under Curzon, is of some importance; for Godley's twenty years' experience necessarily carried much weight with a new Secretary of State.

Soon after landing, Curzon suffered a sharp attack of his spinal trouble, aggravated by severe pain in the leg. The strain of public engagements and of disagreements with the Cabinet, his desire to push through many outstanding items of Indian business, together with his own inability to relax, prevented him from finding any real rest during his first months at home. In mid-August he was writing to Rennell Rodd:

> My holiday has been greatly spoiled by illness from which I am not yet free. I have worked too hard in bygone years. I hope the godchild goes well. I have not been strong enough to get out to a shop and send him a trophy of my devotion. This shall come sooner or later.[39]

Since the birth of their daughter in the spring, Lady Curzon had been in poor health and spirits. Her dreams of a summer's quiet for them both at the Lord Warden's residence, Walmer Castle, had been dashed when it was discovered to be unfit for habitation. Lady Salisbury, who had died there, always called it 'a dirty old hole'. Though Curzon ordered renovations (one of the main objects being to remove the effects of the Duke of Wellington's *idée fixe* that a lavatory must be placed in every bedroom) it was afterwards found that the work had not been properly done.[40]

On the morning of 20 September, the Curzons' baggage was being moved from the Castle to catch the boat which they were to board at Marseilles. Suddenly Mary Curzon was seized by septic peritonitis followed by blood poisoning. Within a few hours she lay at death's door. Surgeons performed two operations, with the aid of primitive oxygen equipment. Several times her life was given up. Curzon, in a frenzy of fear and devotion, hardly left her bedside. 'I am so proud' he had once written to her,

> when I see you run after, admired and adored. What woman in London combines great beauty with exceptional intelligence, as well as a tact which is an inspiration? The combination is wholly unique and there is no limit to the influence which you can exercise at home, as you have done in India, smoothing down those whom I ignore or offend, and creating our own atmosphere of refinement and devotion.[41]

For ten days she remained at the point of death. Then a chink of light appeared. 'You can judge' Curzon wrote to St. John Brodrick, 'what it has been, the ups and downs, the sudden hope and then the sickening despair. One seems to have lived aeons in a week.'[42] Another near-fatal relapse followed at once. The doctors seemed to have neither explanation nor prescription. Messages of sympathy and hope arrived in shoals from well-wishers the world over. On 7 October Curzon was told that Mary was dying. Yet she pulled through again. Then pneumonia set in. 'The strength cannot go on for ever' he wrote to Brodrick. 'I am worn out with anguish and suspense...I can write no more in my misery.'[43]

She hovered between delirium and lucidity. In one of these latter moments she sent a message of thanks to all those who had befriended her, and addressed to the King and Queen pathetic words of gratitude which, wrote Curzon in transmitting them, 'I feel sure will bring tears to the eyes of Your Majesty, so affecting are they in their sweet simplicity.'

Meanwhile, all plans for return to India had been postponed. Whether Curzon could go back at all had become doubtful. He apologised to Ampthill for the inconvenience and wrote again to the King, who inquired daily: 'Hope is sinking lower and lower within me and the cloud of darkness seems to be settling down.'[44]

After this, Lady Curzon slowly recovered, though her life was not out of danger until November. Curzon said that neither of them would ever set foot in Walmer again. Moreover, the office of Lord Warden, which he forthwith resigned, had proved to cost £1,000 a year, regardless of any living expenses at the Castle. Careful inspection showed that only the demolition of a large part would make the place fit for human occupation.

* * * *

That tendency of the Russians to draw closer to Germany which had disquieted Brodrick was mentioned on 19 October by Lansdowne to Cambon, who replied that William had certainly exerted himself at Petersburg ('vous n'avez pas idée des efforts qu'il a faits') but not with any great result. He thought that the Russians would like to be on good terms with Britain, though one or two incidents – the Tibetan convention and the refusal of the right to coal in British waters – had hurt their feelings.[45] Five days later, news reached London that the Russian Baltic fleet, passing through the North Sea en route for the Far East, had fired upon trawlers from Hull, killing and wounding some fishermen.

Admiral Rojestvensky eventually telegraphed that his ships had been attacked by Japanese torpedo-boats, a story which the Russian government apparently believed. While the British fleets concentrated, Charles Hardinge called upon Lamsdorff, whom he had never seen so excited, 'simply spluttering with indignation at the perfidy of the Japanese, whom he termed "vos chers alliés". However, he soon calmed down...' At one point Lansdowne thought the odds on war about even. Lamsdorff later said that if Britain had used a word of menace, he would have been compelled to yield to the war party.[46]

Hardinge was generally well-informed of Russian proceedings. One of the secret police used to give warning of interesting developments, while a high official of the Foreign Ministry told him everything that went on there. 'He was a gambler like them all' wrote Hardinge simply. In this crisis, however, the Ambassador's attitude stemmed from a belief that the issue did not merit a war which could benefit only Germany. For Britain the alternative to moderation seemed to him 'a long and costly war in Central Asia, for which neither our military forces nor our finances appear to be in a fitting state of preparation.'[47]

The Czar, in his diary, called the British 'our mangy enemies'. He telegraphed to the Kaiser: 'I have no words to express my indignation with England's conduct...Whereas she understands the rules of keeping neutrality in her own fashion, it is certainly high time to put a stop to this. The only way, as you say, would be that Germany, Russia and France should at once unite upon arrangements to abolish English and Japanese arrogance and insolence...'

Within forty-eight hours, the draft of a treaty drawn up by the Emperor and Bülow had been despatched from Berlin 'by Imperial fieldjaeger'. Here was the germ of the abortive agreement signed at Björkö in 1905. Even at this stage, Nicholas and Lamsdorff thought that the French must be told, a view for which they had strong financial and political reasons.[48] Not the least valuable result of Lansdowne's temperate attitude was the preservation of good relations with Russia's ally, France. M. Cambon, naturally enough, could hardly conceal his anxiety lest the British fleet should sink the Russian almost within sight of French ports. He mediated assiduously between Lansdowne and Benckendorff. For the moment, the projected continental combination, like that of 1900, faded out.[49]

The Baltic fleet sailed on towards the East. It was agreed at the Defence Committee that if the Russians occupied a port in the Gulf, or Chahbar, Benckendorff would be reminded of Lansdowne's statement of 5 May, 1903. A superior British force would be assembled. Russia must then withdraw, or fight, in which event her fleet's oversea supply routes would be severed. Should the Russians try to seize coal at Aden or Perim, force would be used.[50] Meanwhile, the position in South and East Persia remained troublesome, for the Persians blocked the work of the commercial mission at Bunder Abbas, obstructed the telegraph system, and ignored Hardinge's remonstrances. The threatened dismissal of the Hashmat-ul-Mulk, Governor of Seistan, caused Lansdowne to say that it would be attributed to his good-will towards the British and might create a situation which would compel Britain to alter fundamentally her policy in Seistan and adjoining regions. Ampthill favoured an equally stiff line, and offered the occupation of Nasratabad if it were needed to secure the Hashmat's retention. The Persians, however, replied that he was a mere petty official, careless, reckless, and addicted to opium. When it was learned that the Governor had experienced no undue difficulty in borrowing £2,000 from the Russian bank at Teheran, the ardour of the authorities in London abated. Lansdowne did allow Arthur Hardinge to hint that his oracular phrase about a fundamental alteration might mean a permanent McMahon commission on that frontier but would go no further, despite a warning from India of the damage to British prestige if the Hashmat fell. This he duly did in the spring of 1905, receiving no support from Lansdowne and precious little from Hardinge.[51]

* * * *

Brodrick's intimacy with Curzon did not revive, during this summer of 1904, on the old basis. No doubt Curzon's recurring illnesses had something to do with it and it is quite probable that after five and a half years' Viceroyalty he expected a degree of deference which Cabinet ministers would be unlikely to accord. Yet that is not the whole explanation. With other friends, Curzon behaved as he always had done. Unquestionably he felt vexed at persistent opposition within the India Office, and at Brodrick's unwillingness or inability to lead in the other direction. They had been at odds over the South African garrison, the Coronation charges, the coolies for South Africa, the remission of tax at the Durbar, the soldiers' pay increase, the military effects of India's foreign policy, the proper treatment of the Amir, the Tibetan expedition, the report of the Police Commission, and to a lesser degree the military administration of India. Although Balfour believed that the differences had not been of a kind to cause Curzon undue anxiety, these were substantial issues, disagreement upon which could hardly be confined within official bounds. Brodrick wrote to say how much he regretted it. 'The result is that I have not had one conversation with you in the last eleven weeks except on business and our official relations thus seem to overshadow private friendship.'[52]

It may well be that Curzon had realised, from talks or from his own observation, what attitude Brodrick was adopting in private towards himself. Certainly he felt that the Secretary of State, knowing very little of India, attached insufficient weight to his opinion and failed to consult him adequately. For his part, Brodrick told the Prime Minister of their relations, in terms none too friendly to Curzon:

> These diatribes descend on me two or three times a week—and Ampthill writes he has been hauled over the coals for alluding in his telegrams to the political considerations in other quarters (Russian) which affect Tibet!

And again, early in September:

> Poor Ampthill writes that George's letters are a series of courts-martial and reproaches and that they look back [sic] to his return much as the boys at 'Dotheboys' did to the return of Squeers after his holiday.[53]

It could hardly be contended by anyone who reads all the letters from Ampthill to Brodrick that this was a fair summary of their purport, but Balfour was not to know that. Brodrick did his best not to upset Curzon further. 'I sometimes wonder' he wrote, 'if you know how often I think of you and the difficulties you so courageously overcome.'[54]

A few weeks before his belated departure Curzon complained of having been kept in the dark about many questions during his leave; though often asked for an opinion, he had hardly ever seen the instructions issued from the India Office. Brodrick replied rather pathetically that he had looked forward to holding the India Office because it would bring him closer to Curzon. Now that expectation had turned sour. Friendship had apparently been withdrawn during the summer, and the feeling of loss was accentuated when Curzon seemed to accuse him of lacking even official consideration. He pointed out all the difficulties caused by Curzon's illness and then by his wife's, adding a list of illustrations.[55] Most of them Curzon immediately showed to be inaccurate. His rejoinder, written on the day that he offered his resignation to Balfour, came close to the core of their estrangement:

> You speak of 'constantly fighting my battles'—a phrase which I once before unsuccessfully deprecated—as though I were an inept person whose unsound proposals were only saved from extinction by the chivalrous defence of the S. of S. If my proposals so frequently want fighting for, why keep me in India at all? Every time that you back up the Viceroy you seem to regard it as a sort of personal favour, for which he ought to thank you. This misconception has coloured the whole of our relations.

Curzon added that he had asked himself whether there was advantage in his continuing as Viceroy, a task which no longer gave him any pleasure and which he intended to lay down at the first opportunity. Brodrick answered at length, but scarcely met the main point. He appealed for a fresh start in their relations.[56] Curzon refused to be impressed by Brodrick's account of the sagacity of the Indian Council. The Viceroy's Council, so he was always being told, were merely his puppets, while the India Council were held up as a body of wise men, from whom he had come to expect disagreement:

> That an attempt made by the Viceroy who since Lord Mayo has probably

known most of the Indian Princes and had most influence with them to give
them an opportunity of stating their own views (committing the Govt. of India
or H.M.G. to nothing) on the subject of Imperial defence should create
'absolute consternation' in the India Office is a sufficient indication of the spirit
which I have described and is exactly what I should have expected.

I will now cease, happy in the consciousness that the struggle will not last
much longer and hopeful that the Council will then get a Viceroy after their
own hearts, i.e. one who by never proposing anything new will never require
them to save the State.

This letter, though it reflects feelings of some bitterness, contains nothing I
hope personal to yourself. I will endeavour to reciprocate the feelings with
which you conclude your letter. But to expect me at the end of the longest
period in office in India for 40 years to derive pleasure from habitual rebuffs is
to ask too much of human nature.

Brodrick asked whether Curzon realised that others had feelings too?
The sensations of the man under the millstone, he replied, are always
different from those of the man seated on the top. 'I am entirely grateful for
your courtesy, and if I have not sufficiently acknowledged this I do so
now.'[57] A few days later they met at a dinner, before which Brodrick was
announced in stentorian tones as 'The Right Honourable Mr Arnold-
Forster.' He sent Curzon, now on the eve of departure, an affectionate letter:

> Your friendship has meant so much to me for nearly 30 years that the shadow
> upon it has given me intense pain. I meant from my heart what I said to you at
> the end of the evening and recognised the generosity of your reply.
>
> If you would let our official relations date anew from today, I do not think
> you would ever regret it.[58]

⋆   ⋆   ⋆   ⋆

Curzon knew that plenty of people did not desire his return to India.
At one stage during his wife's illness, it appeared that a new Viceroy might
well have to be found in a hurry; but as soon as she seemed to be mending,
he decided that he must go back.

> I doubt not [he wrote to Ampthill] that many other men could carry on the
> work with ability and success. But I want to ground a few more indispensable
> things with just sufficient firmness to prevent them from being shaken out of
> the soil...
>
> I regret very little of my work in India, though the methods may often have
> been open to exception. The bulk of it I would certainly do again, even if I
> knew of the storms ahead, and in my conscience I have never wavered and
> least of all do I waver now.[59]

Obstacles loomed up ominously. The mission to Kabul, headed by an officer whom he thought unsuitable, would soon leave Simla; Kitchener had only withdrawn his resignation temporarily; and the Secretary of State seemed to find a peculiar satisfaction in disagreeing on most of the matters to which Curzon attached importance. He used to wonder whether he was really a Viceroy coming out for a second term, or some impertinent tyro who knew nothing of India. 'However' he told Ampthill, 'I must not trouble you with these petty matters which you will probably attribute to overstrung nerves.' Godley too feared that Curzon might well find the Cabinet or the India Council trying to bar the way. In a sympathetic farewell, he proffered two pieces of advice:

> You really are (and I think you know that you are) too apt to regard as enemies or fools or both, those who, from perfectly honourable and patriotic motives, are unable to avoid opposing your measures. I know that this is often caused by your own zeal and desire for reform, which in themselves are wholly admirable qualities: but you must try to think charitably of those in this country who honestly differ from you...I must say again, after a year's experience...that whatever you may think of the S. of S.'s action, or of his language, upon this or that question, you may rely upon it that no S. of S. could be more loyal to you, or more sincerely anxious to support you as far as he can.

The last sentence was of doubtful accuracy; but Curzon did not comment upon it. He merely thanked Godley for these parting words to 'your unruly but not unreasonable proconsul'.[60] Though heartily grateful for his wife's deliverance from death, Curzon felt anguished at leaving her in England. 'Amid all the great misery that we have been through' he wrote to her, 'there shines out the consolation of many happy hours and tender moments and the memory of your beautiful and ineffaceable love. We have been drawn very close by this companionship in the furnace of affliction and I hope that it may leave me less selfish and more considerate in the future. To me you are everything and the sole thing in the world; and I go on existing in order to come back and try to make you happy...It is with a sad and miserable heart that I go, leaving all that makes life worth living behind me...to toil and isolation and often worse. But it seems to be destiny; and God who has smitten us so hard must surely have better things in store.'[61]

From most of the group who bade him official goodbye, Curzon parted silently. With two or three whom he knew best he shed tears.

*   *   *   *

During the outward voyage, Curzon met Francis Younghusband, returning home on leave. They talked long under the stars on board the liner, Curzon wanting to know all about Tibet and recognising much – for instance, the value of securing Bhutanese goodwill – that had not been appreciated in London. Nothing, wrote Younghusband, 'could have exceeded the warmth of Lord Curzon's welcome...and his gratitude to me was quite over-powering. Everything I did was in his eyes perfection. All the things I had been censured for he absolutely approved...'[62]

In London, Younghusband saw Brodrick, who 'in a kind of galumphing way...intended to be cordial'. The Secretary of State charged him with paying insufficient attention to broad considerations, to which Young-husband answered that he should have been allowed to remain at Lhasa to make a more complete settlement. He gathered that some ministers believed the government of India to be out of hand and indifferent to the Imperial effects of its policies.[63] This impression was substantially a just one. Brodrick later told Ampthill that Curzon's whole attitude about Tibet and Afghanistan 'frightened the Cabinet to death. Whereas you...saw the necessity of reducing the indemnity, I believe that Curzon would have declared a protectorate over Tibet without a moment's hesitation.'[64] The King said to Younghusband, 'I approve all you did', while Lansdowne assured him of the government's approval of the business as a whole and of his personal confidence. When Sir Francis remarked that Dorjieff had probably influenced not only the Dalai Lama but the impressionable Czar, Lansdowne replied that from what he heard of the Czar this was very likely so.[65] It appears, however, that the Czar refused an appeal from the wandering Lama to declare Tibet a Russian protectorate.[66]

At Bombay, Curzon was welcomed by many of the princes and an enthusiastic throng. Amidst the pomp, he felt lonely and sorrowful, for it seemed unlikely that his wife would ever return to India. At dinner Lord Lamington, who had been best man at their wedding nine years before, proposed the health of the Curzons and referred sympathetically to Mary's illness. Curzon, overwhelmed, sobbed openly and could not for a few moments utter the first phrases of his response.

Ampthill, looking forward with some trepidation to their encounter, had been encouraged by cordial messages, 'but when I saw him coming up the steps of Government House my old fears revived. He looked sad, worn and sombre and shook hands with everybody with the air of a dying man As soon as the formalities were over, Lady Ampthill and I took him off to breakfast alone with us and we found that at the slightest allusion to his wife he broke down at once.'

However, once the talk turned to politics, Curzon's demeanour changed entirely and he became his old animated self, though Ampthill thought he detected a softened tone and greater tolerance. Still Viceroy, Ampthill felt embarrassed at taking precedence for the remaining twenty-four hours and had imagined that it would be irksome. But Curzon accorded the precedence with complete readiness and grace. No trace of unpleasantness was seen.

> Indeed his whole attitude towards me was perfectly charming and if he had been a newcomer and I a Viceroy with five years' experience he could not have been more considerate and deferential. Nor was his demeanour forced or assumed; it seemed to come quite naturally and I felt quite ashamed of ever having thought that he would behave differently.[67]

Brodrick had repeatedly warned Ampthill that Curzon was jealous of their correspondence and reluctant to allow normal relations between Secretary of State and acting Viceroy. However, during all the hours of private conversation, Curzon did not betray the slightest curiosity about the correspondence, which, Ampthill told Brodrick, perhaps mischievously, 'is strange in the light of all you have told me. But he is to a remarkable degree a creature of moods and I have often thought that he is as variable and neurotic as a woman.'[68]

The outgoing Viceroy, cheered by investment with the GCSI and a flattering tribute from Curzon, departed in a glow of goodwill. Curzon's mood, as he resumed his work alone, was a very different one:

'I have not dared to go into your room for fear that I should burst out crying' he wrote to Mary. 'And, indeed, I am utterly miserable and desolate. Nobody to turn to or talk to, memories on all sides of me and anxiety gnawing at my heart...It is a misery even to tear myself from writing to you and never in my life have I felt so forlorn and cast down.'[69]

SIX

Deadlock at Kabul

BY THE early part of 1904, the Amir had ruled for more than two years. The Viceroy still hoped that he would come to Peshawar, but heard many reports of turbulence in Afghanistan. Habibullah showed himself as tricky and argumentative as his father. Curzon realised the difference of approach between himself and the home government, who insisted on watering down the letters to Kabul and then blamed him for the indifferent result. 'Surrender does not pay with Orientals' he wrote to the King, 'and we never show weakness without suffering for it afterwards.'[1] The divergence was pointed by an important letter of the Amir, dated 1 March, 1904, which contended again that the old agreement had not been personal to Abdur Rahman and which hinted broadly that the issue of railways and telegraphs should not be raised. So long as the British remained faithful, Afghanistan would fight valiantly to repel the Russians. 'When such a large number of Afghan tribesmen have perished, the adversary of the Indian government will not have such strength left as to be able to reach India.' In short, the Afghans alone would do the fighting, while the British furnished money and arms. Should the lack of them cause defeat, futile regret and tardy repentance would be the lot of India.[2]

Curzon thought that this letter might mark a breaking-point. Apparently Habibullah did not wish Britain to fulfil all her obligations. Of course, he could be told that unless he mended his ways, friendly relations would be imperilled; but the Cabinet were not likely to be so firm. Alternatively, the former engagements could be renewed without change. With a strong ruler this might have been feasible, whereas with Habibullah there were serious drawbacks 'for it means the pouring into Afghanistan of unlimited arms and ammunition with our consent, and the acceptance of undefined responsibility for the defence of a country which is incapable of defending itself. It would, moreover, render the Amir unmanageable.'[3]

Habibullah combined a mastery of the smooth phrase and well-turned compliment with persistent demands for further instalments of his subsidy, professing the friendship of himself and his God-granted government for the sublime, illustrious and exalted government of India. They would not, he swore, 'speak to Russia in political matters with any other mouth and tongue than that of the rifle and the sword'.[4] Curzon, thinking that the Amir might profit from a period of reflection upon Japan's successes and British coolness,[5] sent him short but courteous acknowledgments. Ampthill too refrained from debating large issues of policy, though he did complain of incursions by Afghan tribesmen. Habibullah was equal to the occasion:

> I have the honour to inform Your Excellency [he replied] that the mischievous Turis, Waziris, Mahsuds and Dawaris do continuously cross over the frontier to this side, and commit raids on the lives and property of the subjects of the God-granted Government...[6]

It had been agreed that British policy towards Afghanistan should be discussed during Curzon's stay in London. He began the serious debate in a paper which reviewed the main elements of the problem on familiar lines: the Amir understood perfectly well the weakness of his claim that the old agreements were still binding; under them he reaped the preponderant advantage; mere acquiescence would make him intractable. He had lately spoken of having 20,000,000 men, a ludicrous exaggeration, and of serious resistance to Russia, 'childish braggadocio'. The defences of the Herat region, for which part of the subsidy had been ear-marked, were known to be decayed. There must be a candid interchange of opinion with him, on the lines laid down by Salisbury nearly thirty years before: 'The tone to be most avoided is that of cold timidity, the attitude to be maintained is that of cordial but conscious superiority.'

The Amir should not be pressed to build railways and telegraphs, or to lease Afghan Seistan, against his will. A personal meeting with the Viceroy would be preferable; or an officer could visit Kabul.[7] These views were largely accepted by Balfour and Brodrick on 21 July. Brodrick, like Curzon, thought Habibullah must be told that if he met the Russians with his own army, he would probably suffer severe defeat and thereby reduce Britain's capacity to help him later. If the Afghans were certain to fight on the British side, the Prime Minister observed, their aid would be invaluable, but an Amir with a well-trained army of 50,000 could dictate terms at a moment of strain, merely by threatening to throw in his lot with Russia.[8]

The Defence Committee considered whether a trained Afghan army or a rabble would be the more serviceable. Kitchener preferred the trained force, Curzon the rabble. The Secretary, Clarke, believing that the Afghans had good reason to mistrust the British, wished to leave matters as they

were. Possessing large stocks of arms, they had become much more
formidable than in 1879–80, and events in the Far East were unlikely to
make them subservient.[9]

In the early months of 1904, the reports of a political officer restoring
boundary pillars on the Herat frontier, Mr Dobbs, showed that Russians
and Afghans there were communicating freely. Count Lamsdorff's assurance that Russia would not send an agent to Kabul 'at present', or force
direct relations upon the Amir, brought little comfort. It was thought that
the Governor of Herat was in the Russians' pay, and that the Amir had been
in communication with them. Habibullah, becoming hostile to Dobbs'
proceedings, virtually demanded his recall.[10] He returned to India by way
of Kabul, where the Amir complained of the stoppage of ammunition
supplies. Afghanistan was India's shield against Russia: 'And how strange
it is to make your shield of paper instead of steel, so that anyone can thrust
a finger through it!'

It seemed that Habibullah was prepared for a rupture. He spoke constantly of Japan's example, which, being consumed by a vanity inordinate
even by Afghan standards, he was convinced that his country could emulate.
In a document handed to Dobbs, the Amir stated that this would be the
right time to loosen the Russians' grip on Asia while they had their hands
full with Japan. He flattered himself that on his slightest movement the
Turcomans, Uzbegs, and the peoples of the frontier would muck in, and
denied that any political correspondence took place between his officers and
the Russians without his permission. Habibullah inveighed against the
abandonment by the Conservatives, 'an ambitious and proud party', of
Mr Gladstone's policy of non-interference with Afghanistan. He did not
want much help, but would like Martini rifles and an advance of the
subsidy for twenty years. If immediate war were thought unnecessary, he
would, as he said in his letter of 1 March to Curzon, devote himself to the
preparation of his forces. Dobbs remarked that the Amir, who never
travelled more than twelve miles from Kabul, imagined that what he saw
around him prevailed everywhere. In fact, Russian influence was growing
unchecked in Herat and probably in Turkestan.[11]

The King, most unfavourably impressed with these reports, described
the Amir as openly treacherous and disloyal. Curzon commented that he
was only a typical Afghan. He could not see what Habibullah would gain
by breaking with Britain. Evidently the King would have liked a much
stronger policy than his ministers were disposed to follow.[12] Ampthill
advised that with the Amir in his present mood, it would not be wise to
court any further exhibition of petulance. He had never thought Habibullah

likely to attend willingly a meeting with Curzon, whose unequalled knowledge of Afghan affairs, persuasiveness and personal magnetism were apparent in his letters and known to the Amir. Being much impressed with the urgency of the dangers on the frontier, the acting Viceroy proposed that he should be asked without more ado to receive an envoy at Kabul.[13] Balfour concurred, with some reluctance

> for, though I think George expects to get a great deal more out of the Amir by interview than...he ever would have got, still, there can be but little doubt that his personality would have had a powerful effect upon the shifting policy of our very difficult ally.[14]

Realising that the Cabinet would not compel the Amir's presence in India, Curzon agreed that an envoy would go to Kabul. At this stage he expected to be back in Simla by mid-October. The Amir seemed to become more tractable, perhaps because the Russian Governor-General of Transcaspia was trying to establish contact with the Governor of Herat. A letter, which Habibullah sent on to India, announced that a Lieutenant-Colonel of the General Staff would visit Herat to deliver a document and confer about 'certain essential matters regarding Russia and Afghanistan'. Habibullah vowed to thwart Russian designs, characterised the letter as an attempt to re-create the situations of 1840 and 1880, recalled the fate of Sher Ali and observed that 'a wise man cannot be twice bitten by a snake emanating from the same hole'. In order to proclaim Afghanistan's friendship with India, he would send his eldest son, Inayatullah Khan, to meet Curzon immediately upon his return. As the news-writer at Herat had reported the arrival of this letter on 3 August, the Amir had held it back at least a month. Later in September he forwarded another Russian letter, this time written to the Governor-General of Balkh.[15]

∗ ∗ ∗ ∗

In the intervals of his wife's critical illness Curzon drafted out instructions for the envoy. He should speak openly and as a friend, without finesse or criticism; railways should not be mentioned; the permanent location of officers in Afghanistan would not be urged; the agreement of 1880 would be renewed *totidem verbis*, in a form personal to Habibullah. India had given Abdur Rahman, ostensibly for military and defensive purposes, £1,600,000; nevertheless, if his son preferred to meet Russia singlehanded, Great Britain would not press upon him unwanted assistance, but would do what seemed most suitable at the time. If no conditions were to be attached, less than 18 lakhs a year should be ample. The Amir would improve the treatment of the British agent at Kabul and of the news-writers; Afghan frontier officers must be less truculent; as a practical mark of goodwill, intrigues with the Afridis and other tribes beyond the Durand line, with whom Abdur Rahman had bound himself not to interfere, must cease.

To hand over all the arrears, about £400,000, would reward the Amir's obstinacy and might cause him to spend so enormous a sum in a way provocative to Russia. Curzon thought it unlikely that these terms would be refused; but if they were, the Amir should be told that Britain would dispense with an agreement altogether, and would make her own arrangements in future. 'Such a threat would probably bring the Amir to his knees at once. I know of no instance in the history of his father or himself, where the presentation of an ultimatum has not been followed by surrender.'[16]

Brodrick thought that Curzon probably asked too much; and the Prime Minister laid it down

> We do *not* want a strong and efficient [Afghanistan]...her fidelity is doubtful; and her inalienable value to us lies, not in the efficiency of her army, but in her difficult passes and barren ranges.

It would not, therefore, be useful to require that the money be spent on the improvement of the Afghan army. Balfour was prepared to continue the full subsidy for a satisfactory arrangement. Almost all Curzon's conditions he accepted; but since the Amir could probably get arms from other sources, he should be encouraged to obtain through India weapons likely to be least injurious to the British if turned against them. On no account must conditions be laid down which would force Habibullah to make rational use of these arms. 'He cannot do better, in my opinion, than hoard them till they rot in the Cabul magazines.'[17]

The Amir, Curzon reminded Brodrick, must be regarded as an oriental, a master of the arts of open bluff and simulated indignation. A liberal discount must be made for first impressions. Even if an outspoken statement of British policy brought forth no immediate response, it should be uttered; and after all, the negotiators were not on even terms.[18] At this stage, a new element entered into the situation. The military authorities of India favoured a frontier policy a good deal more dashing and thorough than that which Curzon had pursued. Kitchener, like Roberts, placed much store by frontier railways, and wished to take under British protection all the tribes up to the Durand line, a policy which Deane said was impossible without great expense. Curzon cared little for the railways and thought the Afridis more likely to be drawn to the British side by detachment from Kabul than by early absorption.[19] The C-in-C wanted also a close alliance for mutual defence with Afghanistan, to include visits by British and Afghan officers to strategic points, a good deal of advice on their defence, improvement of roads and acceptance of British help from the outset in war. If the Amir maintained his existing policy, the 'empty farce of a one-sided military alliance' should be abandoned. Ampthill took a rather less rigorous view. Habibullah had just sent a more friendly letter; and after a discussion in Council it was agreed that even if he refused a true military alliance, he might be granted the subsidy and limited import of arms.[20]

Unquestionably the stakes were high. Should the mission return empty-handed from Kabul, the old obligations would presumably have lapsed. The British would no longer control Afghan foreign relations or guarantee the country. Habibullah could make an alliance with Russia. The result might be to substitute for a suspicious ally a neutral, or a foe. Instead of a buffer to break the force of invasion, Afghanistan might become a spring-board. If war came, the Indian Army must either remain within the border or invade Afghanistan. The hostility of the Amir might inflame the fanaticism of the frontier tribes, amongst whom serious unrest was reported by Deane. The result of this policy, then, might well be that the Indian Empire must be defended on that very line, the Indus, which had finally been declared unsuitable, notably by Kitchener himself.[21]

Lansdowne, admitting that the existing arrangements were unsatisfactory, doubted whether anything much better would be obtained. He thought the Amir less malleable than Curzon supposed, and Kitchener mistaken in believing that he would concert with the British a plan of defence. The Foreign Secretary agreed with Balfour that Afghanistan should be a friendly but not strong military power:

> In my view, we should be content to meddle as little as possible with the Afghan hedgehog. His bristles will prick our fingers occasionally, but I would treat him kindly and make allowance for his bad manners, provided always that the bristles do not all point our way. This we cannot stand, and the Ameer will quite appreciate our refusal to stand it.[22]

British policy was decided not by the Cabinet but by a meeting at Balfour's home, attended by him, his brother Gerald and Brodrick. Balfour and the India Council observed, in comment upon Curzon's proposal that the size of the subsidy should be proportionate to the British advantage, that this was not a business arrangement with a telegraph company but a bonus to content an eastern potentate. If Habibullah received less than 18 lakhs he would have a grievance; if conciliatory, he would also receive the full arrears. In accordance with Lansdowne's view it was ruled that no restriction should be placed on 'reasonable' import of arms and warlike stores by the Amir. Otherwise, with two important exceptions, the instructions followed Curzon's suggestions and language.[23]

This meant the rejection of Kitchener's policy, though the envoy was empowered to sound the Amir cautiously about telegraphs, the occasional deputation of British officers to Afghanistan and surveys. Curzon had recommended that a formal treaty would be unnecessary; but the Prime Minister believed that the Russians had some regard for a treaty and that they considered the British 'squeezable' about Afghanistan. Britain must fight in defence of the Amir and if the Russians felt sure that she meant business they would be more careful about provoking war. A treaty would leave this policy less vulnerable to changes of government in England.[24]

On the day that these instructions left London, Ampthill telegraphed the considered view of the government of India. Military interests must predominate. A treaty against unprovoked aggression, supplemented by a secret military convention, should be sought. The Amir would give large facilities for concerting defensive plans and in war would place no restriction on the place or time at which military help would be given; he would receive an enhanced subsidy, part of which must be spent on defence.[25]

'When the cat is away' said Curzon, 'the mice will play.' He pointed out that Kitchener's desire to treat Afghanistan as an extension of the Indian frontier, to be defended in a pre-arranged plan by both armies, entailed a complete change of policy: that it would bring responsibilities, the end of which could not be foretold, and immediate retaliation by Russia; that Britain would reap the entire odium of Afghan failure in arms: and that there was not the faintest chance of acceptance or loyal execution by Habibullah. Under the existing agreement, if renewed, the British would always be the sole judges of the place, time and scale of military aid:

> There is no advantage in bribing the Amir to accept this view of our responsibilities. It will be dictated by our necessities rather than by his. On the other hand, there are inconveniences in giving anything like a pledge that might be held to commit us to marching to the relief of Herat.

In short, Curzon believed that political considerations weighed as heavily as military. To leave the Amir alone would mean his making terms with the Russians, who would advance. The frontiers would meet on the Hindu Kush. 'For this…we have neither the men nor the money.'[26] Rigid instructions, Curzon wrote to the Secretary of State, should not be laid down in London. Some elasticity was essential. He deplored the growing tendency to issue orders on minute points of foreign policy, of which the Cabinet might know very little. Brodrick replied:

> Is it not true that what India does in Afghanistan, Persia, Tibet, or on the Chinese frontier has become greatly more the concern of the Foreign Office than it was 10 or 20 years ago? Russia's railways, Persia's difficulties, China's decrepitude, all seem to me to have contributed to this.

Certainly the Foreign Office was more concerned in Asiatic questions, Curzon rejoined, but not necessarily more competent to manage them.[27]

The argument about Seistan was still flourishing. In the spring, Curzon had refused to panic at rumours of a Russian advance on Seistan and troop-movements in Turkestan. Brodrick had asked about a counter-demonstration. Short of sending a force into Seistan, which entailed tremendous logistic problems, the only possibility would be the mobilisation of a division or two on the North-West frontier. This, with Habibullah in his most prickly mood, Curzon did not wish to do.[28] But he did wish to develop Seistan. Balfour, for reasons already described, did not, though Curzon pointed out that Seistan was largely protected to the north and north-east by swamps. He still hoped to sound the Amir for a lease of territory on the left bank of the Helmund, and understood Balfour to agree.[29]

This provision figured in Curzon's draft instructions for the envoy. It was struck out. One adviser of the Secretary of State said that nothing but a threat of war would induce Habibullah even to consider it. The government of India had also given up the idea, earlier favoured by Ampthill. However, his view changed rapidly on the threatened removal of the Hashmat from the Governorship. Kitchener said that though he did not wish, for the moment at least, to make Seistan a point in his strategic line of defence, the existing grip must not be relaxed and might have to be tightened.[30] Curzon appealed to Balfour to allow the Helmund to be mentioned at Kabul. 'I do not myself think that it will produce so much suspicion as the proposal which you have...introduced into the instructions to examine the country between Herat and Kabul. In either case, if suspicion is the result, the idea will have to be dropped.' Balfour demurred, imagining that Curzon's view was held by himself alone. That impression Curzon corrected in a conversation of 9 November, being convinced, according to the Prime Minister's account, that the main line of Russian advance would be through Seistan. That was why he wanted control of the waters; for without it, the Russians could not be dislodged. When Balfour replied that a Russian invasion of Seistan should be made a *casus belli*, Curzon remarked that war or no war he did not see how the Russians were to be got rid of. 'We could not turn them out by force as we should never be locally in superior strength, and they are invulnerable in all other parts of the world.'[31]

The Prime Minister answered that though it might seem hard to find a prize-ring in which England and Russia would fight it out, there must in time of war be developments which would prevent a mere stalemate. Anyway, did not Curzon's argument mean that the whole of Afghan Turkestan and the Herat region would be at Russia's mercy, whatever the British did? Curzon said that this was true. Those regions were past praying for. 'Two leaves of the artichoke will go anyhow. Let us try to save the third.'[32] Balfour then relented. He also agreed that disbursement of all the arrears should depend upon the Amir's attitude and that in any event payments should be spread over at least three years.

There remained the selection of an emissary to the court of the Amir. From the moment he parted with Sir Hugh Barnes, the Viceroy judged that Mr Dane would not be an adequate replacement as Secretary to the Foreign Department; for, though zealous, he lacked method, balance and capacity to draft. What was worse, there was no better man available, under the system whereby no one remained longer than a few years in the Foreign Department. After seven months' experience, Curzon told Godley that Dane seemed to develop no sort of aptitude for the post, 'always going off at half cock, or full cock, and even at no cock at all'.[33] In the spring of 1904, he had warned Brodrick that if an envoy were sent to Kabul it should be not Dane but Barnes, 'the only officer in India whom I could thoroughly trust'. This advice he had repeated during the summer in London. However, Barnes refused on grounds of health. That left only Dane, whom Ampthill commended as resourceful and knowledgeable, though impetuous.[34]

Meanwhile the Amir was whiling away the time by stirring up the Afridis. Colonel Deane, on tour along the frontier, noticed among all the tribes bandoliers full of cartridges from Kabul. He urged that the mission be announced at once. Believing that the time was auspicious, Ampthill agreed; Curzon thought that after so long a delay, a few weeks more would not matter much. He would be held responsible for success or failure at Kabul, and wished to go over all the ground with Dane. However, Brodrick supported Ampthill and the arrangements for Dane's journey were pressed forward.[35]

*   *   *   *

Fear of war with Russia, and hope of eventual accommodation with her, cannot have failed to dispose the Ministers in London against stiff treatment of the Amir. 'We have our share of special anxiety' wrote Brodrick on 26 October, 'in contemplating the large Russian forces which are assembled in Trans-Caspia and our own unpreparedness for war.' Ampthill took an even more definite view: 'There can be no doubt that the Russians mean to fight us as soon as they get a convenient opportunity, for the great military preparations in Trans-Caspia can have no other object.'[36]

Well after the Russians had backed down over the Dogger Bank crisis, Brodrick described them as feeling 'absolutely certain of vanquishing us in Afghanistan'. Such apprehensions were much exaggerated. That the British should entertain them will surely have been one of Russia's objects. Some weeks before, Lamsdorff had indicated that the military authorities hoped to cause the British some bad moments in Afghanistan should the Far Eastern war spread.[37]

Ampthill, who had imagined that the Cabinet would lay down a bold and clear-cut line for the talks at Kabul, subjected the instructions to a blistering criticism. It hardly seemed worthwhile to send a mission at all if it were merely to renew old agreements and compose a few disputes. Military considerations, which should predominate, had been virtually omitted. The Cabinet's desire that Afghanistan should be weak, yet a formidable barrier, seemed self-contradictory, ran directly counter to the opinion of Kitchener and portended ultimate absorption by Britain and Russia.[38]

Perhaps anticipating these disappointments, Curzon asked the Viceroy to remember that the Cabinet had wanted to do as little as possible and had all along been anxious to give way to the Amir without even a struggle. Much talking had been needed to overcome this tradition. An heroic policy was as impossible in London as it would prove unpractical at Kabul. At most, some excrescences and anomalies would be rubbed off and a fresh start made.[39] The Cabinet were persuaded, Brodrick explained, that nothing a convention could achieve would make the Amir's troops battleworthy. If Britain took any responsibility for them she would end by taking all. He acknowledged that the Russians must be kept out of Kabul, and that the British must choose their own battleground, as Kitchener wished. The Secretary of State insisted that no repetition of Younghusband's proceedings could be tolerated. Ampthill duly passed the admonition to Dane:

> With this I must leave you to your difficult task of discriminating between instructions which have received the sanction of the Secretary of State and those which have not, if the latter should be sent to you![40]

★   ★   ★   ★

Dane presented Habibullah with a motor-car, several boxes of sporting equipment and a cinematograph. He found that the Amir followed European ways, attired by day in a frock coat and at dinner in a dress suit. His Highness read *The Times* with avidity, making annotations in blue pencil. Just as the mission arrived a thief was caught and crucified, remaining alive for three days without bread or water. He was then cut down, hanged from a gibbet and finally suspended by the feet.

Curzon resumed the Viceroyalty as the talks began. The problems of communication were similar to those which had caused Younghusband such tribulations. From Kabul messages had to be carried for five days to Landi Kotal, whence they were telegraphed to Calcutta. There they had to be studied and circulated; the more important must be summarised and sent forward to London. Assuming the most rapid despatch of business, Dane could hardly expect an answer in less than a fortnight. Curzon, regretting infinitely that they had been unable to talk, explained the situation in London, and asked him to remember that the Amir's object was 'to maintain Afghanistan independent, not to treat it as a mere pawn on the chess-board of Indian military defence'.[41]

The story of the negotiation at Kabul is a tangled one. At the first interview, Habibullah talked excitedly about the activity of the Russians, who were pushing their railway forward. He intended to oppose them on the line of the Hindu Kush. Knowing that the danger was now much greater than in the time of his father, he would ask such help as he could receive without detriment to his honour or religious prestige. Dane did not think it possible to discuss for the moment the Amir's intrigues with the Afridis and other issues.[42]

Soon afterwards, Habibullah sent an unsigned memorandum. Its contents must have surprised Dane more than a little, for after describing Russia's vulnerability and weakness, the Amir proposed that Britain and Afghanistan should forthwith turn her out of Asia, while she was well occupied elsewhere. He would raise a *jehad* of Turks, Persians and other Moslems. The world of Islam would revolt. He hinted broadly that the real business of the British, should they prefer to await the invasion of Afghanistan, was to supply arms and cash, adding saucily that the British troops would in any event be needed to prevent risings in India, where they had failed to reduce tribes under their sway for seventy or eighty years. If the terms were right, the Amir would accept a treaty personal to himself. Then there would be no friendship with Russia. Dane regarded this memorandum as fairly satisfactory. Curzon, in a masterly understatement, commented to Brodrick, 'I do not altogether share this view, since it reveals Amir as holding singu-

Lord Kitchener and Staff at Delhi

The Entrance to Muscat Harbour

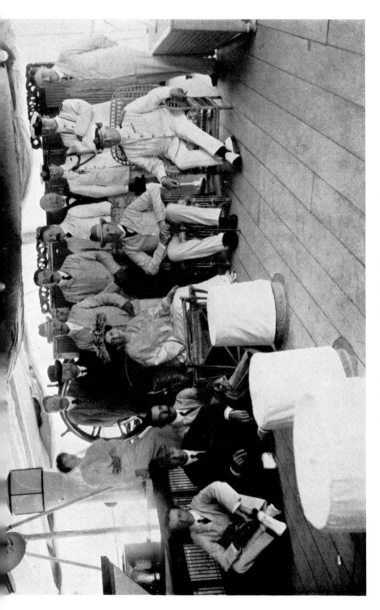

Lord and Lady Curzon with staff on the Persian Gulf tour

The Landing at Kuwait

British and Indian troops escort Col. Younghusband into Lhasa,
4 August, 1904. (From a drawing by L. Rybott)

The Potala Pass, Lhasa
(From a drawing by L. Rybott)

The last phase of the attack on the Tse-chen monastery, two miles west of Gyantse fort, 1904

Arthur James Balfour

Lord Ampthill

larly ill-balanced views about position of Russia and our policy and his own ability to dictate terms.'[43]

On 22 December, Dane ruled out on his own authority an immediate attack on Russia and refused to discuss the number of troops with which Britain could assist Afghanistan. He impressed upon the Amir again that he could not hope to resist unaided. When Habibullah retorted that he could do nothing until he knew the terms of the proposed treaty, Dane spoke according to the instructions approved by the Cabinet. Habibullah fished repeatedly for a larger subsidy and, when Dane talked about the import of arms, asked suspiciously what was meant by 'a reasonable quantity'?[44]

Four days later, the Amir reacted sharply to this talk. He professed willingness to carry out his father's obligations, but if the agreements had lapsed, did not understand why Dane should discuss the various questions, nor why he should answer. He had believed that they were to concert measures for thrusting back Russian aggression. Dane replied that His Highness had misapprehended the object of the mission and that the engagements with Abdur Rahman had always been treated as personal. Privately, he attributed the more hostile atmosphere to the proposed limit on the import of arms and the reassertion of the right to control Afghanistan's foreign relations. Probably Habibullah also realised that the lapse of the agreements deprived him of an indefeasible claim to arrears of subsidy.[45]

Curzon surmised that Dane had opened the talks in too dashing a fashion. He had inquired whether the Amir admitted the Afghans' inferiority to the Russians? If so, would he expect to receive military assistance from the British? The first admission Habibullah was unlikely to make; and the second question needed much care, for Britain's freedom to give or withhold such help according to her judgment had always been insisted upon. On reading that the envoy had also asked whether the Amir would adopt a really friendly attitude' towards the construction of railways within the British border, Curzon could scarcely believe his eyes. 'Really,' he minuted, the next thing will be to ask him if he consents to the reorganisation scheme of the Commander-in-Chief.' Habibullah replied that his attitude must be held in abeyance until he knew what increase of aid would be forthcoming![46]

The position of the negotiator at Kabul must in the circumstances have been delicate. Describing in ample detail the growing menace from Russia, Dane had employed the arguments used by the government of India in October to justify a policy of close military alliance. He then followed with the very different conclusions of the British Cabinet. The Amir found in this something of bathos. Probably, as Curzon and others had long

6

suspected, he had a spy in the Foreign Department. Indeed, all the grandiose
proposals for an onslaught upon Russia may have constituted nothing
but a bluff, to justify discontent upon certain rejection. At any rate, the
Afghans' attitude had changed abruptly. Dane made preparations for the
return to India. Habibullah, unabashed, gave orders for the immediate
collection of supplies to facilitate his journey.

*   *   *   *

On 2 January, the Japanese took Port Arthur after prolonged assaults.
The Baltic Fleet limped out, by easy stages from one repair or coaling
station to another, towards its doom. At lunch, the Chief of the General
Staff remarked to the Secretary for War, 'I wonder where this Russian
Fleet has got to? When we last heard of it, it was in the Bight of Benin.'
Arnold-Forster found this amusing, since the Fleet was actually in Mada-
gascar and had left the Bight of Benin in November.[47] Three weeks later,
Bloody Sunday symbolised discontent at the Far Eastern defeats and the
failings of Tsardom. Mr Brodrick prayed earnestly that the naval works at
Sebastopol might suffer heavily from incendiarism or that Russia should
receive some other quietus which would keep her out of mischief abroad
for five and twenty years.[48]

The effects of the Russo-Japanese war were felt not only in the Far East
and in Europe, where the naval and military balance was moving in
Germany's favour as Russia weakened, but throughout Asia, where the
thrill and the lesson of victory over a white foe were experienced everywhere. At Kabul, the Amir sent to Dane on 1 January an astonishing note
by the Afghan Council of State, which expressed surprise that the question
of expelling Russia from Asia or resisting her advance had not so far been
discussed. Old engagements could be reaffirmed, with a separate agreement
to provide for military collaboration. The British would build a railway to
Seistan along the Helmund and help to build forts on the Oxus; both
powers would operate gunboats on the Oxus river; British troops would
build and hold defences in Afghan Seistan. These and other proposals
depended upon the supply of arms, with funds for any desired increase in
the Afghan army; if they were not acceptable, the tribes must be summoned
from all over Afghanistan.

Curzon could not tell whether Habibullah was bluffing or joking or
serious. What seemed certain was that Dane was not the man to cope with
such an emergency. Something must be patched up, so that he could be got
away from Kabul. Brodrick had earlier telegraphed that Dane's return

without a treaty would be a serious misfortune. Any reasonable concession about arrears and arms might be made, so long as it did not entail 'an admission that any claim hitherto denied by us can be made as of right'.[49] This seemed a modest programme; yet, to Curzon's eyes, it would be unwise to snub the Amir when he seemed genuinely alarmed about Russia and 'anxious to conclude some sort of military alliance with us that will combine the impossible features of making us pay for everything and be responsible for everything, while we are to do none of the actual fighting until it is too late'.

He hoped that the Amir would make an agreement, once he understood that the full subsidy and arrears would be paid. Then the two of them might talk about military co-operation.[50] Reluctantly, Brodrick assented. It was thought imperative in London, he telegraphed, that the Amir be told there was no intention of discussing an attack on Russia. Habibullah had again asked for rifles. He appeared keen that the offer of posts and a railway on the western frontier should be accepted.[51] A few days later, however, the messages from Kabul bore less reassuring news. Habibullah had refused to discuss control of his foreign relations and the subsidy until the original agreement had been strengthened. Dane said the former condition was vital, and told him in terms of British intentions about the subsidy and importation.[52] The response was unsatisfactory. Habibullah accused Dane of acting contrary to instructions. If he should now withdraw his objections to the renewal of engagements, it would appear that he had been dishonourably influenced by the promise of the subsidy and arrears of £400,000, which he was pleased to characterise as 'paltry', and the other benefits, 'worldly carrion'. He might even be held capable of being bribed from his promises.

The Amir, Dane reported, was in the hands of violently xenophobic counsellors, who distorted words and wrote the memoranda issuing in their ruler's name; even in meetings he seemed to play a subordinate role. Unless the instructions were modified, Dane suggested, he should threaten a break, or return to India for consultations. Otherwise his stay at Kabul would last indefinitely, Habibullah's object being to get the whole subsidy, ample quantities of arms and free import without any return: 'I realise the necessity of securing the conclusion of a treaty in some form, and I have done everything in my power to induce Amir to see reason. As long, however, as he refuses to discuss any question until his view of the permanent nature of former engagements is accepted or rejected, I can do nothing.'[53]

The talks had clotted up. Insistence upon a dynastic, as distinct from personal, engagement may well have reflected the weakness of Habibullah's position. Dane thought him vain, lazy and liable to be supplanted at any moment by Nasrullah, but hesitated to rebut his arguments vigorously, having detected signs that the Cabinet would concede almost anything to obtain a treaty of sorts. Yet he had no hope of bringing the Amir to reason unless allowed to speak bluntly. Twice Habibullah had hinted that there was another party upon whom he might rely.[54]

During these weeks Kitchener had a separate source of information at Kabul in the person of Major Malleson, the officer whom he had brought to the Intelligence Department. His private letters describe Dane as having disclosed all his hand at the beginning, as alternately cringing and blustering, volatile, self-deceiving; talking perpetually about himself, 'egotistical, flighty, erratic, indiscreet, slippery, foolish, and flabby'. No doubt Malleson wished to impress Kitchener; probably he felt a military man's contempt for a civilian; almost certainly he failed to realise all Dane's difficulties.

It appears from Malleson's account that after waiting more than a week for an interview, Dane tried to foresee the future by opening the Bible at random. On each occasion he found disquieting references to crucifixion. Mr Dobbs, asked to try his hand, hit upon a passage showing that a mighty prince from the north put the enemy to flight and smote them sore. In desperation the same procedure was attempted with Pepys's diary, which revealed 'Lord Falmouth, the plenipotentiary to the Moors, had been foully murdered by them, with all his following. Nor did I find anyone there present who regretted this event'.

Whether for these or other reasons, Dane asked Dobbs to remove his furniture so that the door connecting their suites would allow instant flight in the event of attack. Dobbs refused. Other members of the staff were soon infected. The shorthand writer refused to go out, and insisted on sleeping in the room of a clerk. Dane and the Amir, Malleson thought, resembled Sir Lucius O'Trigger and Bob Acres, each in a mortal funk; Dane of the Amir and the Amir of the British Empire.

Evidently Dane had had enough. On 30 January he conveyed to the Amir the decision that there could be no immediate attack on Russia. He then dissected Habibullah's recent performances, nailing down a succession of quibbles, perversions and untruths. When Nasrullah refused to believe, unless he saw the original, that Abdur Rahman had signed a certain document, Dane flared up and attacked him vehemently. Another bystander said with the most insolent air that his religion would prevent him from mixing with a representative of the British.[55] Even before he learned of these developments, Brodrick lamented that the Amir's mind seemed 'to have diverged altogether from the ordinary course and I suppose these Russian troubles when they reach him will make him still more impracticable'.[56]

Curzon too had surmised that each Russian defeat increased Habibullah's intractability. Dane had not the authority or quick-wittedness to handle him, while the nervous condition of the authorities in London was pathetic.[57] The Amir's attitude, Curzon believed, had been encouraged by the Cabinet's persistent timidity over the previous three years. Reminding Balfour that the proposal about Seistan, which had been thought almost certain to estrange the Amir, had now emanated in even more precise form from Habibullah himself, he asked whether India's view of Afghan questions might not often be more correct than London's.

> I feel certain that if during the past three years we had sometimes been allowed to speak plain language to him, instead of avoiding the controversial points and indulging in generalities, we should not now have found him puffed up with conceit as he is...I still hope that we may not leave Kabul bootless; and I think myself that even at the last moment a firm stand, if we are permitted to make it, will probably bring him to reason. But my own view is that the occasion...would never have arisen had we shown a little more mettle...
>
> I am not complaining. I am only asking that if there have been mistakes in the past they should not be repeated.[58]

The whole of the Viceroy's Council, especially Kitchener, felt that a halt should be called. Curzon recognised that the Amir might already have entered into secret relations with Russia, but doubted whether he would abandon the policy pursued from the time of Dost Mohamed with only one break, which had cost Sher Ali his throne and his life. Even if Habibullah or Nasrullah wished to ally at once with a power of whose defeats they knew, and which they boasted of being able to repel, opposition within Afghanistan might well prove fatal. Much more probably the Amir was trading upon British weakness:

> I do not know [Curzon wrote to Brodrick on 2 February] whether you are satisfied with the position at Kabul. To me it seems a profoundly humiliating one for a great power. That our representative, sent there in order to negotiate a treaty by which this petty potentate will be the recipient of our bounty, and by which he obtains the advantages of British protection, giving practically nothing in return, should be treated as Dane has been—his arguments misrepresented, his statements of our intentions ignored, and his civility met with impertinence—is, in my opinion, a spectacle neither creditable to ourselves nor capable of being tolerated.

The Viceroy remarked that he knew of only one way of dealing with any oriental power, which was to say that beyond a certain point there must be no trifling. Until that point was reached, diplomacy never effected much at Teheran, Kabul, Lhasa or Pekin.[59] However, he can have cherished little hope by now of any firmness on the Cabinet's part; and within twenty-four hours, a telegram from Brodrick clearly indicated an intention to yield. The interruption of negotiations, it stated, could not fail to have a disturbing effect and might, if the Russians' preparations in Tashkent meant anything, precipitate them into action. 'A deplorable display of timidity and vacillation' minuted Curzon. 'But I do not know that we had a right to expect anything else.'[60]

As for the Russian troop movements, Charles Hardinge and the Military Attaché doubted their existence. 'I am quite convinced' Hardinge wrote, 'that at the present moment the Russian Government have no desire to provoke a conflict with us...' Equally, a reported collision between Afghans and Russians was discounted by Sanderson: 'Oriental newsagents think it necessary to send news of some kind, and if an Afghan trooper had crossed the Oxus, and been sent back with a kick in his backside, the incident would be quite sufficient for a swarm of alarmist rumours.'[61]

By early February Habibullah had stated that the British clearly had no intention of dealing fairly with Afghanistan; that the insistence on the personal nature of the old engagements and subsidy was unjust; that the real object of the British was to establish intimacy between their agent at Kabul and Afghan Sirdars and destroy the autonomy of the Afghan government.

Dane sent in a repudiation at once. The Amir, however, read out his own draft, saying 'If a single thing is altered in that, I shall have to refer the matter to my whole nation'. He was confined to bed with a severe attack of gout at this time, causing Dane to wonder whether insistence of certain counsellors on the dynastic nature of the agreements might stem from their desire to secure all the advantages should Habibullah die suddenly. The Afghans would not budge on this point; Dane doubted whether an ultimatum would make them recede. Habibullah, indeed, told him that while a treaty might help the British in dealing with Russia, Afghanistan did not need it. He would 'accept' an assurance similar to that of 1880. The British draft 'would cause all his relations with Foreign Powers to disappear'.[62] Since Abdur Rahman had specifically forsworn such relations, and since Habibullah had just said he would abide by his father's policy, this made no sense in formal terms. The threat, however, was clear enough.

It is not necessary to follow here all the Amir's confused and self-contradictory claims. The gist of them was that he intended to concede nothing and to get as much as he could, a very natural ambition. He implied that he would consider himself free to overstep British control of his political relations. The British should be grateful, since the old agreements had lapsed, that he had not invited a Russian agent to Kabul or taken back territory ceded earlier. If they would give up those regions, he would have no further claim to a grant in money or in kind. There was a good deal more on similar lines, in transmitting which Curzon commented

> No Amir has ever before addressed British government in such insolent tone. His Majesty's Government will be able to judge from this message of nature of Afghan pretensions and prospects of future friendship with such an ally.[63]

The Amir's proposal meant in effect that the old engagements would be confirmed on a permanent basis. He would then discuss the subsidiary points, but would evidently make no concession on any of them. These terms, the government of India pointed out, were irreconcilable with the Cabinet's instructions, would be dangerous to India and fatal to British prestige. Dane, they proposed, should tell the Amir that if he would not resume discussion on the basis of the British draft, the mission would leave. Probably Habibullah would then give way; but even a rupture would be preferable in the long run to the results of complete surrender. 'We should have sacrificed every means of applying pressure and should leave Kabul without a single point to our credit.'

If the home government wished to compromise, Dane might sign an agreement identical with that of 1880, provided the Amir signed an acceptance as his father had done; and both might sign a repetition of the Durand agreements. The Amir must give a clear undertaking that he would honour the Durand agreement, which he had openly said he would continue to violate, about non-interference with the tribes. Otherwise Afghan intrigues with the Afridis would lead to another Tirah campaign.[64]

This telegram faced the Cabinet with an unpleasant decision. It also brought into sharp focus Curzon's view that the Amir was a master of cunning and sharp bargaining, of bogus indignation and facile dialectics, whose pretensions would increase until curbed. When Brodrick regretted that the Amir's mind had 'diverged from the ordinary course' Curzon observed that Western governments made a great mistake in regarding potentates like the Amir, and their institutions, as if they were European. There was nothing 'ordinary' or 'European' in the Amir:

> You cannot even in dealing with him get on to the platform of mutual intelligibility and common sense. There is no contact between the two points of view or the two states of mind. That is the meaning of those of us who say that

it is useless to treat people of this description as though they were versed in the methods of European politics. They are not. They are only half-tutored savages with a veneer of civilisation, and the sole way to get on with such individuals is by the exercise of personal influence tempered with fear.[65]

Long before this letter reached London, the issue was decided. Brodrick's personal view seems to have agreed in substance with that of the Viceroy's Council. So, at least, he indicated to Ampthill.[66] Roberts, however, thought that if Dane left Kabul without a treaty, Habibullah would throw in his lot with Russia, the tribes of the frontier following suit. Godley predicted ferment in India, especially among Pathans in the Army, tribal risings, the permeation of Afghanistan by Russia. In his covering note, Brodrick told the Cabinet that the government of India clearly wished to break off the negotiations for the moment. This can hardly be called a fair summary of their telegram. On the other hand, Brodrick stated, 'Indian administrators' (by which term he presumably meant certain members of the India Council) thought that though the Amir's terms were one-sided a 'friendly arrangement' would be 'of the utmost benefit' to British policy on the North-West frontier.[67]

The Cabinet, which met twice on 15 February, had therefore to choose between different estimates of the Amir's mind and reactions. They knew of the feelings with which Curzon would see his advice overruled, and did not in any case wish to oppose the authorities on the spot. But they feared that the government of India were still making a false estimate of the Amir's temper, and blenched at the thought of a game of bluff from which Habibullah would emerge successful. It is unlikely that most members of a weak Cabinet would have strong views on this subject; probably the lead came from Balfour. In his report to the King, he illustrated the argument from Tibetan experience. The Cabinet remembered, he wrote, 'that each stage on the road to Lhasa was to be the "last"; though it was not till Lhasa itself was reached that the Llamas gave in.'

On all counts the Prime Minister could not have chosen a less happy analogy; for it was Curzon and his colleagues who had advised that no business would be done except at Lhasa, and the Cabinet which had insisted on a series of halts now admitted to have been futile. 'In Mr Balfour's judgment,' the report continues, 'the Amir will never really show himself "malleable" until he has been thoroughly frightened by the Russians—and the Russian defeats by the Japanese have encouraged the idea in his ill balanced brain that *he* can go and do likewise.'[68]

Brodrick therefore telegraphed that if control of Afghanistan's foreign relations could be secured, no 'question of form' should stand in the way.

Should Dane leave without a treaty, the Amir might foment disturbances on the border or turn to Russia. The Lord Chancellor advised that there would be no need to sign again the Durand or other agreements, and pronounced the Amir's draft binding. Dane was to accept it, and concede all arrears of subsidy and free importation of arms.[69] Balfour sent assurances that the Cabinet had earnestly desired to support the Viceroy, recognising the difficulty in which he had been placed by Habibullah's conduct. The legal view had convinced them that the main ends could be served without withdrawal of Dane. Even if Habibullah were brought to terms by the threat of withdrawal, there would be no greater security for their observance than was provided by the Amir's own draft.

It was impossible, Brodrick telegraphed, to exaggerate the reluctance felt by everyone in the Cabinet to face the situation which would be caused by a withdrawal. He assured Curzon that he had put his views before the Cabinet with all the force he could command, confiding to Ampthill that Curzon's attitude to everyone in England, and his 'impracticability' even in small matters like those concerning Walmer Castle, had made a deep impression.

> Insensibly if a man makes himself impossible on one question or another with everyone with whom he has to do much business, it in the long run impairs the weight of his opinion.
> You have seen so much of Curzon's work that you can understand better perhaps than anyone what I mean. My fear is that he is sailing very close to the line, and will come in for a tumble some day.[70]

Curzon replied that Dane's departure had been envisaged as a last resort. The control of all external relations, and the personal nature of the agreement, which the Cabinet believed the Afghan draft to secure, were contested by the Amir, to whom what was law to the Lord Chancellor was not sacrosanct in the same sense. The reply, considered by the Cabinet, took a different view:

> We attribute importance to meeting Amir in a friendly spirit and to restoring his confidence in our intentions, without which he is unlikely to observe faithfully any Treaty that can be imposed on him.[71]

As the Amir had so far failed to meet a single point, it was thought in Calcutta that the telegram had more relevance to a Blue-book than to the facts. The government of India's view did not change. They pointed out that they too wished to meet the Amir in a friendly way and to give way on points which were not vital.[72]

In the latter part of February, the atmosphere at Kabul had improved somewhat. The Amir shrewdly passed to Dane two letters from Russia, adding that although he had no obligation, since the British said the agreements had lapsed, he declined to separate himself from them. The return from India of Inayatullah Khan probably helped. Dane later judged that if he had presented an ultimatum at this stage it would have led to agreement.[73] Even now the negotiation hung fire. Brodrick had repeatedly spoken of 'renewal' of the Amir's engagements. This, Dane telegraphed, might endanger the whole treaty. Should he allow 'continuance'? Curzon explained again the importance of the issue; but Brodrick agreed at once to 'continuance'.[74]

Eventually the treaty was concluded on 21 March. The Amir agreed that in the engagements which his late father

> that is, Zia-ul-millat- wa-ud-din who has found mercy, may God enlighten his tomb! concluded and acted upon with the exalted British Government, I also have acted, am acting and will act upon the same agreement and compact, and I will not contravene them in my dealing or in any promise.

As the Amir was signing, a secretary upset ink upon the parchment. All efforts to erase the stain failed. But, said he, 'it's the contents of the Treaty which we care about, and not its looks. This is only a mole on its face.'

Mr Dane knew his Hafiz. 'I would give all Samarkand and Bokhara for the Indian-dark mole on the face of my lady-love' he quoted. One of the courtiers asked whether, now Dane had the mole, Afghanistan might have Samarkand and Bokhara. 'The Amir' Dane rejoined, 'has kept the mole copy for himself.'[75] On this more felicitous note the mission set off for home.

*   *   *   *

The Amir styled himself 'Independent King of the State of Afghanistan and its Dependencies' with the title of 'His Majesty'. There was nothing to indicate that he had abandoned his contention that the treaty was permanent, or that the British government had accepted it. He had agreed, at least in words, to British control of his foreign relations. No progress had been made about Russo-Afghan communications, nor in the military question. It was five months since the home government had stated that a refusal to admit British troops would be a repudiation of the old engagements. The conditions for the renewal of the annual subsidy and for the payment of arrears, laid down by Balfour and Brodrick in October, had been abandoned. As for the frontier tribes, Habibullah promised not to go beyond his father's principles.

Dane did not pretend to be very pleased, though he felt confidence in the Amir's willingness to behave well. Curzon said that he would have resigned had it been possible to give a public explanation.[76] Whether his policy would have produced better results must remain open to doubt, since it was never tried. In this instance, however, he had taken much care to see that the line pursued was examined and approved at home. Most of the important letters to Habibullah had been vetted, and toned down, by the home government. In June, 1902, Salisbury and Lansdowne had asked for it to be made abundantly plain that the old agreements were personal. Mere renewal had never, until this point, been the Cabinet's object.

Nonetheless, Godley soon began to write about the 'forward policy', seeming to forget that the terms on which India had wished to insist were those of the home government itself. 'Of course,' Curzon answered, 'the man who stands still finds himself before long in a more forward position than the man who has retreated...'[77] Godley also remarked that consciousness of abnormal military weakness and of disorganization at the War Office had much to do with the Cabinet's attitude. He contrasted the proven Japanese capacity for self-sacrifice, discipline and thrift with the doubt that the British still possessed the same characteristics.[78] Admitting the charge, and believing that the British were growing stale, flaccid and nerveless, Curzon still saw no reason 'why we should tremble like an aspen leaf at every faint growl that emanates from the bear's den. Sometimes they are only the stertorous breathings of physical repletion and obesity, frequently the premeditated snarl that is merely intended to warn the rival denizens of the forest away.'

It was a moot point, he conceded, how far in questions involving foreign powers the Viceroy should conceive himself as the agent, or as the quasi-independent adviser, of the Cabinet. He recognised that resignation would not have affected their policy. On the next occasion, however, the decision would be different, for there must be a limit to the overruling of the government of India.[79] 'I have known all along' he had written to Godley a little earlier, 'that, with a moribund government with fear of Russia on the brain, there could be no other ending.' This letter, though strictly private, was later passed to Balfour and quoted by him, inaccurately, against its author.[80]

Brodrick solemnly assured the Governor of Bombay that there was no question of fear of Russia. The point on which they differed from Curzon 'who has got Russia on the brain', was not whether Afghanistan would be driven into Russia's arms but whether a friendly Afghanistan could be secured by the methods he proposed. This description of the Cabinet's attitude may be accurate, but Brodrick should not have been surprised if Curzon and others derived a different impression from the numerous references to Russian troop movements, British military feebleness, and the earmarking of the bulk of the Army for India.

The contents of Brodrick's letter are chiefly of interest for the attitude of mind they reveal. Curzon's visit to Kabul in 1894, he stated as a fact, was supposed by the Amir to have been a deliberate spying-out of 'the nakedness of his land'. The Viceroy had negotiated for five and a half years with Afghanistan 'on his own terms' but could not show 'a single point' gained. The Amir could no longer be kept 'in subjection', whereas Curzon had throughout tried to make him 'practically a British vassal'. Brodrick wished that every member of the Viceroy's Council could know how utterly during these negotiations the Cabinet's views had 'been travestied by the Viceroy'. The letter does not explain how this could be so. The telegrams and despatches from London were seen in full by all members of the Viceroy's Council. It would seem inconceivable that Brodrick failed to realise that fact, though his capacity to credit the inconceivable must not be under-rated. Within a few months he was to state repeatedly that Curzon manipulated the press of India.

Brodrick asked Lamington to keep the letter absolutely secret, adding, 'I do not in the least want to run Curzon down behind his back'.[81]

Curzon could not realise, Brodrick's memoirs assert, that such matters as Tibet and Afghanistan, involving peace or war, 'were the concern of the whole Cabinet and that in regard to these, once a decision was given the affair was *chose jugée*.'[82] This hardly meets the point; and nowhere is it explained how terms modified and endorsed by the Government in October had become a proof of Curzon's obstinacy and belligerence by March. Lord Esher, in daily contact with Balfour and the Defence Committee, made in his journal for 7 March an entry that needs no comment:

> That the 'forward party' in India, headed by Curzon, believed that a war with Afghanistan and the occupation of Kandahar by us while Russia is in difficulties is the right policy, there can be very little doubt, and that some pretext will be found in a comparatively short time to bring on a war is more than probable.[83]

The Secretary of the Defence Committee, Sir G. Clarke, thought that while Amir had behaved very well, Dane had proved just about the worst agent Curzon could have found and had 'all but made a war'. It was only because the Viceroy despised soldiers, he pronounced, that he had not chosen a good frontier officer. The King, knowing the facts, told Curzon simply that Dane was not the right envoy and that the home government were responsible.[84]

* * * *

At the end of January, another Blue-book on Tibet was produced, four and a half months after the signature of the Lhasa Convention. Presumably this step indicated the Parliamentary weakness of the government. Incredible as it seems, the decision was apparently Brodrick's alone. The Prime Minister wrote in a spirit of wondering detachment:

> St John is really very odd just now. I cannot imagine why he has washed all our and Younghusband's dirty linen in public by giving the whole corre-spondence to the world...The view we took of Younghusband's behaviour was sufficiently emphasised to the Indian government and the Indian official world by the character of the decoration which Younghusband received. Why we should go further I am quite unable to understand![85]

Brodrick's purpose is not established. It may be that he wished to read the government of India a public lesson, a warning that Dane must not behave as Younghusband had done. Certain newspapers received advance copies of the Blue-book, with a memorandum from Brodrick pointing to the consistency of the Cabinet's policy and the disobedience of Younghusband. *The Times* was not thus favoured, perhaps because a private letter Brodrick had sent Chirol on publication of the earlier Blue-book had produced an effect very different from that intended.

When *The Times* commented severely on this latest performance, Brodrick asserted that it was unfair to hold him mainly responsible either for the publication or for the policy, a statement which Chirol gathered from another source to be untrue. He rejoined that Younghusband's alleged error of judgment had after all only given the government more than they asked for. Brodrick disclaimed any personal feeling against Younghusband, adding that if only he could have seen him earlier the trouble would probably not have occurred. Of this utterance Chirol failed to seize the meaning.[86] Lee-Warner, one of Brodrick's principal advisers at the India Office, congratulated *The Times* on its protest against 'the most mis-chievous and uncalled-for publication that had ever within his knowledge been issued from a public Department'.[87]

In the Blue-book, some of the more important telegrams were doctored;

the message of unqualified support sent immediately after Younghusband signed the convention was excised; the innumerable telegrams about Russian intrigues were deliberately cut out, so that whole expedition appeared motiveless. Curzon remarked to Godley that it provided 'the most striking evidence that I have yet seen of the almost paralysing influence that Russia exercises over the nerves of British Governments'.[88]

On receiving privately a copy of Brodrick's letter to the editors, Curzon wrote with his habitual candour to ask for an explanation. On the assertion of the home government's unwavering constancy of view, he observed that many of the issues had still been so open in June, 1904, that he had attended the Cabinet to discuss them, and Lansdowne had assured him that nothing prevented the permanent occupation of Chumbi. Brodrick had also told the press that the points in the convention modified by the home government were those most strongly resented by the Tibetans and which would certainly have led to trouble. Whence, Curzon asked, came this evidence?

But the letter raised much wider questions:

> You constantly depict yourself to me as waging battles in the Cabinet or elsewhere on behalf of myself or the Government of India: although I have frequently but unavailingly deprecated the phrase—as implying that the proposals of the Viceroy or the Government of India are so normally unsound as to be incapable of being carried out without a struggle—I have always been grateful for that support...

What became of all this when the same Secretary of State invited the London press to join him in censuring the government of India and the Viceroy, of whom he should be the champion? Might not the Viceroy by the same token tell the Indian papers of his disagreements with the home government and solicit their support?

> I have heard myself called disloyal by members of the government because I dared sometimes to hold an opinion different from theirs and declined to surrender it. But at least I have never disclosed or advertised the fact: nor has a hint of it ever escaped from me into the public press: though I might have been a hero in India half a dozen times over had I allowed the real history to transpire. Is the Secretary of State to be bound by a less rigid rule?

Curzon could not bring himself to believe that Brodrick, 'most loyal of men', could really manufacture a press opposition against the government of India. Nothing he had ever written to Brodrick, he confessed, had cost more sincere pain. It was unwise and undeserved that India should be represented as erring against propriety for disagreeing with the Cabinet, and that Younghusband should be criticised for failing to carry out instructions at a time when it was impossible to do so. Yet it was not at Younghusband, nor at Ampthill, that Campbell-Bannerman and others were directing their shafts:

> Though I was lying ill at home at the time, and had nothing to do either with the indemnity, or the 75 lakhs, or the 75 years, or the visits to Lhasa—it is at me… that the attacks have been aimed: and your conduct has had the result of fixing a public slur upon the Viceroy who, as you know, had no more to do with these particular occurrences than your own valet, and whose advice on the main issue has never wavered from the start, and will assuredly be justified by events.[89]

What Curzon pardonably failed to realise was that Brodrick genuinely believed him to be responsible for Younghusband's actions. The Secretary of State's reply to this letter largely begged the question and did not alter Curzon's view that the gratuitous publication of a censure upon the government of India necessarily compromised its reputation and weakened its authority. 'I doubt not that its effect is thoroughly appreciated at Kabul.'[90]

Such an episode, as Curzon had forewarned Brodrick, must affect their relations. Receiving just afterwards another letter from the Secretary of State, again representing the heavy struggles needed to get the government of India's proposals through the machine at home, Curzon asked whether there might not be something amiss in the temper and knowledge of those shaping these decisions? Brodrick spoke of the Indian views as being those of one man; Curzon retorted that they were nothing of the kind. The presumption at the Office seemed to be against India's proposals, a complete inversion of the principle on which Indian government was conducted in theory, or, hitherto, in practice:

> I often wonder if your advisers at the India Office desire secretly to drive me to resign: and I have many times been pondering during the past few weeks whether you also contemplate this as a result of one and a half years of our co-operation. If so, I do not think it will be very difficult to attain that end.[91]

After the arrival of Curzon's strong complaints about the proceedings at Kabul and the Blue-book, Godley chided him with allowing emotions to cloud judgment. Some who deserved gratitude were castigated, and the authorities treated in a highly impolitic way. The Viceroy was indignant because he had been overruled 'on a point of diplomacy'; yet 'if your diplomatic treatment of the Amir is not more judicious than that which you apply to the "heads of administration" in and near Whitehall, it is highly probable that H.M. Govt. were right to do as they did'. He recalled their earlier correspondence, when Curzon had said he wanted India to cease to be a dependency and become the greatest member of the Empire. Godley disagreed that Indian independence was desirable; but the authorities in London had a right to ask that the Viceroy's attitude should resemble that prescribed for the Amir, strong, friendly and independent. Let the Viceroy be strong by all means, and independent if he could manage it, but let him also be friendly. Pains should be taken to conciliate Ministers, who would then be much happier; and Curzon would have a far better chance of receiving justice. Godley knew well that no one could speak or write more charmingly and irresistibly than Curzon, when he chose. He asked that this gift be now exercised.[92]

Curzon took this, wrongly it appears,[93] to be a complaint against expressions used in his private letters to Godley. He denied writing words calculated to wound, though he had certainly attacked policies. He had tried to place himself in the position of the home government, very likely without success. Would Godley imagine the position of a Viceroy beginning his second term, who found his authority lowered by the Blue-book, subjected to the Afghan experience and simultaneously plunged against his will into the military question, which might compel resignation; all this happening without sympathy or support from superiors at home, who did not seem to realise the dimensions of the problem or understand the Indian Government's point of view:

> Fancy yourself further at such a moment racked with constant pain and continually discharging business (as your present correspondent is now doing) from bed. Finally depict yourself overwhelmed at the same juncture with torrents of abuse and persecution from the native community whom you had toiled so hard and sacrificed so much of your leisure and health to serve.
>
> Perhaps, my dear Godley, philosopher as you are, a cry of human pain and bitterness might have been wrung from you at such a moment; and you would have felt badly had an almost contemptuous rebuke come to you from six thousand miles across the sea.[94]

SEVEN

The Military Department

THE ASSERTION that in 1904 Curzon left England knowing the Cabinet's view on Indian military administration to clash with his own[1] is unfounded. His opinions had been set out in the memorandum circulated to them on 2 November, and expressed personally to the Prime Minister and Brodrick, both of whom had been asked not to bring the question forward. Balfour evidently had a strong penchant for Kitchener, and had given Curzon in writing a very broad hint that the C-in-C's popularity and prestige must affect the issue. Curzon imagined, correctly, that the Cabinet had not even begun to consider the question; he also presumed, quite wrongly, that they would not overrule the government of India on a question of its own constitution.

In accordance with the procedure Curzon had suggested, the subject was put before the government of India. Brodrick's despatch begged the question from the start by implying that the failure of India to provide for mobilisation on a scale sufficient to meet a European enemy was attributable to 'dual control'. He did not conceal from Curzon that he was privately informed about Kitchener's proceedings, though neither at this nor at any later stage did he reveal the link through Lady Salisbury. The C-in-C, he wrote, on 1 December was

> disturbed in his mind as to his present position. I have not encouraged him in the ultimatums which he is developing a disposition to send. At the same time the idea of his reorganisation of the Indian Army has evidently caught on tremendously with the press and people in this country, and he could not well be in a stronger position for a battle as to his rights if he decides to embark on it.[2]

On the first day of his second term, without awaiting the despatch, Curzon set the machine in motion. The C-in-C, who explained that personal considerations, by which he had never been animated, should be excluded,[3] supposed momentarily that he might carry Curzon on the merits: 'my case' he wrote to Lady Salisbury, 'is an extremely strong one

and George N. does not much like to be on the losing side.'[4] Kitchener did
not, however, have to rely entirely upon the intrinsic strength of his argument. His threats of resignation had produced a considerable effect at home.[5]
Roberts, transmitting them to the Prime Minister, advised that Kitchener
knew little or nothing about the feelings and history of the Indian Army;
that not even Kitchener, with exceptional ability and powers of work,
could fill both posts in India; and that no officer likely to succeed him could
hope to do it.[6]

On 28 December Brodrick telegraphed to ask whether the government
of India could reply to the despatch in time for a commission from home to
begin work before the hot weather, 'because it appears, from indications
that have reached me from various quarters, that Lord Kitchener is becoming
increasingly restless.'[7] This message surprised Curzon, with whom the
C-in-C had spent Christmas. In some hours of talk on military subjects,
the question had not even been mentioned. Kitchener had already had the
papers a fortnight and had submitted nothing.

The Military Member would probably require at least as long to make
his reply; then each of the six civilian members of Council must note, the
Council discuss the issue and the despatch be framed. It could hardly leave
India before the end of February; nor, Curzon told Brodrick, would undue
haste 'be beneficial to the side to which I understand you to incline'. On the
same day, Kitchener wrote to Lady Salisbury: 'If you see St J.[ohn] please
tell him I am very grateful for the way he has backed me up. I do not write
to tell him so as C. might object.'[8]

Brodrick replied that he and the Prime Minister were convinced of
Kitchener's determination 'to make a test question of something before
long'. If no inquiry from home could begin until the end of 1905, 'he will
think his opportunity has come to make a crisis, and to appeal to public
opinion here.'[9] The Secretary of State had already begun to search for
members of this commission. Godley and Roberts declined at once, a fact
which did not prevent Brodrick from stating later that they had accepted.[10]
They too pointed out that in practice the business could not be put through
before the hot weather began, Godley hoping that Curzon would leave
India in the spring.[11]

Brodrick, deeply impressed by the threat of Kitchener's early resignation,
had already invited Roberts to tell Kitchener privately that it was intended,
should the view of the government of India go against him, to appoint a
small commission at once.[12] The Secretary of State pressed Curzon to
accelerate the procedure, so that the gist of the reply could be telegraphed
home early in February. If it should not reach London until mid-March,

and be unfavourable to Kitchener, no inquiry could be held in India before November by any commission sent from home; in which case either the decision must be made in London or Kitchener's resignation 'which will certainly be tendered' be accepted. Hamilton would be willing to go to India in March, but must return in April. Alternative choices were unlikely to be so favourable: 'My mind is more open than the Prime Minister's, and I am therefore especially anxious that the inquiry should be held by Lord George Hamilton.'[13]

Curzon again explained the difficulties. Kitchener's minute had not reached the Military Department until 5 January. Elles was at work upon his reply. It would not be fair to create the impression that the Cabinet were acting upon Indian views, which had not even been formulated. If the home government wished to appoint a commission at once, they should do so on their own responsibility. Any orders would be loyally obeyed.[14] Brodrick seemed to accept this suggestion, but the proposal fell through when Lansdowne told Hamilton about the Indian climate.[15]

Brodrick informed Curzon that Lord George had absolutely refused to go out after the beginning of February. Hamilton, however, wrote to say that his view about the procedure tallied with the Viceroy's. He had been told that the inquiry would last a fortnight, but on seeing the telegrams, had realised that the matter was not yet ripe. He could not remain in India until the autumn. If the question were still unsettled, he would go out then, but by the autumn much might happen:

> The government are utterly discredited in the constituencies, and a smash may come at any moment. Balfour's success in keeping his majority together has been purchased by the loss of character and reputation. He is looked upon as a clever verbal conjurer without conviction or principle.[16]

Although Brodrick's private letters about the commission were out of date by the time of receipt, they contain material of interest. He indicated clearly that information was flowing freely along unofficial channels by every mail. He wished, or so he wrote, to keep Kitchener but not to concede what was unreasonable. The opinion of an independent and expert committee 'would, if unfavourable to Lord Kitchener, make the action he proposed difficult to sustain and detrimental to his future'. Lord George valued Curzon's opinions immensely and had been strongly opposed to undue concentration of power in the C-in-C at home; quite justifiably, Brodrick congratulated himself on persuading Hamilton, 'a masterpiece from your standpoint'. The British public, largely forgetting other soldiers, were 'almost ready to swear to almost anything Kitchener says. This will not last, but in any conflict it would have a most serious effect.'[17]

The timetable suggested would in any event have been impossible. For Hamilton and his colleagues to master the papers, interrogate the officials, investigate the details of departmental procedure and arrive at conclusions in less than a month was out of the question, especially in March when the budget engrossed the attention of everyone. Curzon told Brodrick that he would be content for the question to be judged at home, on its merits:

> Please do not think that I am treating you as a partisan in the matter, for I know full well that you have kept your mind open, and that you are, so to speak, the Chairman of the Jury whom we are about to address. But I think you will admit that the impression generally conveyed by your letters is that, whatever opinions you may ultimately form, the pressure exerted by Kitchener will be so great that, irrespective of the merits, you will be forced to yield to it.[18]

Had Curzon resumed his post in October, 1904, the commission would no doubt have visited India in the following spring. It was a disaster for him that it did not, for Hamilton would almost certainly have reported in a sense hostile to Kitchener's plan. Brodrick accused Curzon later in 1905, and again in his memoirs, of deliberately delaying the government of India's despatch and of proposing that the commission should travel out in May.[19] Both charges are false.

*   *   *   *

Curzon had originally intended to leave India for good during the spring of 1905, by which time most of the outstanding reforms should have taken effect. When he did not reach Calcutta until mid-December instead of early October, that course was hardly feasible. Once the talks at Kabul reached deadlock, Curzon dismissed the notion of early departure. 'I could not run away' he wrote to Balfour, 'or be suspected of running away at such a time.'[20] Moreover, to his amazement and joy, the doctors allowed Lady Curzon to travel again to India.

The other factor which might have determined the decision was the political situation at home, but it held little to attract Curzon. He had no desire to be a minister for a few months in a discredited Cabinet, and anyway felt the need for a good rest. The reports reaching him could not be called alluring.[21] Arnold-Forster's reforms had broken down, and his department was reported to be a greater administrative shambles than ever. There was in his ward, said an inmate of a workhouse, 'that amount of disorder, discomfort, horse-play, and foul language a-going on all day, that we all calls it the War Office.'[22]

George Wyndham had to resign his office in painful circumstances, after a controversy described by Alfred Lyttelton as 'not cricket'. This, Arnold-Forster observed mirthlessly, was the worst state of affairs known to a Lyttelton. Balfour had thought that the government might well be beaten in Parliament during February. Early on 8 March, the Cabinet agreed that should they be defeated that night on the tariff question, resignation would follow at once. Only the belated decision of the Free Food Conservatives saved the day; but the fall could not be long postponed. Not until 16 March did Balfour judge that he might survive Easter.[23] These were the circumstances of the government having to face the Indian military question and the threatened resignation of the most celebrated living soldier.

★   ★   ★   ★

The division of duties between the C-in-C and Military Member in India resembled that between the General Staff and the War Office in most European countries. It rested upon a separation of training and planning for war, and supply. The C-in-C was responsible for the personnel of the Army—for appointments, promotion, discipline, intelligence, distribution of troops, manœuvres, the conduct of war; the Military Member for army finance, contracts, ordnance, stores, clothing and the manufacture of a whole range of warlike stores. The C-in-C, alone with the Viceroy and the Governors of Madras and Bombay, was addressed as 'Your Excellency'. He drew the same pay as the head of an administration, but was not, in the legal or constitutional sense, head of the army in India. That was the function of the Governor-General in Council, whom the Military Member represented by delegated authority in those matters which were not collectively decided by the Council. For the manner in which this power was exercised he was responsible to all his colleagues on the Council, including the C-in-C. The Military Member, then, provided a second military opinion; but he also advised on broader grounds. Most military proposals in British India carried political and financial overtones; the possibility of unrest or even mutiny, the vital importance of consulting religious, historical or caste scruples, the growing criticism in the Indian press of extravagant military expenditure. Army Headquarters normally possessed no particular motive for economy and military spending was by far the largest item in the budget.

The special circumstances of India must be borne in mind when comparisons between British and Indian practice are attempted. No doubt the Viceroy's Council fulfilled the functions of a Cabinet in the sense of bringing together the responsible heads of department and producing a decision at the highest level; but the Honourable Members were not ministers, with an independent political standing or a following in the press. Nor was the Secretary of State for War in England normally a soldier. The C-in-C at home, before his post was abolished in 1904, could travel from one end of the country to the other in a day and was commanding an army of his own countrymen. The C-in-C in India, if he was to know his officers and men, must spend some months of the year on tour and was commanding troops whose customs, religions and language he might not understand in the least.

Kitchener seems to have imagined that he was proposing an adaptation to Indian conditions of the Army Council. The crucial difference was that the Council administered, but did not command, the British Army. Kitchener wished to do both, the C-in-C alone representing this concentration of powers on the Viceroy's Council. The members of the military council he proposed to set up would have no vote or right of dissent. The Secretary to the government of India in the Military Department would lose the right of free and independent access to the Viceroy. In contradiction of some earlier proposals, and of his assurances of six months before, Kitchener demanded the suppression of the Military Membership of Council. No real distinction, he contended, could be drawn between executive and administrative functions: 'In an Army maintained for war, the true executive functions and responsibility of a Commander-in-Chief consist in the careful administration of its fighting power in all its branches and services.'

A good deal of Kitchener's case rested upon the supposed imminence of the Russian menace. A part of his minute deserves quotation as a classic expression of that conviction which weighed so heavily with the Defence Committee and especially with Balfour:

> Slowly but surely the deserts of Central Asia, which were once believed to be an impenetrable barrier, have been crossed by a great European Power. They are now spanned by railways which have only one possible significance; and we have every indication that our Northern neighbour is pushing forward her preparations for the contest in which we shall have to fight for our existence...

The C-in-C asserted that the Military Member was 'really omnipotent in military affairs', having 'power to interfere with the decisions of the Commander-in-Chief or to prevent his wishes being carried out even in questions of discipline and training'.

He repeated previous complaints of dilatory procedure and gratuitous interference, pointing especially to the failure to provide adequate transport even for the field army of four divisions. Some charges in this minute, which reached Elles and Curzon on 5 January, broke down at once. Kitchener alleged that despatches were drafted and telegrams sent without reference to the C-in-C; but all important despatches went to him in first draft, as did the draft of every important telegram, unless it expressed his stated views. Army Headquarters were shown not to be blameless in delaying the despatch of business; files had frequently remained there six or nine months, and one case at least had been with the Quartermaster's department for three years. Of 1,559 proposals put forward by Army HQ in Kitchener's first two and a half years, 96 were refused by the Military Department alone, 15 by the Military and Finance Departments together, 11 by the Viceroy in Council. 1,260 were accepted. Three instances of faulty co-ordination, cited by Kitchener as justifying a change of system, would not bear investigation: in one, Kitchener's staff were shown to be guilty of slackness and in another he had failed to consult the Director-General of Ordnance. Ampthill, during whose Viceroyalty some of these supposed obstructions had occurred, had no hesitation in saying that Kitchener had misrepresented the facts.[24]

Replying on 24 January, Elles pointed to a considerable number of such misstatements. Not the least telling passage was his refutation of the charge that the Military Department could not bring to bear the enlightened and fresh experience possessed by Army HQ. As it happened, Kitchener had made no serious attempt to introduce officers of Indian experience into his own staff, upon which there was in 1905 only one officer of the Indian Army who had ever commanded a regiment, let alone a division or an army. In the Military Department, none of the five senior officers had done less than 13 years' regimental duty, two had done 23 and 24 years, all had attended Staff College and four had served in Army HQ itself.

For the admitted fact that the Army was not fully equipped for mobilisation, which Brodrick had attributed to dual control, the Military Department, Elles argued, was not to blame. The responsibility lay with the whole government, and even more, with the British government. In 1896, on the proposal of the Military Member, Elgin's Council had told Hamilton that until re-equipment of certain field divisions was undertaken, the Indian field army was not ready for war. The absence of a proper transport organisation had been clearly shown in the Chitral expedition of 1895. It was understood that it would be useless to place in the field an army of more than four divisions until a transport service for those divisions was provided. Between 1894 and 1900, the government of India had been able to spend on special military needs less than one-sixth of the sum it was allotting in 1905. In 1899, Curzon and his colleagues, at the instance of Collen, had proposed re-equipment on a very large scale. Only a part of their programme had been sanctioned in London. Collen returned to the charge in 1900, but only about one in three of his proposals was authorised. Again he and Palmer had recorded their dissatisfaction with the mobility and efficiency of the Indian Army. Those were the years of the famine. Nevertheless, military spending in Curzon's time rose by nearly 40% to £20,757,032 in 1905-6, with further heavy expenditure in prospect as Kitchener's redistribution scheme was implemented.[25]

After a conversation early in the new year, Curzon reported to Brodrick that the C-in-C showed no sign of being in a hurry or of annoyance at delay. Nor did he seem 'at present to be vexed or mortified as to his own position. On the contrary, he talks in rather triumphant tones about all that he has accomplished and the success with which he has wheeled his various victims into line.'[26]

Though frequent letters and telegrams from Brodrick described Kitchener as resolved to leave unless an inquiry began promptly, another long meeting failed to reveal, to Curzon at least, any evidence of such determination. It is almost certain that for the moment Curzon believed Kitchener's letters to Roberts to be the sole source of Brodrick's information; and also that Kitchener was being careful not to reveal too much of his intentions to Curzon. At this interview the Viceroy stated that he could not support the indictment against the Military Department. Kitchener, according to his own accounts, said he felt it his duty to resign if overruled, which Curzon accepted as the natural consequence:

> He was quite nice about it [wrote Kitchener to Hatfield] and said politely that he would not have opposed the change I recommended had he any certainty that I would remain on...
>
> So I am preparing to pack up. I shall leave India with considerable regret...
>
> I can, however, quite see Curzon's side of the question. The change I propose would certainly make it more difficult for him to interfere in every day military affairs, and thus it possibly touches in some small details the Viceregal prerogative. Perish the Empire sooner than allow such sacrilege to be perpetrated.[27]

Brodrick having just telegraphed again, Curzon was emphatically assured by Kitchener that nothing he had written justified Roberts's impression and that he was in no state of mental agitation.[28] In a letter of the following day, 20 January, the Secretary of State confessed that he was trying to extricate himself from a position of great difficulty. Balfour had declared that he would not 'go to war with Russia with the present divided system of control...' The Viceroy's account of Kitchener's temper contrasted strangely with the letters written by him ever since the resignation of September. Brodrick stated that he had received these opinions 'first-hand' and did not believe that Kitchener would wait until 1906 'to have affairs placed in some respects on a different footing'. This was not, Brodrick stressed,

> a contest between your views and my own; your mind is made up, while mine is open. All I am endeavouring to do is to secure that we shall not lose our Commander-in-Chief on a point on which he has a full right to be satisfied and on which, if trouble should ensue, he will have every support from the public, when they realise that he put forward his complaint in June, 1904, resigned in September, 1904, and could get no inquiry appointed by the Government at home, despite all promises, until say November of 1905.[29]

This assurance of impartiality, contrasting strangely with Balfour's earlier assertion that Brodrick strongly favoured abolition of the existing system,[30] was accepted by Curzon. Meanwhile, Kitchener sustained his private pressure week by week. The Council, he agreed, must discuss the case, though their decision was a foregone conclusion, 'as they cannot afford to go against the Viceroy'. He took care to inform Sir G. Clarke that he would leave if he did not get his way. Curzon had accepted, he told Roberts, 'that on this question I resign and has so arranged that I shall be free in May next'.[31]

These letters provided reinforcement to a step Kitchener had taken earlier in the month. Before his minute on the military system had reached Curzon or Elles, it was on its way to London. Godley, already predisposed in favour of Kitchener's view, found the paper excellent; Brodrick was much impressed. General Stedman, Military Secretary at the India Office, from whom both received it, professed himself wholly convinced. Clarke, to whom Kitchener sent the paper, was already on his side.[32] As Godley later admitted to Ampthill, those who read the note were converted before they heard the other side. Curzon, of course, knew nothing of the uses to which this supposedly secret document was being put, though he did learn from Brodrick that Kitchener was corresponding with Stedman.[33]

Late in January, it became known that the C-in-C was asking Generals holding Indian commands for their opinions of his minute. When Curzon explained that he thought this procedure irregular, since the question concerned no one but the government of India at this stage, Kitchener said he had asked Roberts whether, if the favourable opinion of Indian Generals were obtained, his opposition to the abolition of the Military Department would be withdrawn. Did not the difficulty arise, the Viceroy then inquired, from this correspondence with Roberts, not a member of the government but possessing an influence which was the avowed reason for wishing to obtain his support? Having asked to see the Generals' views, Curzon learned that Kitchener had not in the least meant to imply that he was collecting these opinions for Roberts. They were requested 'quite privately and were for myself alone, and were not intended for anyone else'.[34] In fact, Kitchener had sent them in the previous week to Lady Salisbury, whom he begged to warn everyone of the privacy of his letters. 'St J[ohn] is the one I am afraid of as he may without intending it make my position most uncomfortable by an indiscreet reference in his letters to Curzon.'[35]

The Viceroy did not for a minute believe Kitchener's assurance. The opinions of the Generals, he wrote to Brodrick, had been sought to influence others' judgment. Roberts was consulted by the home government, sending to Kitchener minutes not shown to the Viceroy and soliciting information; Kitchener was prepared to act behind the back of his colleagues in order, through Roberts, to persuade the Prime Minister, Secretary of State and Cabinet. Curzon understood their desire not to have a row with the C-in-C:

> No one recognises more clearly than myself the sort of artificial prestige that attaches to a great soldier or the degree of the pressure that he is in a position to apply. But do not let a full recognition of this fact tempt the authorities at home into an attitude of positive unfairness to my colleagues and myself, and above all pray remember that, as Secretary of State, it is your duty to see that justice is rendered not to a single one of us, but to the entire body.[36]

A few days after this episode, Curzon heard that Kitchener had sent to London the views of Generals on another subject. Opinion in London, wrote Brodrick, was 'all the other way, and I know only too well the methods by which Kitchener impressed his personality on these proposals'.[37]

★   ★   ★   ★

In his minute dated 6 February, Curzon admitted the increasing gravity of the position to the North-West, but refused to argue the abstract merits and demerits of the military administration of India. He had little difficulty in showing that much of Kitchener's account was inaccurate, a proposition which he illustrated from the C-in-C's own experience in India. Noting by junior officers on proposals emanating from the C-in-C had been stopped; the issue of all Indian Army orders, and executive command of the supply and transport corps, had been transferred to him. Numerous other steps had been taken to help forward his reforms. The redistribution of the Army, and its massive rearmament, constituted by far the largest military measure undertaken in India since 1857. All this scarcely suggested that Kitchener had been hampered at every turn.

A Viceroy did not in practice consult only the Military Member or C-in-C. On all important questions, the views of both were taken in writing. If they disagreed, the Viceroy conferred with them together. The C-in-C always had independent access to him; if dissatisfied with the action of the Military Department, he could at any time bring any subject to the Council or insist that it be referred at once to the Viceroy; if overruled he had the right to record his dissent and bring it to the attention of the Secretary of State. In brief, Curzon refused to accept as a recognisable version of the truth the bald assertion that the Military Member was 'really omnipotent in military affairs'. Should the Military Membership be abolished, on the other hand, the C-in-C would become the initiator and sole judge of policy, limited only by a financial sanction rendered less effective in the absence of expert military advice.

Kitchener proposed that in time of war the C-in-C, the Chief of the General Staff, and the Quartermaster-General should all take the field. This would leave as military adviser to the government of India an acting C-in-C, whose only high-ranking colleague would be the Director-General of Ordnance. How, Curzon asked, would the Viceroy get military advice when the C-in-C was on tour or commanding the army in war? An acting C-in-C could be no real substitute, might disagree with his superior in the field and would lack prestige:

> In such a case the military authority and competence of [the] Government would be perilously impaired, and in war as in peace the supreme power would presently be found in the possession of the real Commander-in-Chief.

Already the C-in-C had charge of training, housing, discipline, inspection, movements and other large areas of the army's activities. He should know every division and brigade, should be in personal touch with the officers. He was also head of the Intelligence Department and a member of Council. These duties were more than enough for one man. That he should also control the administrative and spending departments, correspondence with other departments, preparation of military budgets and the mass of administrative routine was unpractical. If anyone could work such a system it would be Kitchener; but

> administrative systems are not constructed to test exceptional men, but to be worked by average men. If the proposal of the Commander-in-Chief were to be accepted, it is conceivable that as long as he remained in India it might enjoy a temporary vitality. I hazard the confident prediction that it would not long survive his departure.

This was the first significant question, Curzon noted, on which he had dissented from Kitchener's view. He would willingly consider any reasonable reform, but could not support the abolition of the existing system on a single unsupported indictment. The file then passed to other members of Council, amongst whom Sir D. Ibbetson contributed the most interesting observations. He thought that two main elements would contribute to establish the despotism he feared. First, the highly technical nature of most military matters made it difficult for laymen to exercise effective control. Dealing with revenue questions, he had often felt embarrassed when inviting the Viceroy to take a certain line; for the issues were so complicated, and depended so largely on conditions peculiar to India, that no one but an expert could form an independent judgment. In such instances, he had suggested that the Viceroy should consult another expert, not from unwillingness to accept responsibility but because the Viceroy was otherwise placed in an awkward position. Second, the vital importance of military questions lent special force to military advice. The Council might overrule him on a point of revenue policy without apprehending disaster, even if he were right; but if the sole military adviser, responsible for the army on which the security of the British Empire rested, said that certain proposals were vital, they could hardly be turned down.[38]

The other colleagues all noted in a sense hostile to Kitchener's proposal, but it is hard to resist the impression that they were wasting their time. Forwarding a copy of his minute to Lady Salisbury early in January, Kitchener had asked her to obtain the Prime Minister's opinion, so that any suggestions he might make could be incorporated during the discussions.[39] This is a good illustration of the significance of the connexion; and on 14 February Balfour telegraphed in cypher:

> I think your paper…[group omitted by cypherer] and am unable to see what answer can be made to it[40]

Kitchener was delighted. 'Please thank A.J.B. for his very kind message' he wrote to Lady Salisbury. 'It was a great relief to me to feel that he approved of the course I have taken.' The tone of this letter is markedly more confident. Kitchener seems to have felt, rightly as it transpired, that he had the game in his hands. He did not intend, on seeing the views of his colleagues, to 'enter into any controversy here' but would send home some notes: 'these may be useful to St J[ohn].'[41] Kitchener acknowledged the good fortune which had made Marker Private Secretary to Arnold-Forster at the War Office. Messages could thus be transmitted in complete safety, or so Kitchener imagined; and believing that Curzon would have nobbled them, he expressed relief that no commission should be coming out. 'As long as I am backed at home,' he wrote to Marker, 'I have no fear of the ultimate result.'[42]

On 21 and 22 February *The Standard* carried articles describing Kitchener's redistribution scheme, which was an official secret, and alleging that he was hampered at every turn by Indian worship of red tape and by the malignant opposition of the Military Department. Curzon, on tour in Assam, tele-graphed that since the scheme had met with generous support from the government of India at every turn, and since statements to the contrary seemed calculated to prejudge the issue of military administration, he pro-posed to issue an official denial. The C-in-C replied that he was 'very much annoyed' at the articles, which he thought 'most unfortunate' but unworthy of contradiction.[43] Brodrick said that since they had attracted no attention, there was no need to act.

Kitchener admitted that a good many people at home were aware of his views, 'but as you know I have taken up the question on larger lines than any question of delay in carrying out my proposals...' Though Curzon did not yet realise it, Kitchener himself was the source of *The Standard*'s inspira-tion in the previous month he had arranged with the Editor, Mr H. A. Gwynne, that Major Marker would show him the minute of 1 January. Gwynne had written 'a very nice letter promising the support of the Standard'.[44]

*　　*　　*　　*

Kitchener was not impressed by his colleagues' opinions. The remarks of Elles seemed 'pretty personal'; which was all to the good, 'as it is better it should come from him without any cause'. Curzon's note he thought able, but lacking in new arguments 'and the Council looking out for Lt. Gover-norships follow like sheep the lead given by H.E.'[45] On the night before the case came to Council, Curzon talked long with the C-in-C, admitting openly that he had the support of the Prime Minister and other high authorities in London and that owing to his peculiar prestige the chances of persuading the jury were in any case very high. It appeared to Curzon that Kitchener had now given up this hope. Even his reputation could not be improved by a demonstration that he had made unfounded charges, without backing among his colleagues. Kitchener knew that although the Cabinet seemed to entertain little respect for Indian views on foreign policy, it would be unprecedented to overrule their colleagues in India in a matter of this kind: 'In fact' Curzon wrote to Brodrick, 'he sees that it is not impossible that the home Government might in such a case suddenly find themselves with no Government of India at all, and only a Commander-in-Chief, a situation which would also be without precedent.'

At the Council on 10 March, Kitchener found himself in a minority of one. He read out a curt expression of regret that his colleagues disagreed, and refused to debate the issue further. Elles then asked whether he had the others' support. Each member said that in his view Kitchener's allegations had collapsed, that Elles's vindication was complete and that the Council should associate itself wholeheartedly with him.[46] Curzon defended the Military Member. 'He was so eloquent' commented Kitchener, 'that he made us all see a sort of halo appear round Elles's head through which his few remaining hairs protruded.' Incredibly, Kitchener thought the case had gone well for him.[47] He drew up a minute of dissent, asserting baldly that his arguments remained 'uncontroverted and...I believe, incontrovertible'. The question was one of vital importance to the Empire at large. While its resources would be placed at the disposal of India 'in the only great war on land in which we are likely to be engaged' that war would be fought under the Indian military system. There was no argument to which the Cabinet was more susceptible.

Kitchener also stated Elles to have shown that the power of the Governor-General in Council was delegated to the Military Member personally and could be exercised by him without reference to the Council or the Viceroy; that he could therefore override the views of the C-in-C, even in executive functions and command; and that the Military Member exercised these powers according to circumstances and to his own inclination. Curzon pointed out that none of these assertions was true. Should Kitchener insist on recording them, the other members of Council must contradict him. The C-in-C immediately withdrew,[48] and the despatch, drafted by Curzon and stiffened at various points by his colleagues, was sent on 23 March.

Personal relations between Viceroy and C-in-C remained harmonious, although Curzon told Kitchener that he should not try to sway the decision by threatening resignation. No doubt fortified by the knowledge of Balfour's support, the C-in-C retorted that the scales would be balanced if the Viceroy also threatened to resign.[49] Curzon made a suggestion for resolving the difficulty. 'Elles's term' he said to Kitchener, 'is drawing towards its close. He has stated that he would not be unwilling to go. What would you say if the government were to select as his successor a Military Member with whom you could work and who was imbued with your own ideas? Could you work with him?'

If Curzon's record is accurate, Kitchener replied, 'Oh, certainly,' failing to realise for the moment that he had given away his case against the Department. He then said he would like time for reflection. After ten days, he replied that he did not think Curzon's plan would succeed. Duplication of work would continue: 'I do not think I should be giving you a perfectly loyal opinion if I said otherwise. I can, however, assure you that, if the decision of the government at home is against my proposals, I will not resign without the most careful consideration of all the circumstances.'

This, as Curzon remarked, was a refusal, but not a very downright one.[50] It came immediately after the arrival of yet another disturbing letter from Brodrick. Lord Roberts had indicated that unless Kitchener were given some satisfaction shortly, he would resign; Brodrick had himself seen a letter in which the C-in-C gave the date of his probable return to England; and he accused Curzon of entirely failing to discover 'what is apparent to those who receive letters from him'. Curzon at once gave these extracts verbatim to Kitchener, pointing out that they were in flat contradiction of the C-in-C's own assurances to himself, and that the constant repetition of these views by Brodrick placed him as Viceroy in a difficult position.[51]

Kitchener must have been hard put to it to find a suitable reply, for he was writing of resignation almost every week. However, he referred to a conversation in January, when he had said that he would wait until the spring. He had told Roberts on 26 January that if the decision went against him, he would probably leave India in May. (In fact, that letter said Curzon had arranged for him to be free in May. See above, p. 185.) The object, he now explained solemnly, was that Roberts should be prepared when the government consulted him about a successor. Brodrick might be told he would wait patiently for a decision in May.[52]

After the despatch had gone to London, Curzon sent to the Prime Minister on 30 March a long and significant letter to be read in conjunction with it. He asked Balfour to believe that this was not a mere matter of departmental reform, for the issue affected the control vested by Statute in the government of India over military affairs. Kitchener was usually supposed to be a strong man, capable of impressing his opinions upon others, and the tendency of civilians was to accept the dicta of great soldiers on military affairs. How was it that the Council, which had backed ungrudgingly his schemes of reorganisation, and Curzon himself, who had strongly urged his appointment, should all decide his proposals to be dangerous? Was there anything in Elles which should make them turn to him as military adviser?

Why should I, who have been Viceroy for the longest period for half a century, feel so strongly on the matter that I could not consent to remain head of the administration if what I regard as a fundamental principle of the administration were destroyed? Why should Ampthill, who went up to Simla to act for me with a perfectly open mind and who might have been supposed likely to fall under the influence of his most powerful counsellor, write to me... in the following terms:—

'Even during my brief time at Simla the Military Department saved us from several dangerous mistakes which with Lord Kitchener as the sole military adviser of the government we should neither have seen nor been able to avert and I thus received practical proof that the Military Department is essential to the proper administration of the Army in India...'

Curzon recounted Kitchener's various attempts to destroy the Military Department, the persistency and pettiness of his campaign, his discourtesy towards Elles: 'It is simply because Kitchener cannot brook that his schemes (which I can assure you are not uncommonly framed in the most startling ignorance of Indian conditions with which his subordinate officers have not the courage to acquaint him) should be criticised and their flaws sometimes exposed by a General officer of inferior prestige and rank.'

The Viceroy appealed for the dispassionate consideration to which government of India were entitled. Should the home government overrule them, 'I could not accept so striking a proof of want of confidence in the government which I have now administered for over six years.' He regretted that Kitchener had been allowed to presume upon his prestige, but was keen to keep him. Telling Balfour of the recent proposal that Elles be replaced by an officer acceptable to Kitchener, and of his eventual refusal, Curzon judged that the C-in-C expected the decision to go against him. If this were so, and if some similar suggestion could be repeated, Curzon thought he could be persuaded to stay.[53]

Balfour returned neither acknowledgment nor reply. Not until he returned to England did Curzon discover that he had either failed to read the letter, or had completely forgotten it.[54] A very different reception awaited Kitchener's communications. Before Curzon wrote to Balfour, the C-in-C had received 'capital' tidings from Stedman at the India Office;[55] and he had by then taken further steps, in strictest secrecy, to get the decision he craved. On 8 March, two days before that meeting of Council at which he refused to discuss the military question, Kitchener sent to Stedman a commentary upon the views of Elles and Curzon. If he replied to them officially, he argued, 'it would necessarily lead to almost endless further discussion' without being likely to produce any change in their views. Kitchener reiterated that the lack of proper equipment of the field army was directly attributable to the system. 'On the one side we have power without responsibility, and on the other responsibility without power.'

It is needless to describe in detail the 'letter', which consisted of forty typed pages. Some of its statements were obviously untrue, some doubtful; some scored very palpable hits, others were self-contradictory. Elles was accused of deliberate lying and of suppressing documents which would alter the whole case. The argument that a single military adviser could not cope with the business Kitchener rejected. With equal facility he brushed aside the suggestion that the frequent absence of the C-in-C would clog the business. The tone of the letter was generally tendentious, occasionally condescending. 'I leave the Military Member to select either horn of this dilemma which he may prefer.' As the Military Member was completely unaware of the letter, he could hardly select either horn. 'I advocate progress, he opposes it, and we both agree that the present system of administration prevents it.'

The letter then cites the views of Generals, all of whom approved with slightly differing degrees of heartiness. These were the opinions which Kitchener had refused to Curzon in the previous month on the grounds that they were strictly private to himself. Hearing that the question was likely to reach the Cabinet, Kitchener hoped that Brodrick would use some of this material 'so as to ensure the Cabinet not coming to a decision without a correct appreciation of the case from all points of view'.[56]

Kitchener's subordinate, Beauchamp Duff, later explained this procedure by the absurd argument that 'no reasoned minute of dissent by Lord Kitchener stood any chance of transmission and that the attempt to force one through meant nothing but endless delay'.[57] Sending a copy of the letter at once to Lady Salisbury, Kitchener once again foreshadowed resignation if Elles were not got rid of: 'Those at home who would rather I stayed on should I think fully realise this as being final and not blame me if I can stand no more.'[58]

The letter was soon put to good use. It was given to Godley. Another

7

copy was passed by Kitchener to Clarke, who found it 'absolutely un-answerable' and handed it to Esher, who thought likewise. 'I do not think' he wrote immediately to Kitchener, 'that, when the pinch comes, the government will view calmly your departure from India.' Balfour read every word of the letter and was 'very much impressed'.[59]

A little later, Kitchener forwarded further observations to Stedman. He admitted on this occasion that he had been able to achieve some results—in defiance of the system—and that there had been one or two exceptional Cs-in-C and Military Members able to work together. As for the danger of military autocracy, it was a myth and no one knew it better than Curzon, whom he accused of purposely prolonging a dangerous and wasteful system for his own benefit:

> All military power falls nominally into the hands of the Civil Members of Council but actually into those of the Viceroy personally—and when a Viceroy believes, rightly or wrongly, that like Napoleon he combines the highest talent for military administration with genius for civil government such a situation may appear peculiarly advantageous to him. But if this be the object aimed at it could be more cheaply and directly attained by abolishing both the C-in-C and the Military Member and making the Army over technically as well as practically to Civilian control.[60]

* * * *

In mid-April the despatch about military administration reached Brodrick. The considerations which influenced him at this stage may be traced most clearly in the correspondence with Ampthill, now returned to Madras. Having been Viceroy, having seen Kitchener's methods and endured one of his resignations, but free from the personal animus which was believed to inspire Curzon's attitude to Kitchener, he received Brodrick's confidences. Ampthill had already told Godley that if he could only come to India and see the perfunctory manner in which Kitchener did his work and his utter unreasonableness whenever he could not prevail immediately, he would realise how necessary was the control of the Military Department:

> The real truth is that Lord Kitchener gets his own way far too much, as there is hardly a soldier who will dare to express an opinion contrary to his; Lord Kitchener's own Staff admit this in moments of confidence, as also their own fear of disagreeing with their Chief.[61]

Brodrick assured Ampthill, as he had assured Curzon, of his open mind, 'although Curzon has done all he can to prejudice it by the vehemence of his invectives against us for not taking his opinion or for wishing to investigate Kitchener's grievance.'

This sentence is of some note, as revealing Brodrick's state of mind. Perhaps it reflects his irritation that the plan for a commission had fallen through. The fairness of the remark can be judged only by those who have read all the telegrams and letters, but it hardly seems a balanced account of Curzon's attitude. After all, he had written to Brodrick weekly for three months about each stage of the business, had recognised the weight which must attach to Kitchener's opinion and had himself proposed the procedure, accepted by Balfour and Brodrick, for investigating the grievance. Brodrick stated that he had heard 'through a private source' that the military question had passed Council, in a sense unfavourable to Kitchener. He understood, doubtless from the same source, that Curzon would not let Kitchener see the minutes written in reply to his.[62] Ampthill, who must have been astounded that any Secretary of State could credit such a story, explained patiently the system by which the government of India's business was done. He added that Kitchener disliked papers and detail, worked in a slipshod way, was no genius and should be allowed to go.[63]

Brodrick acknowledged that unless an Indian officer could be given a position of prominence and 'semi-independence' he could not see what check could be kept on an inexperienced C-in-C under a new Viceroy. Yet if the system were good, why was it agreed that the Indian Army needed an immediate expenditure of £15m and that there was a shortage of stores, supply and transport, a situation which he described simply as 'the result of dual control'?[64]

The real answers were simple enough; that the money had not previously been available, that the Indian Army had not been shaped for war against Russia, that the home government had several times refused India's requests to re-equip and that the proposal to increase the field army by reducing garrisons had not been conceived by Kitchener, but by Curzon and Palmer. At no stage do Brodrick, Godley, Esher and Balfour seem to have grasped these facts. Ampthill pointedly invited Brodrick to ask his Council why, when they were Lieutenants-Governor and members of the Viceroy's Council, the police and education were not reformed? They would not reply, he surmised, that in their day the government of India was rotten. The Cabinet at home was increasing its military spending each year. Was that because the system of government had previously been faulty? Because new equipment, training and methods of administration were being introduced, the civilian Secretary for War and the Cabinet were not going to be abolished? The friction and delay of which Kitchener complained 'so far as they exist are but the wholesome application of the brake to his impetuous progress. A Commander-in-Chief of a different temperament would find nothing to chafe at in the action of the Military Department.'[65]

On another occasion, Ampthill told the Secretary of State that he had never been able to make Kitchener understand the constitutional practice and principle. To his 'narrow comprehension' nothing was apparent except the fact that a soldier junior in rank was able to criticise his proposals, though the rank of the Military Member was not germane to the real question. The highest officers of the British Army did not object to the control of Mr Brodrick, a Yeomanry Major?[66] In a letter which crossed this in the post, Brodrick admitted that 'all you say of Kitchener is true, but you will never induce people here to believe that a dual system, in which the junior gives orders to the senior, is a correct one'.

Here, Ampthill answered, was 'a lamentable misconception'. Once again he explained the main elements of the question, protesting, not for the first time, that Brodrick's constant references to the 'Kitchener-Elles business' obscured the issue. He told the Secretary of State to dismiss from his mind the belief that Curzon's attitude was dictated by *amour propre* or by anything but a desire for the good government of India.[67] Learning that Brodrick had deliberately kept Curzon in the dark about the progress of the military question in London, Ampthill begged that he should write frankly to the Viceroy. Brodrick's explanation — 'he values nothing on these subjects except complete subservience to his views' — Ampthill rejected:

> There is nothing which he resents more than reticence in others. He expects the same candour which he himself metes out, and prefers open disagreement to silent hostility.[68]

One more exchange in this running battle of views may be cited here. There was a strong feeling, wrote Brodrick in mid-May, that though financial and political restraints should be imposed on the C-in-C, his advice 'on purely military matters' should not be checked by 'another soldier of less eminence'. Ampthill's reply recalled an instance during his Viceroyalty, when Kitchener had suddenly pronounced that since Indian followers were not to be trusted on active service, ammunition mules should be led by soldiers. The Staff at HQ, 'in a chorus of unthinking hero-worship,' applauded. The government of India were asked to approve; but the Military Department then pointed out that the followers were reliable, that the proposal would cost some thousands of fighting men and a considerable sum, and that Indian soldiers would absolutely refuse, on grounds of caste, to do syces' work. When the file was referred back to Kitchener, he flew into a passion at being overruled on a 'purely military' matter. Was the Military Member's criticism, Ampthill asked, uncalled for and improper? If the administrative departments of the Army were not to raise such questions, who was? Would a Viceroy, or the financial authorities, be alive to such objections?[69]

*   *   *   *

During the spring, Ian Hamilton and Victor Brooke left for London, both well primed by Kitchener, who was informed that Nicholson, Roberts and 'a party of old Indians' were working against him.[70] The newspapers owned by Mr Pearson, the *Daily Express* and *The Standard*, indicated in late April that if Kitchener did not get his way he would resign. *The Standard* carried an article 'from our Military Correspondent', who had clearly been shown official papers. Ian Hamilton added his voice to the chorus. Much more important, *The Times* now took up Kitchener's cause in earnest. The Military Correspondent, Colonel Repington, who had been for some time in intimate liaison with Major Marker, had asked Kitchener in January whether a member of the staff could furnish information? Kitchener suggested Birdwood. From one source or the other, Repington too received allegedly secret documents from India, upon which he began to base articles.[71] In view of the powerful influence of the press, and of the special position of *The Times*, Kitchener had cause to congratulate himself.

His mood during this period seems to have fluctuated a good deal. The frequent letters to Lady Salisbury, Marker, Birdwood and others contain an amalgam of self-justification, haughtiness, uplift, depression, horror at the misrepresentations and low methods of others, cheap sneers at Curzon and Elles, threats of early resignation and bluff humour. When Curzon minuted that if the C-in-C took the field, the government of India must still have a reliable military adviser, Kitchener derided the notion:

> There is...a point that would not I think occur to Curzon's mind. It might be even more important to win the war than to advise the Viceroy. I feel that it is almost lèse majesté to suggest this.[72]

The publicity in the English press, or the indiscretions of his partisans, led to consequences which Kitchener had probably failed to foresee. By early May, rumours that he had resigned were circulating freely. Brodrick, asked in Parliament whether it was so, found himself in an obvious dilemma and failed to answer. The news reached India in a few hours. Curzon asked Kitchener whether it would not be well to issue an official disclaimer? Kitchener replied immediately that a denial was 'forced upon us by the circumstances of Brodrick's silence upon the subject. I cannot imagine why he did not deny it.'[73]

Brodrick told Curzon, in all seriousness presumably, that although plenty of people had learned the facts of Kitchener's resignation, he did not know whence the newspaper paragraphs emanated.[74] Ten days after Kitchener's public denial, the misrepresentations in the press had reached such proportions that Curzon decided to pin him down more tightly. The gist of the press comment was that the C-in-C's reorganisation and re-equipment had been thwarted or delayed by his colleagues. Curzon proposed that this falsehood be controverted by the Governor-General in Council. Kitchener chose to put out a communiqué himself. It did not escape the notice of Elles, or of Curzon, that its terms made nonsense of a large part of Kitchener's own charges.[75]

In a talk which Curzon described as 'long and extremely friendly' Kitchener expressed astonishment at learning that the Viceroy, and perhaps the other colleagues, would not accept overruling from home on the military question. When Curzon directly challenged some of Kitchener's allegations, he replied, 'But you cannot expect me to deny what I have once said.' Curzon then commented that it seemed rather absurd that two men like themselves, who agreed on nine points of the law, should break each other over the tenth, however important. 'You admit that the government of India have given you everything for which you have asked, though you may dislike the agency through which they have done so. What you are really condemning, therefore, is not any immediate or practical flaw in our system, but its remote and hypothetical consequences at some future date when it is subjected to the strain of war with Russia. Surely on such a point it should be possible to arrive at a compromise?'

'Dear me' Kitchener replied, always according to Curzon's account, 'I would jump at any compromise. You won't find any difficulty on my part if it comes to discussing a compromise. But, after what you have said, the government are not likely to give me the chance.'[76]

There may have been something in this. On the day after the conversation, Kitchener told Marker that he felt 'a sort of presentiment' that the case would go against him. He also discerned that the Viceroy had no idea what was going on in London.[77]

Since mid-March, Curzon had heard nothing from any Minister about the military question, but Clinton Dawkins, recalling that occasion in 1902 when Kitchener vowed to have everything in his own hands, gathered that he had made some impression in London by playing the Russian scare for all it was worth.[78] In May, Curzon recorded sadly that he had received not a single word of support, sympathy or even understanding from the Secretary of State or any of the Cabinet:

> I imagine that they are anxiously considering whether they would lose more by Kitchener's resignation or mine. Indeed I have heard authoritatively that this is their attitude. Military prestige is so much greater than civilian that the result may be anticipated. I have had so little help or backing from the present Secretary of State that I am quite ready to go, and to be relieved of a task which he has for some time been engaged in rendering distasteful to me.[79]

EIGHT

The Crisis

CURZON'S HALF-WRATHFUL, half-despairing protest of 1902 against the inconveniences of departmental detachment had been provoked by a suggestion which, in its later development, did more than anything else to inflame his relations with the Congress party. For some thirty years proposals to redraw the boundaries of Bengal had circulated in the offices of the government. The first step, of 1874, was to create a chief commissionership in Assam, but that district had a population of only 4 million, while the numbers in Bengal rose at the rate of about half a million each year. Though this problem did not figure among Curzon's early lists of reforms, he and Hamilton had concluded by the spring of 1902 that Bengal was too large a province.[1] Unquestionably, vast regions across the Ganges had been badly administered. Inquiries revealed widespread crime, corruption among the police, extortion by absentee landlords and a scandalous neglect of education. The Lieut.-Governor was supposed to rule 189,000 square miles and $78\frac{1}{2}$ million souls, 30 million more than the population of the United Provinces and nearly 40 million more than that of Madras. Districts of Bengal could hardly be added to either of those charges.

There remained among Bengal's neighbours the Central Provinces and Assam. Like Lord George, Curzon wished to promote the development of Assam, which depended on officers borrowed from Bengal, and, to an unhealthy degree, upon a single industry run largely by imported labour. The Lieut.-Governor of Bengal, Sir A. Fraser, represented the advantage of placing under Assam part of eastern Bengal, a hotbed of 'the purely Bengali movement, unfriendly if not seditious in character, and dominating the whole tone of Bengal administration'. The Viceroy at first adopted this plan, recognising that it would be locally unpopular and resisted by all the eloquence of the Bengali press. Moreover, it would still leave Bengal with a far larger population than that of any other province.[2] A tentative proposal on these lines, published in December 1903, was ill-received.

Yet the serious difficulty remained. The permanent settlement of land revenue in Bengal meant that the close link between revenue officer and the people was lacking, while the sheer size of the province swamped the Governor with work and produced an undue reliance upon the secretariat. 'I suppose' wrote the new Secretary of State, Brodrick, in 1904, 'you have never contemplated cutting up Bengal, and making a new province, making the Bengal Government a smaller affair altogether?' At that moment Curzon was about to tour East Bengal, where he recommended eloquently the solution already ventilated.[3] Fears that East Bengal would 'take over' Assam he dismissed as groundless, but the Chief Commissioner of Assam pointed out that opinion there remained hostile. Dacca was difficult of access from the Assam valley. There existed no community of feeling among the peoples.

The prediction of energetic opposition was soon justified. Curzon found in Bengal a full-scale campaign, with hundreds of illiterate Indians holding placards, frequently upside down, printed in Calcutta and sent along in advance. The tour strengthened his determination to press ahead. In the whole of Mymensingh, with a population of 4 million, there was but one British executive officer. The quality of the men sent to these regions seemed indifferent.

Opposition originated chiefly at Calcutta, especially from businessmen and lawyers. As Fraser remarked, separation of East Bengal from the rest of the province would probably liberate it from the political direction of Calcutta. The areas then proposed for transfer contained five Mohammedans for every two Hindus. 'It is not therefore right that these districts should be dominated by the Congress party in Calcutta...' He described the effort being made to consolidate East and West Bengal into one political organisation, to include Mohammedans as well as Hindus, disciplined, or terrorised, from Calcutta. 'All sorts of methods are being employed to achieve this end. It is not an end, I think, which the true well-wishers of the people can desire to further...'

Curzon, on the point of going for his holiday in England, was convinced that the original proposal should be modified in favour of a new province of East Bengal, to which Assam would be appended, under a Lieut.-Governor.[4] During his absence detailed proposals were put forward from Simla and accepted by the local governments. Curzon was not consulted by the India Office or by Brodrick.[5] The new province would have a population of 31 million, with three Mohammedans to two Hindus. The remainder of Bengal, with some 50 million, would then become, at least in the administrative sense, a more manageable proposition. Of the $41\frac{1}{2}$ million who spoke Bengali, more than half would be placed in the Eastern province. This policy was predictably unpopular with Hindus and especially in Calcutta, where it was believed to be a blow aimed at the city's primacy, a punishment for the prominent part taken by its citizens in the Congress. Mohammedans, who would for the first time find themselves in a majority in a province of British India, generally favoured partition.

The government of India understood the strength of the objection that while Bengal united was a power, Bengal divided would pull in several directions. Shortly after Curzon's return they told Brodrick that it could not be for the lasting good of any people that 'public opinion or what passes for it should be manufactured by a comparatively small number of people at a single centre and should be disseminated thence for universal adoption, all other views being discouraged or suppressed'.

They did not believe that rearrangement of administrative boundaries would stifle Bengali feeling, or prevent the growth of a genuine sense of community. It would be desirable to encourage the growth of local centres of opinion and 'to preserve the growing intelligence and enterprise of Bengal from being cramped and stunted by the process of forcing it prematurely into a mould of rigid and sterile uniformity'.[6]

Privately, Curzon admitted the justification for complaints against the partition in its first form; but opposition to the revised version had become, as it seemed to him, purely the outcry of the Congress party, inspired by political motives. The party was manipulated throughout Bengal, and indeed throughout India, from Calcutta.

> Its best wirepullers and its most frothy orators all reside here. The perfection of their machinery, and the tyranny which it enables them to exercise, are truly remarkable. They dominate public opinion in Calcutta; they affect the High Court; they frighten the local government; and they are sometimes not without serious influence upon the Government of India. The whole of their activity is directed to creating an agency so powerful that they may one day be able to force a weak Government to give them what they desire.

A measure which would dethrone the city as the centre of successful intrigue, or weaken the influence of its lawyers, who had the whole organisation in their hands, was intensely resented by them.[7] Antagonism expressed itself with extreme virulence. Curzon had already deplored the tendency to gross exaggeration, the attribution of evil motives and the feasting upon words characteristic of the Indian press, though realising that extravagant language did not always reflect extravagant thought. The speech which he delivered at Calcutta University in February, 1905, was in essence a protest against immoderation, both in abuse and hyperbole, and a plea for mental independence among the élite, who should cultivate a truly national public opinion and fight not phantasms but India's real enemies, 'backwardness, and ignorance, and antiquated social prescriptions'. He remarked that the highest ideal of truth was largely a Western conception, but explicitly rejected any claim that Europeans were 'universally or even generally truthful, still less...that Asiatics deliberately or habitually deviate from the truth. The one proposition would be absurd, and the other insulting.'[8]

The qualification went unheeded, in Calcutta anyway, and a Hindu with a good memory quoted to the general amusement passages from Curzon's book on the Far East, which described the falsification of age and other personal particulars in his interview with the President of the Korean Foreign Office. Curzon intimated to Godley that the uproar did not cut much ice in India, the object being to press on a radical government, expected to assume power in London soon, the recall of the Tory Viceroy before partition took effect. The methods used confirmed his conviction. 'The tricks and arts of political agitation are no new thing to us in England but I doubt if we have anything quite so squalid, so mendacious, or so mean as the practice of the same gentle art in modern Bengal.'[9]

Ampthill may well have been right in supposing that the furious outcry was a riposte for Curzon's recent crushing, in his best Parliamentary style, of Mr Gokhale in a discussion of the Universities Act.[10] The purpose of that Act had not been, as its more extreme critics supposed, to make the universities subservient to the government, but rather to encourage residence and corporate life in schools and colleges; to improve the teaching and lessen the tyranny of mere examination; to reduce swollen senates and enhance the power of the professionals; and to insist upon a stricter standard in the official recognition of secondary schools. All this was easily misrepresented and Curzon believed the opposition to be hollow.[11] The bill was put through; whereas the assent of the home government to the partition of Bengal was still awaited as the military question moved to its climax.

Curzon knew well that he had nothing to gain personally. He was already *persona ingrata* to the Congress party, who for the remainder of his time would pour forth vilification and scorn. 'You can scarcely have any idea' he wrote to Brodrick, 'of the utter want of proportion, moderation or sanity that characterises native agitation in this country. Starting with some preposterous fiction or exaggeration, the Bengali, after repeating it a few times, ends by firmly believing in its truth. He lashes himself into a fury over the most insignificant issues, and he revels in his own stage thunder in the happy conviction that owing to the circumstances of the case it can provoke no reply.' All 'these petty volcanoes' screamed unendingly; constant repetition of such invective tended to sway the minds of the educated, 'and I doubt not in my own case that the impression exists among them... that I, who am regarded in England as ultra-Indian, am in India ultra-English, and inspired by the most dangerous and reactionary designs.'[12]

Brodrick and his advisers believed that the government of India undervalued the substance of the opposition; but they admitted the problem and could provide no preferable solution. In this somewhat grudging fashion assent was given early in June.[13] The extent to which Curzon and his colleagues were swayed by political motives will remain a subject of argument. Partition had first been taken up to secure more efficient administration. Probably that desire dominated throughout; in other words, political considerations alone would not suffice to justify either partition or its abandonment. There was good reason to anticipate that both parts of Bengal would now be better run; and, as Curzon explained to Brodrick's successor, Bengali nationality, so far as it was a factor to be encouraged, would benefit by being the predominant force in two administrations instead of one:

> In so far as it is an unscrupulous and by no means innocent form of political agitation, engineered at Calcutta and worked by blackmail, the boycott and other nefarious means, it will suffer, with results that will be of immense advantage to the purity and honesty of public life in India.[14]

*   *   *   *

Between the earnest discussions of the Defence Committee about the scale of reinforcement to India, and the ability to provide it, yawned a wide gap. Arnold-Forster, having abandoned the larger part of Brodrick's scheme, was gripped by the Chancellor's insistence on economy. Efforts to render the Volunteers more efficient, a herculean task in which Balfour did not exert himself unduly, excited much criticism. A cartoon showed the Secretary for War, in the shape of a dog, snapping at one of them. Mr Bull addressed the Prime Minister: 'Your dog has got loose and is biting that Volunteer!' To which the Prime Minister, his back to the scene, replied airily: 'The Volunteer has my sympathy, but I do not conceive it to be my duty—especially during the Recess—to interfere with the freedom of Arnold-Forster's individual action.'

Kitchener's request for a reinforcement of about 150,000 men in the first year of war caused Arnold-Forster to repeat the view that the criterion must be not India's demands but England's capacity.[15] Beside this crucial problem of policy, he had to contend with frequent interferences: 'I suppose soon I shan't be able to ask my Private Secretary to tea without consulting the King, the Cabinet, Lord Esher and the Committee of Defence, Sir George Clarke, the Army Council collectively and Sir J. W. Murray individually.'[16]

The War Office he described as 'a perfect caravanserai', in which there existed a feeling 'that the whole organisation is a congeries of unallied and independent units, of men who look to everyone but their chiefs for inspiration, and to everyone but their colleagues for confidence'.

The Prime Minister, who at least thought he knew what purpose the Army was supposed to serve, set up a committee including himself, Clarke and Esher, to investigate its recruitment and structure. Arnold-Forster, on the strength of assurances given by Esher and soon broken, acquiesced.[17]

By late March, a state of crisis had been reached. Balfour made proposals which the Army Council seemed likely to accept, but Arnold-Forster was known to be incubating a clutch of powerful criticisms. Meanwhile, the Army Council could not place their views before Balfour, nor he his before them; which, Clarke observed, 'seems an absurd situation'. He also condemned as pure verbiage Arnold-Forster's plan,[18] to which both the Secretary for War and Lansdowne appeared to commit the government at the moment when Balfour was circulating a memorandum criticising the scheme. 'It is difficult to work with a Chief like this' lamented Arnold-Forster. 'Why does he not stick to something he understands?'

Learning that the Prime Minister's paper was being hawked round the clubs, Arnold-Forster protested vigorously. Balfour professed much sorrow and astonishment: 'but what he expects,' noted the Secretary for War, 'if Esher and Clarke are let loose with a private document, I do not know.'[19] The argument reverberated throughout the summer, until Balfour's government was evidently near the end of its tether. He confessed that one of his keenest disappointments as Prime Minister had been the failure to find a method which would provide greater power of expansion in war at lesser cost in peace.[20]

Against this background of intrigue and dissent the Defence Committee pursued its seemingly endless debate about the reinforcement of India. The resumed discussions proved to be no more fruitful of effective decision. The figure of 148,000 men to go to India in the first year was accepted in April, 1905, as a basis for planning, but not taken seriously by Clarke, who still thought it utterly impossible that so many men should be required so soon. Kitchener even claimed that India might need between 300,000 and 400,000 more men in the second year.[21] How these vast forces were to be fed and maintained in Afghanistan no one seemed to know. Camels would probably die in that terrain; Lord Roberts advised that bullock-carts would be unsuitable; the General Staff then challenged his estimates.[22] All this assumed, of course, that the men were available in these numbers, of which development there was neither sign nor likelihood.

Nevertheless, Balfour announced to the House of Commons on 11 May that Monroe doctrine for Afghanistan on which he had decided two years before:

> If...by laxity, by blindness, by cowardice we permit the slow absorption of the Afghan Kingdom in the way that we have necessarily permitted the absorption of the various Khanates in Central Asia; if Russian strategic railways are allowed to creep closer and closer to the frontier which we are bound to defend; then this country will inevitably pay for its supineness by having to keep on foot a much larger army than anything which any of us can contemplate with equanimity...[23]

The cost of implementing this policy continued to be disputed. Clarke ridiculed equally the figures of the General Staff and of Kitchener. Five divisions could not be maintained around Kabul, and to keep them at fifteen marches from a railhead would need well over three million camels. Keen officials calculated that the total number of camels required to deliver n loads r stages might vary with the formula $14n \left(\dfrac{(15)^r}{13} - 1 \right)$[24]. A memorandum produced by Kitchener, or at least in his name, indicated that the views of the authorities at home, and the decisions taken about Afghanistan in the previous autumn, had made no material difference to his policy. He contended that if the Amir would not make a military alliance the obligation to defend Afghanistan must be abandoned. India must sooner or later occupy all the tribal territory up to the Durand line. Colonel Deane advised that this would take three years of fighting by two divisions and would not even then provide a defensible line. Kitchener's predictions of troop movements – including Russia's placing 150,000 men on the Kabul-Kandahar line in a year, with 50,000 on a second line, and India's placing 100,000 before Kabul and Kandahar in four months – were curtly dismissed by Clarke.[25]

None of these estimates led to a firm basis for action. Since Russia was soon to suffer complete defeat at the hands of Japan, they seemed the more fantastic. Balfour did not consider that he had pledged even a reinforcement of 100,000 men.[26] The provision of a definite and dependable degree of British aid to India was no more settled in 1905 than in 1914 or 1939. In the event, it was India that provided assistance, and on a huge scale, to Britain. This continuing failure, and the size of Indian demands, caused the

Cabinet to search in an unexpected quarter for support. In March the notion of strengthening Anglo-Japanese obligations, so that Japan would help to defend the frontiers of Afghanistan, was first discussed. The Japanese refused. However, the proposal survived, although it carried certain dangers. As Arnold-Forster and Balfour pointed out, it was inadvisable that the defence of a part of the Empire should rest mainly upon a foreign power; and British help to Japan must be by sea only.[27] Probably in order to secure British acquiescence in a virtual protectorate over Korea, Japan later accepted this enlargement of the treaty's scope. It was henceforth to operate if either ally were at war with one power.

*   *   *   *

On the military question, informal consultations in London had already begun. Roberts judged that Curzon had gone as far as he could to meet Kitchener, whom it would be better to lose than to run any risk of the trouble that might arise if the Viceroy's Council had no officer of Indian experience.[28] He tartly rebutted, in a minute of 10 April, 1905, some of the C-in-C's main arguments:

> Lord Kitchener very justly urges that an army divorced from its departmental services cannot exist as an efficient fighting machine, but in doing so he assumes that divorce rather than connubial fellowship is the inevitable result of close official association.

Neither Marlborough nor Wellington nor Moltke had controlled in peacetime the services essential to the armies they led in war. The only commanders he could think of who had been autocratic in this respect, Roberts added pointedly, were Alexander, Caesar, Frederick the Great and Napoleon; 'but they were actually, or virtually, Dictators as well as Commanders.'[29]

A committee was set up to recommend a solution. Brodrick took the chair. Godley and Stedman were the secretaries and the other members White and Roberts, both former Cs-in-C; Lord Salisbury who, as Brodrick nicely expressed it, 'has had some special opportunities of learning the ins and outs of this particular subject';[30] of the India Council, Sir J. Mackay, a merchant, and General Sir John Gordon, whose senior military position in India had been Brigadier-General in Bengal, and who left in 1887; and Sir Edward Law, whose fury at the military system has been recorded, a close friend of Kitchener. Ampthill regretted his failure to forewarn Brodrick that Law was 'a hopeless crank and the very incarnation of cussedness', animated by strong personal dislike of Curzon, with 'a morbid and distorted mental outlook'.[31] The committee contained no former Viceroy, Secretary of State or Military Member. In the latter category Brodrick considered Generals Brackenbury and Collen, but was 'afraid we should overweight the Committee with men who have already a parti pris'. Kitchener felt it unfair to put in 'such a partisan' as Roberts![32]

This body met early in May. Roberts later told Curzon that he regarded it as packed, and that at the first meeting he had protested against its composition and instructions.[33] A sub-committee (Godley, Mackay, Gordon and Law) tried, in the words of its Secretary Stedman, to engineer the disappearance of the Military Member.[34] It proposed, within forty-eight hours, a Defence Committee under the Viceroy, to deal with military questions on the initiative of the C-in-C. The project was killed stone dead by a withering minute of dissent from Roberts, who then joined the sub-committee.[35] It later recommended that a military department be retained to deal with stores, remounts and the like. Recent friction was attributed to the Military Department's having become 'too powerful and busying itself unnecessarily about strictly Army matters'. The Military Member must not have the power to block any proposal put forward by the C-in-C. The members of the sub-committee, Roberts noted, were evidently bent upon letting Kitchener have his way.[36]

The exact chronology of the proceedings, and the role played by the full committee, are not easily established. Through Roberts, Lady Salisbury was informed of developments. Kitchener had given her to understand two months before that he would not in the least mind having a second military member of Council. 'I shall not say anything about this here, but Brodrick ...might insist on my accepting it and so give them something.' This officer would not interfere with the C-in-C's work and would admittedly have nothing to do once a strong headquarters staff were established; 'but at first, until my scheme was in working order, it would give a sense of security and would meet almost all Curzon's arguments.' He asked Lady Salisbury to let Brodrick know of this.[37] Kitchener's secret letter to Stedman was circulated to the committee and to the authorities whom they consulted, the majority of whom imagined that Curzon had seen it.[38]

Among them was Lord Cromer, the most celebrated of British proconsuls and well acquainted with Kitchener, before whose threat of resignation on a minor issue he had refused to quail. In 1899, when Kitchener's methods seemed to have brought the Egyptian army near to rebellion, Cromer had written to Rennell Rodd: 'You know how secretive the Sirdar is. He does not tell me everything, and I am not confident he knows much about it himself. He terrorises all his people and does not encourage them to speak the truth...Kitchener must remember that he has to deal with human beings and not with blocks of wood or stone.'[39]

This was in substance the opinion at which Curzon and Ampthill had independently arrived. Cromer, who admired Kitchener's powers as an efficient military organiser, now advised that it would be a grave error to abolish the post of Military Member. Brodrick, who had said that great weight would attach to Cromer's opinion, did not welcome it. The government at home, he replied, had been profoundly concerned at the conditions found by Kitchener in India. 'For years there had been large surpluses,' yet circumlocution and the cumbrous machine had prevented these surpluses from being used 'even partially for non-recurring expenditure'. Though both assertions were inaccurate it must be assumed that Brodrick believed them. He knew, the letter continues, of Kitchener's methods: 'On the other hand, he is dealing with a Viceroy who takes little interest in the army and has apparently allowed matters to drift...'

This was the exact opposite of Kitchener's contention that Curzon interfered perpetually in army matters, and was in any case a travesty. Brodrick also stated, *inter alia*, that the Military Member issued orders 'so far as I can make out, in nine cases out of ten, without consulting the Viceroy or anyone else'; and that Curzon kept the despatch under consideration for four months in Calcutta.[40] The last statement was false, and Brodrick must surely have known it. Anyway, his letter made no difference to Cromer's attitude.

Among the others whose opinion was sought, Elgin, Brackenbury, Collen and Lansdowne advised against the abolition of the Military Membership. The Foreign Secretary confessed himself appalled at the idea: 'But the India Office (which is strongly anti-Curzon) has gone off at score in the other direction and I think they have captured Balfour.'[41]

As a former Viceroy, Lansdowne wrote a minute which was circulated to the Cabinet. One or two sentences were altered at the request of Brodrick, who thought he went too far in accepting Elles's explanations.[42] Nevertheless, he pointed to a tendency 'to make a case for a change by looking through a microscope at every available case of inter-Departmental dissension'. Lansdowne repudiated both the assertion that the C-in-C and Military Member had traditionally pulled in different ways and Kitchener's statement that the two offices had been 'trained to jealousy and antagonism'.[43] The opinions of Lansdowne and Roberts carried weight, and Brodrick remarked to Frank Maxwell, Kitchener's ADC, that it would be difficult to persuade his colleagues to pass over them. The view would develop that it was Kitchener's personal inability to work with Elles which

had created the difficulty. Of course, he added, those who had really studied
the question knew that this was not so; and Maxwell learned from Stedman
that the India Office was 'solid for Lord K's views'.[44] Sir G. White, who
had earlier been inclined to back Kitchener,[45] agreed with Roberts; at
which Brodrick tried to persuade him to recant, saying that he was 'disappointed' with the minute. 'Such an expression' White wrote to Roberts,
'disposes of the "open mind" he professes.' Simultaneously, Brodrick again
assured Curzon that he had till now kept an open mind, but indicated that
this meant not an open mind about the merits, but about the practicability
or form of a change. Not until the last day or two had he seen his way at
all clearly. He did not indicate the nature of this vision.[46]

The report of the committee was based in essentials upon the revised
report of the sub-committee. Salisbury, being ill, played no part. White
went away on 19 May. This left, beside the sub-committee, only Brodrick
himself. Ironically enough, it was the two former Cs-in-C who had found
themselves, in White's phrase, 'practically dissentients'. To his embarrassment and anger, Gordon produced from the archives of the War Office a
personal letter in which he had long before said that the finance of the
Indian Army should be left to the C-in-C. He surmised, years later, that
this letter might have been the reason for his membership of the committee. 'As it seemed to me, the forces of the India Office were arrayed
against Lord Curzon from the beginning.'[47]

A goodly number of errors appear in the report. Clearly, documents
other than those officially presented had been circulated.[48] It implied that
important proposals of the C-in-C had been turned down without reference
to the Viceroy or Council. Rejecting Kitchener's desire to assume all the
duties of the Military Member, the committee accepted that on questions
of principle the Military Department had done its best to meet the C-in-C.
Kitchener's reorganisation scheme had been endorsed in India and at home,
and implemented, within a few months, a fact which refuted 'any suggestion of deliberate obstruction by the Military Department as representing
the Government of India'. All the same, the committee thought that the
Military Member had in recent years tended to become more an expert
adviser than a civil administrator, giving an authoritative independent
opinion on 'purely military questions'. On these subjects the C-in-C's
proposals should no longer be subjected to expert criticism by another
member of the Council.

On 24 May Brodrick passed to the Cabinet 88 foolscap pages of printed
documents on the military dispute. Two days later, the report of the committee was ready. In his covering note, the Secretary of State advised that

one man could not fulfil all the duties proposed by Kitchener. Yet the Military Member had lately established a position 'embarrassing to the Commander-in-Chief and destructive of rapid or effective administration'. Elles would be replaced 'by some less distinctively military administrator', who would concern himself with questions of contract, provision of clothing and so on.[49] These papers reached most members of the Cabinet on Monday, 29 May.

On that morning *The Times* carried an important article by Colonel Repington, prefaced by a statement that no part of its contents had been received from Kitchener or officers under his command. In fact, the article made extensive use of Kitchener's letter to Stedman of 8 March, replied in detail to Curzon's minute and cited the Generals' opinions. The source of Repington's information on this occasion is not known. Probably it came from Marker and Birdwood; Curzon was later told that the price of Repington's support was Kitchener's backing for an application to rejoin the Army, from which he had been obliged to resign. The Editor of *The Times*, G. E. Buckle, supported Kitchener. Others, like Moberly Bell and Chirol, who took the opposite view, could make no impression.[50] *The Times*' article was at once telegraphed to India. In this fashion Curzon and his colleagues first became aware of the Generals' opinions. He reminded Kitchener of the written promise that these opinions were for his own eye alone. Yet it seemed that they had been used to influence opinion in London. Was *The Times*' correspondent correctly informed? Curzon added that the Generals' views should not be quoted to the public in England while the Viceroy remained in ignorance of what they might have said. Was there not some reason to fear that the privacy of which Kitchener had assured him had been breached, and that some of his entourage had repeated their former indiscretion?

Kitchener's reply was a masterpiece of its kind:

> I really do not think I can be held responsible for what the papers publish.
> It is now nearly five months since I asked some Generals for their opinions.
> In the same paper I see the opinions of Lord Roberts and Sir G. White against my proposals are also stated.
> I have had a good many spontaneous letters from officers of Indian experience at home stating the views they hold and I have little doubt officers in India have written home privately on the same subject.
> I do not know to what former indiscretion of my entourage you allude.

Curzon pointed out that this begged the question. Kitchener answered that in their letters to him the Generals had not used the words appearing in the telegram, though they had agreed with his own views. He did remark that not all the Generals were being consulted. *The Times* stated the contrary, and Kitchener made the astonishing comment that if their correspondent 'is quoting from my private letters, he is therefore in this inaccurate as well as mistaken'.

The C-in-C did not explain how it could even conceivably be the case that his correspondence should be appearing in an English newspaper. He wrote immediately to Marker, hoping that Stedman would 'destroy private letters now and see that anything I have told him privately is not left on record...' The suggestion that the Generals' opinions had been leaked by himself or his staff he dismissed in the next breath as absurd.[51]

On 30 May the Cabinet endorsed the solution of the military question proposed by Brodrick's committee. The only member with Indian experience, Lansdowne, acquiesced, though he said later in the year that he would have left the government sooner than consent to Kitchener's proposals.[52] There can be little doubt that the threat of Kitchener's resignation influenced an enfeebled government. His skilful manipulation of the press, and careful supply of papers to those who would shape the decision, played their part. Brodrick, for all his protestations of an open mind, had obviously felt for some time that large changes must be made. This is not to suggest that the solution was dictated, at least consciously, merely by a desire to keep the C-in-C at all costs. It was while the committee was sitting that Balfour announced British determination to fight for Afghanistan. The fear of a war with Russia under the existing system of Indian administration, to which Kitchener constantly referred, will certainly have moved the Cabinet. Colonel Repington was not alone in pointing to Russia's success in transporting and supplying a vast army over a single steel track far distant from European bases.

As usual, Lord Esher had taken a hand. Kitchener's retirement, he told the Prime Minister, must be averted. It was 'the broad fact' that for ten years Military Members had had the opportunity to carry out the reforms now initiated by the C-in-C. Starting from this incorrect premise, Esher made the obvious deduction. With the aid of the letter to Stedman, he advised the King in the same sense. Kitchener appreciated the value of this support.[53] Nevertheless, there is no reason to doubt that Clarke was substantially right to tell Kitchener that the decision 'depended mainly on Mr Balfour's support of your views, which he completely grasped after reading the papers you sent me'.[54]

On 31 May Marker telegraphed an abbreviated but largely correct account of the Cabinet's verdict. The C-in-C replied that he was 'quite pleased', but to Lady Salisbury expressed himself delighted, for he had feared things were going badly:

> I am so happy at the result I do not know what to write...I hope you will tell A.J.B. how grateful I am...you might tell St J. he has my very best thanks for all he has done. I know he must have worked hard in my favour against a lot of opposition...[55]

That night, 1 June, the Curzons were to dine with Kitchener. Hubert Hamilton looked forward to studying their faces. He guessed, rightly, that they knew nothing of the decision reached in London.[56] A week later arrived Brodrick's letter of 18 May, which still contained nothing about the merits of the military question. Curzon recognised that their conceptions of the weekly correspondence diverged. In Lord George's time, Viceroy and Secretary of State had expressed their innermost feelings. Realising that such frankness was not desired, Curzon had desisted. Now, at last, Brodrick explained that since he had not been asked for his personal opinion on the military question he had not given it. Having written on the subject week after week without receiving any reply, Curzon could hardly take this seriously and said so.

Brodrick also commented in his letter that having spent nearly fifteen years 'dealing directly with soldiers, I feel to have a claim to a greater knowledge of their idiosyncrasies in administration than any civilian now in political life. And I have felt it very useless to write where I could not convince.'

Curzon responded at once that he did not contest Brodrick's great knowledge of military affairs, or affect to possess similar knowledge, though he did know India and Indian administration.[57] When that day's work was done, he wrote from Naldera to a more congenial correspondent:

> Far below me the whisper of the wind through the pines comes humming up from the gorge of the Sutlej: absolute peace reigns both in earth and sky, where the crescent moon is slowly dipping to the horizon: everyone else in the camp is asleep, and I am enjoying one of the few restful and happy hours that Simla ever gives me.

The long delay, Curzon presumed, meant that a new constitution was to be sent out. To Ampthill's question about spending another summer in India, he rejoined that he would not do it for millions sterling:

> By next spring—unless I go before—my work will be done, and I shall turn my back on these shores. The seven best years of my life will have gone. I shall never regret, but would not repeat them.[58]

*   *   *   *

The Cabinet's decision, in the shape of a despatch dated 31 May, arrived at the end of the third week in June. Being based on the reports of the committee and the sub-committee, it reproduced most of their mistakes of fact, and was written by Brodrick. He, like the committee and the Prime Minister, was convinced that the Military Department had materially increased its duties in recent years, a conclusion at variance with Curzon's. The document bore evident marks of the haste in which it had been drafted. Most of paragraph 6 was taken up with a lengthy refutation of an argument which had never been advanced; other parts were self-contradictory. In effect, it placed the blame for friction upon Elles and the Military Department. Brodrick ruled that junior officers were not to note upon the military proposals of the C-in-C, evidently not knowing that the practice had been stopped in 1903. The government of India and the Viceroy were taken to task for failing to make alternative proposals or to realise how many obstacles stood between the C-in-C and military autocracy. The Finance Member and other members of the Viceroy's Council, the Military Department of the India Office, the India Council and the Secretary of State provided ample safeguards:

> Bearing in mind all these processes which, though familiar to Your Excellency, do not appear to have been fully weighed in the Despatch, it is difficult to understand how the absence of a second military expert in Council would produce a military autocracy, or violate a fundamental principle of our constitution.

The Secretary of State made great play in the despatch, as he had done in his paper to the Cabinet, of an incident of 1904 concerning small arms ammunition. He conceived that a prolonged delay had been caused by the dilatoriness of the Military Department, and had been cut short only by his own intervention. As it happened, the documents supposed to be before him did not substantiate this account. No doubt Kitchener or one of his staff had remedied the deficiency. The rest of the file, which showed that within five days of receiving sanction in August, 1904, the government of India ordered 23,000,000 rounds of such ammunition, was probably not sent to London; or if it was, Brodrick made no mention of it.

However, the Military Member was to exist no more. A Military Supply Member would join the Council. The despatch stated, at various points, that he was not to give 'expert opinions on military questions'; his functions were to be limited to supply; he must realise that his duties were to be 'more of a civil than of a military nature'; he would not be able to veto any proposal put forward by the Commander-in-Chief; he was specially to advise on 'questions of general policy as distinct from purely military questions'; if the C-in-C were of the British Army, the Military Supply Member must be 'an officer of considerable Indian experience and of administrative capacity, and intimately acquainted with the characteristics of the Native Army'. The duties of this officer 'would be essentially those of a civilian administrator with military knowledge and experience'. In Parliament, Brodrick stated that the new Member might be a soldier or a civilian. He was, then, to possess 'military knowledge and experience' although he might be a civilian; he must often be an officer of long Indian experience, but his duties were to be those of a civilian administrator; he was 'specially to advise...on questions of general policy', although the C-in-C was to be the sole expert adviser.

Nothing in the despatch indicated what would be a 'question of general policy' and what a 'purely military' question. Into which category would the absorption of frontier tribes, or Kitchener's reorganisation scheme, fall? Who would determine, Curzon wondered, when the storekeeper should blossom into the adviser? The subordinate status of the new Department was clearly marked out. Its Secretary was to have no higher rank than Colonel, whereas the opposite number in the Army Department would be a Major-General. In any case, if the Military Supply Member exercised his supposed power of advising on 'general questions', his criticisms would evidently be resented and he would surely be accused of obstructing the sole military adviser. Indeed, his position in this respect would be worse than that of civilian members of Council, each of whom was entitled to criticise every proposal coming before them. Sir Hugh Barnes, now translated to the India Council, explained repeatedly that all members of the Council were equally responsible for all acts of the government of India, but Brodrick seemed not to understand.[59] Under new organisation three Secretaries to the government, instead of one, would be dealing with military affairs. Each must have access to the Viceroy.

No copy of the reports of the committee and sub-committee was sent to India. No trace of the opinions of Cromer, Lansdowne, Brackenbury, Collen and others appeared. But Curzon had already heard from Lansdowne that he had done his best to thwart the 'insensate' proposal to discard the Military Member, and by the mail bringing the despatch Roberts wrote privately that people at home, no doubt influenced by the press, took Kitchener's side. Had it not been for the strong opinion expressed by everyone who knew the working of Indian government at first hand, the Military Member's position would have been abolished; whereas under the new scheme there would still be on the Council an officer who knew the traditions and idiosyncrasies of the Indian Army.[60]

Both Godley and Brodrick took care to let Curzon know that the decision was strongly approved in a 'higher quarter'. The King himself wrote that he hoped it might prove satisfactory both for Curzon and for the C-in-C: 'he is a man of such importance, and especially in India just now...'[61] Brodrick genuinely believed he had hit upon a durable solution, which would 'stand any amount of hammering'. He attached the highest value to the check imposed by the India Council, felt 'practically assured' that control over Kitchener's proceedings in respect of the Native Army would be strengthened.[62] Ampthill was not in the least moved. It was a victory, he wrote to Godley, not for Kitchener but for the 'young lions of Army Headquarters' who used him for their own ends, and especially for Mullaly, a schemer and wire-puller of none too scrupulous a description'. For some reason, Brodrick was much taken aback to learn of Ampthill's view. There was a 'consensus of opinion' at home, he replied, that the 'results of the old system were as bad as the principle'.[63]

Curzon brushed aside, with the aid of Roberts's letter, the protestation that the solution had been arrived at purely upon the abstract merits. Kitchener, he wrote, had in practice triumphed, 'although a disembowelled Military Member has been left to prevent me from resigning'. This he was ready to do. Indeed, he regretted his failure to resign before the decision was known.[64] The first step would be to see whether some modifications could be agreed with the home government. Failing them there could be, Curzon predicted, only two results. Either the Military Supply Member would be found so useless that there would soon be a demand that he be replaced by a civilian; or the independence of the C-in-C would be so soon established that the new system would break down irretrievably. England from the Prime Minister downwards, Curzon wrote to Clinton Dawkins, would make any sacrifice in deference to a whisper from Kitchener:

> I have long since ceased to extract any pleasure from my task, and I yearn to hand over and be at rest. I would come at once if I thought that Milner would succeed me. But I fear some subservient member of a Cabinet whose second ablest member recently confessed publicly his 'colossal ignorance of India'.[65]

The annual debate on the Indian Budget took place at home just as the despatch reached Simla. Brodrick gave a condensed version of his scheme, but no hint of the Indian government's views. He refrained from paying the customary tribute to the Viceroy, an omission remedied by Haldane, who spoke handsomely of Curzon's work. At this the opposition cheered heartily. 'Unless something quite unforeseen happens,' Haldane wrote, 'I doubt whether there is any one the Opposition would rather see in your great office than yourself.'[66] After the debate, a blocking motion was placed upon the Order paper, so that the military issue was never discussed.

Two days later, on Brodrick's insistence and precluding any possibility of modification or rejoinder, the minutes of Kitchener, Elles and Curzon, with the despatches of 23 March and 31 May, were published. Sharp-eyed observers did not fail to note that many of Kitchener's arguments, and some of his *ipsissima verba*, were already familiar from the press campaign.[67] This was the second time in six months that the home government had published controversial Indian papers; a habit, Curzon remarked, less in accord with their traditions than with those of the *Daily Mail*.[68] Light relief was provided only in *The Standard*'s comment that 'Mr Brodrick's reputation has been more than maintained by the masterly Despatch now published'.

The manner in which the government overruled the wishes of their colleagues in India, and the tone of the despatch, were severely commented upon in almost every organ of the Indian press, which described the result as a great triumph for Kitchener. This surprised Brodrick. 'I hope Curzon will not take up the same line.'[69] The Viceroy was actually discussing with his civilian colleagues whether they should all resign. Two said they would stand by him if the rest did the same. The three others decided that they did not wish the whole Council to go. This meant that if Curzon acted he had to do so alone. Arundel and Ibbetson urged he should set aside for the public good his wish to retire.[70]

On 25 June, Curzon told the C-in-C that unless some modifications were accepted he intended to go. Kitchener, feeling that the home government had done much for him, and that if Curzon resigned he should have no reasonable excuse, said that he himself would resign rather than let Curzon do so. He contested Curzon's forecast of the way in which the decision would work out, but assented to various modifications, notably that the Secretary in Army Department should be of the rank of Major-General, not Colonel; and that important changes of organisation should be discussed in the mobilisation committee or some other body on which the Supply Member had a seat. Curzon refused to concede Kitchener's view that the Supply Member would have 'most important duties', but agreed that there should be no duplication of work. Kitchener allowed that on submission of any case to the Viceroy by either department he might refer the case to the other for advice. When Curzon insisted that the new Member must always be a soldier and the new department retain the old title Kitchener replied that though he could not consider the alterations to be improvements, 'there are none that I am not willing to accept in deference to your wishes'. All this is admitted in Kitchener's own account.[71]

After a meeting of Council, Curzon telegraphed to the Prime Minister that the government of India regarded the scheme of 31 May, unless modified, as mischievous and unworkable. Kitchener's resignation had been refused. They had agreed on the modifications, designed to give greater status, and the right of offering independent advice, to the Military Member, but without departing from the 'general principles' approved by the Cabinet. If these could not be accepted, he wished to resign.[72] As Brodrick pointed out to his colleagues, these were serious changes. A telegram sent on behalf of Stanley, later Lord Derby, in the War Office cypher, asked whether Kitchener had really accepted such 'great and most serious alterations'. He replied to Balfour, through the same channel, that he had agreed out of desire to avoid Curzon's resignation, suggested that if the Cabinet refused to retain the title 'Military Department' Curzon could not depart on that issue alone, somewhat minimised one of the other conditions and opined that the others fell

within the four corners of the despatch...I think they should be conceded, otherwise I believe the Viceroy will resign.

I hope we may and we ought to get on but as long as Elles is here we shall have difficulties.

Kitchener added, in response to Stanley's question, that he did not know the contents of Curzon's telegram beyond the conditions.[73] Since the telegram followed the lines of a discussion in full Council, there was not much pith in this; but the Cabinet did not know that fact, nor did Curzon know anything of this latest exchange. Balfour thereupon telegraphed his extreme surprise at the version given of Kitchener's view, which seemed quite inconsistent with his published minute. He was asked to send privately a statement of his reasons.[74] Marker had already wired that Kitchener's friends felt he had given too much away. 'It is really not much' he told Lady Salisbury on 29 June, 'and we can put things right when he goes.'[75]

The Prime Minister's telegram placed Kitchener in something of a difficulty, since he had committed himself and the reply had to go through Curzon. On 30 June, the two reiterated the demand for modifications. Kitchener added to the draft in his own hand:

Above proposals are so cordially agreed to by both of us that if His Majesty's Government are not able to accept them, Lord Kitchener desires to associate himself with any action that I may take in the matter.[76]

Meanwhile, Brodrick, who seems to have been truly astonished that the solution should be considered a victory for Kitchener, did not take Curzon's threatened resignation seriously, and even blamed him for telegraphing to Balfour. The sentiment that the Viceroy brought everything and everyone into hot water was growing apace, Brodrick told Ampthill. To Curzon he wrote that his resignation was not desired:

> But supposing it was not you who were in question, but Lord Dalhousie or any other administrator of the past, do you think that any Government would surrender a point in which they really believed, in order to secure for a few months extra the presence of a Viceroy who disagrees with them on as many subjects as you have recently disagreed with the Government...?[77]

Before this specimen of tact arrived, Curzon had given up writing the weekly private letter. He made no reply, therefore, but cannot have been much surprised. Kitchener, realising that he was held to have conceded too generously, informed Lady Salisbury that the latest interview with Curzon had been a stormy and violent encounter, in which the Viceroy had broken down. Kitchener had been so surprised that he said he would associate himself with Curzon's 'other puerile requests...I could have bitten my tongue out for making such a stupid remark but really I suppose I was rather excited with the discussion. I was prancing up and down his room talking to him very straight...' His explanation to Marker is similar, with the additional argument that Curzon's resignation was 'not advisable on the papers as they stand'. Moreover, Curzon had now swallowed the title 'Military Supply Department' and Kitchener feared that if he went back on the modifications, the Viceroy would follow suit on the designation.[78] The C-in-C's story of excitement, collapse and harsh words is probably an exaggeration or fabrication, for Curzon, with no cause to be kind, states that at none of these conversations did the other lose his self-control.

It seems that Kitchener never understood the purport or purpose of the modifications; indeed he was soon telling Lady Salisbury that there had not been any modifications.[79] Yet they could hardly have been spelt out more clearly. On 1 July Balfour telegraphed in a conciliatory way that it had never been desired to limit the right of the Viceroy to consult whom he pleased. The modifications of detail were accepted. So that there should be no mistake, Curzon telegraphed again that he and Kitchener contemplated that the Military Supply Member should be available for consultation by the Viceroy at his discretion upon all questions, without the limitations laid down by Brodrick; otherwise the modifications would be valueless. Curzon told Balfour of the overwhelming unanimity of opinion in India, in which the soldiers largely joined, against the new organisation. The changes proposed were in his view the minimum required to make it at all viable: 'I hope that importance of concessions will not be minimised when they are officially announced. This would only produce renewed outbreak of public feeling here.'[80]

The new Member should therefore be 'available for official consultation by the Viceroy on all military questions without distinction, and not only upon questions of general policy, or when cases are marked for Council'. All important changes in military organisation, conditions of service or customs affecting the Native Army proposed by either Military Department, must be discussed by the Mobilisation Committee, of which both officers would be members.[81] Curzon told Brodrick, who clearly had his eye on imminent publication, that the modifications could not truthfully be described as being designed to make the scheme work effectively, for the government of India doubted whether even the modified scheme would work:

> Although our proposals are not inconsistent with principles of your scheme, which we had no alternative but to accept, they do to some extent challenge policy, in so far as they attempt to provide Viceroy and Council with alternative military advice.[82]

Nothing could be plainer. 'My colleagues' Brodrick told Roberts, 'think him unreasonably violent but he has no idea of resigning.'[83] Whether the colleagues really thought so, or whether Brodrick was using them as a lightning conductor, is a matter for speculation. The government, having taken up the military question at Kitchener's behest, and having produced a solution similar to that which he had outlined to Lady Salisbury in March, found that he had sided with Curzon. Evidently Balfour felt the absurdity of the position. 'K is a traitor' he wrote on 11 July.[84] Three days later, however, Brodrick wired that the recommendations from India did not contravene the despatch of 31 May and in some respects exactly fulfilled it. The Viceroy had the right to consult any member of his Council on any subject. The C-in-C and Military Member must advise him if invited to do so, though neither could have any special claim to be consulted.[85] The issue, it now seemed, was resolved.

*   *   *   *

In his telegram of 26 June, Curzon had protested against the 'invidious and derogatory' form in which the decision was conveyed, with the curt order to institute the new organisation by 1 October and with no provision for consultation. He felt that the despatch singled him out for criticism. Kitchener, he told Balfour, had called it 'nasty' and 'insulting'. It seemed to be Brodrick's object to humiliate the Viceroy before the community of which he was head; yet 'To ignore a public opinion in India about an Indian subject—so unanimous and emphatic as this—is to weaken British rule and its instruments in this country.'[86]

The divergence between Indian and English opinion now revealed, and the apparent indifference of the home government to the views of those who knew India well, Curzon wrote to the King,

> are omens of serious significance for the future. It has hitherto been generally assumed that the Government of India are not merely constituted but competent to advise the Home Government about Indian affairs. If their advice is publicly disregarded, and if they are further exposed as they have been both in this case and in that of the Tibetan Blue-book, to open rebuke for doing what is after all only their duty, their position in India will be a very difficult one, and their prestige will disappear...[87]

Early in July, *The Standard* insinuated that articles in the *Times of India* were inspired by Curzon, adding that similar indiscretion had been imputed, without foundation, to Kitchener. The *Daily Express*, also owned by Mr Pearson, published a communication from its 'Simla correspondent', who stated that 'All the correspondents at Simla are registered and unless we send only what the Government wishes known, we are 'black-listed', and if we send views that the Government does not wish known, we are practically debarred from getting any news at all.'

This falsehood was at once derided by the Indian press. Its significance, however, is that Brodrick believed it.[88] In mid-June Stedman had arranged that cypher messages from Kitchener should, if necessary, reach the Secretary of State.[89] No doubt this was the source of his conviction. What was said in these telegrams is unknown and will very likely remain so; but on 5 July Hubert Hamilton told Lady Salisbury that he detected 'evident signs' of a press campaign 'craftily engineered from the precincts of Viceregal Lodge'.[90] At some point during the summer an Indian offered the Viceroy copies of Kitchener's cypher messages to Marker. According to his own account, Curzon refused to look at them.[91] Probably this is true. Had he known the contents his tactics would almost certainly have been different. Brodrick, convinced that Curzon was conveying selected telegrams to the press, stated in all seriousness to Ampthill that in the military question 'any public opinion there is in India has been manufactured at

Simla, while not a single thing has escaped through us here'.[92] Ampthill at once denied it with his customary candour: 'there is not a soul who has had any experience of this country who would not laugh at the idea.' As Curzon commented later in the same connexion, if Brodrick could believe this he could believe anything.[93]

The Secretary of State announced the modifications to Parliament as though they were entirely within the original intentions of the government. Within a few hours the statement was known throughout India. In this case, there was no reason why Curzon should have threatened to resign, and on the following day he explained in the Legislative Council what had happened, referring only to the published facts, and pointing, in Kitchener's presence, to the C-in-C's agreement with all the representations made by the government of India. The Viceroy refused to discuss the durability or merits of the new organisation, which was not of their creation:

> All that we have been in a position to do is to effect the removal of some of its most apparent anomalies and to place its various parts in more scientific relation to each other. We have converted the position of the Military Supply Member into one of greater efficacy and utility. We have very considerably strengthened the guarantees for civil supervision and control. In the last resort I expect that the new system, like the old, will depend in the main upon the personal equation...[94]

There was nothing of substance in the speech which had not been put to the Secretary of State and accepted. Only one phrase — 'We were very glad to make this discovery', applied to Brodrick's assurance that the modifications chimed with the Cabinet's original intent — could give a legitimate ground of mild offence. However, the summary telegraphed in a few sentences by Reuter was seriously misleading. A former Secretary for India, Sir H. Fowler, put down a question on 19 July. That morning the Cabinet decided to telegraph for the full text, believing nevertheless that *The Times'* report was almost certainly accurate. If so, Balfour reported with unwonted intemperance, the speech was

> deplorable in taste and temper...no such public exhibition of disloyalty to the Home Government has ever yet been made by an Indian Viceroy...how the Government are effectively to defend against an unanswerable charge one who has left no means unused, legitimate and illegitimate, to defeat their policy, it is difficult to see. On personal grounds even more than on public grounds, Mr Balfour is deeply grieved...[95]

Curzon's 'tampering with the press' and 'tortuous course with Kitchener' had made a very bad impression, Brodrick noted on the same day. The

Cabinet understood that a reprimand would mean Curzon's resignation. 'I fear it will come to this.'[96] In the House, the Secretary of State did not suggest a suspension of judgment but merely announced that he had wired for the text. A leading Liberal, asked why Fowler had spoken severely, replied, 'It was a protest against Imperialism.'[97] On the next day the government were beaten by four in a fairly full House.

When the compromise between Kitchener and Curzon was reached, Elles asked that the unpublished despatch demanding his retirement be cancelled. He would then resign, but would accept no money. Brodrick refused. Elles thereupon declined to resign. The Secretary of State felt certain that Curzon was influencing Elles in this sense, so that he should be placed in the position of being dismissed.[98] That despatch, Curzon's conditional resignation and his further telegram when he and Kitchener agreed on the modifications had all leaked out. Brodrick telegraphed to inquire whether Curzon knew the names of those responsible, and if so, 'whether you think it desirable to take any steps to make them amenable under the Official Secrets Act'. The implication appeared to be that Curzon should apply the Act to himself. 'Can you conceive' he asked Ampthill, 'anything in an official telegram more spiteful, or yet more puerile?'[99]

Curzon replied that so far as he knew the telegrams had been seen by no unauthorised person; he had not concealed his intention to resign if modifications were not made; the conferences between himself and Kitchener, and Brodrick's request for Elles's early resignation, were known to the whole Council and many other officers and soon became public property in Simla. But disclosures had also taken place in England; for instance, *The Standard* announced on 29 June that Curzon's resignation had been telegraphed to the Prime Minister, although that fact had not transpired in India. Moreover, Kitchener's threatened resignation had long been public property at home. Curzon now knew, and told Brodrick, that the C-in-C's supposedly confidential minute had been given to pressmen and used in articles long before it was officially published. The Viceroy added that he did not see how the Official Secrets Act could be applied.[100] He had also learned that Kitchener had supplied privately to the India Office a long and hostile commentary on the minutes of himself and Elles.

The days passed with no reaction from London to the full record of Curzon's speech. He lived from day to day under a cloud of apprehension, explaining to Ampthill that while no idea of insubordination had been in his mind, he had certain duties:

I had to explain to the Indian public why I had offered to resign, what were the flaws...which I had been struggling to correct, and to what extent they were being corrected. I was anxious to make clear that I did not overrate the value of the amendments, that I felt bound to disclaim responsibility for the scheme as amended.[101]

Curzon hated the squalor of this unsought controversy, though he hardly appreciated, as yet, all its ramifications:

> I never sought it [he wrote to Lamington on 24 July]. I implored Balfour and Brodrick not to bring it on. But they would do anything first to prevent Kitchener from resigning here, and secondly to prevent him from coming home. And thus I have been dragged against my will into this dirty mud-pond, in which everyone gets bespattered and the larger aspects of the case are obscured by personal revilings and trivial issues.[102]

He felt also the indignity, after long and distinguished tenure of the Viceroyalty, of being treated thus by a man ignorant of India, 'who would never have had the chance of being a failure as Secretary for India if he had not already been a failure as Secretary for War.'[103] In his own account of these events, published long after Curzon's death, Brodrick admitted Kitchener's secret contacts with himself and the Cabinet, but alleged that 'a most prominent politician' acted in England for Curzon.[104] The reference is presumably to Lord George Hamilton, who had been out of office for nearly two years, and whose role cannot be seriously equated with that of Lady Salisbury, Marker and Stedman. Moreover, Balfour and Brodrick seem to have accepted, at least until it was too late, almost everything that Kitchener and his confidants said. Lord George, on his own initiative, pointed out courteously that the speech at Simla, Curzon's justification for not resigning, was undeserving of censure.

Brodrick took little notice. He informed the Cabinet that Curzon had 'gratuitously volunteered' his statement, of which 'the Simla public' were previously warned, and asserted, despite Curzon's denial, that a campaign against the Cabinet's policy had been 'assiduously dictated for the Indian newspapers, which were supplied from day to day with the subject-matter of confidential telegrams until the Prime Minister himself telegraphed urging the Viceroy to keep communications secret'. Curzon, he added, had been 'counting for months on the fall of His Majesty's Government and the advent of a Government who may recall Lord Kitchener for work at home. The division of last week will encourage this hope.'

In all probability, this judgment was mistaken. There is nothing in Curzon's papers to indicate that he banked upon the government's fall. Meanwhile, Brodrick, having taken steps to find out whether Kitchener gave his authority for everything about which he had been quoted, learned 'through private sources' that the telegrams of 26 June and 6 July had not been shown before despatch to the C-in-C, though they cited his opinions. Moreover, Kitchener's and Curzon's accounts of their interview differed sharply.[105] Neither of these eminent men, Balfour thought, emerged from the controversy with any credit whatever; but since they had reached a working agreement which left untouched 'the essence of the proposals which, largely in consequence of Lord Kitchener's views, the Government have pressed upon the Viceroy' the Cabinet decided not to condemn Curzon's speech.[106]

NINE

Resignation

AT THIS POINT, just before the final crisis, Brodrick remained convinced that Curzon was manipulating the newspapers. Undoubtedly this was the burden of the clandestine cypher messages. 'The press agitation out here' wrote Hubert Hamilton to Lady Salisbury on 26 July, 'is all manufactured at Viceregal Lodge. There is really no public opinion but it is amusing to watch the effort that is being made to pretend there is one.' Brodrick told Knollys that he had received 'very precise' information, through 'non official channels' of the imparting of private telegrams to Indian papers.[1] He resented Curzon's efforts to overthrow the decision by 'appeals to popular prejudice', and even accused him of a 'sedulous campaign' at home. Lawrence denied indignantly the notion that the Viceroy instigated leakages to the press. Brodrick sent for him and said that Curzon had gone out to India pledged to the abolition of the Military Department, and 'other things equally refuted by the published correspondence'.[2]

Seven thousand miles distant, and depending on letters always three weeks outdated, Curzon probably failed to comprehend how deeply rooted this conviction of Brodrick's had become. Realising that he was accused of inspiring the *Times of India*, he expressed stupefaction.[3] Lovat Fraser, the Editor, never had a private conversation with Curzon in India, never received secret information from Curzon or his staff, and was not asked for support. Later, Brodrick made the highly libellous charge that Reuters had been subsidised by Curzon from official funds, a process which 'largely accounted for the indignation telegraphed from India at Kitchener's proceedings'.[4] In fact, the Indian press abounded with criticisms of the home government's performance, but Reuter's extracts were generally bowdlerized in the opposite interest. Reuter's agent at Simla, Curzon learned, had heard from Baron de Reuter that there was no choice, on account of the Cabinet's pressure.[5] Mr Gwynne, whose support was so helpful to Kitchener, had until recently been foreign director of the firm.

There remained one other crucial ingredient of the military tangle: Elles's successor. Curzon had no doubts. He had long since described Sir Edmund Barrow as 'the most capable of our young Generals both in the office and in the field'; two years later, in January, 1903, he advised Lord George that Barrow was the only possible man for the post of Military Member should Elles go; and when Barrow left that department in the autumn the Viceroy warmly commended his broadmindedness, freedom from bias and high ability. 'I have never worked with any military officer with greater satisfaction, or parted from him with greater regret.'[6] Thereafter Barrow commanded the Peshawar Division. Not one of the Generals consulted by Kitchener, he took Curzon's side in the military argument,[7] and was, by any standard, one of the more distinguished soldiers of the Indian Army. After the Peshawar Division, he commanded the Southern Army, and then became Military Secretary at the India Office and a member of the India Council. Curzon now wished to appoint him as Military Supply Member.

It happened that Barrow was about to go on leave to England. Curzon asked him to call *en route* to Bombay, but the General was intercepted by Kitchener, whom Curzon had already told that he thought Barrow the right man for the new post; and if Barrow's accounts are accurate, Kitchener at this interview rehearsed the prospects on the assumption that he would be appointed. Barrow refused to discuss the issue until he had talked with Curzon. 'Let me impress on you one thing' said Kitchener (according to Barrow); 'that if you accept you urge Lord Curzon to get you put into office at once. I cannot get on with Elles and this scheme has got to be got into working order by the 1st October...Besides it is only proper that the man who is going to work the new system should help to frame it.'

The General replied that he could hardly tell the Viceroy how to conduct the government. Moreover, Elles was a friend of twenty years' standing, with whom he was actually staying. Then, said Kitchener, he would make the suggestion, to which Barrow rejoined he would be ready to surrender his leave. He believed that Kitchener was quite prepared to cooperate with him. 'We shall get on all right together.'[8]

From this interview Barrow went immediately to Viceregal Lodge, where he recounted what had happened. Curzon remarked that the post was not in his gift, but that he would now recommend Barrow's name to Brodrick. Sir Edmund said he doubted the permanence of the scheme, and reported Kitchener to have spoken likewise. As for giving up the leave, Elles had already been asked to stay on until 1 October. Barrow had better take his holiday. On the next day, Kitchener told Curzon that he should get rid of Elles and set Barrow to work at once. He thought Barrow almost too good a man for the billet and would prefer to have him as his own Chief of Staff. Curzon expressed surprise and asked whether that would not be rather hard on General Duff, who would doubtless expect the promotion? Moreover, whom would Kitchener contemplate as Military Supply Member? The C-in-C suggested Egerton, at which Curzon laughed, he was an elderly and apoplectic General with no administrative experience. He asked why Kitchener did not take Egerton as Chief of his Staff? 'Oh no, I don't want a duffer' said Kitchener.[9]

Curzon told the C-in-C there was no need to cancel the leave already sanctioned, informing Barrow to that effect in writing and adding that he believed Barrow would be able, with unfailing Viceregal support, to rehabilitate the department which it had been sought to destroy.[10] Barrow, having seen Kitchener and Curzon again, left Simla with the conviction that Kitchener would be willing to have him as a colleague in Council.[11]

Curzon wrote at once to London, expressing the hope that Barrow would be appointed and that Balfour would see him. 'He is absolutely honest and will tell you nothing but the truth.'[12] Unfortunately, the Prime Minister failed to act upon this request. On the same day, Kitchener told Marker that he did not know quite what to say about Barrow's appointment:

> I think highly of Barrow but as an old Mily. Dept. Secretary he naturally does not believe in the change and considers the new system will not last long. Whether it is wise to put in a man with these views seems to me doubtful. He is able and gets on well with other officers but he has no special knowledge of or ability as regards the special duties of his office.[13]

A letter from one of Kitchener's staff, which found its way to the Prime Minister, contains similar statements: to Curzon's desire to make Barrow the new member Kitchener 'could not object and had nothing to say'; Barrow had 'many good points' but no special aptitude for the new post; Curzon had offered Duff as Chief of Staff. The writer stated that Curzon was determined to wreck the scheme if possible, that Barrow would in practice maintain the old system and that Kitchener had been 'too conciliatory'. Hubert Hamilton wrote in similar terms to Lady Salisbury.[14]

Most of this account is based upon letters and memoranda of Curzon and Barrow. Kitchener, by contrast, later declared he told Sir Edmund on 8 July that he had not the least idea whom Curzon would propose; but that whoever was appointed should be on hand to see the new arrangements worked out. However, it is known from one of Kitchener's own letters that

Curzon had suggested to him on 25 June Barrow or Wolfe Murray for the new post, and an account which Kitchener set down at the end of the year is shown from his own letters to be inaccurate, at least in part.[15] The conflict of evidence cannot be wholly resolved. It may be that Kitchener's letters to Stedman, almost all of which appear to have been destroyed at his request, would shed fresh light. Perhaps Curzon interpreted Kitchener's apparent acquiescence as genuine agreement. Possibly both Curzon and Barrow were lying, though it seems hard to believe that in those circumstances Curzon would repeat his version so widely and ask the Prime Minister to question Barrow, or that Barrow would independently confirm it at home. The balance of probability is that Kitchener was treading warily at a moment when he had blotted his copybook in London, while giving Balfour and Brodrick every encouragement to reject Barrow. Moreover, as we now know, he had telegraphed secretly to London, some weeks before, in favour of Gen. Scott. Stedman had then doubted whether Brodrick could agree, since the despatch decreed that the new Member must possess intimate knowledge of the native army; but that chance was still open and, as Hubert Hamilton later admitted to Lady Salisbury, Kitchener desired Duff as Chief of Staff and did not want Curzon to oppose him.[16] Alternatively, his main motive may simply have been to get rid of Elles forthwith.

On 16 July Curzon received a private letter from Brodrick, containing the utterly unexpected remark that he intended to nominate a Military Supply Member from England and anticipated that Curzon would acquiesce, since he had 'twice given way' to the Viceroy over recent nominations to the Council. In fact, Brodrick had only appointed Curzon's candidates after himself suggesting four others, to all of whom Curzon had agreed in succession and to at least two of whom the posts had been offered. The Viceroy therefore pointed out in courteous language that this was scarcely a candid statement of the case. He seems to have made no impression on Brodrick, who repeated and published the charge, but not the denial. Curzon also telegraphed that he proposed to recommend General Barrow, who 'would be acceptable both to Lord Kitchener and myself' and more likely than anyone else to inaugurate the new system successfully.[17]

Immediately upon this followed the row about the speech in the Legislative Council. To a private telegram, Curzon replied on 29 July that he feared his position had never been quite understood at home. Though the controversy had been none of his seeking, he had been singled out for criticism and the government of India treated 'with a lack of public consideration which has characterised recent utterances, from Tibetan Blue

Book onwards, and which has produced deplorable impression in this country'.

There had ensued the discussion by telegram of the modifications, in which the Cabinet first expressed surprise, then asked for a change of language and finally belittled the concessions made. After eleven days Curzon was still in suspense about the nature of the public reply the government proposed to make about his Simla speech. 'Any expression of censure' he telegraphed, 'would have been followed by immediate resignation...My view...is that I have been treated throughout, however unintentionally, with extreme lack of consideration, while my speech is universally regarded in India as having been characterised not by impropriety but by self-restraint.'

Curzon offered his resignation. If he was to give the new organisation a chance, he was entitled to the support of the Secretary of State and of the Cabinet, in Parliament and in India, instead of the treatment he had received since the previous December.[18] This long telegram, which again represented the danger of so marked a divorce between Indian and British opinion, was omitted from the published papers.

Barrow arrived in London at the end of July. It appears that Brodrick had for some time been inclined to favour Kitchener's original candidate General Scott. He learned from 'a number of private sources' that Curzon was taking steps to defeat the new scheme, and stated that Curzon had summoned Barrow, offered him the post and sent him on short leave, 'and this without saying a word to the Secretary of State, with whom the appointment rests'.[19] As it happened, Curzon had done nothing of the sort. Barrow's leave had long been sanctioned and Curzon had told both him and Brodrick in writing that the appointment lay with the home government. This point was especially emphasised by Barrow in conversation with the Secretary of State. Brodrick's insistence upon Barrow's opposition to the scheme probably derives from the emphasis which Kitchener and his staff placed upon the General's remark that he was not confident that it would last. They had made no mention of Kitchener's own observation in the same sense; but Barrow later repeated it to Balfour and Brodrick.[20]

Curzon soon realised that the vessel which took Barrow home must also have borne letters from Army HQ, for on 1 August Brodrick telegraphed that he 'was advised' that Barrow's admitted capacity would find more appropriate scope in the Frontier command or in the post of Chief of Staff to Kitchener, if the Viceroy and C-in-C thought him fit. This, unless Curzon's account is false, was the proposal that Kitchener had put to him three weeks before. He naturally suspected, therefore, that Brodrick's suggestion was not entirely self-inspired; and wondered who had advised that Barrow would be unsuitable as Military Supply Member? Evidently the Secretary of State intended to allow no discussion, for the telegram ended, 'This is also the view of the Cabinet who are not willing to appoint General Barrow. I hope to telegraph...very shortly the name of the officer we propose for the Military Supply Department.'[21]

He complained that Curzon's budget speech of the previous March, and his speech of 18 July, did not seem calculated to allay feeling in India, which had been inflamed by Curzon's intention to resign and by 'daily disclosures' in the press. The despatch of 31 May had been conceived in no invidious spirit and the colleagues thought that they had reason to complain that Curzon should have treated the Cabinet's action as being taken on their own initiative, after the meeting at the House of Commons in August 1904, and the agreement between Balfour and Curzon about procedure. Curzon replied that he did not wish to pursue the controversy; but it was the truth that the home government had insisted upon taking up this question, as Balfour's letter of 3 November, 1904, showed.[22]

Simultaneously, an important debate was held in the House of Lords. Brodrick had just expressed surprise that Ampthill should think the military system defensible, assuring him that 'no one looking at it from a distance seems to think so at all';[23] but it very soon appeared that some did think so. Indeed, Brodrick appealed to Roberts on the same day to say nothing which might be cited as justifying Curzon's attempts to endow the Military Supply Member with the authority of his predecessor. But Roberts replied that his sympathy lay with the Viceroy, whose position would be lowered in Indian eyes by recent events. If Kitchener had 'had his own way, as the members of the Sub-Committee were evidently bent on letting him have, I should have been surprised if there were not trouble in India. As it is, I hear on good authority there is a great deal of dissatisfaction throughout the Indian Army'.[24]

In the debate, therefore, Roberts stated that the Viceroy must not be dependent on the advice of a single soldier. A former Viceroy, Lord Ripon, described Brodrick's despatch as the greatest rebuff inflicted on the government of India since Ellenborough's despatch to Canning about the affairs of Oudh. On behalf of the government, Lansdowne said that they had decided against Kitchener's demand for the disappearance of the Military Member, who would 'remain very much in the position which he had always occupied'. Thus the Secretary for India was prepared to break the Viceroy for carrying out what the Foreign Secretary described as the decision of the Cabinet. It would be hard to imagine either a more

extraordinary position or a more natural interpretation of the telegram
sent to India on 14 July.

Curzon telegraphed that if the new Member was to give general military
advice, as agreed by the home government and now explicitly reaffirmed by
Lansdowne, he should be an officer of the highest qualifications. In such
circumstances the Viceroy was entitled to expect that unless there were
strong reasons to the contrary, his candidate would be appointed. Barrow's
name had been put forward with the full knowledge of Kitchener, who had
said he wished to have Duff as Chief of the Staff: 'and if any contrary advice
has reached you I cannot accept its validity.'[25]

At that moment Kitchener was advising Marker by letter, and almost
certainly by telegram, that Duff would be an ideal Chief of Staff:

> For goodness' sake don't let me have Barrow as C. of S. I could not trust
> him a yard and you know how openly I speak sometimes...I would far rather
> see Barrow Military Supply Member *outside* my office than C. of S. *inside*.
> I should never be able to sleep on both ears if he were.
>
> Of course Scott would make an A1 M.S.M. but I doubt Curzon ever agree-
> ing. He is as obstinate as anything you like and will look on Scott as not having
> sufficient knowledge of the native army and he and I would agree which is of
> course what C. does not wish.[26]

At about this time two telegrams from the C-in-C to Marker were
shown to Brodrick, who wrote out a message for transmission in code to
Kitchener. It deprecated any support for Barrow, who had already been
warned of the unfavourable effect on his pension which acceptance of the
new post would entail:

'I am quite sure' commented Stedman to Kitchener, 'that you do not
believe in Barrow (clever man though he may be) to the extent of wishing
to go out of your way to get him made Hon. Mem.'[27]

Brodrick then telegraphed officially to Curzon that having held positions
in the Military Department, Barrow could hardly be expected to inaugurate the new system with an open mind. In the opinion of his military
advisers (principal amongst whom was Stedman) it would be well to
choose a Member with technical experience, to stand him in good stead in
the 'heavy charge' of the manufacturing departments. 'Will you consult
Kitchener' the telegram goes on, 'as to who in his opinion is the best
qualified man for the post, and let me know his views? We will willingly
consider any names you and he desire to put forward...we must avoid any
appointment which would in our opinion tend to reproduce previous
difficulties.'

As Curzon had already made it plain that he wanted Barrow, this message in effect indicated that Kitchener would nominate the new Member, though it stated again that such appointments rested with the Secretary of State, and that he had twice deferred in 1905 to the Viceroy's view when 'no point of principle was involved'. Evidently the telegram was framed for publication: the Cabinet, it said, had 'accepted' General Elles's resignation 'with great regret'.[28]

Kitchener and Curzon met on the next day, 5 August. The C-in-C, according to Curzon's account, had more than once said that he had been severely taken to task from home for giving the game away in July. Of course, Curzon had no means of learning that the Secretary of State had warned Kitchener not to support Barrow. Chirol, who saw much behind the scenes, gathered that Kitchener had received, from a lady friend, intelligence about the Cabinet's temper which induced him to change his mind about Barrow, in the belief that Curzon could be overthrown.[29] At all events, Kitchener now denied entirely any arrangement about Duff and Barrow, abusing the latter. This, Curzon records, was his first disagreeable interview with the C-in-C, who trembled violently throughout: 'he lost all command of himself, raged and blustered, and eventually stalked out of the room, not however before he had mentioned as his ideal Military Supply Member a dear placid old dummy named General Scott, Director-General of Ordnance...'

Curzon asked what the C-in-C would do if Scott, under the new arrangements, criticised any of his proposals? 'Criticise them! General Scott criticise me! I wish you to know that I should resign at once.'[30]

Kitchener also remarked that it was not his business to recommend members of the Viceroy's Council. Curzon disputed his version of the facts. 'Used as I am to Kitchener's complete indifference to truth,' he noted, 'I was somewhat shocked and surprised.'[31]

The C-in-C's account cannot be reconciled with Curzon's at a number of points. It records Curzon, not himself, to have lost control:

> He said that I had brought all this on him, that he would make it unpleasant for everyone including myself if he resigned, that I was prejudiced against Barrow, to which I replied that I was not in the least but I did not think him suitable for the special post...

Kitchener's note maintains that he had all along held this opinion: that he had not been more explicit in July because he understood Barrow to have told Curzon that he did not believe in the durability of the scheme, which Curzon admitted; and that he, the C-in-C, was determined to abide by

Brodrick's despatch. He did not, it seems, take seriously Curzon's remark that he would resign if Barrow could not be appointed;[32] but there he was mistaken, for the Viceroy wired at once that the Cabinet clearly denied him the confidence which would enable him to serve with advantage, and that they attached to the modifications a meaning fundamentally different from his own. The chief point was that the new Member

> should not merely be purveyor of stores...but should be qualified, in words of your own despatch and as reaffirmed by Lord Lansdowne...to give advice on questions of general military policy to Governor-General in Council.

The Viceroy picked holes in the telegram. If Barrow did not possess an open mind, why was he offered to Kitchener as Chief of the Staff? If the Military Supply Member were to advise on general military questions, why was it desired to obtain an officer distinguished for technical knowledge of military supplies, knowledge which Barrow anyway possessed in exceptional degree? The position, Curzon added, had now reverted to that of June. He could only introduce the new organisation with the co-operation of the best qualified officer and the support of the Cabinet. If that could not be given, his resignation should be placed at once before the King.[33]

Curzon's telegram, which repeated Kitchener's remark that it was not his job to recommend members of the Council, did not mention General Scott. However, Brodrick knew from a secret message that Kitchener had again suggested Scott's name. Informed by Stanley that he was supposed to have acquiesced in Curzon's description of the original scheme as 'mischievous and unworkable', Kitchener protested that he had done nothing of the kind. Later in the evening, 6 August, he telegraphed again: 'please ask friends not to believe anything Viceroy says regarding me or my views.' And yet again the following morning:

> Since hearing of the unwarrantable lies that have been told about me, of which I had not the faintest conception, I do not believe in any protestations of loyalty. The only one General in India who would help to wreck Secretary of State's scheme has been chosen, and I think now, deliberately for the purpose.[34]

This, as Kitchener knew, confirmed Brodrick's own opinion. The timing of the messages could not have been improved. They were printed and circulated immediately to the Cabinet. 'Some amazing private telegrams from Kitchener' noted Arnold-Forster, '...every one of them, as it seems to me, rendering Curzon's behaviour more detestable.'[35] Clarke had already weighed in with the Prime Minister against Barrow. Godley did the same with Brodrick:

To allow the Viceroy, at a critical moment, to force upon you a nominee of his own, with the hardly concealed purpose of modifying the policy of H.M. Government..., would be, I submit, to act unconstitutionally and in direct contravention of the intentions of Parliament.

The Viceroy has no *right* to be even consulted...[36]

The force of this argument depends, of course, on the real nature of the government's policy. If it was correctly expressed in the Cabinet's telegram of 14 July and Lansdowne's speech, then Curzon did not want to modify it substantially; but if, after all, the Military Supply Member was to be a purveyor of stores, then Curzon had no intention of staying. Brodrick, who had but recently been so confident that Curzon had no intention of going, now realised that a new Viceroy might have to be found in a hurry. He had also adopted a new explanation, probably under Godley's inspiration. 'Curzon' he noted on 5 August, 'is getting so alarmed at the storm his proposals for partitioning Bengal have raised, that it is possible he may seek relief.'[37] In his report to the King after the Cabinet's meeting of 8 August, Balfour took up the same theme:

The tremendous storm which Lord Curzon's proposal for dividing Bengal has raised in India, and the consequent unpopularity which will attach to him during the Prince of Wales' visit, may induce him to grasp at any expedient for relieving himself of a task which has now become distasteful to him for other reasons besides those which spring from his relations to Lord Kitchener and the Home Government.

Balfour thought Curzon extremely sensitive 'to even the gentlest comment' and his language violent; he was convinced, like Brodrick, that Kitchener's name had been unwarrantably used. All this the Prime Minister attributed to the combined effects of overwork, climate and ill-health. He felt alarmed lest Curzon might 'get us into quite unnecessary trouble with the Amir of Afghanistan—a calamity the magnitude of which it would not be easy to measure'.[38] The Cabinet, Balfour telegraphed, could not understand Curzon's position. They gathered, from an unnamed source,

that General Barrow has no great liking for the system which you wish him to administer and would prefer an office which would not withdraw him from a distinguished career of active service. Anxious, therefore, as we are to make your task a light one, it does not seem that General Barrow's appointment would be the most effectual method of attaining that end.[39]

This message puzzled Curzon a good deal. Not until the position was beyond rescue did he learn from Barrow that on the night before the Cabinet he had called on Brodrick, who gave me to understand that you and he were at variance on the subject of my appointment about which there was something like a deadlock. He clearly wanted me to pull him out of a hole, by saying that I personally did not want the appointment and would be content with Chief or Staff or any other sop. I equally clearly gave him to understand that he was not in a position to offer me that appointment, as Lord K. would insist upon nominating his own man, and further that I was not open to a bargain.

When Barrow eventually saw the telegrams, he told the Prime Minister in writing how he had clearly explained to Brodrick that although he did not agree with the home government's views, he would loyally act by them if appointed; and that Kitchener himself had said the modified system would never work.[40] This made the origin and value of the Cabinet's information clear enough. The Prime Minister's telegram contained no answer to Curzon's question whether the Supply Member was to possess the authority and capacity to advise on broad military questions.

Brodrick had by now persuaded himself that Curzon wanted to resign immediately because he feared, on account of unpopularity in Bengal, to receive the Prince of Wales in November; 'and he wants to saddle us with his resignation...I wish I felt any real confidence in his fairness and uprightness. One must try and think these aberrations are due to ill-health.'[41]

Meanwhile, a file had been started at Simla to work out the new organisation. When Elles proposed that one of the Supply Department's four officers should study cases referred from the Army Department by the Viceroy, Kitchener objected that this would mean the creation of a new Military Department 'for the express purpose of reconsidering and criticising the opinions recorded by the Commander-in-Chief on military questions'. He could not allow the creation of a 'bureau'. Elles protested that the right of the Viceroy to consult the Supply Member had been a key point in the recent exchanges and that the C-in-C's proposals in effect meant the reduction of the Supply Member to the role of a Director of Stores without any stores to look after.[42] These papers were before Curzon when he telegraphed his resignation on 5 August and again when he replied to Balfour's message of 8 August. In putting forward Barrow's name, he explained, he was trying not to subvert the prerogatives of the Secretary of State but to maintain the view he had held from the start, that the government of India should have a second military adviser.

Under Kitchener's proposals, Curzon went on, all stores, whether mobilisation or peace, would be transferred to the C-in-C, who would also take the lion's share of the Ordnance, Supply and Transport, and Army Remount departments; the existing staffs at Army HQ would be largely

increased, while the much-vaunted Secretary to Government would have
no functions beyond correspondence and signing papers. The Military
Supply Member was not to criticise opinions recorded by the C-in-C on
military questions.

'It is estimated,' Curzon commented, 'that under these conditions the
Military Supply Member will not have two hours' work a day.' It would be
better to dispense with the department altogether than to waste public
money in such a manner, for the cumulative effect of these proposals,
allegedly based on Brodrick's despatch, would be the concentration of all
military power at Army HQ. In fact, Kitchener was reverting in practice
to the plan which the home government were supposed to have rejected.
If Curzon were to continue as Viceroy, he must have consistent support
from home and the co-operation of a trusted colleague as Military Supply
Member; and if that support could not be given, he must again ask for
relief.[43]

The Cabinet met at once. Afterwards Brodrick telegraphed that the
Secretary of State's right to nominate members of the Viceroy's Council
must be upheld, and that it was from a desire to consult Curzon's wishes
that the Cabinet asked him to confer with Kitchener. They placed the
utmost value on the Mobilisation Committee's ability to furnish the Viceroy
with far more useful advice on the C-in-C's proposals than any individual
could give. The new Member should have special experience for the work
of the Supply Department, but should not be in the line of promotion to
'the highest posts of a purely military nature'. The Cabinet's policy had
been laid down after 'the most exhaustive consideration' by Brodrick 'with
all authorities on the subject in this country'. Nothing should now be
proposed which would 'appear to re-establish the old conditions'.[44]

Reflecting upon the events of the previous two months, Curzon thought
he had made three mistakes; not to have resigned when the despatch first
arrived, to have believed the Cabinet sincere in accepting the modifications
and to have trusted Kitchener, whom he had now found to be without
truth or honour.[45] He refused to preside over a system which appeared to
have no parallel in the world and to combine in one mass the duties of
C-in-C and War Minister. He believed that the majority of his colleagues
would reject Kitchener's latest proposals. The matter would then be referred
to London, coupled in all probability with Kitchener's resignation, after
which, no doubt, India would be overruled again. Curzon pointed out on
12 August that he had still received neither an assurance of support
nor any explanation of the principles now to be applied in Indian military
administration:

I am reluctantly driven to the conclusion that the policy of His Majesty's Government differs fundamentally from what I thought had been agreed upon with the Government of India, and is based upon principles which I could not conscientiously carry into execution. In these circumstances my ability to act with advantage as head of the Indian Government has ceased to exist, and I beg you again to place my resignation in Prime Minister's hands.[46]

Balfour, having wagered half a crown that Curzon would not resign, had retreated to Gloucestershire. 'If he *will* go', he wrote, 'he *must* go.' And a day or two after, 'Life would be tolerable but for its Viceroys.'[47] After Milner had refused the succession, Lord Minto, who had long announced his candidature, was chosen.[48] Balfour then telegraphed that he thought the principles clear and the support given. Brodrick wired his regret, asserting that he and his colleagues had tried to give 'constant support' to reforms, 'including partition of Bengal, on which we recently adopted your proposals'. He repeated the bare statement that he had twice in a year accepted Curzon's nominations to seats on the Council. Curzon replied:

I am not now concerned to speak of the earlier years of my administration, but looking back upon more recent events I reflect with sorrow how little justification there has been for the claim which you make of having rendered me constant support.[49]

All these telegrams, which Brodrick intended to publish, were shown on 17 August to Kitchener, who suggested that for the words 'would be acceptable both to Lord Kitchener and myself', referring to Barrow, should be substituted: 'I am under the impression he would be acceptable to Lord Kitchener as well as myself.' Curzon's telegram of 10 August, summarising his military proposals, Kitchener repudiated as wholly inaccurate. Not intended for publication, it had been prepared with much labour. Curzon, taking care to have his Private Secretary present, agreed to telegraph that Kitchener disputed its truthfulness, but warned him that every statement would be substantiated. Kitchener then produced a long minute and demanded its publication.[50]

'It is...evident' he wrote to Lady Salisbury on 17 August, 'he is not going to resign under any circumstances.' Three days later he learned that the announcement was imminent. 'I am deeply grieved at the news', Kitchener assured the Viceroy, 'as I had hoped up to the last moment that your resignation might have been avoided.'[51] Curzon wrote simultaneously to his principal colleagues and subordinates. Their replies reveal a personal affection, gratitude for kindnesses and appreciation of his work which must have been a source of comfort.

At home, Sandars arranged for Godley to show telegrams and talk indiscreetly to the Editor of *The Times*, who had already been subject to lobbying by Ministers and their spokesmen.[52] Godley confessed afterwards to having made an impression. 'I earnestly hope', he wrote to Sandars, 'that every facility is being given to Curzon to come home as soon as possible. My own view about his health is not a cheerful one: I strongly suspect that he has paralysis.'[53]

The paralysed Viceroy was meanwhile going through all the recent papers on the Military Supply Department, while Kitchener pressed for publication of his minute. Curzon proposed that the documents should be sent to Brodrick by mail for decision. Kitchener insisted.[54] Curzon wired accordingly to Brodrick, twice deprecating further publication on personal grounds, though not on any other. The Secretary of State replied that while he did not want publication he did not see how it could be avoided if Kitchener thought his views misrepresented. This telegram was not shown to Kitchener, either because Curzon could not bear to deal with him further, or because by publication Kitchener would place himself in a ridiculous position.

If there was one thing Curzon could do supremely well, it was to summarise accurately and lucidly masses of detail. He vindicated the original précis, which Kitchener had described as 'a most malicious libel',[55] very largely by quoting from papers written, or at least signed, by Kitchener himself. The C-in-C was shown to have contradicted his own statements of only a few days before. Presumably his well-known distaste for careful reading of files had brought him to grief. Curzon concluded his rejoinder by reaffirming that all military power would be concentrated at Army HQ. Most of this could not be disputed. One final quarrel ensued, however, on the subject of some figures which Kitchener swore were missing from the file when he minuted upon it. Curzon sent for the papers and replied that the figures had been printed, Kitchener's attention being especially drawn to them by a green slip.[56] Duff virtually accused the Military Department of moving the slip after the file had been returned; but the fact is that the relevant note did go to Army HQ. It appears that Kitchener had relied on a separate copy, given privately, and had not looked out the file.[57] He expressed the utmost horror at Curzon's shameful treatment of him:

Everyone knows out here that I never saw the paper. It was hid away in a big

Military Department file and it was through no carelessness of mine that I did not see it...

I shall have nothing further to do with him until he goes.

I should like to call him out and rid the world of such a − −. In the old days I suppose I should have done so.[58]

When he found himself severely criticised in *The Times* for the publication, Curzon asked that his protest against it, and the telegrams omitted from the Command Paper, should be made known. Brodrick requested him, on public grounds, to refrain.[59] Curzon agreed. 'Nothing' he wrote to his brother 'has been more honourable to me than the final episodes, and so far from regarding them as a humiliation or failure, I look upon them with pride...Please do not think...that I am fuming with vexation or anger. I have, indeed, been wickedly treated, as you will subsequently learn when the facts are before you. But I am perfectly serene...'[60]

Kitchener's nominee, General Scott, was appointed Military Supply Member.

*   *   *   *

Curzon's long letters of 19 and 27 July did not reach Balfour until the crisis was over. For eight months the Prime Minister had not sent a single line; but now he answered at once, with an assurance that Curzon had done Brodrick an injustice. The last six months, unpleasant for the Viceroy, had been unquestionably wretched for the Secretary of State. Balfour cited two letters of Curzon to Brodrick, both of which he misinterpreted, and another letter to Godley, which he misquoted. The language, Balfour observed, had not always been of a kind common in friendly correspondence; but now he desired to save from the wreck all that was possible of amity and esteem:

If these priceless possessions have been threatened by the form in which either my colleagues or I have carried out what we believe to be our duty, I deeply deplore it. If anything that has been done or said by you gives cause to regret, I wish only to forget it. Of one thing only shall I be mindful—that for nearly seven years, in sickness and in health, you have devoted with untiring energy your splendid abilities to the service of India and of the Empire. And this is enough.

For these generous and affectionate sentiments Curzon thanked him warmly.[61] The correspondence with Brodrick was not, however, resumed; and at a distance of more than sixty years it is unlikely that all the disputes about Curzon's resignation will be resolved. Nonetheless, there can be no substantial doubt that he was badly treated. Balfour's familiar reluctance to intervene, and refusal to answer letters, played their part, but it is clear that a good deal of his opinions and information derived from Brodrick, the springs of whose attitude remain concealed. That he was somewhat wrong-headed, credulous and obstinate is undeniable. Even Sir G. Clarke confessed that Brodrick's methods, of which he had seen a good deal at first hand, were indefensible. To Chirol he seemed 'simply unspeakable in his mean-ness and lying...' and to Dawkins 'essentially the temperament of the worst kind of schoolmaster...always wanting to send somebody "a lesson" '.[62]

Godley testified that Brodrick had strained every nerve, 'according to his lights', to avoid a row, but detected in him an 'abnormal sensitiveness'.[63] In this there is much truth. His long experience at the War Office, the painful end of his time there, and confidence in the excellence of his solution of the military controversy, no doubt made Brodrick the more resentful when Curzon demanded its modification, when he had to bear other Ministers' reproaches and when another failure seemed to loom.

Milner, who had ample experience of Kitchener's methods at first hand, once remarked that he was 'a liar and a bad liar, for he doesn't recollect today the lie which he told yesterday', absolutely autocratic and observing no contract.[64] In another's kindly phrase, Kitchener seemed to 'have moments of impulse in which he writes one thing to one person and another to another'.[65] There is still room for doubt at some points in the story, but again there can be no question that Kitchener lied to Curzon and to others. That he, and Balfour, Brodrick and Godley all conceived them-selves to be acting in the highest public interest is not contested. Had Brodrick been more perceptive, Balfour more decisive, Godley more knowledgeable or Kitchener less devious, the situation could hardly have developed as it did. That all were biased in greater or lesser degree against Curzon must be accounted a failure of management on his part. Whether any degree of tact or submission could have overcome a weak Cabinet's reluctance to face the resignation of the C-in-C remains questionable.

Probably Brodrick never realized how comprehensively he had been misled. Balfour, invited again by Curzon to verify the facts, did admit in mid-October that Barrow's evidence certainly went to show 'that K. did not behave straightforwardly about the appointment of the new Military Member...'[66]

Brodrick's subsequent allegation that Curzon was recalled not on account of the military controversy, but because he claimed to direct the foreign policy of India with insufficient regard to its Imperial effects,[67] seems implausible. Foreign affairs were indeed abnormally quiet after the Kabul negotiation, and Curzon would in any event have left India no later than the spring of 1906. It was unlikely that any vital issue of foreign policy would arise before then. For the same reason, the decision on the military issue could little affect Curzon's own convenience. But his conception of India's place in the Empire was incompatible with the overruling of the government of India on its own constitution and the publication of rebukes:

> The post of Viceroy of India is not one which any man fit to hold it would resign for any but the strongest reasons. When you remember that to me it was the dream of my childhood, the fulfilled ambition of my manhood, and my highest conception of duty to the State, when further you remember that I was filling it for the second time..., you may judge whether I should be likely heedlessly or impulsively to lay it down...I resigned for...two great principles; firstly, the hitherto uncontested, the essential, and in the long run the indestructible subordination of military to civil authority in the administration of all well-conducted states, and, secondly, the payment of due and becoming regard to Indian authority in determining India's needs.[68]

TEN

Epilogue

IT HAD BECOME customary for a retiring Viceroy to receive the Garter or
an advancement in the peerage. In 1904 Balfour expressed some doubt
whether the Liberals, if in office at the material time, would confer an
honour; but Curzon was informed in the King's name that the Viceroy
stood outside party politics. Should the Liberals be in power, His Majesty
would press the point on them.[1] When Curzon resigned a year later, the
King telegraphed:

> Most warmly do I thank you for your invaluable services to your Sovereign
> and your Country and especially to the Indian Empire.

He wished the government to grant an Earldom forthwith; but Brodrick,
convinced that the Viceroy intended to launch a bitter attack upon himself
and the Cabinet, demurred, once more accusing Curzon of trying hard to
break off British relations with Afghanistan in the previous February, of
deliberately upsetting the Tibetan policy and of tortuous conduct during the
recent crisis. Sandars opposed an honour vehemently,[2] while Balfour,
acknowledging Curzon's services in handsome terms, advised that an immediate award would encourage the dangerous conviction that India was not
in any vital sense subject to the control of Parliament and Cabinet.

Knollys retorted to Sandars on 9 September that Curzon had been sent
back to India when his views on the military question were known; that
he had not been 'practically dismissed'; that his first five years should not be
forgotten; and that Curzon and Minto could not be placed on the same
level. The King represented that this was a case for magnanimity. 'The fact
is' wrote Sandars after an interview with him, 'that all the evidence at
present before H.M. is pro-George: but still his attitude can, I think, be
easily modified under adroit management.'[3]

King Edward appealed to Curzon:

> Though I deeply regret that you were unable to be in accord with views
> expressed by my Government at home, I cannot but hope that on your return

243

you may consider it advisable in the interests of the British Empire at large, and especially as regards India, not to enter into any further controversy regarding the different issues...which compelled you to resign...It is always inadvisable to wash one's dirty linen in public.[4]

The confident belief that the Viceroy would be afraid to receive the Prince of Wales in November proved unfounded. Both the Prince and the King thought that the royal party should be greeted by Curzon. Eventually, it was arranged that Minto should arrive a week after the Prince. The King telegraphed that 'In face of considerable opposition and after laborious correspondence' he had by personal intervention secured this plan.[5] Curzon accepted it immediately. Nothing was done about an honour, ostensibly at least because Curzon might continue the controversy and Balfour felt unable to make a bargain. Though Curzon bowed to the King's wish that he should not indulge in recriminations, his reply seems to have been misinterpreted, and private accounts from India spoke of his bitter hostility to Brodrick and the India Office.[6]

'I am not going to say all I think in a letter:' wrote Schomberg McDonnell; 'never has anything been so shocking or disgusting...The only redeeming feature in all this sordid business has been the attitude of the King...'[7]

*   *   *   *

Minor clashes with the India Council continued to the end. 'I have been much astonished' remarked Sir Hugh Barnes, recently appointed, 'at the attitude of hostility to all that comes from Your Excellency which is assumed by several Members of Council.' Another wrote in September, 'I have been already long enough in the India Office to appreciate the thorns with which your Excellency's path has been strewn.'[8]

The campaign against the petition of Bengal was carried on, in its later stages, to the accompaniment of intimidation, occasional attacks on Europeans and allegations that the blood of sacred animals had been used to purify salt and sugar. Curzon, recognising that Bengali aspirations in their extreme form were inconsistent with British rule, deplored the tactics of Brodrick, whose public statements indicated that the measure might not be pushed through, that the home authorities did not like it and that it had been a sop to the Viceroy. Brodrick, receiving many telegrams which described the agitation as more fierce than any in recent times, suggested a short postponement. This could only be achieved by an amending Act and Curzon replied that the opposition had been 'converted into a purely political movement organised by a small and disloyal faction on anti-British lines…If any concession were made at the eleventh hour to such an agitation, it would at once assume a serious character; the government of India would forfeit the respect of all classes; and a premium would be placed on similar tactics in future.'[9] The partition was carried through on 16 October. Nevertheless, Curzon's last weeks in India were cheered by countless expressions of sympathy, gratitude and support. He superintended every detail of the forthcoming royal tour, continued to despatch the daily business, and visited again some of the monuments which his reverence had helped to rescue. At Lahore, the Lieut.-Governor trailed round after His Excellency, muttering 'damned rot'. Arriving at the Pearl Mosque, Curzon asked what it was. Sir C. Rivaz had no idea; nor had others, questioned in turn. Curzon then inquired of the sentry:

Can *you* tell me what it is?
''Indu mosque, sir,' said a Cockney voice.

This incident, comments a bystander, had the happy result of making the official world take 'a more enlightened interest in the remains of Mogul rule in Lahore'.[10]

Shortly before leaving Simla for good, Curzon attended a conference of the Directors of Public Instruction. Already the reforms of earlier years had begun to fructify. Education, he said, was needed in India not so much as the vehicle of culture but as the key to all national advance and prosperity,

the sole stepping-stone of every class of the community to higher things. It is a social and political, even more than an intellectual, demand, and to it alone can we look to provide a livelihood for our citizens, to train up our public Servants, to develop the economic and industrial resources of the country, to fit the people for the share in self-government which is given to them, and which will increase with their deserts…[11]

Having received the Prince and Princess of Wales at Bombay, Curzon, with a few days to spare before Minto's arrival, determined to visit Agra, the city he loved best of all. Every corner of Shah Jehan's palace was inspected. The Taj Mahal and the other noble buildings had now been expertly restored. 'If I had never done anything else in India' he had once told Mary, 'I have written my name here and the letters are a living joy.'[12] On his return to Bombay, Curzon was given a dinner at the Byculla Club. The concluding passage of his speech expresses perfectly his conception of Empire:

A hundred times in India have I said to myself, Oh that to every Englishman in this country, as he ends his work, might be truthfully applied the phrase 'Thou hast loved righteousness and hated iniquity.' No man has, I believe, ever served India faithfully of whom that could not be said. All other triumphs are tinsel and sham. Perhaps there are few of us who make anything but a poor approximation of that ideal. But let it be our ideal all the same—to fight for the right, to abhor the imperfect, the unjust or the mean, to swerve neither to the right hand, nor to the left, to care nothing for flattery or applause or odium or abuse—it is so easy to have any of them in India—never to let your enthusi- asm be soured or your courage grow dim, but to remember that the Almighty has placed your hand on the greatest of his ploughs, in whose furrow the nations of the future are germinating and taking shape, to drive the blade a little forward in your time, and to feel that somewhere among these millions you have left a little justice or happiness or prosperity, a sense of manliness or moral dignity, a spring of patriotism, a dawn of intellectual enlightenment or a stirring of duty where it did not exist before—that is enough, that is the Englishman's justification in India. It is good enough for his watchword while he is here, for his epitaph when he is gone. I have worked for no other aim. Let India be my judge.

★   ★   ★   ★

Minto's ship was delayed by adverse currents. Curzon, who had set aside a day for intimate conversation with him, spent the time preparing a long note on the main problems of the moment. The ceremonial reception of the incoming Viceroy was postponed until the morrow. Minto landed privately in the late afternoon and went to Government House, where Curzon greeted him informally. These proceedings, widely attributed to Curzon's egotism, gave rise to much cruel gossip. The likelihood is that the cancella- tion resulted from a genuine misunderstanding. Minto believed otherwise, and did not hide his opinion from the King or Brodrick, though he made no complaint to Curzon.[13]

The Governor of Madras had been asked by Brodrick to convey the message that the Viceroy had misunderstood and deeply injured him. Ampthill, who found Curzon unusually calm and dispassionate, did his best, but with no success.[14] Knowing that Curzon was to call at Cairo, Brodrick sent Lord Cromer an account of the military controversy. Among his more startling statements were allegations that Curzon had refused requests from London to prevent delays in the military system; that under him the army had clearly declined; that he had never taken any interest in army matters; and that the Military Member had continually rejected Kitchener's proposals without reference to anyone.[15] Whether Brodrick

knowingly falsified the facts, or, as seems more probable, failed to the last
to grasp them, matters comparatively little; for Cromer disagreed. Nevertheless, the rumour that he had supported Brodrick was widely spread in
London. Meanwhile, it was not only Brodrick who looked with some
apprehension on Curzon's return. Kitchener believed Curzon to possess
copies of all his cypher telegrams, a fact which understandably made him
'very unhappy'.[16]

The King was anxious that Balfour and Brodrick should greet Curzon
at the station. Brodrick immediately arranged to be at some hours' distance
from London, and urged that Balfour should also find the hour inconvenient. Outraged by Curzon's remark at the Byculla Club that he had the
support of most of the army, Godley spoke up in the same sense.[17] The
returning Viceroy who, like Dalhousie, had left India without a syllable of
thanks, therefore received no official welcome at Charing Cross on
3 December. On 4 December the roof of the station fell in. 'How like
St John!' exclaimed Lady Curzon, 'to bring it off a day too late!'

★　　★　　★　　★

Curzon at once assured the King's secretary that he would not air his
grievances in public. 'Nothing' wrote Knollys, 'could be more satisfactory
than his attitude.'[18] It must have been hard to maintain this self-denying
ordinance, for Curzon acquired a good deal of information about the
methods by which he had been brought down. Copies of Kitchener's two
secret letters to Stedman were handed over by the Manager of *The Times*.
A number of the experts consulted by Brodrick said that they had advised
against the policy he had adopted; and the papers had been abstracted from
the India Office. Curzon knew of the existence, and perhaps the contents,
of Kitchener's secret telegrams, and of the means by which the press
campaign had been organised. It seems incredible, in all the circumstances
here described, that Brodrick should have been 'extremely confident and
eager for the fray'.[19]

The retirement of the Cabinet coincided with Curzon's return. He had
some reason to hope that the incoming Liberal government might reverse
the decision on military administration. The arrangements for the Mobilisation Committee, by which the Cabinet had set such store, seemed somewhat
doubtful, for Kitchener proposed to omit the Military Supply Member!
Brodrick had to telegraph that the constitution of the Committee required
attention.[20] Kitchener immediately threatened resignation should Brodrick's scheme be upset,[21] while Curzon supplied the new Secretary of State

with a documented account of the controversy, including the celebrated letter to Stedman. 'The story is indeed outrageous' Morley replied, '—almost too ugly for belief...I do understand your profound indignation. And I may say that the thing confirms my resolution to deal faithfully with him...'[22]

Repington worked hard on Morley, avowing picturesquely that the former system was like having two Secretaries of State for India in the Cabinet. At one lunch, Ian Hamilton happened to have a letter from Kitchener highly complimentary to Morley, in whose pocket it went away. 'I think you must allow' wrote Repington to Marker after further treatment, 'that we have looked after J.M. for you.'[23] Minto had already refused some proposals of Kitchener, who was made to acknowledge the absolute supremacy of the civil power; but he believed the Commander-in-Chief straightforward and generally backed him. Morley, who felt no keenness to face the resignation of both, decided after all to confirm the previous decision with minor but significant alterations. He remarked that even a tentative and dubious scheme was better than indefinite prolongation of the row.[24]

This was for Curzon a miserable time. Repington in *The Times* attributed his ignorance of the Generals' opinions to the probable intervention of the Military Member and was only with some difficulty compelled to recant.[25] A conversation with Balfour showed that he had throughout believed Curzon in some way pledged to accept the decision of the government and therefore guilty of ill-faith in resigning; and when Curzon pointed out that this view was inconsistent with his memorandum of 2 November, 1904, and letter of 30 March, 1905, Balfour admitted the first charge and could remember nothing of the letter.[26] After accepting the King's argument that a returning Viceroy should not plunge into the strife of the Commons, Curzon found himself debarred from the Lords by Campbell-Bannerman's refusal to recommend for a peerage a Conservative whom Balfour had pointedly refrained from honouring. Recalling the King's assurances of 1904 that the Viceroy would be treated as beyond party politics, Curzon represented the unfairness of exclusion from Parliament for the best years of his life. The fact that he alone of recent Viceroys had received no recognition must cast a reflection upon his administration.

The King did his best, but on Bannerman's renewed refusal felt that it would be constitutionally improper to press further. Moreover, the Prince of Wales had returned from India a violent partisan of the C-in-C. During the tour he had gossiped indiscreetly against Curzon and the 'antiquated old fossils' of the Viceroy's Council. In London he used what Morley described as 'most unmeasured language' against Curzon, who was well aware of it. The Prince said to Charles Hardinge that Curzon had never done a single thing right in India. Hardinge at once objected.[27]

All these troubles, however, counted as nothing beside Curzon's anxiety for his adored wife. Her recovery in 1905 had proved no more than a false dawn; and she had long felt a premonition that India would kill her, 'as one of the humble inconsequent lives who go into the foundations of all great works, great buildings and great achievements.'[28] During the summer of 1906 her strength ebbed steadily away. She died in July at the age of thirty-six, and was buried at Kedleston:

> I have seen it coming and dared not avow it to her or even to myself...We lay her to rest peacefully, no one here, no show. This is as she would have wished.[29]

In anguish Curzon exclaimed that his life was a failure and a misery, for she had been his one resource and comfort since they left India, and before then his only friend and trustiest adviser. 'Every man's hand' he said pathetically, 'has long been against me, and now God's hand has turned against me too.' He hid at Kedleston, finding some comfort in the well-loved surroundings and the many messages of affection and sorrow. 'For the time I am stunned and know not where to turn...Some day I must look up again...The children keep me at home. For they are all that I have.'[30]

★   ★   ★   ★

Ten years separated Curzon's resignation from his return to office as a member of the coalition Cabinet in 1915. A good deal of that decade he spent outside the arena of party politics, upon his duties as Chancellor of Oxford, as a Trustee of the National Gallery, and as President of the Royal Geographical Society. Believing that a British Army might well be needed in Europe, and that a tiny force of regulars was no sufficient protection, Curzon enthusiastically but unavailingly seconded Roberts's campaign for national service, and thereby detached himself from the official Conservative leadership. In 1908, largely on account of Lansdowne's goodwill, he took his seat in the Lords as an elected Irish peer.

Conditions which had played a dominant part in the last years of the Viceroyalty changed swiftly. Morley and his Liberal colleagues set their faces resolutely against large military spending in India, so that the nine divisions and many other features of Kitchener's scheme were never completed. They opposed equally any policy but the most timid in the buffer states. These attitudes, coinciding with Russia's external battering and domestic turmoil, not to say her need for the London money market, provided the setting for the agreement which Russia had disdained before. The Liberal government, by conceding in effect that Britain should have no special position in Tibet, had already thrown away the remaining fruits of Younghusband's mission in a manner which Curzon, during prolonged negotiations with the Chinese in 1905, had refused to allow.[31] For Russia, bad relations with Britain meant greater dependence on Germany. The abortive treaty signed at Björkö in the summer of 1905, and other methods by which Germany had taken advantage of Russia's embarrassment, gave point to this lesson.

In that uneasy interval between the dismissal of Delcassé and the Algeciras conference of January 1906, Balfour, Lansdowne and Clarke had agreed on a fresh effort to make terms with Russia. The Czar and Lamsdorff seemed willing, and would have realised the more fully after 1904–5 that their depleted naval strength would be at British mercy in war. The chief of the Russian General Staff declared that the idea of invading India was 'a mere phantasy that had never been seriously entertained by responsible Russians'. Probably that was true;[32] but a treaty would mean abandonment of the threat, however remote. Isvolsky, Lamsdorff's successor, did not wish to bind Russia too tightly to Germany or Britain in European questions.[33] The agreement of 1907 was not an alliance.

Curzon took objection mainly to the Persian terms. Morley and Grey had deliberately foregone the opportunity to offer a Persian loan on the security of the Southern customs and the revenues of Seistan. Grey's aim during the negotiations was strategic, not commercial. Eleven of the twelve main towns fell within the Russian sphere. Too late the Foreign Secretary realised that the British line did not cover Herat; and it was in general less advantageous than that proposed by Curzon in 1899.[34] Whether the agreement would really secure India depended upon Russia's willingness to abide by the terms. 'You can't keep an elephant out of a potato-plot' commented Spring-Rice, 'by tying a parchment to his trunk.' Curzon's similar view received a good deal of confirmation in succeeding years. Very shortly the commanding officer of the Cossacks at Teheran threatened to bombard the British Legation. Sazonov, replacing Isvolsky as Foreign Minister, realised that England, on account of European interests, would make sacrifices in Asia to keep the agreement alive.[35] Russia traded upon that fact, and had by 1914 virtually occupied Northern Persia.

Amir Habibullah persistently refused to recognise the agreement. In 1908 his forces attacked Landi Kotal and crossed into India. Minto feared that Britain might soon be forced into war with him, but the Afghans withdrew.

While Habibullah lived no open clash occurred. His successor, Amanullah, declared a holy war in 1918 and was soundly beaten. As for Tibet, the Dalai Lama's return in 1910 led to a Chinese invasion and caused him to flee again, but this time southwards to British protection. After the Chinese upheaval of 1911 the Tibetans appealed for British support. By 1914 it was agreed that Tibet would in practice be treated as independent of China.

Curzon continued to follow closely the convolutions of the military question. In the summer of 1907, he learned of certain alterations in the official record of his military administration. From the revised version many episodes reflecting credit on Curzon, Elles and Palmer had been expunged, together with references to Kitchener's plan for homogeneous brigades, his original redistribution and his change of attitude about reserves of ammunition; the celebrated case of the 9th Lancers had been rewritten. The reply of the government of India to Curzon's protest stated that Kitchener had nothing to do with all this, but Minto's Private Secretary admitted that the C-in-C was in fact responsible. On the Viceroy's order, the revised version was withdrawn.[36]

The position of the Military Supply Member, who became known as the Director of the Army and Navy Stores Ltd, soon proved to be very much what Curzon had predicted. Within eighteen months, Morley was considering the abolition of the post; and in 1909, shortly before Kitchener left India, the entire military organisation was placed under the C-in-C, as he had long desired. It therefore fell to the Liberals to set up the form of administration against which they had inveighed so vigorously in 1905. The strongest protests, apart from Curzon's, came from those like Lansdowne who had brought about his resignation. Under the new system, the C-in-C of an army of 225,000 men, scattered over a huge area, was responsible at the highest level for every question of supply, training and planning, and simultaneously supposed to be taking his full share in the civil government of India.[37]

After the debate, Brodrick sent Curzon an appealing note:

> You told me, in reply to my question, that some day you would not be averse to seeing me.
>
> While you were speaking, I could not help thinking how many mists have gathered round this difference between us, and how large an element of misunderstanding there has been.
>
> I do not mean that I think I could ever remove from your mind the sense of injury under which you have laboured, any more than you could recall what have seemed to me cruel thrusts now continued for four years.
>
> But somehow lately I have looked back more than ever to old days...I ask

myself whether anything justifies life passing away in bitterness and neglect after 30 years of unstinted friendship.

It has been your edict and you must decide...

But Curzon could not bring himself to the point of full reconciliation:

> I would sooner leave things as they are and not rake up the past. Too much is involved that touches the innermost springs of my being and I have been too deeply scarred to wish to reopen the wounds.

So their co-operation was not resumed until August, 1914, when together they pressed Asquith's government to bring Indian troops to France. One of Curzon's last public acts was to persuade Brodrick to resume his seat on the Opposition front bench.[38]

*   *   *   *

Long before then, the reorganisations of 1905 and 1909 had been put to a bitter test. Their effect had been to centralize all important questions at Army HQ and to create in the Viceroy's Council complete dependence in everything military upon the competence and energy of one man. Sir E. Barrow was appointed to the Southern Command where, as he wrote, he commanded nothing but his own small staff, possessing responsibility without power and authority without information.[39] So far was the policy carried that the Northern and Southern Army commands were afterwards left unfilled. There existed in the whole Indian Army no authority higher than a General of a division until Army HQ was reached, and no one on the frontier capable of commanding two or more divisions if war suddenly broke out. Every important issue now came to the C-in-C through two separate channels nominally within the same department. Often the one contradicted the other.[40]

By 1911, it appears, a return to the old system was being considered. Kitchener's successor as C-in-C, Sir O'Moore Creagh, a distinguished fighting soldier, was generally thought to be unequal to his task. This was the situation which Curzon and his colleagues had foreseen when they pointed to the need for a system which men of ordinary ability could work; and in private Kitchener went far to admitting it. 'I am afraid I miscalculated the possible harm that incapacity might achieve' in 'this critical time of supreme Hd. Qr. inefficiency.'[41] Charles Hardinge, who followed Minto as Viceroy, states baldly in his memoirs that by 1912 chaos prevailed in the military system. He insisted upon the appointment as C-in-C of Sir Beauchamp Duff, who had made a fine reputation as an administrator.[42]

History has a way of producing ironical situations; but in the tragedy about to be played in Mesopotamia, India, and London, the irony could not have been more fully rounded. At the apex of the military system in India stood Duff, Kitchener's *alter ego* in the controversy of 1905, operating a system especially designed to cope with the stresses of war. In the Cabinet at home, Kitchener was Secretary for War, secretive and mistrusted by the civilians, most of whom would no doubt have been glad to get rid of him had they only seen the means. Balfour, after painful experience, called him 'a great hustler but not a good organiser'.[43] Beside Balfour, there were prominent in the government Lansdowne and Austen Chamberlain, leading members of the Cabinet which had sanctioned the solution of 1905, and Asquith and Lloyd George, Prime Minister and Chancellor in the Cabinet which abolished the Military Supply Membership in 1909. To preside over the inquiry into the breakdown of India's military administration came first Lord Cromer and then Lord George Hamilton, both of whom had supported Curzon in 1905. At the head of the Military Department of the India Office was none other than General Barrow.

Early in the war, Curzon and Kitchener found themselves at one in believing that it would last long, and that Indian troops should be used in the Middle East and Europe. After the successful start to the campaign in Mesopotamia, Kitchener agreed that the advance to Baghdad, about which the Viceroy's Council were not consulted, should be undertaken. Curzon protested but was overborne. In the end, more than a quarter of a million troops were committed. Meanwhile, the sufferings of the force almost defied description; gangrene and cholera ran riot; hospital ships and medical supplies were lacking. Inquiries from Austen Chamberlain, Secretary for India, received reassuring replies from the Viceroy. Sir B. Duff found himself in the dilemma to which Curzon had pointed in 1904 and 1905, and which Kitchener had contemptuously dismissed as unreal. If he took command of the troops, or even went to the port of embarkation, to whom would the Viceroy and his civilian colleagues turn for military advice?

It is true [telegraphed Hardinge in March, 1916] [that] Commander-in-Chief has not visited Bombay since the outbreak of war, and I venture to submit that it has been quite impossible for him to do so. The situation on the frontier and elsewhere has been far too critical for me to have allowed him to leave Headquarters when rapid and decisive action might be necessary at any moment.[44]

As Duff explicitly admitted to the Commission of Inquiry, his dual duties could not be carried out in time of war. As sole military adviser of the government of India he must remain at Delhi and Simla; and because he must stay there, he knew far less about events in Mesopotamia than did laymen in Bombay. It is true that the Indian Army was already depleted on a scale not foreseen by Kitchener, and that his scheme had not precluded, in theory, the appointment of a deputy to represent the C-in-C at the seat of government. As a practical solution, this had drawbacks which Duff evidently felt disinclined to accept. For instance, would it be feasible to find at short notice a man with sufficient experience and authority to advise a small cabinet of civilians on all questions of supply, strategy, intelligence and internal security? Would the Council be able to attach the right weight to such advice? And what would happen if the replacement disagreed with his absent chief?

To Curzon, who had always contended that no one man could do the administrative business of a War Office and simultaneously manage a campaign, none of this came as any surprise. Correspondents and his own observation had convinced him that Indian military administration had broken down even before the war; and like everyone else, he regretted deeply that it should have needed the Mesopotamian campaign to demonstrate the completeness of the collapse:

> I sometimes wonder [he wrote to Chamberlain] if my colleagues who went against me in 1905 now realize exactly what I was fighting against and for—after their experience of my then Commander-in-Chief in his present capacity...[45]

Certainly Chamberlain made no attempt to contest the charge. He told the Commission that the organisation had disintegrated through excessive concentration. The intention had been to abolish the Military Member; but in fact the C-in-C had disappeared. The report accepted Duff's view that the duties could not be performed by one man, and revealed a method of administration incredibly cumbrous, weighed down with paperwork and minute-writing, centralised to an absurd degree. 'This astounding system has only to be described to be condemned.' The transport question, formerly the work of the Military Member, had not been properly gripped. Hardinge had not been told of vital deficiencies. He had trusted the only available military advice; but the whole object of Kitchener's reform had been to compel him to do so.[46] Chamberlain, the Minister technically responsible, resigned, showing clearly in his speech that he regretted the decision of 1905. Another prominent member of Balfour's Cabinet, Lord Lansdowne, said that he 'deeply regretted' that decision, and believed the old system to have been in principle 'entirely sound'. Brodrick, who had then accepted Curzon's resignation rather than allow the Military Supply Member any role beyond that of purveying stores, was driven to explain how important he had always thought it that the government of India should have two military advisers.[47]

Curzon himself made a moderate, urbane and dignified speech, omitting the personal aspects. A quite surprising variety of people felt it prudent to alter their views. J. S. Sandars discovered that in the quarrel with Kitchener Curzon had been right, and had been overruled because he showed 'no wisdom, equity or moderation in his treatment of the matter'. Lord Esher wrote innocently that Kitchener's proceedings were 'not untinged by methods which the Israelites inherited from Jacob and the statesmen of the Renaissance from Machiavelli'. *The Times* recanted, but contrived to adopt a posture fulfilling its Editor's definition of a mugwump as an individual who sits upon a fence with his mug on one side and his wump on the other.[48] Meanwhile, Austen Chamberlain, having read all the papers about the mission to Tibet, had summoned Younghusband and said he now realised grave injustice had been done in 1904. The KCSI was awarded forthwith.

★   ★   ★   ★

Since it has now become common to conceive of the European Empires in Africa and Asia merely as instruments of oppression and exploitation, it is well to record here that between 1893–4, when Lansdowne closed the mints to the free coinage of silver, and 1904–5, Curzon's last complete year as Viceroy, capital invested in Indian railways increased by 56%, by joint-stock companies in industry by 23%; savings banks deposits grew by 43%, deposits in other banks by figures between 71% and 130%, the sums on which income tax was assessed, progressive exemptions notwithstanding, by 29%. India's imports in those eleven years went up by 35%, her exports by 48%. In Curzon's first five years, the revenue swelled from £68½m to £83m despite plague and famine, and the debts of India by £16m; but £20m were spent on railways and £2¾m on irrigation, the increased revenue from which amply serviced the extra debt. Net imports of bullion into India, a country from which the wealth was supposed to be fast draining away, rose from £25m in 1894–9 to £46m in the next five years.

In citing such figures, Curzon did not pretend that there were not abuses, injustices, blots on the record, grave symptoms of future trouble. No Viceroy saw more clearly that India must have, and that quickly, better communications, all-round improvements of education, methodical development of industry and commerce, scientific study of agriculture. Eight out of every ten Indians were then dependent upon the land, pitifully

poor, at the mercy of the elements and of the usurer. If it was a fault, it was
at least an understandable and honourable fault, that Viceroys and civil
servants should believe them to be the real India. In Curzon's last months
as Viceroy, after the salt tax had again been reduced, a scheme to standardise
the methods of remitting land revenue in time of famine was brought
forward. This, he minuted,

> will be of the utmost importance to the great mute pathetic cultivating class—
> the backbone of the country and the main instrument of its economic sub-
> sistence...For such services Government receives no gratitude.
>
> It is lucky if it escapes abuse. But relief and comfort will be brought thereby
> in times of stress to countless humble homes, and if praised by no other tribunal
> Government will have the silent approval of its own conscience.[49]

The educated minority of Indians, articulate and conscious of a long
history of high civilisation, were then just beginning to contest the British
right to rule India. The sense of grievance and the stirrings of national,
rather than regional, consciousness doubtless owed something to the partition of Bengal but much more to the defeat of Russia by an Asiatic power.
In Curzon's time, the size of this movement was still small. Britain could
govern India only through Indians' goodwill; and the Viceroy himself was
accustomed to the end to wander about the slums and narrow streets of
Calcutta quite alone, or with an ADC.

One day, the owner of a celebrated Indian paper came to Walter
Lawrence, then Curzon's Private Secretary, and said

> We do not ask for Home Rule now, nor in ten years, nor in twenty, but all
> we ask is that he will not shut the door of hope upon us. Ask him to say that
> perhaps in fifty years India may be self-governing.

Much moved by his earnestness, Lawrence put this to his master.
Curzon, who had a high respect for the visitor, thought long before he said,
'No, I will say nothing, for it might embarrass my successor if I raised any
hopes or expressed any opinion as to when self-government will come.'
And, when Lawrence said it must happen some day, 'It will not come in
my time and I cannot say what may happen in the future.'[50]

Curzon realised quite well that Indians were indispensable to the higher
levels of the administration, not least for their knowledge of the languages,
the people and the country. He hoped, vainly, that a better educated India
would be more content to accept British dominion, or at least partnership.
'We are ordained to walk here in the same track for many a long day to
come. You cannot do without us. We should be impotent without you.'

In a country so deeply crevassed, in which slumbering hatreds might so readily be inflamed, the developing force of nationality presented peculiar pitfalls. Nationalism in its highest and least selfish form, which he habitually called patriotism, Curzon thought indispensable to the life of any man or nation; but unless it were broadly conceived in India, the consequence would be not unity but division:

> It should not be a question of India for the Hindus, or India for the Musulmans, or, descending to minor fractions, of Bengal for the Bengalis, or the Deccan for the Mahratta Brahmans. That would be a retrograde and dissolvent process. Neither can it be India for the Indians alone...[51]

Curzon understood that the presence of the British had affected the whole structure of Indian life. From the mingling of the two cultures, he hoped, would emerge a more cosmopolitan and less exclusive conception of nationality, with European and Asiatic elements. Perhaps that ambition, which seemed less and less real or worthy in the later and more bitter stages of the struggle for emancipation, has not been entirely falsified. Where Curzon and his contemporaries failed was in anticipating an ample span in which to bring about adjustments. Australia, New Zealand, South Africa and Canada were achieving with every passing year a greater degree of independence. With India, that process was temporarily reversed. The view of the India office, Brodrick told Balfour, was that 'the Secretary of State can check any appointment and can direct every farthing of Indian expenditure'.[52] He once wrote that Curzon regarded the Secretary of State not as the Minister responsible to Parliament for the government of India but as the Viceroy's diplomatic representative at the Court of St James; while Balfour claimed that if Curzon's view were admitted, India would be raised to the position of an independent and not always friendly power.[53] There is some truth in both remarks; and on the whole time has justified Curzon's contention that it was unpractical and undesirable to rule India in detail from King Charles Street.

That habit, noticeable under Brodrick, became still more pronounced under so advanced a Liberal as Morley. Learning that Minto had refused to take an official of the Treasury as his Private Secretary, Curzon congratulated him on his wisdom:

> You will realise that the home ideal of a Viceroy is that he should be a Treasury Clerk also. I have not a doubt that before long you will be resisting this contention.[54]

This proved to be so. Morley interfered perpetually in small matters,

9

reacted with horror to Minto's request that the government of India be fully consulted before an agreement was made with Russia, and insisted upon the sole right of the Secretary of State to appoint members of the Viceroy's Council. His Under-Secretary, Montagu, indeed described the Viceroy as the Secretary of State's 'agent'. Minto told the King's Private Secretary that had he not been on the point of return, he would have felt bound to ask for an official inquiry into the relations of the Viceroy and Secretary of State, for the India Office had far overstepped the powers it could wisely assume.[55] The tendency doubtless reflected Morley's autocratic spirit; and it was in any event impossible that India should continue to be thus governed, not least because of that developing public opinion the significance of which Sir Arthur Godley had disputed.

By the reforms of 1909, the Legislative Councils in India, and the elected element within them, were largely increased in size; for the first time an Indian member was appointed to the Executive Councils in Madras and Bombay, and to the Viceroy's Council. Curzon, who had been forewarned by Morley, did not take serious exception and acknowledged the advantages. In their estimates of the results, however, the two differed. To Curzon it was clear, though Morley denied it with vehemence, that these changes would lead to a Parliamentary system, and he could not persuade himself either that the whole sub-continent could be held together in a policy so alien to its traditions, or that the majority of Indians would benefit:

> Remember that to these people...representative government and electoral institutions are nothing whatever...The good government that appeals to them is the government which protects them from the rapacious money-lender and landlord...and all the other sharks in human disguise...I have a misgiving that this class will not fare much better under these changes than they do now...I am under the strong opinion that as government in India becomes more and more Parliamentary—as will be the inevitable result—so will it become less paternal and less beneficent to the poorer classes of the population.[56]

At the time, it was believed that the new arrangements would endure for a considerable period. However, the First World War meant a rapid change of emphasis. Not only did India contribute on a massive scale, by voluntary enlistment, but the allies' espousal of self-determination inevitably quickened Indian desire for another step in that direction. 'We are really making concessions to India' Curzon wrote in June, 1917, 'because of the free talk about liberty, democracy, nationality and self-government which have become the common shibboleths of the Allies, and because we are expected to translate into practice in our own domestic household the sentiments which we have so enthusiastically preached.' He realised the force of the argument and agreed with Austen Chamberlain that self-government within the Empire, with the safeguards of British justice and power, was the right goal for India. By this he meant not that uniformity was possible or that all British administrators would be withdrawn within the foreseeable future, but rather a continuous increase in the share taken by Indians in governing their country. The rate of advance would be measured by their capacity, as tested by experience, the judges of that rate the British Government. Not until India proved herself, and possessed the armed force to repel attack, could she be fully self-governing.[57]

It was Curzon who drafted the formula announced in August, 1917:

> The policy of His Majesty's Government, with which the Government of India are in complete accord, is that of increasing association of Indians in every branch of the Administration and the gradual development of self-governing institutions, with a view to the progressive realisation of responsible Government in India as an integral part of the British Empire.

Whether he understood that 'responsible government' would be taken to mean Parliamentary Government in the Western sense is doubtful. In the later shaping of the Montagu-Chelmsford reforms he played little part. Like many another British administrator of India, fearing that the relaxation of control must bring a lowering of standards, the growth of corruption and danger to minorities, Curzon had no desire to hasten the day of departure which would portend the end of the British Empire in Asia. Speaking for the last time about India, in 1924, he pointed out that the reforms, instead of satisfying the aspirations of those for whom they were intended, had encouraged their hostility. A general impression of weakness on the part of the government of India had been produced. Racial and sectional antagonisms were reviving, the ancestral cauldron boiling up again:

> And you see what is at the back of it all. What democracy means to these shrewd people who look below the surface is not a fair chance for the Moslems; it means Brahmin ascendancy, and that means the ascendancy of a highly accomplished oligarchy framed on the strictest lines of creed and caste.[58]

The embers of more recent controversies – whether it was unavoidable that the sub-continent should be split up in 1947, that the renewed partition of Bengal should come in so terrible a form, that communities which had lived side by side should fall upon each other with pitiless ferocity, that the deaths and injuries by violence in the first weeks of independence should far outnumber those suffered in the whole history of British India – need not be raked over here. Now that twenty more years have passed, the nature of the Anglo-Indian connexion may be viewed in a calmer atmosphere. The British defended India from invasion and civil war and provided her with railways, roads, canals, irrigation and access on favourable terms to the London money-market. India became, in effect, a free-trade area the size of Europe, and what had been in the eighteenth century a geographic expression acquired a cohesion without which India and Pakistan in their present form could not exist. India gave Britain much enhanced status, especially in Asia; a huge market and a safe field of investment; supplies of raw material, particularly cotton; and in both world wars service of such distinction that it may justly be called indispensable to the survival and triumph of the allies. There were, in this long story, many acts of unwisdom or injustice, many failures of imagination or sympathy, but its culmination, as Mr Nehru acknowledged, was a fine civil service, a Parliamentary system, the rule of law and individual freedom.

To the day of his death Curzon followed eagerly the affairs of India. He regretted his silence in 1905, declaring that his whole career had been prejudiced.[59] It was, nevertheless, one of much distinction and has not yet been assessed at its true worth. Nor does the accepted picture of Curzon do him justice. In Sir Harold Nicolson's telling phrase, he 'loved and suffered with the eternal intensity of boyhood'.[60] Moreover he was rarely free from racking pain. Genuine kindness, generosity and devotion to the public service tended to be obscured by irritability or thoughtlessness. His real qualities would flower only when circumstances were auspicious. Usually, and especially to those who did not know him well or who lacked self-confidence, he appeared stony, cold, hard, the embodiment of English aristocratic aloofness carried to the point of caricature.

That his mood was infinitely variable, and that he often behaved harshly and tactlessly, is not in doubt. Ampthill surmised pertinently that had Curzon not been the first of his family to attain any kind of eminence he would have been saved many mistakes; but on taking over the Viceroyalty, it is right to add, Ampthill had soon discovered among subordinates and colleagues a real respect for Curzon's staggering powers of work, and a personal affection for him.[61] Many of those who served under Curzon found him the reverse of inconsiderate or unbending. 'I feel absolutely broken and dejected' wrote Walter Lawrence in 1903, 'at the idea of leaving you. Whatever the future may hold—and it seems dreary and empty enough now—I shall never have a chief whom I shall admire and love as I have admired you.'[62]

A friend once remarked that it was Curzon's misfortune to have the manners of minor royalty without its habitual incapacity. He enjoyed telling good stories against himself, and part of the legend which has gathered around his name was his own doing. He loved to act up to it. When Queen Mary was due to visit Oxford, the Domestic Bursar of Balliol sent a menu, beginning with soup. It came back endorsed with a solitary sentence in the Chancellor's hand: 'Gentlemen do not take soup at luncheon.'[63]

Common to the late Victorian apologists of Empire—Dilke, Salisbury, Rhodes, Cromer and Milner among them—was a deep-seated belief in the ability of the British to guide other countries uprightly. Curzon shared that confidence as a young man, and was confirmed in it during the Viceroyalty. He would contrast the standards of the ICS favourably with those at home. 'In India' he noted in 1921, 'I was magnificently served. The whole spirit of service there was different. Everyone there was out to do something.' Asked whether a young man should try for the Home or Indian Civil Service, he replied without hesitation that whatever good was in a man would show itself in India, whereas in England it might be forever interred in files. Further, since men do not know why they exist or whither they go, the only purpose of life must be to do good. Where could that be better accomplished than in India?[64]

At the end of his life, Curzon used to say that he had derived more satisfaction from his other interests, architecture, paintings, history and literature, than from politics. India was the exception. Like Burke, he valued that part of his work the most, for the labour and for the spirit in which it had been done, and on his deathbed he expressed the hope that the full story of his administration should be told. In the years after his resignation, there came a time when some Indian papers pictured Curzon as a kind of ogre who had detested and oppressed the people, torn up the proclamation of 1858, lived only for tawdry display, shattered Bengal, had even been idle. Feeling all this deeply, he was nevertheless sustained by a belief that service to India was not to be accomplished without suffering and by the stream of letters from Indians, some grateful for services, some still appealing to him as a source of justice, others saying that they had found a spark of inspiration in his example. He professed himself content to be judged, when the mists of passion had uplifted, by the test of results. Finally

> I knew what I had done and been. Great as may have been my errors, I had yet striven conscientiously and manfully for India and I cared not what the world might think or India say so long as I had this self-absolving spring of conviction within me.[65]

Abbreviations used in notes

FULL TITLES of books and articles, with place and date of publication, are printed in the bibliography at the end of this volume, where the unpublished MS. collections upon which I have drawn are also listed. Usually, letters and documents are to be found in the papers of those to whom they are addressed. The main exception is Curzon's Viceregal papers, amongst which are printed copies of most of his outgoing letters. I have not thought it worthwhile to cite the number of each file from which a document is taken, since the handlists are generally clear. For instance, Curzon's letters to and from Queen Victoria and King Edward VII are printed in Curzon Papers 135 and 136; Schomberg McDonnell's letters to him are in C.P.14. Where a document might not be readily located, I have given the file number.

It is not uncommon to find minor differences of wording between copies of the same telegram. In such instances, I have followed whichever version seemed most likely to be authentic; and I have occasionally standardised spelling or inserted punctuation marks. Square brackets enclose my interpolations.

The abbreviations used in the notes are:

A.P.   Ampthill papers.
A.F.P. Arnold-Forster papers.
B.P.   Balfour papers.
A.C.P. Austen Chamberlain papers.
J.C.P. Joseph Chamberlain papers.
C.P.   Curzon papers.
C.P.2   Curzon papers (that part of the collection until recently held at Kedleston).
G.P.   Godley papers.
H.P.   Hamilton papers.
K.P.   Kitchener papers.
L.P.   Lansdowne papers
M.P.   Midleton (Brodrick) papers.
R.P.   Roberts papers.
S.P.   Salisbury papers.
S.P.2   Salisbury papers held at Hatfield.

Notes

Chapter I: Kitchener's Debut

1. Parl. Deb., H. of L., 5th ser., vol. 22, cols. 852–3; Lord Curzon, *Private Correspondence relating to the Military Administration of India, 1902–1905* (C.P.412), p. 1; Frank Maxwell to Lady Salisbury, n.d., but spring, 1905, S.P.2; G. de S. Barrow, *The Fire of Life*, p. 84; Lord Birdwood, *Khaki and Gown*, p. 137; Curzon to Hamilton, 3 Dec., 1902.
2. Lawrence's diary, 21 and 23 Oct., 30 Nov., 2 Dec., 1902.
3. Curzon to Hamilton, 3 Dec., 1902.
4. Lady Curzon to Kitchener, 9 Dec., 1902, K.P.26.
5. C.P.412, pp. 1–2.
6. Kitchener to Lady Cranborne, 10 Dec., 1902, S.P.2.
7. Kitchener to Roberts, 17 Dec., 1902, 12 Jan., 1903, R.P.
8. Curzon to Hamilton, 13 Jan., 1903.
9. Kitchener to Lady Cranborne, 25 Jan., 1903, S.P.2.
10. Curzon to Roberts, 5 Feb., 1903; Kitchener to Lady Cranborne, 12 Feb., 1903.
11. Kitchener's memo. of 26 Feb., 1903 (copy in Birdwood papers); Curzon to Hamilton, 26 Feb., 1903.
12. Roberts to Kitchener, 19 Feb., 1903, K.P.28; Kitchener to Roberts, 12 March, 1903; cf. Sir G. Arthur, *Life of Lord Kitchener*, vol. II, p. 124.
13. Curzon to Cromer, 19 March, 1903.
14. See Curzon's minute, 3 May, 1903, in Military file II, C.P.2.
15. Curzon to Hamilton, 7 May, 1903.
16. Hamilton to Kitchener, 5 June, 1903; Curzon to Hamilton, 5 Jan., 1900, Hamilton to Lansdowne and reply, 5 and 6 Jan., 1900, Hamilton to Brodrick and reply, 21 Jan. and 1 Feb., 1901, H.P.56.
17. Curzon to Kitchener and reply, 12 and 13 May, 1903.
18. Curzon to Kitchener and reply, 13 May, 1903.
19. Kitchener to Lady Cranborne, 13 May, 1903; Kitchener to Roberts, 28 May, 1903; Roberts to Kitchener, 4 June, 1903.
20. Curzon to Hamilton, 14 May, 1903.
21. Curzon to Kitchener, 16 May, 1903. File of this correspondence in the Birdwood papers.
22. Curzon to Hamilton, 21 May, 1903; C.P.412, p. 4.
23. Curzon to Kitchener, 20 and 24 May, 1903.
24. Curzon to Hamilton, 21 May, 1903.
25. Kitchener to Lady Cranborne, 21 May, 1903.

26. Curzon to Kitchener and reply 24 and 25 May, 1903; Curzon to Kitchener, 25 May, 1903.
27. Curzon to Hamilton, 28 May, 1903.
28. Curzon to Hamilton, 4 June, 1903.
29. Hamilton to Curzon, 4 June and 28 May, 1903.
30. Hamilton to Curzon, 11 June, 1903.
31. Hamilton to Curzon, 19 June, 1903; Curzon to Hamilton, 24 June, 1903.
32. Curzon to Hamilton, 9 July, 1903.
33. Kitchener to Lady Cranborne, 16 and 23 July, 1903.
34. Kitchener to Roberts, 30 July, 1903; Kitchener to Lady Cranborne, 29 July, 1903.
35. Kitchener to Lady Cranborne, 6 Aug., 1903.
36. Kitchener to Roberts, 24 March, 1903; Curzon to Kitchener, 13 Sept., 1903 (original in Birdwood Papers); Kitchener to Roberts, 25 Jan., 1903; C.P.412, p. 6.
37. Curzon to Brodrick, 2 July, 1903.
38. Brodrick to Curzon, 22 June, 1900.
39. Curzon to Brodrick, 19 July, 1900.
40. Hamilton to Curzon, 16 March, 1899; Lyttelton to Curzon, 5 Aug., 1900.
41. Curzon to Brodrick, 1 Aug., 1901.
42. Brodrick to Curzon, 26 Sept., 1901.
43. Brodrick to Curzon, 14 March, 1902 and 13 June, 1902.
44. *Studies of Yesterday*, pp. 54–5.
45. Brodrick to Curzon, 6 Nov., 1903; McDonnell to Curzon, 26 Oct., 1902; Dawkins to Curzon, 20 Feb., 1903.
46. Brodrick to Curzon, 16 Sept. and 17 Oct., 1902.
47. Selborne to Curzon, 4 Jan., 1903; Knollys to Curzon, 5 Feb., 1903; Selborne to Curzon, 24 April, 1903.
48. Earl of Midleton, *Records and Reactions,* pp. 145, 149.
49. Sir P. Magnus, *King Edward the Seventh,* pp. 324–5.
50. Curzon to Hamilton, 19 Feb., 1903.
51. Hamilton to Curzon, 13 Feb., 1903.
52. K. Young, *Arthur James Balfour,* p. 229.
53. Hamilton to Curzon, 27 Feb., 1903.
54. Brodrick to Curzon, 27 Feb., 1903; Curzon to Brodrick, 19 March, 1903.
55. Hamilton to Curzon, 5 March, 1903.
56. Hamilton to Curzon, 13 March, 1903.
57. McDonnell to Curzon, 29 April, 1903.
58. Hamilton to Curzon, 27 March, 1903.
59. Brodrick to Curzon, 17 May, 1903.
60. Curzon to Brodrick, 17 June, 1903.
61. Hamilton to Curzon, 15 July, 1903; Curzon to Hamilton, 22 July, 1903; minute by Kitchener, 20 July, 1903, C.P.2, Military file II, folder marked 'Defence of India'; Kitchener to Roberts, 27 and 30 July, 1903.
62. Curzon to Hamilton, 29 July, 1903; Government of India to Secretary of State, 30 July, 1903, C.P.2, Military file II, 'Defence of India'; Curzon to Brodrick, 19 Aug. 1903.
63. Hamilton to Curzon, 14 and 6 Aug., 1903.
64. Curzon to Brodrick, 30 July, 1903.
65. Brodrick to Curzon, 29 July, 5 Aug., 1903; Curzon to Brodrick, 10 Sept., 1903.
66. Brodrick to Curzon, 19 Aug., 1903; Curzon to Brodrick, 10 Sept., 1903.
67. McDonnell to Curzon, 4 Oct., 1903.

68. Hamilton to Curzon, 7 and 15 May, 1903.

69. Earl of Balfour [Gerald Balfour] to Austen Chamberlain, 14 Oct., 1935, A.C.P.

70. Balfour to Knollys, 16 May, 1903, RA R23/64.

71. Hamilton to Godley, 2 June, 1903, G.P.6B.

72. Curzon to Brodrick, 14 May, 1903; Brodrick to Curzon, 4 June, 1903.

73. Hamilton to Curzon, 5 June, 1903.

74. McDonnell to Curzon, 13 June, 1903, C.P.14; Balfour to King Edward VII, 9 June, 1903, RA R23/67; cf. M. V. Brett (ed.), *Journals and Letters of Reginald, Viscount Esher*, vol. I, pp. 410, 412.

75. Hamilton to Curzon, 25 June, 1903; Lord George Hamilton, *Parliamentary Reminiscences and Reflections*, vol. II, p. 323; Lady V. Hicks Beach, *Life of Sir Michael Hicks Beach*, vol. II, p. 195.

76. Ian Malcolm to Curzon, 4 Aug., 1903; B. E. C. Dugdale, *Arthur James Balfour*, vol. I, pp. 345-52.

77. Hamilton to Curzon, 20 Aug., 1903.

78. Curzon to H. O. Arnold-Forster, 10 Sept., 1903.

79. Lord Newton, *Lord Lansdowne*, p. 298.

80. B. E. C. Dugdale, *Arthur James Balfour*, vol. I, p. 357; Austen Chamberlain to Mrs. Dugdale, 21 Nov., 1929, A.C.P.

81. Hamilton to Curzon, 16 Sept., 1903.

82. Hamilton to Curzon, 24 Sept., 1903; B. Holland, *The Life of Spencer Compton, Eighth Duke of Devonshire*, vol. II, pp. 347-8, 352-3, 369-70. See also the discussion of these events in W. S. Churchill, *Great Contemporaries*, and A. Gollin, *Balfour's Burden*.

83. Hamilton to Curzon, 16 Sept., 1903; Curzon to Hamilton, 15 Oct., 1903; Ampthill to Godley, 28 Oct., 1903.

84. Roberts to Brodrick, 3 and 13 Sept., 1903; Brodrick to Roberts, 4 Sept., 1903, R.P.; D. James, *Lord Roberts*, p. 395; Roberts to Kitchener, 10 Dec., 1903.

85. Brodrick to Roberts, 4 and 6 Sept., 1903; Brodrick to Curzon, 6 Nov., 1903.

86. G. Monger, *The End of Isolation*, p. 171, f.6; Lord Chilston, *Chief Whip*, p. 313; Brodrick to Roberts, 29 Sept., 1903; Brodrick to Curzon, 6 Nov., 1903.

87. Balfour to King Edward VII, 30 Sept. and 4 Oct., 1903; King Edward VII to Balfour, 1 and 4 Oct., 1903, RA R23/99-102.

88. Brodrick to Curzon, 9 Oct., 1903; Curzon to Dawkins, 11 Nov., 1903 (original in Lawrence Papers).

89. Brodrick to Curzon, 6 Nov., 1903.

90. Balfour to King Edward VII, 30 Sept., 1903, RA R23/99.

91. Ian Malcolm to Curzon, 6 Oct., 1903.

92. Hamilton to Curzon, 24 Sept., 1903.

93. Curzon to Hamilton, 23 Sept., 1903; Brodrick to Curzon, 29 Sept., 1903.

94. Curzon to Dawkins, 11 Nov., 1903.

95. Curzon to Sir E. Law, 17 June, 1903.

96. These developments are conveniently summarised in an India Office memorandum, of which there is a copy in Austen Chamberlain's Papers, dated 9 April, 1917; cf. Curzon to Godley, 23 Sept., 1903.

97. Printed copies of the speeches are in Lawrence's Papers; for Curzon's high opinion of Lawrence see Curzon to King Edward VII, 15 October, 1903 and Curzon to Hamilton, 16 Sept., 1903; Sir W. Lawrence, *The India We Served*, p. 209.

Chapter II: The Buffer States

1. Curzon to Hamilton, 19 Dec., 1902, 13 and 30 Jan., 1903; Curzon's note of 24 Dec., 1902, enclosed in Government of India to Secretary of State, 8 Jan., 1903, C.P.399.
2. Lord Newton, *Lord Lansdowne*, p. 271; Gooch and Temperley, op. cit., Vol. IV, pp. 576–7.
3. Balfour to King Edward VII and Knollys to Balfour, 19 and 20 Feb., 1903, B.P.; Curzon to Hamilton, 8 Jan., 1903.
4. Lansdowne to Sir C. Scott, 21 Feb., 1903, C.P.399.
5. Curzon to Hamilton, 19 March, 1903.
6. Hamilton to Curzon, 13 Feb., 1903.
7. Lansdowne to Curzon, 24 April, 1903.
8. Maj. J. A. Douglas to A. Hardinge, 4 June, 1903, enclosed in Hardinge to Lansdowne, same date, C.P.352; Habibullah to F. Martin, enclosed in Sir A. Martin to W. R. Lawrence, 28 March, 1903; Habibullah to Curzon, 27 June, 1903; India Office to Foreign Office, 7 Aug, 1903, F.O.539/87; minute by Curzon, 5 July, 1903, C.P.399.
9. *Krasnyi Arkhiv*, vol. II, pp. 31–2.
10. War Office memoranda of 4 and 14 Oct., 1902, A. Hardinge to Lansdowne, 17 June, 1903, memorandum by Intelligence Dept., War Office, 9 April, 1903, memorandum by Brodrick, 4 Nov., 1902, C.P.2, Foreign Affairs file II.
11. A. Hardinge to King Edward VII, Dec., 1902, RA W43/30.
12. Hamilton to Curzon, 6 Jan., 1903.
13. Hamilton to Godley, 30 Dec., 1902, and 1 Jan., 1903, G.P. 6B.
14. Selborne to Curzon, 4 Jan., 1903.
15. Hamilton to Curzon, 25 Feb., 1903; minute by Curzon, 25 Feb., 1903, C.P.2, Foreign Affairs file II, folder marked 'Proposed loan to Persia'; minutes by Cranborne and Lansdowne, 27 Feb., 1903, S.P.2. Curzon to Earl Percy, 5 March, 1903.
16. Knollys to Balfour, 31 March, 1903.
17. A. Hardinge to Curzon, 30 April and 1 May, 1903; on Persian engagements to Russia and Great Britain, see Hardinge to Lansdowne, 14 May, 1903, C.P. 360.
18. Memorandum by Chirol, 16 Dec., 1902, enclosed in Curzon to Lansdowne, 3 April, 1903, Sanderson to Lansdowne, 20 April, 1903, C.P.2; Lansdowne to Curzon, 24 April, 1903.
19. Curzon to A. Hardinge, 5 April, 1903; A. Hardinge to Curzon, 28 May, 1903. cf. Hardinge to Lansdowne, 26 May, 1903, L.P.22.
20. Minute by Curzon, July, 1903, C.P.2, Foreign Affairs file II; Curzon to Lansdowne, 19 Aug., 1903.
21. Notes of conference of 19 Nov., 1902, C.P.2, Foreign Affairs file II.
22. Dawkins to Curzon, 13 April, 1903.
23. Gooch and Temperley, op. cit., vol. II, pp. 187–9, 196; memorandum by Lansdowne, 14 April, 1903, Cab. 37/64/24; Dawkins to Curzon, 26 April, 1903.
24. Parl. Deb., 4th ser., H. of L., vol. 121, col. 1348.
25. Hamilton to Curzon, 5 June, 1903; Curzon to Hamilton, 4 June, 1903; Lansdowne to Scott, 6 May, 1903, C.P.2, Foreign Affairs file II.
26. Curzon to Dawkins, 3 April, 1903; Curzon to Lansdowne, 20 June, 1903. Cf. minute by Curzon, 10 Jan., 1904, in Foreign Dept. Proceedings, March 1904, and

Government of India to Secretary of State, 4 Feb., 1904, C.P.2, Foreign Affairs file II.

27. Hamilton to Curzon, 5 and 27 March, 1903; cf. minute by Roberts, 9 Feb, 1903, Cab. 6/1/4.

28. Godley to Curzon, 23 April, 1903.

29. Hamilton to Curzon, 22 May, 1903.

30. Hamilton to Curzon, 5 and 11 June, 1903.

31. Hamilton to Curzon, 30 April, 1903.

32. Memorandum by Balfour to Curzon and Kitchener, undated, covering his memoranda on Indian defence, 30 April and 20 May, 1903, C.P.2, Military file II; cf. War Office memorandum, 22 May, 1903, Cab. 6/1/18.

33. Kitchener to Lord Cranborne, 7 June, 1903; Curzon's minute of 29 June, 1903, C.P.2, Foreign Affairs file II; Documents Diplomatiques Français, ser. 2, vol. II, p. 491; Balfour to King Edward VII, 21 July, 1903, RA R23/75 and 76; memorandum by Lansdowne, 24 July, 1903, Cab. 37/15/44; Hamilton to Curzon, 30 July, 1903. Cf. Curzon's minute on Mekran, 9 Oct., 1903, C.P.338. For a military report on Seistan see C.P.378.

34. Memorandum by Curzon and Kitchener, 7 Aug., 1903, C.P.2, Military file II; on irrigation see C.P.359, especially McMahon to Dane, 13 July, 1903, and 25 Sept., 1904; G. N. Curzon, Russia in Central Asia, p. 379; Kitchener to Lady Salisbury, 23 July, 1903; Hamilton to Balfour, 6 Sept., 1903.

35. A. Hardinge to Lansdowne, 3 March and 20 July, 1903, 20 June, 1904, L.P.22; Hardinge to Curzon, 24 July, 1903; Gooch and Temperley, op. cit., vol. IV, p. 376.

36. Curzon to Lansdowne, 30 June, 1903; Balfour to King Edward VII, 21 July, 1903, RA R 23/75.

37. Brodrick to Curzon, 10 Nov., 1903, summarising Secretary of State to Government of India, 6 Nov., 1903, C.P.2, Foreign Affairs file II; minute by Curzon, 14 November, 1903, C.P.359. For Lansdowne's assurances to the French, see Documents Diplomatiques Français, ser. 2, vol. IV, p. 102.

38. Curzon to Lansdowne, 20 June, 1903.

39. Curzon to Brodrick, 17 Dec., 1903; Curzon to C. Hardinge, 21 Nov., 1903, Hardinge Papers 3. For the record of the conversation see C.P.399, folder marked 'Maskat', and for trade statistics C.P.359; on the tour in general, V. Chirol, Fifty Years in a Changing World, pp. 168–70.

40. Lieut-Col. C. A. Kemball to Dane, 2 Oct., 1903, C.P. 359; Curzon's speech to the Trucial Chiefs, 21 Nov., 1903, C.P.399.

41. Record of the interview, C.P.399; Curzon to Brodrick, 17 Dec., 1903. On Mubarak and Nejd, see H. St J. Philby, The Heart of Arabia, vol. I, chap. III; and for an Intelligence Branch report on Kuwait, see C.P.383.

42. This and the description of the arrival at Kuwait are taken from Marquess Curzon, Tales of Travel, pp. 247–50.

43. For the earlier telegrams see C.P.359; Curzon to Brodrick, 10 Dec., 1903; Curzon to Chirol, 28 Jan., 1904; A. Hardinge to Lansdowne, 14 Feb., 1904; Sir A. Hardinge, A Diplomatist in the East, pp. 314–16; Curzon to Kitchener, 7 Dec., 1903, Birdwood Papers.

44. Curzon to Brodrick, 25 Nov., 1903; Curzon to Earl Percy, 30 April, 1903.

45. Curzon to Brodrick, 17 Dec., 1903, and 7 Jan., 1904.

46. Chirol to Curzon, 7 Jan., 1904.

47. Curzon to Brodrick, 21 Nov., 1903; Curzon to C. Hardinge, same date, Hardinge Papers 3.

48. Spring-Rice to Curzon, 17 Sept., 1903.
49. Spring-Rice to Lansdowne, 12 Oct., 1903, F.O. 539/88; for a convenient summary see Lansdowne to Spring-Rice, 5 Nov., 1903, C.P.296.
50. Habibullah to Curzon, 19 and 21 Sept., 1903.
51. Curzon's minute, 21 Oct., 1903, C.P.399; Government of India to Secretary of State, 29 Oct., 1903, C.P.213.
52. Habibullah to Curzon, 19 Sept., 1903; Curzon to Hamilton, 9 Sept., 1903.
53. Curzon's minute, 15 Oct., 1903, 399; Curzon to Brodrick, 7 Nov., 1903.
54. Gooch and Temperley, op. cit., vol. IV, p. 306.
55. ibid., pp. 183–8; Brodrick to Curzon, 3 and 6 Dec., 1903; Curzon to Ampthill, 26 Nov., 1903; Lord Newton, *Lord Lansdowne*, p. 287; Lord Zetland, *The Life of Lord Cromer*, p. 284; *Documents Diplomatiques Français*, ser. 2, vol. IV, p. 239.
56. Brodrick to Curzon, 4 and 11 Dec., 1903; Balfour to Brodrick, 17 Dec., 1903, B.P.
57. Secretary of State to Government of India, 25 Dec., 1903, C.P.399; Curzon to Brodrick, 24 Jan., 1904.
58. Gooch and Temperley, op. cit., vol. II, pp. 213, 223; *Krasnyi Arkhiv*, vol. 2, p. 48; C. L. Seeger (ed.), *The Memoirs of Alexander Isvolsky*, p. 131. See also I. H. Nish 'Korea, Focus of Russo-Japanese Diplomacy' in *Asian Studies*, April, 1966.
59. Balfour to Selborne and Arnold-Forster, 21 Dec., 1903, Balfour to Selborne, 23 and 29 Dec., 1903, Balfour to Lansdowne, 21 Dec., 1903, memorandum by Lansdowne, 24 Dec., 1903, B.P.; cf. Cab. 37/67/92 and 93.
60. Memorandum by Balfour, 29 Dec., 1903, Cab. 37/67/97.
61. Memorandum by Selborne, 26 Feb., 1904, with addendum by Lansdowne, A.C.P.
62. C. Hardinge to King Edward VII, 27 May, 1904, Hardinge to Lansdowne, 25 May and 6 Dec., 1904, Hardinge Papers 6; *Documents Diplomatiques Français*, ser. 2, vol. II, p. 90.
63. Balfour to Selborne, 6 April, 1904.
64. *Krasnyi Arkhiv*, vol. 53, p. 5.
65. Government of India to Secretary of State, 4 Feb., 1904, and Foreign Department Proceedings, March, 1904, Nos. 1–21, C.P.2, Foreign Affairs file II, 'Persia' folder.
66. Memorandum by Balfour, 22 April, 1904, Cab. 37/70/57, cf. his memorandum of 24 Nov., 1903, Cab. 6/1/32; note by Kitchener, 23 April, 1904, C.P.359; Brodrick to Kitchener, 29 April, 1904, K.P.22.
67. Kitchener to Lady Salisbury, 30 June, 1904.
68. A. Hardinge to Lansdowne, 20 June 1904; cf. Hardinge to Lansdowne, 1 Feb., 1904 and 16 July, 1905, and Sir A. Hardinge, *A Diplomatist in the East*, p. 285; Hardinge to Curzon, 3 March, 1904.
69. Minute by Curzon, 11 April, 1904, C.P.2, Foreign Affairs file II; Curzon to A. Hardinge 8 April, 1904; Dane to Col. A. H. McMahon, 20 April, 1904, C.P.209; Hardinge to Lansdowne, 15 April, 1904, McMahon to Hardinge, 10 June, 1904, C.P.2, Foreign Affairs file II; Hardinge to Lansdowne, L.P.22; *Documents Diplomatiques Français*, ser. 2, vol. IV, pp. 94–5.
70. A. Hardinge to Lansdowne, 6 June, 1904; A. Hardinge to C. Hardinge, 20 June, 1904. See also *Documents Diplomatiques Français*, ser. 2. vol. IV, pp. 130–5.
71. A. Hardinge to Lansdowne, 21 June, 1904 and enclosures, C.P.359.
72. A. Hardinge to Curzon, 7 March, 1905; A. Hardinge to King Edward VII, 10 Sept., 1904, RA W44/202.

73. *Krasnyi Arkhiv*, vol. 53, pp. 13–37; G. A. Schreiner (ed.), *Entente Diplomacy and the World*, p. 474.

Chapter III: Younghusband's Mission

1. Sir C. Bell, *Portrait of the Dalai Lama*, pp. 61–2; P. L. Mehra, 'Tibet and Russian Intrigue' in *Journal of the Royal Central Asian Society*, vol. XLV, pp. 34–5.
2. C. Hardinge to Sanderson and reply, 13 and 19 Nov., 1902, Hardinge Papers 3.
3. Minute of Curzon's interview with the Prime Minister of Nepal, 31 Dec., 1902, C.P.344; cf. Curzon's MS. addition to his letter to Hamilton, 1 Jan., 1903.
4. Minutes by Lieut.-Col. W. R. Robertson and Roberts, 25 and 30 Sept., 1902, C.P.344.
5. Government of India to Secretary of State, 8 Jan., 1903, C.P.344.
6. Hamilton to Curzon, 14 and 28 Jan., 1903.
7. Curzon to Hamilton, 29 Jan., 1903.
8. Curzon to Hamilton, 12 Feb., 1903.
9. Hamilton to Curzon, 13 Feb., 1903.
10. Hamilton to Curzon, 19 Feb., 1903.
11. Balfour to King Edward VII, 19 Feb., 1903, RA R23/43.
12. Hamilton to Curzon, 27 Feb., 1903.
13. Curzon to Hamilton, 26 Feb., 1903.
14. Hamilton to Curzon, 19 Feb., 1903.
15. Curzon to Hamilton, 12 March, 1903.
16. Secretary of State to Government of India, 27 Feb., 1903, C.P.2, Foreign Affairs file III.
17. Hamilton to Curzon, 11 April, 1903; Curzon to Hamilton, 13 April, 1903.
18. Hamilton to Curzon, 15 April, 1903.
19. F. Younghusband, *The Light of Experience*, p. 286; G. Seaver, *Francis Younghusband*, pp. 202–3; Curzon to Hamilton, 7 May, 1903. The account of the Younghusband mission's adventures in Tibet is chiefly based on P. Fleming, *Bayonets to Lhasa*; Sir F. O'Conor, *Things Mortal* and *On the Frontier and Beyond*; G. Seaver, *Francis Younghusband*; F. Younghusband, *India and Tibet* and *The Light of Experience*; and the article by Lieut-Col. L. A. Bethell (under the nom-de-plume 'Pousse-Cailloux') in *Blackwood's Magazine*, Feb., 1929.
20. Hamilton to Curzon, 28 May, 1903. The decision was reached over the heads of the officials at the India Office; see Godley to Curzon, 29 May, 1903.
21. Younghusband to Dane, 17 and 23 July, 6 Aug., 1903, C.P.344.
22. Curzon to Hamilton, 12 Aug., 1903; Curzon to Lansdowne, 19 Aug., 1903; cf. memorandum by Younghusband, 17 Aug., 1903, C.P.344.
23. Curzon to Hamilton and reply, 16 and 20 Sept., 1903.
24. Hamilton to Curzon, 1 Oct., 1903.
25. P. Fleming, *Bayonets to Lhasa*, pp. 89–90.
26. Curzon to Brodrick, 26 Oct., 1903.
27. Brodrick to Balfour and reply, 27 Oct., 1903.
28. Memorandum by Brodrick, 20 April, 1904, Cab. 37/70/56; Godley to Ampthill, 29 April, 1904; cf. Wyndham to Balfour, 24 April, 1904.
29. Brodrick to Curzon, 29 Oct., 1903.

30. Memorandum by Brodrick, 4 Nov., 1903, F.O. 17/1746; G. Monger, *The End of Isolation*, p. 142.
31. Curzon to Brodrick, 3 and 4 Nov., 1903. For Curzon's early desire to move to Gyantse, see his letter to Hamilton, 21 May, 1903.
32. Brodrick to Curzon, 6 Nov., 1903 (two telegrams).
33. Balfour to King Edward VII, 6 Nov., 1903, RA R24/21.
34. Brodrick to Curzon, 6 and 13 Nov., 1903.
35. Government of India to Secretary of State, 5 Nov., 1903, C.P.344; Curzon to Brodrick, 4 Nov., 1903.
36. Curzon to Brodrick, 11 Nov., 1903.
37. Brodrick to Curzon, 4 Dec., 1903.
38. Curzon to King Edward VII, 10 Dec., 1903; Younghusband to Dane, 9 Dec., 1903, C.P.344; cf. the papers in C.P.112.
39. Sir C. Bell, *Portrait of the Dalai Lama*, pp. 61–3.
40. *Krasnyi Arkhiv*, vol. V, p. 19; Kuropatkin's memoirs, cited D. J. Dallin, *The Rise of Russia in Asia*, p. 42.
41. Younghusband to Curzon, 1 and 20 Jan., 3 Feb., 1904; Younghusband to Dane, 13 and 31 Jan., 1904, C.P.344.
42. Minute by Curzon, 22 Jan., 1904, C.P.344.
43. Curzon to Younghusband and reply, 23 Jan. and 3 Feb., 1904.
44. Curzon to Brodrick, 31 Jan., 1904; see Command Paper 1920.
45. Younghusband to Dane, 1 April, 1904, C.P.344; P. Landon to Curzon, 4 April, 1904.
46. Brodrick to Curzon, 7 April, 1904; Curzon to Brodrick, 5 and 15 April, 1904; Curzon to Younghusband, 4 April, 1904, Gen. Macdonald's report, 12 April, 1904, C.P.342.
47. Brodrick to Curzon, 15 April, 1904.
48. Younghusband to Curzon, 16 April, 1904.
49. Minute by Dane, 25 April, 1904, C.P.344; Brodrick to Curzon, 28 April, 1904.
50. Curzon to Brodrick, 20 April, 1904.
51. Younghusband to Dane and to Ampthill, 5 May, 1904, C.P.344.
52. Ampthill to Brodrick, 6 May, 1904, and minute by King Edward VII; cf. his minute on Ampthill to Brodrick, 7 May, 1904, M.P.50072.
53. D.D.F., ser. II, vol. V, p. 47; Curzon to Brodrick, 29 April, 1904.
54. Balfour to King Edward VII, 4 May, 1904, RA R24/86.
55. Balfour to King Edward VII, 10 May, 1904, RA R24/87.
56. Brodrick to Ampthill, 13 May, 1904.
57. D.D.F., ser. II, vol. V, p. 137; Lansdowne to Spring-Rice, 4 and 10 May, 1904, Lansdowne to Benckendorff, 14 May, 1904, Lansdowne to C. Hardinge, 17 May and 2 June, 1904, C.P.344; Gooch and Temperley, op. cit., vol. IV, pp. 189–90, 308, 310.
58. Brodrick to Ampthill, 30 April, 1904; Ampthill to Younghusband, 2 May, 1904; Younghusband to Curzon, 15 and 31 May, 1904; cf. Younghusband to Ampthill, 3 and 12 June, 1904, A.P.34/1.
59. Minutes by Kitchener and Elles, 25 and 26 May, 1904, C.P.344; Ampthill to Brodrick, 2 and 9 June, 1904.
60. Younghusband to Dane, 7 June, 1904; Dane to Younghusband, 14 June, 1904; P. Fleming, *Bayonets to Lhasa*, p. 196; Ampthill to Younghusband, 13 June, 1904; Younghusband to Ampthill, A.P.34/1.

61. Kitchener's minute, 14 June, 1904, C.P.344; Kitchener to Lady Salisbury, 16 June, 1904.

62. Curzon to Ampthill, 26 May 1904; Younghusband to Curzon, 18 June, 1904, referring to Curzon's letter of 26 May, to him; Curzon to Brodrick, 21 Feb., 1905.

63. Lansdowne to Roberts, 25 May, 1904.

64. Curzon to Ampthill, undated but probably 17 June, 1904.

65. Memorandum by Curzon, 25 June, 1904, C.P.342; cf. Curzon to Brodrick, 27 June, 1904.

66. Brodrick to Ampthill, 1 July, 1904.

67. Curzon to Ampthill, 1 July, 1904.

68. Government of India to Secretary of State, 30 June, 1904, C.P.344.

69. Curzon to Ampthill, 4 Aug., 1904.

70. Ampthill to Younghusband, 11 July, 1904; M. Gilbert, *Servant of India*, p. 19; Brodrick to Ampthill, 22 July, 1904; Curzon to Ampthill, 19 July, 1904.

71. Brodrick to Curzon and reply, 6 and 8 July, 1904, B.P.49721.

72. M. Gilbert, op. cit., p. 17; Younghusband to Curzon, 12 July, 1904.

73. Younghusband to Curzon, 25 July, 1904.

74. Younghusband to Dane, 4 Aug., 1904, C.P.345.

75. Secretary of State to Government of India, 5 Aug., 1904, C.P.2, Foreign Affairs file III.

76. Younghusband to Curzon, 6 Aug., 1904; Younghusband to Dane, 19 Aug., 1904; Ampthill to King Edward VII and to Brodrick, 1 and 3 Sept., 1904, RA W2/101 and 102; Chirol to C. Hardinge, 21 Sept., 1904, Hardinge Papers 7.

77. Balfour to King Edward VII, 15 Aug., 1904, RA R25/22.

78. Ampthill to Brodrick, 18 and 31 Aug., 5 Sept., 1904.

79. Younghusband to Dane, 2, 4 and 27 Sept., 1904; Younghusband to Curzon, 2 Feb., 1905; Younghusband to Ampthill, 26 Sept., 1904.

80. Ampthill to Brodrick, 11 Sept., 1904; Ampthill to Younghusband, 11 Sept., 1904; Brodrick to Ampthill, 12 Sept., 1904; cf. Ampthill to Brodrick, 28 Dec., 1904, A.P.7.

81. Brodrick to Ampthill, 13 Sept., 1904.

82. For Younghusband's explanation of his motives, see his memorandum of 18 Oct., 1904, and Younghusband to Dane, 24 Sept., 1904, C.P.345.

83. Brodrick to Ampthill, 16 Sept., 1904; Younghusband to Ampthill, 24 Sept., 1904; see the summary in Government of India to Secretary of State, 27 Oct., 1904, C.P.345.

84. Brodrick to Ampthill, 3 Oct., 1904; Secretary of State to Government of India, 2 Dec., 1904.

85. Brodrick to Salisbury, 15 Sept., 1904, B.P.

86. Curzon to Brodrick, 18 Sept., 1904.

87. C. Hardinge to Lansdowne, 18 Aug., 1904; Lansdowne to C. Hardinge, 24 Aug., 1904, L.P.24; Brodrick to Ampthill, 2 Sept., 1904.

88. Brodrick to Ampthill, 22 Sept., 1904; Lansdowne to C. Hardinge, 27 Sept., 1904, C.P.345; C. Hardinge to Lansdowne, 27 Sept., 1904, L.P.25.

89. Balfour to Lady Salisbury, 4 Oct., 1904.

90. Note by Balfour, 4 Oct., 1904, in Lansdowne file, B.P.

91. Brodrick to Knollys, 5 Oct., 1904, RA W2/166; Lansdowne to C. Hardinge, 4 Oct., 1904, H.P.7.

92. Brodrick to Knollys, 6 Oct., 1904, RA R25/29.

93. Chirol to C. Hardinge, 4 Oct., 1904, Hardinge Papers 7.

94. Ampthill to Brodrick, 12 and 20 Oct., 1904; Government of India to Secretary of State, 6 and 27 Oct., 18 Nov., 1904. C.P.2, Foreign Affairs file III.
95. Ampthill to King Edward VII, 7 Nov., 1904.
96. Brodrick to Curzon and reply, 24 and 25 Oct., 1904, M.P.50076.
97. Brodrick to Ampthill, 4 Nov., 1904.
98. Godley to Ampthill, 4 and 11 Nov., 1904.
99. Brodrick to Ampthill, 18 Nov., 1904; Brodrick to Roberts, 16 Dec., 1904; memorandum by Brodrick, 22 Nov., 1904; Brodrick to Curzon, 1 Dec., 1904.
100. Secretary of State to Government of India, 2 Dec., 1904 (two despatches), C.P.345; R. Ritchie to A. Hirtzel, 2 Nov., 1906, Morley Papers 43.

Chapter IV: Kitchener's Threat

1. Sir J. E. Wrench, *Alfred, Lord Milner*, p. 215.
2. Balfour to Hamilton, 12 Sept., 1901, H.P.47.
3. Balfour to Knollys, 5 Nov., 1903, RA R24/17; for the Elgin commission's reports, see Command Papers 1789, 1790, 1791 and 1792.
4. Brodrick to Curzon, 6 Nov., 1903.
5. Arnold-Forster to Roberts and reply, 12 and 13 Feb., 1904, R.P.
6. Esher to Roberts, 22 Feb., 1904.
7. Roberts to Ian Hamilton, 28 Feb., 21 March and 4 May, 1904; for the Esher committee's reports, see Command Papers 1932, 1968 and 2002.
8. Kitchener to Lady Salisbury, 2 March, 1904.
9. Minutes by Devonshire, 2 and 21 Nov., 1900, Cab. 37/53/71; cf. Cab. 1/2/55; Selborne to Curzon, 13 July, 1901.
10. Memorandum by Arnold-Forster, 20 Oct., 1902; memorandum by Selborne and Brodrick; 10 Nov., 1902, Cab. 37/63/152; Lord Midleton, *Records and Reactions*, p. 141; B. E. C. Dugdale, *Arthur James Balfour*, vol. I, p. 367; memorandum by Balfour, 29 February, 1904, Cab. 37/69/33.
11. Note by Clarke on the Imperial Defence Committee, 10 Oct., 1905, B.P.
12. Balfour to King Edward VII, 4 Dec., 1903, RA R24/44.
13. Parl. Deb., H. of C., vol. 139, cols. 618-19.
14. Curzon to Brodrick, 20 April, 1905. On the Defence Committee see also F. A. Johnson, *Defence by Committee*; Lord Hankey, *The Supreme Command*, Vol. I, especially pp. 45-59, and *Diplomacy by Conference*, pp. 12-14, 83-104.
15. Hubert Hamilton to Lady Cranborne, 9 Aug., 1903.
16. Hubert Hamilton to Lady Salisbury, 12 Nov., 1903.
17. Kitchener to Lady Cranborne, 25 June, 1903.
18. Balfour to Kitchener, 3 Dec., 1903, original in Birdwood Papers.
19. Curzon to Brodrick, 14 Jan., 1904.
20. Curzon to Brodrick, 23 Feb., 1904; Kitchener to Lady Salisbury, 24 March, 1904.
21. This concerned the appointment of the Q.M.G., India. By the time Curzon's recommendation reached London, the appointment had already been gazetted, Kitchener having telegraphed directly to the War Office. See Curzon to Brodrick, 22 and 24 March, 1904; Brodrick to Curzon, 23 March, 1904.
22. Curzon to Brodrick, 14 April, 1904.
23. Ampthill to Brodrick, 12 May, 1904.
24. Ampthill to Brodrick, 9 June, 1904.
25. Elles to Ampthill, 14 June, 1904, A.P.34/1.

26. Ampthill to Brodrick, 16 June, 1904; Kitchener to Ampthill, 10 June, 1904.

27. Elles to Ampthill, 7 Aug., 1905, A.P.21.

28. Brodrick to Ampthill, 1 July, 1904.

29. Balfour to Curzon, 23 June, 1904.

30. Ampthill to Brodrick, 7 July, 1904; Ampthill to Godley, 16 June, 1904; Kitchener to Lady Salisbury, 7 July, 1904.

31. Ampthill to Brodrick, 20 July, 1904.

32. Elles to Ampthill, 23 July, 1904.

33. Memorandum by Ampthill, 27 July, 1904, A.P.34/1; Ampthill to Brodrick, 17 Aug., 1904; Kitchener to Lady Salisbury, 22 Sept., 1904.

34. Balfour to Kitchener, 3 Dec., 1903, original in Birdwood Papers; cf. Balfour to Esher, 14 Jan., 1904.

35. Curzon to Brodrick, 5 April, 1904; cf. Kitchener to Lady Salisbury, 17 Dec., 1903. See C.P.244 and C.P.2., Military file II, for papers on the defence of India.

36. T. H. von Laue, *Sergei Witte and the Industrialisation of Russia*, p. 231; minutes by Kitchener and Curzon, 16 and 20 Jan., 1904, Foreign Department Proceedings, Nos. 1–21, 1904, C.P.2, Foreign Affairs file II; comments by Kitchener on War Office memorandum on the Defence of India, 15 Feb., 1904, C.P.2, Military file 1, folder marked 'Defence of India'.

37. Ampthill to Brodrick, 18, 27 and 31 May, 4 and 10 June, 1904.

38. Ampthill to Kitchener, 8 June, 1904; War Office to Kitchener and reply, same date, A.P.34,1; S. L. Gwynn, *Letters and Friendships of Sir Cecil Spring-Rice,* vol. I, p. 409.

39. Lord Newton, *Lord Lansdowne*, pp. 313–14; Roberts to Kitchener, 11 Aug., 1904; Brodrick to Ampthill, 12 Aug., 1904.

40. Brodrick to Ampthill, 18 Aug., 1904; Brodrick to Ampthill, 29 Aug., 1904, repeating C. Hardinge to Foreign Office, 26 Aug., 1904; Curzon to Ampthill, 18 and 23 Aug., 1904.

41. Ampthill to Brodrick, 2 and 5 Sept., 1904.

42. Roberts to Kitchener, 2 March, 1904; Defence Committee's 36th meeting, Cab. 2/1; Balfour to Roberts, 10 April, 1904; memorandum by Arnold-Forster, 28 April, 1904, A-F.P.

43. G. Monger, *The End of Isolation*, p. 168; Arnold-Forster to Austen Chamberlain, 18 June, 1904, A-F.P.

44. Balfour to Roberts, 12 July, 1904, R.P.

45. Defence Committee's 47th meeting, Cab. 2/1; memorandum by Colonel Mullaly, 28 July, 1904, Cab. 6/2/64.

46. Maj.-General Sir G. Younghusband, *A Soldier's Memories in Peace and War*, p. 241.

47. Kitchener to Lady Salisbury, 9 June, 1904; for other examples, see Kitchener to Lady Salisbury, 7 and 28 July, 1904; for Brodrick's correspondence with him, see K.P.22.

48. See, e.g., Kitchener to Roberts, 30 March, 27 April, 9 and 16 June, 1904, R.P.; Sir G. Arthur, *Life of Lord Kitchener*, vol. II, pp. 199–200; cf. Kitchener to Brodrick, 15 July, 1902.

49. L. S. Amery to Clarke, 19 May, 1904; Clarke to Amery, 22 May and 6 June, 1904, Amery Papers.

50. Clarke to Amery, 9 June, 1904; cf. Clarke to Amery, 18 July, 1904, Amery Papers.

51. Clarke to Balfour, 23 July, 1904; on Mullaly see G. de S. Barrow, *The Fire of Life*, pp. 98ff; on Malleson see Colonel R. Meinertzhagen, *Army Diary, 1899–1926*, p. 154.

52. Roberts to Kitchener, 1 July, 1904; M. V. Brett (ed.), *Journals and Letters of Reginald, Viscount Esher*, vol. II, p. 59.
53. Curzon to Ampthill, 4 Aug., 1904; cf. Roberts to Kitchener, 5 Aug., 1904; Brodrick to Curzon, 20 Jan., 1905, Cab. 37/77/96; Balfour to Lady Salisbury, 4 Oct., 1904.
54. Godley to Brodrick, 5 Aug., enclosed in Brodrick to Balfour, 8 Aug., 1904.
55. Brodrick to Ampthill, 5 Aug., 1904.
56. Note by Clarke for Balfour on Indian Military Administration, enclosed in Clarke to J. S. Sandars, 5 Aug., 1904.
57. Repington to Marker, 18 July and 25 Aug., 1904; Kitchener to Marker, 14 July, 1904, Marker Papers.
58. Brodrick to Ampthill, 28 Sept, 1904; Roberts to Kitchener, 5 Aug., 1904; Ampthill to Brodrick, 5 Sept., 1904.
59. Ampthill to Brodrick, 16 Sept., 1904; Kitchener to Lady Salisbury, 14 Sept., 1904.
60. Curzon's minute, 11 Jan., 1904, in C.P.2, Military file III, folder marked 'Redistribution of the Indian Army'; Curzon to Kitchener, 2 Feb., 1904; Kitchener to Lady Salisbury, 27 April, 1904.
61. Brodrick to Curzon and reply, 4 July, 1904.
62. Brodrick to Ampthill, 8 July, 1904; Clarke's note for Balfour on the Defence Committee's discussion of 8 July, 1904, B.P.
63. Elles to Ampthill and reply, 16 Sept., 1904, A.P.34/1; Ampthill to Brodrick, 21 Sept., 1904.
64. Kitchener to Brodrick, 21 Sept., 1904.
65. Ampthill to Brodrick, 28 Sept., 1904.
66. Kitchener to Arnold-Forster, 23 Sept., 1904; see M.P.50072 for the telegrams.
67. Kitchener to Ampthill and reply, 23 Sept., 1904.
68. Ampthill to Brodrick, 24 Sept., 1904.
69. Kitchener to Ampthill and reply, 24 and 25 September, 1904.
70. Arnold-Forster's diary, 24 Sept., 1904; Brodrick to Ampthill, 25 Sept., 1904; Ampthill to Brodrick, 25 Sept., 1904.
71. Ampthill to Brodrick, 28 Sept., 1904.
72. Lady Salisbury to Balfour, 27 Sept., enclosing Colonel Mullaly to herself, 26 Sept., 1904, B.P.
73. Kitchener to Lady Salisbury, 28 Sept., 1904, Ampthill to Brodrick, 28 Sept., 1904.
74. Minute by Maj.-General Grierson, 29 Sept., 1904, and Lord Hardwicke to War Office, 22 Oct., 1904, A-F.P.; for other reports see F.O.539/88; Kitchener to Curzon, 13 Oct., 1904.
75. *Summary of Lord Curzon's Administration in the Military Department*, p. 8, C.P.414; Brodrick to Knollys, 7 Oct., 1904, RA W2/167.
76. *Krasnyi Arkhiv*, vol. 18, p. 21; vol. 53, pp. 7, 18.
77. Arnold-Forster to Curzon, 8 Sept., 1904, C.P.226.
78. Brodrick to Balfour, 5 Oct., 1904; cf. Brodrick to Cromer, 20 Dec., 1905, Cromer Papers 7.
79. Brodrick to Ampthill, 13 Oct., 1904.
80. Balfour to Lady Salisbury, 4 Oct., 1904.
81. Balfour to Brodrick and reply, 8 and 9 Oct., 1904.
82. Brodrick to Ampthill, 20 Oct., 1904.
83. Gooch and Temperley, op. cit., vol. IV, pp. 27, 35; Lieut.-Colonel Napier to C. Hardinge, enclosed in C. Hardinge to Lansdowne, 10 Nov., 1904, C.P.295 (a) and F.O.539/88; *Krasnyi Arkhiv*, vol. 53, pp. 7–8.

84. Brodrick to Curzon, 1 Nov., 1904; memorandum by Curzon, 2 Nov., 1904, C.P.2, Military file III.

85. Balfour to Curzon, 3 Nov., 1904.

86. Curzon to Balfour, 3 Nov., 1904.

87. Balfour to Brodrick, 10 Nov., 1904; cf. Curzon to Brodrick, 19 Jan., 1905.

88. Brodrick to Kitchener, 13 Oct., 1904; Kitchener to Brodrick, 9 Nov., 1904; Kitchener to Roberts, 27 Nov., 1904; Sir G. Arthur, op. cit., vol. II, pp. 201-2.

89. Repington to Marker, 11 and 23 Oct., 1904.

90. Memorandum by Curzon, 'Redistribution of the Indian Army', C.P.2, Military file II; Curzon to Kitchener, 4 Nov., 1904.

91. Brodrick to Curzon, 7 Nov., 1904.

92. Defence Committee's 57th meeting, Cab. 2/1; Roberts to Kitchener, 23 Nov., 1904; note by Clarke, 24 Nov., on Defence Committee's discussion of 22 Nov., 1904; memorandum by General Grierson, 5 May, 1904, Cab. 6/1/50.

93. Memorandum by Balfour, 19 Dec., 1904; cf. Clarke to Roberts, 3 Oct. and 4 Dec., 1904.

Chapter V: Interlude in England

1. Curzon to Brodrick, 2 Oct., 1903.

2. Curzon to Brodrick, 4 Nov., 1903.

3. Brodrick to Curzon, 11 Nov., 1903; Curzon to Brodrick, 15 and 16 Nov., 1903.

4. Brodrick to Curzon, 20 Nov., 1903.

5. Brodrick to Curzon, 26 Nov., 1903.

6. Curzon's minute, 28 Dec., 1903, C.P.280; Curzon to Brodrick, 2 Jan., 1904; Brodrick to Curzon, 7 April, 1904.

7. Lawrence to Curzon, 25 Nov., 1903.

8. Curzon to Godley, 17 Dec., 1903.

9. Godley to Curzon, 27 Nov., 1903.

10. Curzon to Godley, 17 Dec., 1903.

11. Curzon to Godley, 4 Jan., 1904.

12. Godley to Curzon, 28 Jan., 1904.

13. Godley to Curzon, 1 Jan., 1904; cf. Godley to Curzon, 8 Jan., 1904.

14. Curzon to Godley, 27 Jan., 1904.

15. Godley to Curzon, 26 Feb., 1904.

16. Godley to Ampthill, 25 Nov., 1904; cf. Godley to Curzon, 3 March, 1904.

17. Curzon to Dawkins, 9 March, 1904.

18. Brodrick to Curzon, undated, C.P.9.

19. Cited Ronaldshay, The Life of Lord Curzon, vol. III, p. 394.

20. Ampthill to Godley, 28 Oct., 1903, A.P.23.

21. Ampthill to Godley, 5 May, 1904.

22. Ibbetson to Curzon, 25 April, 1904; Curzon to Ibbetson, 26 April, 1904.

23. Hamilton to Curzon, 9 July, 1903.

24. Memorandum by Lansdowne, 10 Sept., 1903; see G. Monger, The End of Isolation, p. 133.

25. Selborne to Balfour, 12 May, 1904.

26. Curzon to Lansdowne, 5 May, 1904; Curzon to Ampthill, 23 Aug., 1904.

27. Sir T. Raleigh (ed.), Lord Curzon in India, vol. I, p. 49; Lord Ronaldshay, The Life of Lord Curzon, vol. I, pp. 34ff.

28. Selborne to Curzon, 22 July, 1904; Godley to Curzon, 21 July, 1904; cf. Sir W. Lawrence, *The India We Served*, p. 254, where the reference is almost certainly to Godley.

29. Memorandum by Arnold-Forster, 23 Feb., 1904; Arnold Forster's diary, 19 April, 1904.

30. Curzon to Ampthill, undated but probably 17 June, 1904.

31. Arnold-Forster's diary, 19 July, 1904, 12 Aug., 1905.

32. Curzon to Ampthill, 26 May, 1904.

33. Curzon to Ampthill, 10 June, 1904.

34. M. V. Brett (ed.). *Journals and Letters of Reginald, Viscount Esher,* vol. II, p. 59; Curzon to Ampthill, 23 June 1904; Curzon to Clarke, 13 Aug., 1904, Sydenham Papers.

35. Godley to Ampthill, 29 March and 29 April, 1904.

36. Godley to Ampthill, 17 June, 1904; Brodrick to Ampthill, 24 June, 1904.

37. Balfour to Curzon, 28 May, 1904; Godley to Brodrick, 8 Aug., 1904; Curzon to Balfour, 4 Dec., 1904; Balfour to Curzon, 1 Jan., 1905.

38. Godley to Ampthill, 19 May, 1904.

39. Curzon to Rennell Rodd, 18 Aug., 1904, Rennell Papers.

40. Schomberg McDonnell to J. S. Sandars, 31 Oct., 1904, RA W35/26b.

41. L. Mosley, *Curzon,* p. 116.

42. Curzon to Brodrick, 1 Oct., 1904.

43. Curzon to Brodrick, 11 Oct., 1904.

44. Curzon to King Edward VII, 12 and 14 Oct., 1904, RA W63/133, RA W64/1.

45. Lansdowne to C. Hardinge, 19 Oct., 1904, Hardinge Papers 7.

46. C. Hardinge to Lansdowne, 27 Oct., 1904, Hardinge Papers 6; Lansdowne to C. Hardinge, 29 Oct., 1904; Lord Newton, *Lord Lansdowne,* p. 317.

47. Lord Hardinge, *Old Diplomacy,* p. 108; C. Hardinge to Knollys, 24 Nov., 1904, Hardinge Papers 6.

48. *Dnevnik Imperatora Nikolaya,* p. 177, cited H. Seton-Watson, *The Decline of Imperial Russia,* p. 216; N. F. Grant (ed.), *The Kaiser's Letters to the Tsar,* pp. 138–9; *Die Grosse Politik,* vol. XIX, p. 4.

49. P. Cambon, *Correspondance,* vol. II, pp. 165–76; Chirol to C. Hardinge, 1 Nov., 1904.

50. 57th and 61st meetings of the Defence Committee, Cab. 2/1; Governor of Bombay to Ampthill, 3 Dec., 1904, citing Brodrick to the Governor, 13 Nov., 1904, A.P.34/1.

51. Ampthill to Brodrick, 2 Nov., 1904; Government of India to Secretary of State, 22 Dec., 1904, C.P.2, Foreign Affairs file II; A. Hardinge to Curzon, 7 Jan. and 31 March, 1905.

52. Balfour to Brodrick, 6 Sept., 1904; Brodrick to Curzon, 5 Aug., 1904.

53. Brodrick to Balfour, 8 Aug. and 3 Sept., 1904.

54. Brodrick to Curzon, 3 Sept., 1904, M.P.50076.

55. Curzon to Brodrick, 30 Oct., 1904; Brodrick to Curzon, 31 Oct. and 1 Nov., 1904.

56. Curzon to Brodrick, 3 Nov., 1904; Brodrick to Curzon, 4 Nov., 1904.

57. Curzon to Brodrick, 6 and 7 Nov., 1904; Brodrick to Curzon, 6 Nov., 1904.

58. Brodrick to Curzon, 22 Nov., 1904.

59. Curzon to Ampthill, 31 Oct., 1904.

60. Godley to Curzon and reply, 22 and 23 Nov., 1904, G.P.60.

61. Ronaldshay, op, cit., vol. II, p. 360; vol. III, p. 31.

62. M. Gilbert, *Servant of India,* p. 20.

63. M. Gilbert, op. cit., p. 20; Younghusband to Curzon, 16 Dec., 1904.
64. Brodrick to Ampthill, 3 Feb., 1905.
65. F. Younghusband, *The Light of Experience*, p. 111; Younghusband to Curzon, 22 Dec., 1904; M. Gilbert, op. cit., pp. 20–1.
66. D. J. Dallin, *The Rise of Russia in Asia*, p. 148.
67. Ampthill to Brodrick, 20 Dec., 1904.
68. Ampthill to Brodrick, 28 Dec., 1904.
69. Ronaldshay, op. cit., vol. III, p. 31.

Chapter VI: Deadlock at Kabul

1. Curzon to King Edward VII, 21 Jan. and 9 March, 1904. On Afghanistan see especially C.P.293, 294, 295 (a), (b) and (c), 296, 399, which contain copies of the more important documents.
2. Habibullah to Curzon, 1 March, 1904.
3. Curzon to Brodrick, 21 March, 1904; see also the minute by Kitchener, 26 March, 1904, C.P.399.
4. Habibullah to Curzon, 13 Feb., 1 March and 27 April, 1904; on the subsidy see Habibullah to the Viceroy, 18 April, 2 May, 14 May, 11 June, 5 July, 13 and 23 Aug., 1904; for Ampthill's correspondence with him see A.P.46.
5. Curzon to Brodrick, 5 April, 1904.
6. Habibullah to Ampthill, 25 Aug., 1904.
7. Memorandum by Curzon, 18 July, 1904.
8. Godley to Ampthill, 21 July, 1904; memorandum by Balfour, 23 July, 1904, Cab. 6/2/62.
9. Clarke to Balfour, 2 Aug., 1904; note by Clarke for Balfour, 6 Aug., 1904, on Defence Committee discussion of 3 Aug., 1904; cf. Clarke to Balfour, 23 July, 1904.
10. Scott to Lansdowne, 7 Jan., 1904, F.O.539/88; memorandum by Brodrick, 28 March, 1904, Cab. 37/69/50. On Afghanistan Jan.–March, 1904, see Cab. 37/68/16.
11. For Dobbs' reports, see Cab. 6/2/70, F.O.539/88, Ampthill to Brodrick, 24 and 28 Aug., 1904; Ampthill to Kind Edward VII, 1 Sept., 1904; cf. Major Bird's diary, C.P.295(a).
12. Curzon to Ampthill, 7 Sept., 1904.
13. Ampthill to Brodrick, 10 and 31 Aug., 1904, 5 Sept., 1904.
14. Balfour to Brodrick, 6 Sept., 1904.
15. Habibullah to Ampthill, 8 Sept., 1904; Ampthill to Brodrick, 17 and 30 Sept., 1904.
16. Memorandum by Curzon, 5 Oct., 1904.
17. Memoranda by Brodrick and Balfour, 8 and 12 Oct., 1904.
18. Memorandum by Curzon for Brodrick, 15 Oct., 1904.
19. Ampthill to Brodrick, 13 July, 1904; Deane to Ampthill, 23 Aug., 1904, A.P.34/1; Curzon to Brodrick, 5 April, 1904; Roberts to Balfour, 19 July, 1904; Curzon to Kitchener, 4 Nov., 1904, Birdwood Papers.
20. Minute by Kitchener, 7 Oct., 1904; Habibullah to Ampthill, 5 Oct., 1904; Ampthill to Brodrick, 9 and 12 Oct., 1904.
21. For Ampthill's views, see his letters to Brodrick of 5 and 12 Oct., 1904, and his minute enclosed with the latter.

22. Memorandum by Lansdowne, 16 Oct., 1904, Cab. 37/72/126.
23. Brodrick to Curzon, 21 Oct., 1904; aide-memoire for Mr Dane, 20 Oct., 1904; cf. Godley to Roberts, 13 Oct., 1904.
24. Brodrick to Curzon, 21 Oct., 1904; Secretary of State to the Government of India, 21 Oct., 1904, Cab. 37/72/129.
25. Ampthill to Brodrick, 21 Oct., 1904; cf. Government of India to Secretary of State, 27 Oct., 1904.
26. Minute by Curzon, 23 Oct., 1904; Curzon to Godley, 23 Oct., 1904, G.P.22; Curzon to Ampthill, 28 Oct., 1904; Curzon to Kitchener, 4 Nov., 1904, Birdwood Papers.
27. Curzon to Brodrick and reply, 20 and 24 Oct., 1904; Curzon to Brodrick, 25 Oct., 1904, M.P.50076.
28. Minute by Curzon, 5 March, 1904; Curzon to Brodrick, 7 March, 1904, in file 'Foreign Affairs III', C.P.2.
29. Minute by Curzon, 1 June, 1904, in file 'Foreign Affairs III', folder marked 'Persia (g) Railways', C.P.2.
30. Brodrick to Curzon, 21 Oct., 1904; Curzon to Ampthill, 31 Oct., 1904; minute by Ampthill enclosed in Ampthill to Brodrick, 20 Oct., 1904; Ampthill to Brodrick, 28 Oct., and 9 Nov., 1904.
31. Curzon to Balfour and reply, 1 and 3 Nov., 1904.
32. Balfour to Brodrick, 10 Nov., 1904; Curzon to Balfour, 15 Nov., 1904.
33. Lawrence's diary, 11 Dec., 1902; Curzon to Hamilton, 25 Dec., 1902; Curzon to Barnes, 16 June, 1903; Curzon to Godley, 8 July, 1903.
34. Curzon to Brodrick, 20 March, 1903; Godley to Ampthill, 13 June, 1904; Ampthill to Brodrick, 20 Oct., and 3 Nov., 1904; Ampthill to King Edward VII, 7 Nov., 1904.
35. Deane to Ampthill, 2 Nov., 1904, A.P.34/1; Ampthill to Brodrick, 20 Oct., 1904; Curzon to Brodrick, 5 Jan., 1905.
36. Ampthill to Brodrick, 26 Oct., 1904; Ampthill to Curzon, 3 Nov., 1904.
37. Brodrick to Lamington, 18 Nov., 1904, Lamington Papers 1; *Krasnyi Arkhiv,* vol. liii, pp. 13–37.
38. Ampthill to Brodrick, 9 Nov., 1904; Ampthill to Kitchener, 8 Nov., 1904.
39. Curzon to Ampthill, 10 Nov., 1904.
40. Brodrick to Ampthill, 11 Nov., 1904; Ampthill to Dane, 17 Nov., 1904, A.P. 34/1.
41. Curzon to Dane, 9 Dec., 1904.
42. Curzon to Brodrick, 20 Dec., 1904; Dane to Curzon, 17 Dec., 1904.
43. Curzon to Brodrick, 26 Dec., 1904.
44. Curzon to Brodrick, 29 Dec., 1904.
45. Curzon to Brodrick, 2 Jan., 1905.
46. Curzon's minute of 1 Jan., 1905. Copy in C.P.293.
47. Arnold-Forster's diary, 3 Jan., 1905.
48. Brodrick to Ampthill, 26 Jan., 1905.
49. Curzon to Brodrick, 9 Jan., 1905; Curzon to Ampthill, 8 Jan., 1905; Brodrick to Curzon, 6 Jan., 1905.
50. Curzon to King Edward VII, 11 Jan., 1905; minutes by Curzon, 7 and 8 Jan., 1905, C.P.293.
51. Curzon to Brodrick, 10 and 13 Jan., 1905; Brodrick to Curzon, 13 Jan., 1905.
52. Curzon to Brodrick, 23 Jan., 1905.
53. Curzon to Brodrick, 2 Feb., 1905.

54. Dane to Curzon, 25 Jan., 1905, C.P.293.
55. Major Malleson to Kitchener, 24 and 31 Jan., 1905. These and Malleson's other letters from Kabul are in the Birdwood Papers.
56. Brodrick to Curzon, 26 Jan., 1905.
57. Curzon to Ampthill, 25 Jan., 1905.
58. Curzon to Balfour, 26 Jan., 1905; cf. Curzon to Brodrick, same date.
59. Curzon to Brodrick, 2 Feb., 1905.
60. Brodrick to Curzon, 3 Feb., 1905; minute by Curzon, 6 Feb., 1905, C.P.293; cf. Curzon to Balfour, 9 Feb., 1905.
61. Hardinge to Sanderson and reply, 8 and 21 Feb., 1905, Hardinge Papers 6; Hardinge to Lansdowne, 18 Feb., 1905, F.O.539/90.
62. Curzon to Brodrick, 9 Feb., 1905; see minutes and documents in C.P.293 and A.P.73; Dane to Foreign Secretary, Calcutta, 2 Feb., 1905.
63. Curzon to Brodrick, 10 Feb., 1905.
64. Curzon to Brodrick, ibid.
65. Curzon to Brodrick, 16 Feb., 1905.
66. Brodrick to Ampthill, 10 Feb., 1905.
67. Memorandum by Roberts, 'The British Mission at Kabul', 13 Feb., 1905; memoranda by Godley and Brodrick, 14 Feb., 1905, Cab. 37/74/29.
68. Balfour to King Edward VII, 16 Feb., 1905, RA R25/76.
69. Brodrick to Curzon, 16 Feb., 1905.
70. Brodrick to Curzon, 16 and 17 Feb., 1905; Brodrick to Ampthill, 17 Feb., 1905.
71. Curzon to Brodrick, 18 Feb., 1905; Brodrick to Curzon, 21 Feb., 1905.
72. Curzon to Brodrick, 27 Feb., 1905.
73. Dane to Curzon, 18 Feb., 1905; Curzon to Brodrick, 20 April, 1905.
74. Dane to Foreign Secretary, Calcutta, 2 March, 1905; Curzon to Brodrick, 7 March, 1905; Brodrick to Curzon, 9 March, 1903; cf. Brodrick to Ampthill, 10 March, 1905.
75. See the article 'Anglo-Afghan Relations' in *The United Service Magazine*, Sept., 1908, p. 603.
76. Dane to Curzon, 23 and 28 March, 1905; Cab. 37/76/67; for minutes of the Foreign Dept., see C.P.293; Curzon to Ampthill, 2 April, 1905.
77. Curzon to Godley, 16 March, 1905.
78. Godley to Curzon, 3 March, 1905.
79. Curzon to Godley, 23 March, 1905.
80. Curzon to Godley, 2 March, 1905; Balfour to Curzon, 23 Aug., 1905; Curzon to Balfour, 21 Sept., 1905.
81. Brodrick to Lamington, 23 March, 1905, Lamington Papers 1; cf. Brodrick to Ampthill, 7 April, 1905.
82. Midleton, *Records and Reactions*, pp. 200–1.
83. M. V. Brett (ed.) *Journals and Letters of Reginald, Viscount Esher,* vol. II, p. 77.
84. Clarke to Chirol, 13 April and 2 Sept., 1905; King Edward VII to Curzon, 18 April, 1905.
85. Balfour to G. Wyndham, 31 Jan., 1905.
86. Chirol to Curzon, 3 Feb., 1905.
87. Chirol to Hardinge, 6 Feb., 1905, Hardinge Papers 7; cf. P. L. Mehra, *The Younghusband Expedition,* p. 396.
88. Brodrick to Ampthill, 24 Feb., 1905; Curzon to Rodd, 9 April, 1905, Rodd Papers; Curzon to Godley, 2 February, 1905.
89. Curzon to Brodrick, 21 Feb., 1905.

90. Curzon to Brodrick, 30 March, 1905.
91. Curzon to Brodrick, 2 March, 1905.
92. Godley to Curzon, 24 March, 1905; cf. Godley to Curzon, 31 March, 1905.
93. Godley to Curzon, 11 May, 1905.
94. Curzon to Godley, 20 April, 1905.

Chapter VII: The Military Department

1. *The Times*, 21 Aug., 1905; Curzon's MS. note in C.P.412, copy No. 1; Curzon to Chirol, 14 Sept., 1905.
2. Brodrick to Curzon, 1 Dec., 1904.
3. Curzon to Godley, 22 Dec., 1904.
4. Kitchener to Lady Salisbury, 22 Dec., 1904.
5. See, e.g. Brodrick to Roberts, 7 and 27 Dec., 1904.
6. Roberts to Balfour, 26 Dec., 1904; cf. D. James, *Lord Roberts*, p. 420.
7. Brodrick to Curzon, 28 Dec., 1904.
8. Curzon to Brodrick, 29 Dec., 1904; Kitchener to Lady Salisbury, 29 Dec., 1904.
9. Brodrick to Curzon, 30 Dec., 1904; cf. Roberts to Brodrick, 30 Dec., 1904.
10. Brodrick to Cromer, 10 Nov., 1905, Cromer Papers 7.
11. Godley to Brodrick, 26 and 29 Dec., 1904, G.P.7; cf. Godley to Ampthill, undated, but late Dec., 1904, A.P.14; Brodrick to Balfour, 18 Jan., 1905.
12. Brodrick to Roberts, 21 Dec., 1904.
13. Brodrick to Curzon, 16 Jan., 1905.
14. Curzon to Brodrick, 17 Jan., 1905; cf. Curzon to Hamilton, 19 Jan., 1905.
15. Brodrick to Balfour, 18 Jan., 1905; Sandars to Balfour, 21 Jan., 1905.
16. Hamilton to Curzon, 10 Feb., 1905.
17. Brodrick to Curzon, 6 and 12 Jan., 1905.
18. Curzon to Brodrick, 9 Feb., 1905.
19. Brodrick to Cromer, 10 Nov., 1905, Cromer Papers 7; Midleton, *Records and Reactions*, p. 205.
20. Curzon to Balfour, 26 Jan., 1905.
21. See, e.g. McDonnell to Curzon, 14 Jan., 1905.
22. Hamilton to Curzon, 10 Feb., 1905.
23. Arnold-Forster's diary, 27 Feb., 1905; Balfour to Sandars, 22 Jan., 1905; Balfour to King Edward VII, 8 March, 1905, RA R25/90; M.V. Brett, *Journals and Letters of Reginald, Viscount Esher,* vol. II, pp. 80-1.
24. Ampthill to Curzon, 6 July, 1905.
25. Minutes by Kitchener and Elles, 1 and 24 Jan., 1905; cf. Sir G. Arthur, *Life of Lord Kitchener,* vol. II, p. 206; the details of proposals put forward by Kitchener are given on p. 8 of the pamphlet on Indian military administration written by Curzon at Cannes, Jan., 1906.
26. Curzon to Brodrick, 5 Jan., 1905.
27. Kitchener to Lady Salisbury, 19 Jan., 1905; Kitchener to Birdwood 15 and 18 Jan., 1905; Kitchener to Marker, 18 Jan., 1905.
28. Curzon to Brodrick, 19 Jan., 1905.
29. Brodrick to Curzon, 20 Jan., 1905.
30. Balfour to Curzon, 3 Nov., 1904.
31. Kitchener to Clarke, 26 Jan., 1905; Kitchener to Roberts, same date.
32. Stedman to Kitchener, 27 Jan., 1905, K.P.33; Clarke to Kitchener, 18 Nov., 1904;

Kitchener to Clarke, 5 Jan., 1905; Godley to Ampthill, 13 Oct., 1904 and 26 Jan., 1905.

33. Godley to Ampthill, 11 July, 1905; Brodrick to Curzon, 26 Jan., 1905.
34. There is a copy of the Generals' opinions in the Birdwood papers, marked '63'; Kitchener to Curzon, 31 Jan., 1 and 2 Feb., 1905, and replies, same dates.
35. Kitchener to Lady Salisbury, undated but c. 2 Feb., 1905, and 8 Feb., 1905.
36. Curzon to Brodrick, 2 Feb., 1905.
37. Brodrick to Curzon, 26 Jan., 1905; cf. memo. by Roberts on Kitchener's proposal to form class brigades in the event of a large force going to Afghanistan, 13 Feb., 1905, R.P.
38. Minutes by Curzon and Ibbetson, 6 and 15 Feb., 1905. The minutes are printed in the Proceedings of the Military Department. The Birdwood Papers contain copies of some.
39. Kitchener to Lady Salisbury, 5 Jan., 1905.
40. Balfour to Kitchener, 14 Feb., 1905, Birdwood Papers.
41. Kitchener to Lady Salisbury, 16 Feb., 1905.
42. Kitchener to Marker, 15 Feb., 1905.
43. Curzon to Kitchener, 23 Feb., 1905; Kitchener to Curzon, same date.
44. Kitchener to Marker, 12 Jan., 1905; cf. C.P.412, p. 32 and Curzon's manuscript footnote.
45. Kitchener to Birdwood, 3 March, 1905; cf. Kitchener to Marker, 9 March, 1905.
46. Curzon to Brodrick, 16 March, 1905.
47. Kitchener to Lady Salisbury, 14 March, 1905; Kitchener to Birdwood, 12 March, 1905.
48. Curzon to Kitchener, 17 and 19 March, 1905; Kitchener to Curzon, 18 March, 1905.
49. Kitchener to Lady Salisbury, 14 March, 1905; Sir Ian Hamilton's letter in *The Times*, 9 June, 1928; Lady Oxford, *More Memories*, pp. 177–8.
50. Kitchener to Lady Salisbury, 14 and 23 March, 1905; Kitchener to Curzon, 19 March, 1905; Curzon to Balfour, 30 March, 1905.
51. Curzon to Kitchener, 17 March, 1905.
52. Kitchener to Curzon, 18 March, 1905.
53. Curzon to Balfour, 30 March, 1905.
54. See C.P.412; cf. the memorandum by Curzon dated Nov.–Dec., 1922, C.P.2, Box 65.
55. Kitchener to Birdwood, 24 March, 1905; cf. Kitchener to Birdwood, 20 March, 1905.
56. Kitchener to Stedman, 8 March, 1905.
57. B. Duff to Sir G. White, 25 May, 1905, White Papers.
58. Kitchener to Lady Salisbury, 9 March, 1905.
59. Clarke to Kitchener, 31 March and 14 April, 1905, K.P.34; Esher to Kitchener, 1 April, 1905; Stedman to Kitchener, 31 March, 1905 (wrongly dated 1904), K.P. 33.
60. Kitchener to Stedman, 23 March, 1905.
61. Ampthill to Godley, 14 March, 1905.
62. Brodrick to Ampthill, 17 March, 1905. The source may have been Marker; cf. Kitchener to Marker, 23 Feb., 1905.
63. Ampthill to Brodrick, 2 April, 1905.
64. Brodrick to Ampthill, 17 March, 1905; cf. Brodrick to White, 18 April, 1905.
65. Ampthill to Brodrick, 2 April, 1905.

66. Ampthill to Brodrick, 2 May, 1905.
67. Brodrick to Ampthill, 27 April, 1905; Ampthill to Brodrick, 16 May, 1905.
68. Brodrick to Ampthill, 14 April, 1905. Ampthill to Brodrick, 23 May, 1905.
69. Brodrick to Ampthill, 18 May, 1905; Ampthill to Brodrick, 6 June, 1905.
70. Kitchener to Birdwood, 21 April, 1905.
71. See the *Daily Express*, 21 April, 1905, and *The Standard*, 24 April, 1905; see Repington's article of 28 April, 1905, reprinted in his *Imperial Strategy*, pp. 286–94; Dawkins to Curzon, 10 May, 1905; Kitchener to Birdwood, 20 Feb., 1905.
72. Kitchener to Lady Salisbury, 16 Feb., 1905.
73. Curzon to Kitchener and reply, 6 May, 1905.
74. Brodrick to Curzon, 12 May, 1905.
75. Curzon to Kitchener and enclosure, 16 May, 1905; Elles to Nathan and reply, 20 May, 1905.
76. Curzon to Balfour, 18 May, 1905.
77. Kitchener to Marker, 17 May, 1905.
78. Dawkins to Curzon, 14 April, 1905.
79. Curzon to Ampthill, 12 May, 1905.

Chapter VIII: The Crisis

1. Curzon to Hamilton, 30 April, 1902; Hamilton to Curzon, 21 May, 1902; on the partition of Bengal see the thesis of Dr Z. H. Zaidi, C.P.247, vols. (a), (b) and (c), C.P.323, and Command Papers 2658, 2746.
2. Minute by Curzon, 1 June, 1903, C.P.247 (a).
3. Brodrick to Curzon, 29 Jan., 1904; Curzon's speech at Dacca, 20 Feb., 1904, C.P.247 (a).
4. Memorandum by Sir A. Fraser on the political aspect of partition, copy in M.P. 50074; Curzon to Brodrick, 23 Feb., 1904.
5. Curzon to Morley, 19 Feb., 1906, Morley Papers 43; Curzon's letter to *The Times*, 2 July, 1908.
6. Government of India to Secretary of State, 2 Feb., 1905, C.P.247(b).
7. Curzon to Brodrick, 2 Feb., 1905.
8. Sir T. Raleigh (ed.), *Lord Curzon in India*, vol. II, pp. 216, 220–30.
9. Curzon to Godley, 2 and 16 March, 1905.
10. Ampthill to Brodrick, 3 March, 1905, A.P.7.
11. Curzon to Brodrick, 5 April, 1904.
12. Curzon to Brodrick, 23 March, 1904.
13. Secretary of State to Government of India, 9 June, 1905, C.P.247(b).
14. Curzon to Morley, 19 Feb., 1906, Morley Papers 43.
15. Arnold-Forster to Balfour, 17 Dec., 1904; cf. 58th meeting of the Defence Committee, 22 Nov., 1904, Cab. 2/1.
16. Arnold-Forster's diary, 14 Jan., 1905.
17. Arnold-Forster to J. S. Sandars, 24 Jan., 1905; on the committee, see Cab. 37/76/80.
18. Clarke to Roberts, 3, 26, 29 and 30 March, 1905, R.P.; cf. Lord Sydenham, *My Working Life*, pp. 176, 181.
19. Arnold-Forster's diary, 3 and 17 April, 1905.
20. Balfour to Roberts, 12 Aug., 1905, R.P.
21. Clarke to Roberts, 13 April, 1905; Cab. 6/3/77D and 91D; Kitchener to Clarke,

15 June, 1905, Sydenham Papers; on reinforcements for India see the papers conveniently collected in Cab. 6/3/94D.

22. Cab. 6/3/79D and 80D.
23. Parl. Deb., 4th ser., vol. CXLVI, cols. 62–84; see Lord Esher's letter in *The Times*, 22 May, 1905, and Col. Repington's commentary, reprinted in *Imperial Strategy*, pp. 123–34.
24. Cab. 6/3/84D and 89D; Clarke to Kitchener, 7 July, 1905.
25. Memorandum by Kitchener, 19 July, 1905, copy in Morley Papers 37; Clarke to Balfour, 14 Oct., 1905, and enclosure.
26. Esher to Balfour and reply, 3 Oct., 1906; M. V. Brett (ed.), *Journals and Letters*, vol. II, pp. 184–5, 187–92.
27. Balfour to King Edward VII, 23 March and 9 June, 1905, RA R26/3 and 37; memorandum by Arnold-Forster, 2 June, 1905, A-F.P.50317; for the fullest discussion, see I. H. Nish, *The Anglo-Japanese Alliance*.
28. Roberts to Brodrick, 12 March, 1905, R.P.
29. Note by Roberts on Lord Kitchener's minute 'Administration of the Army in India', 10 April, 1905, R.P.
30. Brodrick to Cromer, 12 May, 1905, Cromer Papers 7.
31. Ampthill to Brodrick, 23 May, 1905, A.P. 7; cf. T. Morison and G. T. Hutchinson, *The Life of Sir Edward FitzGerald Law*, pp. 338–40, 349.
32. Brodrick to Roberts, 30 April, 1905; Kitchener to Lady Salisbury, 25 May, 1905.
33. Curzon's manuscript note, C.P.412/1, p. 37.
34. Stedman to Kitchener, 9 June, 1905, K.P.33.
35. Dissent by Lord Roberts from the report of the sub-committee, 11 May, 1905, R.P.; cf. Roberts to Sir J. Mackay, 16 May, 1905, ibid. Some useful papers are collected in G.P.62.
36. Roberts to Brodrick, 31 July, 1905, R.P.
37. Kitchener to Lady Salisbury, 2 and 23 March, 1905.
38. Curzon's manuscript footnote, C.P.412/1, pp. 27–8.
39. Cromer to Rennell Rodd, 4 June, 1899, Rennell Papers.
40. Brodrick to Cromer, 12 May, 1905; Marquess of Zetland, *Lord Cromer*, pp. 245–6; cf. Sir A. Bigge to Minto, 13 April, 1906, Minto Papers.
41. Lansdowne to Cromer, 11 May, 1905, Cromer Papers 7.
42. Lansdowne to Roberts, 19 May, 1905, R.P.
43. Memorandum by Lansdowne, 16 May, 1905, Cab. 37/76/86.
44. Frank Maxwell to Lady Salisbury, undated.
45. White to Roberts, 5 March, 1905; cf. Sir M. Durand, *Sir George White*, p. 412.
46. White to Roberts, 19 May, 1905, R.P.; Brodrick to Curzon, 18 May, 1905.
47. Roberts to White and reply, 10 and 11 May, 1905, White Papers; cf. Elles to Curzon, 22 Jan., 1906, and Command Paper 2718, p. 6.
48. See, for example, the statements that it had been the exception for a Military Member to hold an important military appointment after leaving that office; that the staff of the Military Dept. had increased; that it was a new departure for the Military Member to wear uniform at Council; that the evidence before the committee had made it clear that the discussions between the two departments had been unjustifiably protracted; Command Paper 2718.
49. Memorandum by Brodrick, 26 May, 1905 (wrongly dated '1906'), Cab. 37/77/96.
50. Curzon's manuscript footnote, C.P.412/1, p. 22; Chirol to Curzon, 2 June, 1905; E. H. C. Moberly Bell, *The Life and Letters of C. F. Moberly Bell*, p. 231.
51. Curzon to Kitchener, 31 May and 1 June, 1905; Kitchener to Curzon, 1 June,

1905 (2 letters); Kitchener to Marker, 1 June, 1905.
52. Chirol to C. Hardinge, 3 Oct., 1905.
53. Esher to Sandars, 4 May, 1905, B.P.; Esher's memorandum of 11 May, 1905, RA W39/76; Kitchener to Clarke, 15 June, 1905, 22 Feb., 1906, Sydenham Papers.
54. Clarke to Kitchener, 15 June, 1905.
55. Kitchener to Marker, 1 June, 1905; Kitchener to Lady Salisbury, 1 June, 1905.
56. Hubert Hamilton to Lady Salisbury, 1 June, 1905.
57. Brodrick to Curzon and reply, 18 May and 8 June, 1905.
58. Curzon to Ampthill, 8 June, 1905.
59. Barnes to Curzon, 21 July, 1905.
60. Lansdowne to Curzon, 26 May, 1905; Roberts to Curzon, 2 June, 1905.
61. Brodrick to Curzon, 2 June, 1905; Godley to Curzon, 30 May, 1905; King Edward VII to Curzon, 2 June, 1905.
62. Brodrick to Curzon, 2 June, 1905; Brodrick to Ampthill, 2 and 18 June, 1905.
63. Ampthill to Godley, 4 July, 1905; Brodrick to Ampthill, 14 July, 1905.
64. E. J. Buck, *Simla Past and Present*, p. 56.
65. Curzon to Dawkins, 21 June, 1905.
66. Haldane to Curzon, 22 June, 1905.
67. See, for instance, Younghusband to Curzon, 30 June, 1905.
68. Curzon to Sir E. Satow, 27 July, 1905.
69. Brodrick to Ampthill, 23 June, 1905.
70. Sir A. T. Arundel to Curzon, 25 June, 1905; Arundel to Richards, 25 June, 1905, Richards Papers 2(a); Curzon to Ampthill, 3 Oct., 1905.
71. Kitchener to Stedman, 26 June, 1905, copy in Salisbury Papers, S.P.2; cf. note by Kitchener, 5 Aug., 1905, copy in Birdwood Papers; Curzon to King Edward VII, 6 July, 1905, and to Knollys, 12 July, 1905; Sir P. Magnus, *Kitchener*, p. 219. The only substantial point of difference is that Kitchener states that Curzon had drawn up the modifications whereas Curzon says that Kitchener drafted most of the arrangement himself; Curzon's memorandum, C.P.412/1, pp. 44–5.
72. Curzon to Balfour, 26 June, 1905.
73. These telegrams, and Brodrick's memorandum of 27 June, 1905, are in Cab. 37/78/112.
74. Balfour to Curzon, 29 June, 1905.
75. Kitchener to Lady Salisbury, 29 June, 1905.
76. Kitchener and Curzon to Balfour, 30 June, 1905; Ronaldshay, vol. II, pp. 384–5.
77. Brodrick to Ampthill, 30 June, 1905; Brodrick to Curzon, 30 June, 1905.
78. Kitchener to Lady Salisbury, 6 July, 1905; Kitchener to Marker, 6 July, 1905; cf. Hubert Hamilton to Lady Salisbury, 26 July, 1905.
79. Kitchener to Lady Salisbury, 27 July, 1905.
80. Balfour to Curzon, 1 July, 1905; Curzon to Balfour, 3 July, 1905.
81. Curzon to Brodrick, 6 July, 1905.
82. Curzon to Brodrick, 10 July, 1905.
83. Brodrick to Roberts, 11 July, 1905.
84. Balfour to Lord Salisbury, 11 July, 1905, S.P.2.
85. Brodrick to Curzon, 14 July, 1905.
86. Curzon to Balfour, 19 July, 1905; cf. Curzon to Sandars, 5 July, 1905, B.P.
87. Curzon to King Edward VII, 6 July, 1905.
88. Brodrick to Ampthill, 7 July, 1905.
89. Stedman to Kitchener, 16 June, 1905.
90. Hubert Hamilton to Lady Salisbury, 5 July, 1905.

91. Curzon to Morley, 28 Dec., 1905; Curzon's manuscript footnote, C.P.412/1, pp. 32-3.
92. Brodrick to Ampthill, 14 July, 1905.
93. Ampthill to Brodrick, 1 Aug., 1905; C.P.412/1, p. 52.
94. Copy in Appendix 3, C.P.412.
95. Balfour to King Edward VII, 19 July, 1905, RA R26/52.
96. Brodrick to Lord Salisbury, 19 July, 1905, S.P.2.
97. Lawrence to Curzon, 21 July, 1905. Evidently Fowler misunderstood Curzon's reference to the Act of 1833.
98. Elles to Ampthill, 7 Aug., 1905, A.P.21; Brodrick to Knollys, 20 July, 1905, RA W/9 and 9a and enclosures.
99. Brodrick to Curzon, 20 July, 1905; Curzon to Ampthill, 23 July, 1905; cf. Curzon to Balfour, 27 July, 1905.
100. Curzon to Brodrick, 20 July, 1905. See Collen to Curzon, 30 June and 22 Sept., 1905.
101. Curzon to Ampthill, 23 July, 1905.
102. Curzon to Lamington, 24 July, 1905.
103. Curzon to Ampthill, 23 July, 1905.
104. Midleton, *Records and Reactions*, pp. 204-5.
105. Hamilton to Brodrick, 21 July, 1905; memorandum by Brodrick, 24 July, 1905, Cab. 37/78/112; Brodrick to King Edward VII, 25 July, 1905, RA W4/10; cf. Sir S. Lee, *King Edward VII*, p. 378, and Brodrick to Lord Salisbury, 19 July, 1905, S.P.2.
106. Balfour to King Edward VII, 25 July, 1905, RA R26/55.

Chapter IX: Resignation

1. Hubert Hamilton to Lady Salisbury, 26 July, 1905; Brodrick to Knollys, 28 July, 1905, RA W4/12.
2. Brodrick to Roberts, 27 July, 1905; Lawrence to Curzon, 21 and 27 July, 12 Sept., 1905.
3. Curzon to Lamington, 24 July, 1905.
4. Lovat Fraser's memorandum for Curzon, 26 Jan., 1908; C.P.412/1, p. 52; L. Fraser, *India Under Curzon and After*, p. vi; Midleton, *Records and Reactions*, p. 205; cf. Brodrick to Minto, 13 March, 1906.
5. C.P.412/1, p. 52.
6. Curzon to Hamilton, 14 March, 1901, 13 Jan., 1903; Curzon to Barrow, 22 Sept., 1903; cf. Curzon to Godley, 5 Oct., 1903.
7. Barrow to Curzon, 23 April, 1905.
8. Barrow's note for Curzon, 29 Oct., 1905; cf. Kitchener to Stedman, 26 June, 1905, S.P.2, and Curzon to Balfour, 21 Sept., 1905.
9. C.P.412, pp. 55ff; Curzon to Ampthill, 12 Aug., 1905. According to Barrow's cousin, Sir G. de S. Barrow, *The Fire of Life*, p. 96, and Sir G. Younghusband, *A Soldier's Memories in Peace and War*, p. 242, Kitchener offered Barrow the post of Chief of Staff.
10. Curzon to Barrow, 10 July, 1905.
11. Barrow to Nathan, 13 Aug., 1905; Lawrence to Curzon, 19 Aug., 1905; Barrow to Curzon, 19 Sept., 1905; Curzon to Barrow, 14 Sept., 1905; Curzon to Sir A. Lyall, 5 Oct., 1905.

12. Curzon to Sandars, 13 July, 1905.
13. Kitchener to Marker, 13 July, 1905.
14. Hubert Hamilton to Lady Salisbury, 13 July, 1905.
15. Note by Kitchener on his interview with Barrow of 8 July, 1905, Birdwood Papers; Kitchener to Stedman, 26 June, 1905, S.P.2; letter, probably to Lady Salisbury but first page missing, about Dec., 1905, in Salisbury file, B.P.
16. Stedman to Marker, 22 June, 1905; Hubert Hamilton to Lady Salisbury, 21 Nov., 1905.
17. Brodrick to Curzon, 29 June, 1905; Curzon to Brodrick, 17 July, 1905; Brodrick to Curzon, 4 Aug., 1905; cf. Midleton, *Records and Reactions,* p. 206.
18. Curzon to Brodrick, 29 July, 1905.
19. Memorandum by Brodrick, 31 July, 1905, Cab. 37/78/112; Brodrick to Roberts, 31 July, 1905; Brodrick to Ampthill, 3 Aug., 1905; cf. Brodrick to Lamington, 18 Aug., 1905, Lamington Papers.
20. Barrow to Curzon, 5 Aug., 1905; Barrow to Balfour, 22 Aug., 1905.
21. Brodrick to Curzon, 1 Aug., 1905; Curzon to Ampthill, 12 Aug., 1905.
22. Brodrick to Curzon and reply 1 and 2 Aug., 1905.
23. Brodrick to Ampthill, 27 July, 1905.
24. Brodrick to Roberts and reply, 27 and 31 July, 1905, R.P.; on dissatisfaction in the Indian Army, see also Chirol to Amery, 10 Nov. and 22 Dec., 1905.
25. Curzon to Brodrick, 2 Aug., 1905.
26. Kitchener to Marker, 3 Aug., 1905.
27. Stedman to Kitchener, 4 Aug., 1905.
28. Brodrick to Curzon, 4 Aug., 1905.
29. Chirol to C. Hardinge, 3 Oct., 1905.
30. C.P.412/1, pp. 60–1.
31. Curzon to Ampthill, 12 Aug., 1905.
32. Kitchener's note of an interview with Curzon on 5 Aug., 1905, Birdwood Papers; Kitchener to Amery, 21 Sept., 1905, Amery Papers.
33. Curzon to Brodrick, 5 Aug., 1905.
34. Kitchener to (?) Stanley, 6 and 7 Aug., 1905, Cab. 37/78/112.
35. Arnold-Forster's diary, 7 Aug., 1905.
36. Clarke to Balfour, 5 Aug., 1905; Godley to Brodrick, 7 Aug., 1905.
37. Brodrick to Knollys, 5 Aug., 1905, RA W4/14; for Godley's attitude see Sandars to Balfour, 15 Aug., 1905.
38. Balfour to King Edward VII, 8 Aug., 1905, RA R26/69.
39. Balfour to Curzon, 8 Aug., 1905.
40. Barrow to Curzon, 10 Aug., 1905; Barrow to Balfour, 22 Aug., 1905; Curzon to Barrow, 30 Aug., 1905.
41. Brodrick to Lord Salisbury, 8 Aug., 1905, S.P.2; cf. Brodrick to Ampthill, 11 Aug. 1905.
42. Military Department notes, with minutes by Kitchener, 28 July, 1905, and Elles, 2 Aug., 1905, Birdwood Papers; Elles to Ampthill, 7 Aug., 1905, A.P.21.
43. Curzon to Brodrick, 10 Aug., 1905.
44. Brodrick to Curzon, 11 Aug., 1905.
45. Curzon to Ampthill, 12 Aug., 1905.
46. Curzon to Brodrick, 12 Aug., 1905.
47. Balfour to Brodrick, 14 Aug., 1905; Balfour to Sandars, 16 Aug., 1905, B.P.
48. Sandars to Balfour, 14 and 17 Aug., 1905; Brodrick to Balfour, 16 Aug., 1905; Minto to (?) Lansdowne, 23 Jan., 1903, H.P.61.

49. Brodrick to Curzon and reply, 16 and 17 Aug., 1905.
50. Minute by Kitchener, 17 Aug., 1905, Birdwood Papers; Curzon to Brodrick, 18 Aug., 1905.
51. Kitchener to Lady Salisbury, 17 Aug., 1905; Kitchener to Curzon, 3 Aug., 1905.
52. Chirol to Curzon, 3 Aug., 1905.
53. Godley to Sandars, 22 Aug., 1905.
54. Kitchener to Curzon, 21 Aug., 1905.
55. Kitchener to Marker, 24 Aug., 1905.
56. Kitchener to Curzon and reply, 26 Aug., 1905.
57. For the crucial conversation between General Duff and Colonel Watkis, 28 Aug., 1905, see K.P.31.
58. Kitchener to Marker, 30 Aug., 1905; cf. Kitchener to Lady Salisbury, 30 Aug., 1905.
59. Brodrick to Curzon, 2 Sept., 1905.
60. Ronaldshay, vol. II, p. 389.
61. Balfour to Curzon and reply, 23 Aug., and 21 Sept., 1905.
62. Clarke to Chirol, 2 and 5 Sept., 1905, Sydenham Papers; Chirol to C. Hardinge, 22 Aug., 1905; Dawkins to Curzon, 22 Aug., 1905. On Brodrick see also *The Autobiography of Margot Asquith*, pp. 182–5; there is no good account of Balfour's part in the crisis. The version given in the latest biography, by K. Young, contains little new except the statement (p. 239) that Curzon had formerly been C-in-C of the Indian Army.
63. Godley to Ampthill, 15 Dec., 1905, A.P.14.
64. Chirol to C. Hardinge, 3 Oct., 1905; E. Crankshaw, *The Forsaken Idea*, pp. 96–7.
65. M. V. Brett (ed.), op. cit., vol. II, p. 246.
66. Balfour to Sandars, 20 Oct., 1905, B.P.
67. *The Times*, 20 Nov., 1930; cf. Midleton, *Records and Reactions*, pp. ix–xi and 188.
68. Curzon's speech at the Byculla Club, Bombay, 16 Nov., 1905, Sir T. Raleigh, op. cit., vol. II, pp. 312–32.

Chapter X: Epilogue

1. Knollys to Curzon, 21 Sept., 1904, RA W63/128.
2. Brodrick to Balfour, 4 Sept., 1905; Sandars to Balfour, 5 Sept., 1905.
3. Knollys to Sandars, 9 Sept., 1905; Sandars to Balfour 15 Sept., 1905.
4. King Edward VII to Curzon, 15 Sept., 1905.
5. King Edward VII to Curzon and reply, 28 and 29 Sept., 1905.
6. Lansdowne to Balfour, 23 Oct., 1905; Balfour to Knollys, 24 Feb., 1906; Curzon to Balfour, 24 June, 1906.
7. McDonnell to Curzon, 1 Nov., 1905.
8. Sir H. Barnes to Curzon, 4 Aug., 1905; Sir D. Barr to Curzon, 27 Sept., 1905.
9. Curzon to Morley, 19 Feb., 1906, Morley Papers 43; Curzon to Brodrick, 9 Oct., 1905.
10. Sir M. Darling, *Apprentice to Power*, p. 34.
11. Sir T. Raleigh (ed.), *Lord Curzon in India*, vol. II, p. 65.
12. Sir V. Chirol, *Fifty Years in a Changing World*, pp. 229–31; Ronaldshay, op. cit., vol. II, p. 336.
13. Chirol, op. cit., p. 231; Curzon to Lawrence, 2 Feb., 1906; Curzon to Knollys, 13 Dec., 1905, RA W4/61; Minto to King Edward VII, 26 Nov., 1905, RA W4/54;

Ampthill to Godley, 23 Nov., 1904, A.P.14; Ampthill to Minto and reply, 20 March and 22 April, 1906, Minto Papers; Minto to Godley, 13 April, 1906, G.P.25.

14. Brodrick to Ampthill, 19 Oct., 1905; Ampthill to Brodrick, 6 and 16 Nov., 1905.

15. Brodrick to Cromer, 10 Nov., 1905, Cromer Papers 7.

16. Hubert Hamilton to Lady Salisbury, 2 Nov., 1905.

17. Knollys to Sandars, 26 Nov., 1905; Brodrick to Balfour, 29 Nov., 1905; Sandars to Balfour, 3 Dec., 1905; Godley to Minto ,23 Nov., 1905; Godley to Lawrence, 1 Dec., 1905, Lawrence Papers.

18. Knollys to Lawrence, 8 Dec., 1905, Lawrence Papers; cf. Godley to Minto, 15 Dec., 1905.

19. Godley to Ampthill, 22 Nov., 1905; for the admission that the documents had been removed see Godley to Minto, 9 March, 1906.

20. A. Hirtzel to Godley, 19 Dec., 1905, G.P.7.

21. Kitchener to Lady Salisbury, 14 Dec., 1905.

22. Morley to Curzon, 25 Dec., 1905.

23. Repington to Marker, 2 Jan. and 1 March, 1906.

24. M. Gilbert, *Servant of India*, p. 38; Minto to Morley, 10 Jan., 1906; memorandum by Morley, 5 Feb., 1906, Morley Papers 39; Barnes to Curzon, 7 Feb., 1906; Morley to Curzon, 7 Feb., 1906; Command Paper 2842.

25. See *The Times*, 16 March, 1906; Repington to Marker, 15 March, 1906.

26. Curzon's MS. addition, p. 15, C.P.412/1.

27. Ampthill to Godley, 30 Jan., 1906; Morley to Minto, 3 May, 1906; Godley to Minto, 23 May, 1906; cf. Repington to Marker, 18 May, 1906; Ampthill to Minto, 20 March, 1906. There are many other examples in the Minto Papers; see, e.g., Prince of Wales to Minto, 1 Jan., 1907.

28. Lady Ravensdale, *In Many Rhythms*, p. 16.

29. Ronaldshay, op. cit., vol. III, p. 33.

30. Curzon to Rennell Rodd, undated, Rennell Papers.

31. On the negotiation of 1905, see the papers in C.P.345, and especially Curzon to Brodrick, 26 April, 11 May, 7 and 15 Nov., 1905; Curzon to Satow, 27 July, 1905; Curzon to Selborne, 5 Oct., 1905; Curzon to King Edward VII, 12 June, 1905; A. Lamb, *The McMahon Line*, vol. I, chaps. I–III.

32. Clarke to Balfour and reply, 7 and 11 Oct., 1905; A. Hardinge to Curzon, 10 Oct., 1905; Lansdowne to C. Hardinge, 17 Oct., 1905, Hardinge Papers 7; C. Hardinge to King Edward VII, 31 May and 24 Oct., 1905, Hardinge Papers 6; Lord Sydenham, *My Working Life*, p. 182; Gooch and Temperley, op. cit., vol. IV, p. 530; W. Walsh, 'The Imperial Russian General Staff and India' in *The Russian Review*, April, 1957.

33. F. Lindberg, *Scandinavia in Great Power Politics, 1905–1908*, pp. 74, 98–100.

34. Sir H. Barnes to Curzon, 27 Jan., 1906; Gooch and Temperley, op. cit., vol. IV, p. 292; Curzon's letter in the *Morning Post*, 28 Feb., 1908; see Parl. Deb., H. of L., vol. CLXXXIII, cols. 999–1024, 1335–1353; Lord Curzon, *Persian Autonomy*, passim.

35. S. L. Gwynn (ed.), *Letters and Friendships of Sir Cecil Spring-Rice*, vol. II, p. 102; G. A. Schreiner (ed.), *Entente Diplomacy and the World*, pp. 44–141, esp. p. 99.

36. See the papers on this subject in Morley Papers 43; a copy marked to show the alterations is in C.P.414; memoranda by Curzon, 25 July, 1908, 3 Aug., 1909, C.P.2, Box 2; Minto to Morley, 9 and 28 Oct., 1907; Curzon to Army Dept., India, and reply 5 March and 10 April, 1908, memorandum by Curzon, 30 Aug.,

1916, C.P.2, Box 72, file C/34/5.

37. For the details see Command Paper 4574.
38. Midleton Papers 50077; Brodrick to Curzon, 16 March, 1924, C.P.2, Box 20.
39. Barrow to Curzon, 29 Dec., 1908.
40. See, e.g., R. Blake, *The Private Papers of Douglas Haig, 1914–1919*, p. 23.
41. Kitchener to Birdwood, 24 Jan., 1912; cf. Kitchener to Birdwood, 5 Nov., 1911, 5 Dec., 1911, Birdwood Papers.
42. Lord Hardinge, *My Indian Years*, pp. 65, 86.
43. Lady F. Balfour, *Ne Obliviscaris*, vol. I, p. 358.
44. Hardinge to Austen Chamberlain, 30 March, 1916, A.C.P.
45. Curzon to Austen Chamberlain, 2 April, 1916, A.C.P.
46. See Command Paper 8610, especially the evidence of Mr Brunyate, Part XI, and p. 99.
47. Parl. Deb., 5th ser., H. of L., vol. XXV, cols. 941, 961.
48. J. S. Sandars, *Studies of Yesterday*, pp. 205–6; Lord Esher, *The Tragedy of Lord Kitchener*, p. 11; *The Times'* leader, 6 July, 1917.
49. Minute by Curzon, 24 March, 1905, C.P.281.
50. Sir W. Lawrence, *The India We Served*, p. 234.
51. Sir T. Raleigh (ed.), *Lord Curzon in India*, vol. II, pp. 63, 213, 219–20.
52. Brodrick to Balfour, 13 Sept., 1905.
53. See Brodrick's memorandum, 'The Relations of Lord Curzon as Viceroy of India with the British Government, 1902–1905'. This document was described by him as an 'official narrative', carefully scrutinised by Balfour and others (*Records and Reactions*, preface, p. x). Nevertheless, it contains many inaccuracies. There is a copy in A.C.P.55.
54. Curzon to Minto, 3 Nov., 1905.
55. J. Buchan, *Lord Minto*, p. 228; Minto to Bigge, 5 Jan., 1908, 5 July, 1910. There are numerous other examples in the Minto Papers.
56. Parl. Deb., H. of L., 5th ser., vol. I, col. 132.
57. War Cabinet Memoranda by Curzon, 27 June and 2 July, 1917. Copies in A.C.P.
58. Curzon's speech of 31 July, 1924, Parl. Deb., H. of L., vol. LIX, cols. 154–71.
59. Ronaldshay, op. cit., vol. III, p. 255.
60. H. Nicolson, 'Lord Curzon's Funeral at Kedleston' in *The Spectator*, 4 April, 1925.
61. Ampthill to Godley, 21 Dec., 1905, G.P.39; Ampthill to Brodrick, 19 May, 1904.
62. Among many examples see F. Younghusband, *The Light of Experience*; Lord Sydenham, *My Working Life*, esp. p. 330; Sir J. Tilley, *London to Tokyo*, pp. 91–3, 127; J. C. Grew, *Turbulent Era*, vol. I, pp. 491, 496, 525; W. S. Churchill, *Great Contemporaries*, p. 215; Sir C. Jones, 'Lord Curzon of Kedleston, 1859–1925' in *International Affairs*, vol. 37, pp. 334–7; Sir O. O'Malley, *The Phantom Caravan*, pp. 57–61; the quotation is from Lawrence to Curzon, 1 Sept., 1903.
63. E. L. Woodward, *Short Journey*, pp. 165–6.
64. Ronaldshay, vol. II, p. 4; Sir M. Darling, *Apprentice to Power*, p. 34.
65. Note by Curzon on his work in India, undated, C.P.2, Box Z, C/32/9.

Bibliography

MANUSCRIPT COLLECTIONS—

Amery Papers: By courtesy of the Rt. Hon. Julian Amery.

Ampthill Papers: India Office Library.

Arnold-Forster Papers: British Museum.

Balfour Papers: British Museum.

Birdwood Papers: India Office Library.

Austen Chamberlain Papers: Birmingham University Library.

Joseph Chamberlain Papers: Birmingham University Library.

Cotton Papers: By courtesy of Col. H. Cotton.

Cromer Papers: Public Record Office.

Curzon Papers: India Office Library. The collection described as C.P.2 was seen at Kedleston, but is now at the India Office Library.

Elgin Papers: India Office Library.

Godley Papers: India Office Library.

Hamilton Papers: India Office Library (two collections).

Hardinge Papers: Cambridge University Library.

Kitchener Papers: Public Record Office.

Lamington Papers: India Office Library.

Lawrence Papers: By courtesy of Murray Lawrence, Esq.

Lansdowne Papers: Public Record Office. There are some other papers at Bowood.

Marker Papers: British Museum.

Midleton Papers: British Museum.

Minto Papers: National Library of Scotland.

Morley Papers: India Office Library.

Rennell Papers: By courtesy of Lord Rennell.

Richards Papers: India Office Library.

Roberts Papers: Army Museums Ogilby Trust.

Salisbury Papers: Christ Church, Oxford. Kitchener's letters to Lady Salisbury, and the papers of the 4th Marquess, are at Hatfield.

Sydenham Papers: British Museum.

White Papers: India Office Library.

Royal Archives: Windsor Castle. Copies of the Prime Minister's letters to the Sovereign are also held at the Public Record Office.

Foreign Office, Defence Committee and Cabinet Papers: Public Record Office.

India Office Papers, telegrams and despatches: India Office Library.
I have been unable to trace the papers of Chirol, Repington and Barrow. The
Midleton and Sydenham collections are evidently incomplete.

PUBLISHED COLLECTIONS OF DOCUMENTS
Documents Diplomatiques Français (1871–1914)
  1st series, vols. 15–16
  2nd series, vols. 1–8
Krasnyi Arkhiv, vols. 2, 18, 19, 53, 56, 69. See also EISELE, L. W. *A Digest of the*
  Krasnyi Arkhiv, vols, 31–106 (Ann Arbor, 1955)
DUGDALE, E. T. S. (ed.): *German Diplomatic Documents*, 1871–1914, vol. III (1930)
  (translation of certain documents from *Die Grosse Politik der Europäischen Kabinette,*
  1871–1914, Berlin, 1922–27)
GOOCH, G. P. and TEMPERLEY, H. (eds.): *British Documents on the Origins of the War,*
  vols. I, III, VI. (1927, 1928, 1930)
AITCHISON, C. U.: *A Collection of Treaties, Engagements and Sanads Relating to India*
  and Neighbouring Countries, vols. 11–12, 13 (Delhi, 1933)

SECONDARY WORKS
Dates of publication are given in brackets after titles; unless stated otherwise, the
place of publication is London. Subtitles are not usually given. For a general survey
of the literature, see J. E. FLINT: *Books on the British Empire and Commonwealth: A*
Guide for Students. (1968)
ABDUR RAHMAN, Amir of Afghanistan: *The Life of Abdur Rahman* (ed. S. M. Khan)
  (1900)
ABRAHAM, F.: 'Was Lord Curzon's Indian Policy a Success?' in *The Imperial and*
  Asiatic Quarterly Review, vol. XXVII (1909)
ALDER, G. J.: *British India's Northern Frontier.* (1963)
ALI KHAN, S. S : *Lord Curzon's Administration of India.* (Bombay, 1905)
ALLEN, B. M.: *The Rt. Hon. Sir Ernest Satow.* (1963)
AMERY, RT. HON. J.: *The Life of Joseph Chamberlain*, vols. IV–VI (1951, 1969)
ANDREWS, C. F. and MUKERJI, A.: *The Rise and Growth of Congress in India.* (Bombay,
  1938)
ANSTEY, V.: *The Economic Development of India.* (1929)
ARGOV, D.: 'Moderates and Extremists: two attitudes towards British rule in India'
  in *St. Antony's Papers*, No. 18 (Oxford, 1966)
ARNOLD-FORSTER, M.: *The Right Honourable Hugh Oakeley Arnold-Forster, A Memoir.*
  (1910)
ARTHUR, SIR G.: *Life of Lord Kitchener*, vol. II (1920)
ASQUITH, HON. H.: *Moments of Memory.* (1938)
ASQUITH, M. (Lady Oxford): *The Autobiography of Margot Asquith.* (1920) *More*
  Memories. (1933)
ATKINS, J. B.: 'W. St. John Brodrick' in *The Dictionary of National Biography, 1941–50.*
  (1959)

BALDWIN, RT. HON. S.: *On England.* (1926)

BALFOUR, LADY F.: *Ne Obliviscaris,* vol. I (1930)

BALFOUR, RT. HON. LORD: *Chapters of Autobiography.* (1930)

BALLARD, C. R.: *Kitchener.* (1930)

BALSAN, C. V.: *The Glitter and the Gold.* (New York, 1952)

BANNERJEE, SIR S.: *A Nation in the Making.* (Bombay, 1964)

BARROW, GEN. SIR G. DE S.: *The Fire of Life.* (1942)

BARTON, SIR W.: *India's North West Frontier.* (1939)

BELL, SIR C. A.: *Tibet past and Present.* (1924) *Portrait of the Dalai Lama.* (1946)

BELL, E. H. C. M.: *The Life and Letters of C. F. Moberly Bell.* (1927)

BENNETT, G. (ed.): *The Concept of Empire.* (1953)

BENNETT, T. J.: 'The Past and Present Connection of England with the Persian Gulf' in *Journal of the Royal Society of Arts.* vol. L (1902)

BENTON, SIR J.: 'Irrigation works in India' in *Journal of the Royal Society of Arts,* vol. LXI (1913)

BERESFORD, COL. C. E. DE LA P.: 'Russian Railways towards India' in *Proceedings of the Central Asian Society* (1906)

BETHELL, LT. COL. L. A. :See 'Pousse Cailloux'

BHATIA, B. M.: *Famines in India, 1860–1908.* (Bombay, 1963)

BHATTACHARYA, S.: *Lord Curzon's Impressions of the Indian Administration, 1898–1901* in *Indian Historical Records Commission Proceedings,* vol. 31, part 2 (1955)

BIBDWOOD, FIELD-MARSHAL LORD: *Khaki and Gown.* (1941). *In My Time.* (n.d., c. 1945).

BLAKE, R. (ed.): *The Private Papers of Douglas Haig, 1914–1919.* (1952)

BLOOD, GEN. SIR B.: *Four Score Years and Ten.* (1933)

BLUNT, W. S.: *My Diaries.* (1920)

BODELSEN, C. A.: *Studies in Mid-Victorian Imperialism.* (1960)

BOLSOVER, G. H.: 'Aspects of Russian Foreign Policy, 1815–1914' in R. Pares and A. J. P. TAYLOR (eds.) *Essays Presented to Sir Lewis Namier.* (1956)

BRETT, M. V. (ed.): *Journals and Letters of Reginald Viscount Esher,* 3 vols. (1934–38)

BRIGGS, A.: 'The Political Scene' in *Edwardian England,* ed. S. NOWELL-SMITH, q.v.

BROCKWAY, T. P.: 'Britain and the Persian Bubble, 1888–92' in *Journal of Modern History,* vol. XIII (1941)

BRODRICK, HON. ST. J.: See MIDLETON, RT. HON. LORD

BROWNING, O.: *Memories of Sixty Years.* (1910)

BUCHAN, J.: *Lord Minto: A Memoir.* (1924)

BUCK, E. J.: *Simla Past and Present.* (Bombay, 1925)

BUCKLE, G. E. (ed.): *The Letters of Queen Victoria,* 3rd series, vol. III (1932)

BUSCH, B. C.: *Britain and the Persian Gulf, 1894–1914.* (1968)

CAIRNCROSS, A. K.: *Home and Foreign Investment, 1870–1913.* (Cambridge, 1953)

CALLWELL, GEN. SIR C. E. (ed.): *The Autobiography of General Sir O'Moore Creagh.* (n.d., c. 1924)

CAMBON, P.: *Correspondance,* vol. II (Paris, 1940)

CANDLER, E.: *The Unveiling of Lhasa.* (1905)

CAROE, SIR O.: *The Pathans, 550 B.C.–A.D. 1957.* (1958)

CARTER, LADY V. BONHAM: 'The Souls' in *The Listener,* vol. XXXVIII, (October 30, 1947)

CECIL, A.: 'Arthur James Balfour' in *The Dictionary of National Biography 1922–1930.* (1937)

CECIL, LADY G.: *Life of Robert Marquis of Salisbury,* 4 vols. (1921–1935)
Biographical Studies of the Life and Political Character of Robert Marquis of Salisbury. (n.d.)

CHAKRAVARTI, P. C.: 'Genesis of the Partition of Bengal (1905)' in *The Modern Review,* vol. CV (1959)

CHAMBERLAIN, RT. HON. SIR A.: *Politics From Within.* (1936)

CHAPMAN, M. K.: *Great Britain and the Baghdad Railway.* (Northampton, Massachusetts, 1948)

CHAPMAN, COL. S.: *Lhasa: The Holy City.* (1938)

CHAUDHURI, K. N.: 'India's International Economy in the Nineteenth Century' in *Modern Asian Studies,* vol, 2, Part 1 (1968)

CHILSTON, LORD: 'Balfour: The Philosopher at the Helm' in *Parliamentary Affairs,* vol. XIII (1960). *Chief Whip.* (1961)

CHIROL, SIR V.: *The Middle Eastern Question.* (1903)
Fifty Years in a Changing World. (1927)

CHURCHILL, R. P.: *The Anglo-Russian Convention of 1907.* (Cedar Rapids, Iowa, 1939)

CHURCHILL, R. S.: *Winston S. Churchill,* vol. 1 (1966)

CHURCHILL, RT. HON. W. S.: *My Early Life.* (1944) *Great Contemporaries.* (1947) 'The Story of the Malakand Field Force' in *Frontiers and Wars.* (1962)

COLERIDGE, HON. G. J. D. and the HON. MRS. A. M.: *Eton in the Seventies.* (1912)

COLLEN, MAJ.-GEN. SIR E. :'Lord Curzon, Lord Kitchener and Mr. Brodrick' in *Blackwood's Magazine,* vol. 178 (1905)

COOPER, D.: *Haig,* vol, 1 (1935)

COTTON, SIR H. J. S.: *New India.* (1907) *Indian and Home Memories.* (1911)

COUPLAND, R.: *The Indian Problem, 1833–1935.* (Oxford, 1942)

COURTNEY, W. L. and J. E.: 'Lord Curzon' in *Pillars of Empire.* (1918)

CRANKSHAW, E.: *The Forsaken Idea.* (1952)

CREAGH, GEN. SIR O'M.: See CALLWELL, GEN. SIR C. E.

CROMER, LORD: *Ancient and Modern Imperialism.* (1910)

CUMPSTON, M.: 'Some Early Indian Nationalists and their Allies in the British Parliament, 1857–1906' in *The English Historial Review,* vol. LXXVI, No. 299 (1961)

CURRY, J. C.: *The Indian Police.* (1924)

CURZON, HON. G. N.: 'The Conservatism of Young Oxford' in *The National Review,* vol. III, No. 16 (1884). 'Poetry, Politics and Conservatism' in *The National Review,* vol. VI. No. 34 (1885). 'The Scientific Frontier, an Accomplished Fact' in *The Nineteenth Century* (1888). 'Our True Policy in India—A Rejoinder' in *The National Review,* vol. XIII, No. 73 (1889) 'The Fluctuating Frontier of Russia in Asia' In *The Nineteenth Century,* vol XXV (1889). *Russia in Central Asia.* (1889). 'Leaves from a Diary on the Karun River' in *The Fortnightly Review* (new series),

Curzon, Hon. G. N.—*continued*

vol. XLVII (1890) .'The Karun River and the Commercial Geography of South West Persia' in *Proceedings of the Royal Geographical Society*, vol. XII (1890). *Persia and the Persian Question*, 2 vols. (1892). 'The Chinese Boundary Question' in *The Nineteenth Century*, vol. XXXIV (1893). 'India between Two Fires' in *The Nineteenth Century*, vol. XXXIV (1893). 'A Recent Journey in Afghanistan' in *The Journal of the Royal Institution of Great Britain* (1895). *Problems of the Far East*. (1896). 'The Pamirs and the Source of the Oxus' in *The Geographical Journal*, vol. 8, July, August and September, 1896 and published separately by the Royal Geographical Society, London, 1897. *Speeches in India*. (1904). 'Frontiers' (Romanes Lecture, Oxford, 1907). 'The True Imperialism' in *The Nineteenth Century*, vol. LXIII (1908). *The Place of India in the Empire*. (1909). *Persian Autonomy*. (1911). *Modern Parliamentary Eloquence*. (1913). *Subjects of the Day*. (1915). *Tales of Travel*. (1923). *British Government in India*, 2 vols. (1925). *Leaves from a Viceroy's Notebook*. (1926).

CURZON, MARCHIONESS: *Reminiscences*. (1955)

D'ABERNON, RT. HON. LORD: *An Ambassador of Peace*, vol. 1 (1929). *Portraits and Appreciations*. (1931)

DALLIN, D. J.: *The Rise of Russia in Asia*. (1950)

DARLING, SIR M.: *Apprentice to Power: India 1904–1908*. (1966)

DAS, G.: 'Lord Curzon's Concern for the Past' in *Asiatic Review*, vol. 43, No. 214 (1962)

DAS, M. N.: *India under Morley and Minto*. (n.d., c. 1964)

DAVIES, C. C.: *The Problem of the North West Frontier*. (Cambridge, 1932)

DICKINSON, G. LOWES: 'Oscar Browning' in *The Dictionary of National Biography 1922–30*. (1937)

DUFF, RT. HON. SIR M. E. GRANT: *Notes from a Diary, 1892–1895*. vol. 2 (1904)

DUGDALE, B. E. C.: *Arthur James Balfour*, 2 vols. (1936)

DUNLOP, J. K.: *The Development of the British Army, 1889–1914*. (1938)

DUNN, A. J.: 'British Interests in the Persian Gulf' in the *Proceedings of the Central Asian Society*. (1907)

DOUGLAS, A. C.: *The Life of Admiral Sir Archibald Lucius Douglas*. (Totnes, 1938)

DURAND, COL. A.: *The Making of a Frontier*. (1900)

DURAND, RT. HON. SIR M.: 'The Amir Abdur Rahman Khan' in *Proceedings of the Central Asian Society* (1907). *The Life of Field-Marshal Sir George White*, 2 vols. (1915)

EARLE, E. M.: *Turkey, the Great Powers and the Baghdad Railway*. (New York, 1923)

EDWARDES, M.: 'The Viceroyalty of Lord Curzon' in *History Today*, vol. 12 (1962) *High Noon of Empire*. (1965)

EDWARDS, E. W.: 'The Japanese Alliance and the Anglo-French Agreement of 1904' in *History*, vol XLII (1957)

ELLIOTT, MAJ.-GEN. J. G.: *The Frontier, 1939–1947*. (1968)

ELLISON, LT. GEN. SIR G.: 'Lord Roberts and the General Staff' in *The Nineteenth Century and After*, vol. 112 (1932)

ELWIN, V.: *India's North-East Frontier.* (Oxford, 1959)

ENTNER, M. L.: *Russo-Persian Commercial Relations, 1828–1914.* (Gainsville, Florida, 1965)

ESHER, LORD: *The Tragedy of Lord Kitchener.* (1921)

EUSTIS, F. A. and ZAIDI, Z. H.: 'King, Viceroy and Cabinet: The Modification of the Partition of Bengal, 1911' in *History*, vol. XLIX (1964)

FABER, R.: *The Vision and the Need.* (1966)

FALLS, C.: 'The Army' in *Edwardian England*, ed. S. NOWELL-SMITH, q.v.

FEIS. H.: *Europe, The World's Banker.* (1961)

FIELDHOUSE, D. K.: ' "Imperialism": An Historiographical Revision' in *The Economic History Review*, 2nd series, vol. XIV (1961)

FLEMING, P.: *Bayonets to Lhasa.* (1961)

FRASER, SIR A. H. L.: *Among Indian Rajahs and Ryots* (1911)

FRASER, D.: 'The Strategic Position Of Russia in Central Asia' in *Proceedings of the Central Asian Society.* (1907)

FRASER, LOVAT: 'Gun-running in the Persian Gulf' in *Proceedings of the Central Asian Society.* (1911). *India under Curzon and After.* (1911)

FRASER-TYTLER, SIR W. K.: *Afghanistan.* (Oxford, 1950)

FULFORD, R.: 'The King' in *Edwardian England*, ed. S. NOWELL-SMITH, q.v.

FULLER, SIR J. B.: *Studies of Indian Life and Sentiment.* (1910). *Some Personal Experiences.* (1930)

GALLAGHER, J. and ROBINSON, R. E.: 'The Imperialism of Free Trade' in *The Economic History Review*, vol. VI (1953)

GARDINER, A. G.: 'Lord Curzon' in *Prophets, Priests and Kings.* (1914)

GARVIN, J. L.: *The Life of Joseph Chamberlain*, vol. III (1934)

GASELEE, SIR S. and TILLEY, J.: *The Foreign Office.* (1943)

GIBBS, N. H.: *The Origins of Imperial Defence.* (Oxford, 1955)

GILBERT, M. (ed.): *Servant of India.* (1966)

GILLARD, D. R.: 'Salisbury and the Indian Defence Problem' in K. BOURNE and D. C. WATT, *Studies in International History.* (1967)

GODLEY, HON. E. (ed.): *Letters of Arthur, Lord Kilbracken and General Sir Alexander Godley.* (Cheltenham, privately printed, 1949)

GOLLIN. A.: *Balfour's Burden.* (1965)

GOPAL, R.: *Indian Muslims: A Political History.* (1959). *Lokamanya Tilak.* (1965)

GOPAL, S.: 'Lord Curzon and the Indian Nationalism' in *St Antony's Papers*, No. 18 (Oxford, 1966). *British Policy in India, 1858–1905.* (Cambridge, 1965)

GORDON, D. G.: *The Dominion Partnership in Imperial Defence, 1870–1914.* (Baltimore, 1965)

GOSSES, F.: *The Management of British Foreign Policy before the First World War.* (Leiden, 1948)

GOUDSWAARD, J. M.: *Some Aspects of the end of Britain's 'Splendid Isolation'.* (Rotterdam, 1952)

GRAHAM, G. S.: *The Politics of Naval Supremacy.* (Cambridge, 1965)

GRANT, N. F. (ed.): *The Kaiser's Letters to the Tsar*. (1920)

GRAVES, P.: *The Life of Sir Percy Cox*. (1941)

GRAY, J.: *At the Court of the Amir*. (1895)

GREAVES, R. L.: *Persia and the Defence of India*. (1959) 'Some aspects of the Anglo-Russian Convention and its working in Persia 1907–1914' in *Bulletin of the School of Oriental and African Studies*, vol. XXXI (1968). 'British Policy in Persia, 1892–1903' ibid., vol. XXVIII (1965)

GRENVILLE, J. A. S.: 'Lansdowne's Abortive Project of 12 March, 1901 for a Secret Agreement with Germany' in *Bulletin of the Institute of Historical Research*, vol. XXVII (1954). *Lord Salisbury and Foreign Policy*. (1964)

GREW, J. C.: *Turbulent Era*, vol. I (1953)

GRIFFITHS, SIR, P.: *The British Impact on India*. (1952)

GROVER, B. L.: *A Documentary Study of British Policy towards Indian Nationalism*. (Delhi, 1967)

GWYNN, S. L.: *Letters and Friendships of Sir Cecil Spring-Rice*, 2 vols. (1930)

HABBERTON, W.: *Anglo-Russian Relations concerning Afghanistan, 1837–1907*. (Urbana, 1937)

HAMILTON, RT. HON. LORD G.: *Parliamentary Reminiscences and Reflections*, 2 vols. (1916, 1922)

HAMILTON, I. B. M.: *The Happy Warrior*. (1966)

HAMILTON, GEN. SIR I.: *Listening for the Drums*. (1944)

HAMILTON, J. A. L. M.: (under the nom-de-plume 'the Author of Afghanistan') 'Anglo-Afghan Relations' a series of articles in *The United Service Magazine*, new series, vols. XXXVI, XXXVII, XXXVIII (1908–9)

HANKEY, RT. HON. LORD: 'The Origin and Development of the Committee of Defence' in *The Army Quarterly*, vol. 14 (1927)

HARDINGE, RT. HON. SIR A.: *A Diplomat in the East*. (1928)

HARDINGE, RT. HON. LORD: *My Indian Years, 1910–1916*. (1948)

HARRIS, D. G.: *Irrigation in India*. (1923)

HARRIS, S.: *J. N. Tata*. (1958)

HICKS BEACH, LADY V.: *Life of Sir Michael Hicks Beach*, vol. II (1932)

HINSLEY, F. H.: 'British Foreign Policy and Colonial Questions, 1895–1914' in *The Cambridge History of the British Empire*, vol. III ed. E. A. BENIANS et al.

HOLDICH, SIR T. H.: 'The Perso-Baluch Boundary' in *Geographical Journal*, vol. IX (1897). *The Indian Borderland, 1880–1900*. (1901). *Tibet, The Mysterious*. (1908). *Political Frontiers and Boundary Making*. (1920)

HOGARTH, D. G.: 'George Nathaniel Curzon, Marquess Curzon of Kedleston, 1859–1925' in *Proceedings of the British Academy*, vol. XI (1925)

HOLLAND, B.: *The Life of Spencer Compton, Eighth Duke of Devonshire*, vol. II (1911)

HOLLINGS, M. A.: *The Life of Sir Colin C. Scott-Moncrieff*. (1917)

HOWARD, C. H. D.: 'Spendid Isolation' in *History*, vol XLVII(1962). *Spendid Isolation*. (1967)

HUTTENBACK, R. A.: 'Indians in South Africa, 1860–1914: The British Imperial Philosophy on Trial' in *The English Historical Review*, vol. LXXXI (1966)

ILBERT, SIR C.: *The Government of India.* (Oxford, 1922)

IMLAH, A. H.: 'British Balance of Payments and Export of Capital, 1816–1913' in *The Economic History Review*, 2nd series vol. V, No. 2 (1952)

ISMAY, RT. HON. GEN. LORD: 'The Machinery of the Committee of Imperial Defence' in *The Journal of the Royal United Service Institution*, vol. 84 (1939)

JAECKEL, H.: *Die Nordwestgrenze in der Verteidigung Indiens 1900–1908 und der Weg Englands zum russisch-britischen Abkommen von 1907.* (Cologne, 1968)

JAMES, D.: *Lord Roberts.* (1954)

JOHNSON, F. A.: *Defence by Committee.* (1960)

JONES, SIR C.: 'Lord Curzon of Kedleston, 1859–1925' in *International Affairs*, vol. 37, No. 3 (1961)

JUDD, D.: *Balfour and the British Empire.* (1968)

KARVE, D. G. and AMBEKAR, D. V. (eds.): *Speeches and Writings of G. K. Gokhale.* (1966)

KAZEMZADEH, F.: 'Russian Imperialism and Persian Railways' in H. MCLANE et al (eds.) *Russian Thought and Politics.* (Harvard, 1957). *Russia and Britain in Persia, 1864–1914.* (New Haven, 1968)

KELLY, J. B.: 'The Legal and Historical Basis of the British Position in the Persian Gulf' in St. *Antony's Papers*, No. 4 (1958). *Sultanate and Imamate in Oman* (1959). *Eastern Arabian Frontiers.* (1964). 'Salisbury, Curzon and the Kuweit Agreement of 1899' in K. BOURNE and D. C. WATT (eds.) *Studies In International History.* (1967). *Britain and the Persian Gulf, 1785–1880.* (Oxford, 1968)

KEMP, P. K.: 'The Royal Navy' in *Edwardian England*, ed. S. NOWELL-SMITH, q.v.

KENNEDY, A. L.: *Salisbury 1830–1903.* (1953)

KEPPEL, A.: *Gun-Running and the Indian North-West Frontier.* (1911)

KEYNES, J. M.: *Indian Currency and Finance.* (1913)

KILBRACKEN, LORD: *Reminiscences of Lord Kilbracken.* (1931)

KNORR, K.: 'Theories of Imperialism' in *World Politics*, vol. IV, No. 3 (1952)

KOEBNER, R. and SCHMIDT, H. D.: *Imperialism.* (Cambridge, 1964)

KUMAR, R.: 'Abdul Aziz Al Saud and the Genesis of Saudi Arabia' in *Bengal Past and Present*, vols. LXXLX and LXXX (1960). 'Curzon and the Anglo-Russian Negotiations over Persia, 1889–1901' in *Proceedings of the Indian Historical Research Commission*, (Chandigarh), vol. II (1961). 'British Attitudes towards the Ibadiyya Revivalist Movement in East Arabia' in *International Studies* (New Delhi), vol. II (1962). 'The Jisseh Lease' in *Journal of Indian History*, vol. 42. (1964). *India and the Persian Gulf Region, 1858–1907.* (1966)

LAMB, A.: 'Some notes on Russian Intrigue in Tibet' in *Journal of the Royal Central Asian Society*, vol. XLVI (1959). *British and Chinese Central Asia: the Road to Lhasa, 1767–1905.* (1960). *The McMahon Line*, 2 vols. (1966)

LANDON, P.: *Lhasa; An Account of the Country and the People*, 2 vols. (1905)

LANGER, W. L.: *The Diplomacy of Imperialism.* (New York, 1951)

LATTIMORE, O.: *Studies in Frontier History.* (Oxford, 1962)

LAWRENCE, SIR W.: (under pseudonym 'Anglo-Indian') 'Lord Curzon's Services to India' in *The North American Review*, vol. CLXVII (1903).'India's Dual Problem' in *The National Review*, vol. 43, (1904). 'The British Mission to Tibet' in *The North American Review*, vol. CLXVIII (1904). *The India We Served*. (1928)

LEE, SIR S.: *King Edward VII*, 2 vols. (1925, 1927)

LEE, W. K.: *Tibet in Modern World Politics, 1774–1922*. (New York, 1931)

LEVESON-GOWER, SIR G. G.: *Mixed Grill*. (1947)

LINDBERG, F.: *Scandinavia in Great Power Politics, 1905–1908*. (Stockholm, 1958)

LIPSETT, H. C.: *Lord Curzon in India, 1898–1903*. (1903)

LOBANOV-ROSTOVSKY, PRINCE A. A.: *Russia and Asia*. (Ann Arbor, 1951)

LOW, D. A.: *Soundings in Modern South Asian History*. (1968)

LOWE, C. J.: *The Reluctant Imperialists*. (1967)

LUVAAS, J.: *The Education of an Army*. (1965)

MACKINTOSH, J. P.: 'The Rôle of the Committee of Imperial Defence before 1914' in *The English Historical Review*, vol. LXXVII (1962)

MACLEAN, SIR F. H.: 'Superior Person' in *A Person from England and Other Travellers*. (1958)

MACMUNN, LT.-GEN. SIR G.: *Romance of the Indian Frontiers*. (1933)

MACONOCHIE, SIR E.: *Life in the Indian Civil Service*. (1926)

MAGNUS, SIR P.: *Kitchener: Portrait of an Imperialist*. (1958). *King Edward the Seventh*. (1964)

MAHAN, CAPT. A. T.: 'The Persian Gulf and International Relations' in *The National Review*, vol. XL (1902)

MAJUMDAR, R. C.: *History of the Freedom Movement in India*, vols. I and II (Calcutta, 1962, 1963)

MALCOLM, SIR I.: *Indian Pictures and Problems*. (1907). 'George Curzon' in *The Quarterly Review*, No. 485 (1925). *Lord Balfour: A Memory*. (1930)

MALLET. V. (ed.): *Life with Queen Victoria*. (1968)

MARDER, A. J.: *The Anatomy of British Sea Power*. (1941)

MARLOWE, J.: *The Persian Gulf in the Twentieth Century*. (1962)

MARRIOT, SIR J. A. R.: 'Lord Curzon of Kedleston: A Friend's Tribute' in *The The Fortnightly Review*, vol. 117 (1925). 'Lord Curzon of Kedleston' in *The Edinburgh Review*, vol. 248 (1928). *Memories of Four Score Years*. (1944)

MARTIN, F. A.: *Under the Absolute Amir*. (1907)

MARTIN, P.: 'Figures Indiennes Disparues: Lord Curzon' in *Asie Française*, vol. 25 (1925)

MASON, K.: 'Sir Francis Edward Younghusband' in *The Dictionary of National Biography, 1941–1950*. (1959)

MCMAHON, COL. SIR H.: 'Recent Survey and Exploration in Seistan' in *The Geographical Journal*, vol. 28 (1906)

MEHRA, P. L.: 'Tibet and Russian Intrigue' in the *Journal of the Royal Central Asian Society*, vol. XLV (1958). 'Kazi-U-gyen: "A Paid Tibetan Spy"?' in *Journal of the Royal Central Asian Society*, vol. LI (1964). 'Kazi-U-gyen and Lord Curzon's Letter of 1901: A Footnote' in *Journal of Asian Studies*, vol. XXVI (1967). *The Younghusband Expedition* (1968)

MEHROTRA, S. R.: 'Imperial Federation and India, 1868–1917' in *Journal of Commonwealth Political Studies*, vol. I, No. 1 (1961)

MEINERTZHAGEN, COL. R.: *Army Diary, 1899–1926.* (Edinburgh, 1960)

MENPES, M.: *The Durbar.* (1903)

MERSEY, LORD: *A Picture of Life, 1872–1940* (1941)

MEYENDORFF, A. (ed.): *Correspondence Diplomatique de M. de Staal*, vol. II (Paris, 1929)

MIDLETON, RT. HON. LORD: *Records and Reactions, 1856–1939.* (1939)

MILNER, LADY: *My Picture Gallery, 1886–1901.* (1951)

MILLINGTON, P.: *To Lhassa at Last.* (1905)

MINTO, LADY: *India, Minto and Morley, 1905–1910.* (1934)

MONGER, G. W.: 'The End of Isolation: Britain, Germany and Japan, 1900–1902' in *Transactions of the Royal Historical Society*, vol. 13 (1963). *The End of Isolation.* (1963)

MORLEY, RT. HON. LORD: *Recollections*, vol. II (1917)

MORISON, SIR T. and HUTCHINSON, G. T.: *The Life of Sir Edward FitzGerald Law.* (Edinburgh, 1911)

MOORE, R. J.: *Liberalism and Indian Politics, 1892–1922.* (1966). 'John Morley's Acid Test: India, 1906–1910' in *Pacific Affairs*, vol. XL (1968)

MOSLEY, L.: *Curzon, The End of an Epoch.* (1960)

NEWTON, LORD: *Lord Lansdowne: A Biography.* (1929). *Retrospection.* (1941)

NICOLSON, HON. SIR H.: 'Lord Curzon' in *The Spectator*, No. 5048 (1925) 'Lord Curzon's Funeral at Kedleston' in *The Spectator*, No. 5049 (1925). 'Curzon' in *Foreign Affairs*, vol. VII, No. 2 (1929). *Sir Arthur Nicolson, Bart.* (1930). *Curzon, The Last Phase.* (1934). 'George Nathaniel Curzon' in *The Dictionary of National Biography, 1922–1930.* (1937)

NICOLSON, HON. N.: *Great Houses of Britain.* (1965)

NISH, I. H.: *The Anglo-Japanese Alliance.* (1966). 'Korea, Focus of Russo-Japanese Diplomacy' in *Asian Studies*, vol. IV (1966)

NOWELL-SMITH, S.: *Edwardian England, 1901–1914.* (1964)

NOYCE, F.: *England, India and Afghanistan.* (1902)

O'CONNOR, LT.-GEN. SIR F.: *Things Mortal.* (1940). *On the Frontier and Beyond.* (1931)

O'DONNELL, C. J.: *The Failure of Lord Curzon.* (1903)

O'DWYER, SIR M.: *India as I knew it, 1885–1925.* (1925)

O'MALLEY, L. S. S.; *The Indian Civil Service.* (1931)

O'MALLEY, SIR O.: *The Phantom Caravan.* (1955)

ONSLOW, LORD: 'Lord George Francis Hamilton' in *The Dictionary of National Biography, 1922–1930.* (1937)

PAISH, G.: 'Great Britain's Capital Investments in Individual Colonial and Foreign Countries' in *Journal of the Royal Statistical Society*, vol. LXXIV (1911)

PALMER, A. W.: 'Lord Salisbury's approach to Russia, 1898' in *Oxford Slavonic Papers.* (1955)

PARKER, A.: 'The Baghdad Railway Negotiations' in *The Quarterly Review*, vol. CCXXVIII (1917)

PENSON, DAME L.: 'The Principles and Methods of Lord Salisbury's Foreign Policy' in *Cambridge Historical Journal*, vol. V. (1935). 'The New Course in British Foreign Policy' in *Transactions of the Royal Historical Society*, vol. XXV (1943). 'Obligations by Treaty: Their Place in British Foreign Policy, 1898–1914' in A. O. SARKISSIAN (ed.) *Studies in Diplomatic History and Historiography in Honour of G. P. Gooch.* (1961). *Foreign Affairs under the Third Marquess of Salibury.* (1962)

PHILBY, H. ST. J. B.: *The Heart of Arabia*, 2 vols. (1922)

PHILIPS, C. H., with SINGH, H. L. and PANDEY, B. N.: *The Evolution of India and Pakistan, 1858 to 1947: Select Documents.* (1962)

PHILLIPS, W.: *Oman.* (1967)

PIERCE, R. A.: *Russian Central Asia, 1857–1917.* (Berkeley, 1960)

PINE, L. G.: *They Came with the Conqueror.* (1954)

PLASS, J. B.: *England zwischen Russland und Deutschland.* (Hamburg, 1966)

PLATT, D. C. M.: *Finance, Trade and Politics in British Foreign Policy, 1815–1914.* (Oxford, 1968). 'The Imperialism of Free Trade: Some Reservations' in *Economic History Review*, vol. XXI, No. 2 (1968) 'Economic Factors in British Foreign Policy during the 'New Imperialism'' in *Past and Present*, vol. 39 (1968)

PORTLAND, DUKE OF: *Men, Women and Things.* (1937)

POUSSE-CAILLOUX (LT.-COL. L. A. BETHELL): 'A Footnote' in *Blackwood's Magazine*, vol. CCXXV (1929)

RALEIGH, SIR T. (ed.): *Lord Curzon in India* (Speeches), 2 vols. (1906)

RASTOGI, R. S.: *Indo-Afghan Relations, 1880–1900.* (Lucknow, 1965)

RATCLIFFE, S. K.: 'Curzon in India. Fifty Years after' in *The Contemporary Review*, No. 1079 (1955)

RAVENSDALE, LADY: *In Many Rhythms.* (1953)

RAYA, K.: *Some Desultory Notes on Lord Curzon's Work in India, January 1899–June 1901.* (Calcutta, 1902)

REED, SIR S.: *The India I knew.* (1952)

REPINGTON, C. à'C.: *Imperial Strategy.* (1906). *Essays and Criticisms.* (1911)

REPINGTON, M.: *Thanks for the Memory.* (1938)

RICHARDSON, H. E.: *Tibet and its History.* (1962)

RIDDELL, RT. HON. LORD: *Lord Riddell's War Diary, 1914–1918.* (1933). *Lord Riddell's Intimate Diary of the Peace Conference and After.* (1933)

RIFE, J. B. and GROSER, H. G.: *Kitchener in His Own Words.* (1917)

ROBINSON, R. E. and GALLAGHER, J.: 'The Imperialism of Free Trade' in *The Economic History Review*, vol. VI (1953)

RODD, SIR R. (Lord Rennell): *Social and Diplomatic Memories*, vol. III (1925)

RONALDSHAY, LORD: See ZETLAND, RT. HON. LORD

SALISBURY, LADY (A.S.): *A Memory, 1887–1947.* (privately printed, 1950). *Hatfield 1887–1903.* (MS copy at the Bodleian Library)

SALMON, E.: 'Lord Curzon' in *United Empire*, vol. 16 (1925)

SANDERS, J. S.: *Studies of Yesterday, by a Privy Councillor.* (1928)

SANDHURST, RT. HON. LORD: *From Day to Day, 1916–1921.* (1921)

SANDISON, A.: *The Wheel of Empire*, (1967)

SCHREINER, G. A. (ed.): *Entente Diplomacy and the World*. (1921)

SCHUMPETER, J.: *The Sociology of Imperialisms*, (New York, 1955)

SEAL, A.: *The Emergence of Indian Nationalism*. (Cambridge, 1968)

SEAVER, G.: *Francis Younghusband*. (1952)

SEEGER, C. L. (ed.): *The Memoirs of Alexander Ivolsky*. (1920)

SETON, M. C. C.: *The India Office*. (1925)

SETON-WATSON, H.: *The Decline of Imperial Russia*, (1952). *The Russian Empire, 1801–1917*. (Oxford, 1967)

SHAKOW, Z.: 'The Defence Committee: a Forerunner of the Committee Of Imperial Defence' in *The Canadian Historical Review*, vol. XXXVI (1955)

SIMON, RT. HON. SIR J.: *Comments and Criticisms*. (1930)

SINGH, H. L.: *Problems and Policies of the British in India, 1885–1898*. (Bombay, 1962)

SINGH, S. N.: *The Secretary of State for India and his Council*. (Delhi, 1962)

SINGHAL, D. P.: *India and Afghanistan, 1876–1907*. (Queensland, 1963)

SMITH-DORRIEN, GEN. SIR H.: *Memories of Forty-Eight Years' Service*. (1925)

SPECTOR, I.: *The First Russian Revolution: Its Impact on Asia*. (Englewood Cliffs, N. J., 1962)

SPINKS, C. N.: 'The Background of the Anglo-Japanese Alliance' in *Pacific Historical Review*, vol, VIII, No. 3, (1939)

STEINER, Z. S.: 'Great Britain and the Creation of the Anglo-Japanese Alliance' in *The Journal of Modern History*, vol XXXI. No. 1 (1959). 'The Last Years of the Old Foreign Office' in *The Historical Journal*, vol. 6 (1963)

STIRLING, A. M. W.: *Victorian Sidelights*. (1954)

STRACHEY, SIR J. and LT.-GEN. SIR R.: 'Playing with Fire: Mr Brodrick and Lord Curzon' in *The National Review*, vol. 46 (1905)

SUMNER, B. H.: *Russia and the Balkans, 1870–1880*. (Oxford, 1937). 'Tsardom and Imperialism, 1880–1914' in *Proceedings of the British Academy*, vol. XXVII (1941). *Survey of Russian History*. (1947)

SYDENHAM, LORD: *My Working Life*. (1927)

SYKES, MAJ-GEN. RT. HON. SIR F.: *From Many Angles*. (1942)

SYKES, H. R.: 'Our Recent Progress in Southern Persia and its Possibilities' in *Proceedings of the Central Asian Society*. (1905)

SYKES, BRIG.-GEN. SIR P.: *A History of Persia*. vol. 2. (1921), *The Right Honourable Sir Mortimer Durand*. (1926). *A History of Afghanistan*, vol. 2 (1940)

SWINTON, RT. HON. LORD: *Sixty Years of Power*. (1966)

TEMPERLEY, H.: 'British Secret Diplomacy from Canning to Grey' in *Cambridge Historical Journal*, vol. VI, No. 1 (1938)

TERENZIO, P-C.: *La Rivalité Anglo-Russe en Perse et en Afghanistan jusqu'aux accords de 1907*. (Paris, 1947)

THORNER, D.: 'Great Britain and the Development of India's Railways' in *Journal of Economic History*, vol. XI (1951). 'The Pattern of Railway Development in India' in *Far Eastern Quarterly*, vol. XIV, No. 2.(1955)

THORNTON, A. P.: *Doctrines of Imperialism*, (New York, 1965). *The Habit of Authority.* (1966). *For the File on Empire.* (1968)

THORNTON, T. H.: *Colonel Sir Robert Sandeman.* (1895)

TILLEY, RT. HON. SIR J.: *London to Tokyo.* (c. 1942)

TIMES, THE: *The History of the Times*, vol. III (1947)

TUCKER, A.: 'The Issue of Army Reform in the Unionist Government, 1903–1905' in *The Historical Journal*, vol. IX, No. 1 (1966)

TUNSTALL, B. H.: 'Imperial Defence, 1870–1897' and 'Imperial Defence, 1897–1914' in *The Cambridge History of the British Empire*, vol. III, ed E. A. BENIANS et al.

VANSITTART, RT. HON. LORD: *The Mist Procession.* (1958)

VON LAUE, T. H.: *Sergei Witte and the Industrialization of Russia.* (New York, 1963)

WADDELL, L. A.: *Lhasa and its Mysteries.* (1905)

WALSH, W. B.: 'The Imperial Russian General Staff and India: A Footnote to Diplomatic History' in *The Russian Review*, vol. 16, No. 2 (1957)

WARWICK, LADY: *Life's Ebb and Flow.* (1929). *Afterthoughts.* (1931)

WASTI, S. R.: *Lord Minto and the Indian Nationalist Movement*, 1905 to 1910. (Oxford, 1964)

WHATES, S.: *The Third Salisbury Administration*, 1895–1900. (1900)

WHIBLEY, C.: *Lord John Manners and his Friends*, vol. II (1925)

WILLIAMS, B. J.: 'The Strategic Background of the Anglo-Russian Entente of August, 1907' in *The Historical Journal*, vol, IX, No. 3 (1966)

WILSON, SIR, A.: *The Persian Gulf.* (Oxford, 1928)

WITTE, COUNT S.: *The Memoirs of Count Witte.* (ed. A. YARMOLINSKY) (1921)

WOLF, J. B.: 'The Diplomatic History of the Baghdad Railroad' in *University of Missouri Studies*, vol. XI (1936)

WOLFF, RT. HON. SIR H. DRUMMOND: *Rambling Recollections*, vol. II (1908)

WOLPERT, S. A.: *Tilak and Gokhale.* (Berkeley, Los Angeles, 1962). *Morley and India.* (1967)

WOODRUFF, P.: *The Men who Ruled India: The Guardians.* (1954)

WOODWARD, E. L.: *Short Journey.* (1942)

WOODYATT, MAJ.-GEN. N.: *Under Ten Viceroys.* (1922)

WORTHAM, H. E.: *Oscar Browning.* (1927)

WRENCH, SIR J. E.: *Alfred, Lord Milner, The Man of no Illusions.* (1958)

WRIGHT, C. H.: 'Nicholas II of Russia' in *The Quarterly Review*, vol. CCXLVIII (1927)

YATE, COL. C. E.: 'Baluchistan' in *Proceedings of the Central Asian Society.* (1906)

YOUNG, K.: *Arthur James Balfour.* (1963)

YOUNGHUSBAND, SIR F.: 'Our Position in Tibet' in *Proceedings of the Central Asian Society* (1910). *India and Tibet.* (1910). 'Lord Curzon' in *The Nineteenth Century and After*, vol. 97 (1925). *The Light of Experience.* (1927). *The Heart of a Continent.* (1937)

YOUNGHUSBAND, MAJ.-GEN. SIR G.: *A Soldier's Memories in Peace and War.* (1917). *Forty Years a Soldier.* (1923)

ZAIDI, Z. H.: 'The Political Motive in the Partition of Bengal' in *Journal of the Pakistan Historical Society*, vol. XII, part II (1964)

ZETLAND, RT. HON. LORD: *Sport and Politics under an Eastern Sky*. (Edinburgh, 1902). *On the Outskirts of Empire in Asia*. (1904). *The Life of Lord Curzon*, 3 vols. (1928–29). *Lord Cromer*. (1932). *Essayez*. (1956)

Index

304